T0181553

Lecture Notes of the Institute for Computer Sciences, Social Informatics and Telecommunications Engineering 451

More information about this series at https://link.springer.com/bookseries/8197

Yan Chenggang · Wang Honggang ·
Lin Yun (Eds.)

Mobile Multimedia Communications

15th EAI International Conference, MobiMedia 2022
Virtual Event, July 22–24, 2022
Proceedings

 Springer

Editors
Yan Chenggang
Hangzhou Dianzi University
Hangzhou, China

Wang Honggang ⓘ
University of Massachusetts - Dartmouth
Dartmouth, MA, USA

Lin Yun ⓘ
Harbin Engineering University
Harbin, China

ISSN 1867-8211   ISSN 1867-822X (electronic)
Lecture Notes of the Institute for Computer Sciences, Social Informatics
and Telecommunications Engineering
ISBN 978-3-031-23901-4   ISBN 978-3-031-23902-1 (eBook)
https://doi.org/10.1007/978-3-031-23902-1

This Springer imprint is published by the registered company Springer Nature Switzerland AG
The registered company address is: Gewerbestrasse 11, 6330 Cham, Switzerland

Preface

We are delighted to introduce the proceedings of the 15th European Alliance for Innovation (EAI) International Conference on Mobile Multimedia Communications (MOBIMEDIA) 2022. With the commercialization of 5G communication technology, multimedia services and applications in the mobile environment have grown at an extraordinary rate. The conference EAI MOBIMEDIA 2022 brought together researchers, developers and practitioners from around the world who are studying new technologies, applications and standards for mobile multimedia processing, such as content features analysis and coding, media access control, multimedia flow and error control, cross-layer optimization, Quality of Experience (QoE), media cloud as well as mobility management and security protocols.

The technical program of EAI MOBIMEDIA 2022 consisted of 29 full papers, including 3 best papers in technical sessions at different conference tracks. The conference tracks were: Track 1 - Internet of Things, Wireless Communications and Communication Strategy Optimization; Track 2 - Cyberspace Security on Cryptography, Privacy Protection, Data Sharing, Access Control and Task Prediction; Track 3 - Neural Networks and Feature Learning; and Track 4 - Object Recognition and Detection. Aside from the high quality technical paper presentations, the technical program also featured four keynote speeches. The four keynote speakers were Prof. Yan Zhang from the University of Oslo in Norway, Prof. Shiwen Mao from Auburn University in USA, Prof. Jingyu Yang from Tianjin University in China and Prof. Zhangjie Fu, Nanjing University of Information Science & Technology in China. The four keynote speeches presented the deeper development and wider use of novel mobile multimedia processing technologies, which captured and held the audience's attention and inspired in-depth discussions.

Coordination with the steering chair, Imrich Chlamtac, was essential for the success of the conference. We sincerely appreciate his constant support and guidance. It was also a great pleasure to work with such an excellent organizing committee team, we note their hard work in organizing and supporting the conference. In particular, the Technical Program Committee, led by our TPC Co-Chairs, Zhidong Zhao, Jilin Zhang, Xun Cao, Lei Chen, Jianhua Tang, Jinbo Xiong and Yiming Wu, who completed the peer-review process of technical papers and made a high-quality technical program. We are also grateful to the Conference Manager, Veronika Kissova for her support and all the authors who submitted their papers to the EAI MOBIMEDIA 2022 conference and workshops.

We strongly believe that the EAI MOBIMEDIA 2022 conference provided a good forum for all researcher, developers and practitioners to discuss all science and technology aspects that are relevant to mobile multimedia processing. We also expect that future

EAI MOBIMEDIA conferences will be as successful and stimulating, as indicated by the contributions presented in this volume.

August 2022

Zefei Zhu
Chenggang Yan
Wang Honggang
Lin Yun

Organization

Steering Committee

Imrich Chlamtac   Bruno Kessler Professor, University of Trento, Italy

Members

Honggang Wang   University of Massachusetts, Dartmouth, USA
Yun Lin   Harbin Engineering University, China

Organizing Committee

General Chairs

Zefei Zhu   Hangzhou Dianzi University, China
Chenggang Yan   Hangzhou Dianzi University, China
Honggang Wang   University of Massachusetts Dartmouth, USA
Yun Lin   Harbin Engineering University, China

Technical Program Committee Chairs

Zhidong Zhao   Hangzhou Dianzi University, China
JiLin Zhang   Hangzhou Dianzi University, China
Xun Cao   Nanjing University, China
Lei Chen   Georgia Southern University, USA
Jianhua Tang   South China University of Technology, China
Jinbo Xiong   Fujian Normal University, China
Yiming Wu   Hangzhou Dianzi University, China

Sponsorship and Exhibit Chairs

Ruiping Wang   Institute of Computing Technology, Chinese Academy of Science, China
Yongbin Zhang   Harbin Institute of Technology, China
Liang Kou   Hangzhou Dianzi University, China

Local Chairs

Ying Fu   Beijing Institute of Technology, China
Liang Kou   Hangzhou Dianzi University, China

Workshops Chairs

Guiguang Ding   Tsinghua University, China
Ting Wu   Hangzhou Innovation Institute, Beihang
                                    University, China
Muhammad Alam   London South Bank University, UK
Jingyu Yang   Tianjin University, China
Zhenyu Na   Dalian Maritime University, China

Publicity and Social Media Chairs

Yuebin Liu   Tsinghua University, China
Pierluigi Siano   University of Salerno, Italy
Yanzhao Shen   Hangzhou Dianzi University, China
Liang Zhao   Shenyang Aerospace University, China

Publications Chairs

Yue Deng   Beihang University, China
Shuai Liu   Hunan Normal University, China
Shanshuo Ding   Hangzhou Dianzi University, China
Hui Wang   Hangzhou Dianzi University, China

Web Chairs

Gyu Myoung Lee   Liverpool John Moores University, UK
Yue Gao   Tsinghua University, China
Zeng Yan   Hangzhou Dianzi University, China
Jinli Suo   Tsinghua University, China

Technical Program Committee

Yizhi Ren   Hangzhou Dianzi University, China
Jingyu Hua   Nanjing University, China
Jieren Cheng   Hainan University, China
Hao Peng   Zhejiang Normal University, China
Jun Shao   Zhejiang Gongshang University, China
Cheng Guo   Dalian University of Technology, China

Tong Qiao	Hangzhou Dianzi University, China
Heng Yao	University of Shanghai for Science and Technology, China
Fengyong Li	Shanghai University of Electric Power, China
Ran Shi	Nanjing University of Science and Technology, China
Xianhua Ou	Zhejiang University of Technology, China
Sheng Li	Zhejiang University of Technology, China
Chaogeng Huang	Zhejiang University of Finance & Economics, China
Guangmang Cui	Hangzhou Dianzi University, China
Jufeng Zhao	Hangzhou Dianzi University, China
Kuo Chen	Chongqing University of Posts and Telecommunications, China
Jianhua Yang	Guangdong Polytechnic Normal University, China
Chensheng Yuan	Nanjing University of Information Science and Technology, China
Chenyang Wang	Aalto University, Finland
Xiaoming Li	Tianjin University, China
Wei Yu	Zhejiang Yuexiu University, China
Zhen Wang	Hangzhou Dianzi University, China
Zhen Zhang	Hangzhou Dianzi University, China
Liqin Hu	Hangzhou Dianzi University, China
Gengran Hu	Hangzhou Dianzi University, China
Jibo Shi	Harbin Engineering University, China
Kuixian Li	Harbin Engineering University, China
Chang Liu	Harbin Engineering University, China
Chenggang Cao	Harbin Engineering University, China
Hongtao Li	Shanxi Normal University, China
Biao Jin	Fujian Normal University, China
Zhigang Yang	Chongqing University of Arts and Sciences, China
Yinbin Miao	Xidian University, China
Tao Zhang	Xidian University, China
Qi Li	Nanjing University of Posts and Telecommunications, China
Changguang Wang	Heibei Normal University, China
Hongfa Ding	Guizhou University, China
Hai Liu	Guizhou University, China
Yandie Yang	Harbin Engineering University, China

Contents

Neural Networks and Feature Learning

Object Recognition and Detection

Internet of Things, Wireless Communications and Communication Strategy Optimization

A Novel Cross-Resolution Image Alignment for Multi-camera System

Kuo Chen[1](✉), Tianqi Zheng[1], Chenxing He[1], and Yeru Wang[2]

[1] Chongqing University of Posts and Telecommunications, Chongqing 400065, China
chenkuo@cqupt.edu.cn
[2] Hangzhou Dianzi University, Hangzhou 310018, ZJ, China

Abstract. In complicated computer vision tasks, the multi-camera system is more effective than a single camera owing to the image fusion of multiple cameras, in which the image alignment is the essential first step. Especially, the cross-resolution image alignment caused by focal length difference has been extensively studied. A usual solution is using pyramid based local feature matching to create the mapping between input images with high and low-resolution. However, this kind of algorithm has high time and space complexity and is not applicable to front-end equipment such as the multi-camera system. Therefore, this paper proposes a fast and novel cross-resolution image alignment method based on the approximate focal length difference, including the coarse feature matching in low-resolution and the matching model estimation in high-resolution. At last, two types of test experiments are carried out using the industrial camera and SLR camera respectively. And the experimental results show that the proposed method performs well for cross-resolution image alignment, which can be widely used for multi-camera system.

Keywords: Local feature matching · Image alignment · Multi-camera imaging

1 Introduction

Powered by computer vision and artificial intelligence technology, more visual information and higher-quality images can be obtained by multi-camera system [1], which has been widely used in medicine, industry, remote sensing and other fields. By reasonably fusing the image information between different cameras, higher-quality composite images can be obtained, and panoramic imaging, high dynamic range imaging, extend depth of field imaging, night vision and so on can be realized with multi-camera system [2, 3].

In the process of image fusion between different cameras, the image alignment is the essential first step, which is limited by the possible differences between cameras, such as attitude difference, focal length difference and spectral difference [4]. Currently, the general solutions are pixel based, patch based and local feature based methods [5], among which the most flexible one is local feature based matching. It has a robust alignment effect.

Y. Chenggang et al. (Eds.): MobiMedia 2022, LNICST 451, pp. 3–14, 2022.
https://doi.org/10.1007/978-3-031-23902-1_1

This paper focuses on cross-resolution image alignment, which is image alignment between the long-focus camera and the short-focus camera. For this problem, benefiting from the image pyramid technology, accurate feature points can be extracted on the cross-resolution images by feature detection algorithms such as Scale-Invariant Feature Transform [6] (SIFT), Speeded-Up Robust Features [7] (SURF) and Oriented Fast and Rotated Brief [8] (ORB). Then the final homography matrix can be estimated by using inlier filtering algorithms such as Random Sample Consensus [9] (RANSAC).

However, in order to achieve scale invariance, the existing technologies have designed a complex feature description method, which leads to high time and space complexity. Therefore, this paper studies a novel cross-resolution image alignment method.

2 Related Work

To realize cross-resolution image alignment, local feature detection and outlier removal technologies are involved. This paper briefly discusses the related works of these two aspects.

For local feature detection, many excellent algorithms have been developed. For example, SIFT detects the sub-pixel feature point using difference of Gaussians on pyramids with different scales, and generates the robust feature descriptor by gradient histogram. But its time complexity and space complexity are extremely high. Therefore, SURF uses box filtering, wavelet transform, lower dimensional vector and other techniques to reduce the complexity of SIFT. But there are still some shortcomings in real-time performance. While ORB effectively combines the detection of local extremum feature and binary descriptor and realizes real-time local feature matching. However, to deal with the cross-resolution problem, a complicated pyramid structure is still required.

In the aspect of outlier removal, a global transformation is usually used to judge inliers or outliers, such as RANSAC, in which similar transformation, affine transformation, projective transformation and so on can be used. There are also a series of later improvements of RANSAC [10, 11]. Or the probability of sampling inliers is increased, the speed of iteration is accelerated, and the threshold of inlier discrimination is optimized, etc. In addition, with the development of deep learning technology, there are many excellent feature detection and outlier removal algorithms based on deep learning, such as LF-Net [12], Superpoint [13] and SuperGlue [14], which can only achieve high real-time performance on GPU at present, and cannot meet the application requirements of multi-camera system which needs edge computing.

Inspired by the related works, this paper focuses on the image alignment of long-focus camera and short-focus camera. According to the approximate ratio of spatial resolution between multi-camera images, the high-resolution images are downsampled to the low-resolution scale to realize coarse matching. Then the feature points are filtered and matched iteratively on the high-resolution scale to achieve final accurate alignment.

3 The Proposed Method

As shown in Fig. 1, a narrow field-of-view image with high-resolution is captured by the long-focus camera, defined by I_s, and a wide field-of-view image with low-resolution is captured by the short-focus camera, defined by I_r. Considering the difference in image resolution caused by focal length, this paper designs a method consisting of matching feature point on the low-resolution scale and estimating the alignment model on the high-resolution scale. It is worth mentioning that in the practical application of multi-camera imaging, the non-overlapping areas of images I_s and I_r can be marked in advance to reduce their influence on the final alignment. The approximate ratio of spatial resolution between images caused by focal length can be estimated by geometric measurement and defined by integer k.

In this paper, the image I_s is downsampled to the image I_{s_d}, and the feature points are extracted without complex pyramid structure, as shown in Fig. 1. In order to realize more accurate alignment result, the feature points of the image I_{s_d} are restored to a high-resolution scale after the coarse feature matching, and then the alignment model is estimated in high-resolution.

Normally, restoring feature points from low-resolution scale to high-resolution scale involves two aspects: image texture and spatial coordinate. For the former, it still requires reconstructing the missing image information under high-resolution, which consumes a lot of time and space. Therefore, this paper only restores the spatial coordinates of feature points to high-resolution, which greatly reduces the time and space complexity. And then finds the best alignment in the alignment model estimation stage. For specific implementation methods and steps, please refer to Sect. 3.1 and Sect. 3.2 respectively.

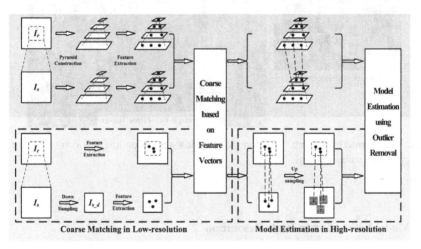

Fig. 1. The flow chart of proposed cross-resolution image alignment. The upper half is the pyramid-based solution, and the lower half is the proposed solution.

3.1 Coarse Matching in Low-Resolution

Firstly, the high-resolution image I_s is downsampled by k to obtain the low-resolution image I_{s_d}, where k is an integer. And the downsampling process does not need interpolation and has high time efficiency. Then, on the low-resolution scale, the feature points on image I_{s_d} and image I_r can be detected using any one fast detection operators without scale invariance. And then the feature point sets P_{s_d} and P_r are obtained respectively. Although the true resolution ratio of images I_s and I_r is not equal to integer k absolutely, which may cause mismatch in sets P_{s_d} and P_r, it can be compensated in Sect. 3.2.

According to the practical application of multi-camera system, descriptor without scale can be used flexibly to get the feature vectors V_{s_d} and V_r corresponding to the feature point set P_{s_d} and P_r. Following the general steps of feature matching, the matching quality is measured by the ratio of maximum and submaximum of feature vector distance, and the search process is accelerated by kd-tree, and then the matched point pair $\left\{P'_{s\_d}, P'_r\right\}$ of image I_{s_d} and image I_r is obtained. It only represents the correspondence of input images on the low-resolution scale. So, in this paper, the feature point P'_{s_d} of image I_{s_d} is upsampled k times on the spatial coordinate to get P'_s, as shown in Fig. 2, which represents the coarse matching of images on the high-resolution scale.

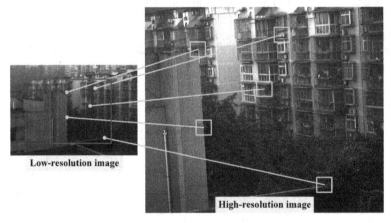

Fig. 2. Coarse matching result. A feature point on low-resolution image is corresponding to a patch on high-resolution image.

3.2   Model Estimation in High-Resolution

As shown in Fig. 2, due to the difference of spatial resolution, coarse matching in low-resolution establishes the correspondence between a feature point of I_r and a patch of I_s. In order to estimate the accurate alignment model, it is necessary to find the pixel-wise correspondence between high-resolution image I_s and low-resolution image I_r. Therefore, this paper designs the following iterative algorithm to estimate the alignment model.

Algorithm1	
1. **Input:**	
2.	I_r: Wide field-of-view image with low-resolution
3.	I_s: Narrow field-of-view image with high-resolution
4.	k: Approximate ratio of spatial resolution
5. **Function:**	
6.	Downsample high-resolution image
7.	Feature detection using FAST and others
8.	Feature descriptor using BRIEF and others
9.	Get the initial matched point pair $\{P'_{s\_d}, P'_r\}$
10.	Upsample feature point P'_{s_d} to P'_s
11.	**for** i=1 to T **do**
12.	Select randomly m feature points in P'_r, and the corresponding m patches in P'_s
13.	Select one feature point for each patch
14.	Estimate the alignment model H_i
15.	Find all inlier sets P_{in} and projection error E_i
16.	**If** the number of P_{in} is large enough and the value E_{in} is small enough
17.	Update current alignment model H_i
18.	Update current projection error E_i
19.	Update T
20. **Output:**	
21.	H: Optimal cross-resolution alignment model

In order to solve the optimum solution, this paper designs an iterative approach to estimate the alignment model inspired by RANSAC. Specifically, firstly randomly select m matched points on the low-resolution image I_r and corresponding m patches on the high-resolution image I_s. And then estimate an alignment model H_i according to these m matching relationships. Decide whether all feature points meet the current mapping relationship of model H_i, except the selected m points, and obtain the inlier set P_{in} and the projection error E_{in} based on a threshold. Because a feature point in the low-resolution image I_r is corresponding to a patch in the high-resolution image I_s, this paper selects the smallest projection error point in a patch as the inlier point. After getting the set of inliers, decide whether to update the alignment model according to the inliers number and projection error until the end of the iteration process, and output the optimal cross-resolution alignment model H.

4 Experiments

In order to verify the validity of the proposed method, this paper designs three test experiments. In test experiment No. 1, a multi-camera system is built, including a 5-megapixel Daheng industrial camera with an 8 mm focal length lens, and a 12-megapixel

Daheng industrial camera with a 16 mm focal length lens. Five groups of wide field-of-view images with low-resolution and narrow field-of-view images with high-resolution images are captured, with resolution ratio 7.4, named as H1, H2, H3, H4, and H5. In test experiment No. 2, a Nikon D7100 SLR camera with an 18–105 mm zoom lens is used. Two groups of cross-resolution test images with resolution ratio 3 are captured, named as D1 and D2. Two groups of cross-resolution test images with resolution ratio 3.89 and 4.17 are captured, named as E1 and E2. Two groups of cross-resolution test images with resolution ratio 5.11 are captured, named as F1 and F2. Two groups of cross-resolution test images with resolution ratio 5.83 are captured, named as G1 and G2. In test experiment No. 3, we used the SLR camera in Experiment No. 2 to capture images of the same resolution with slight displacement, rotation, etc., and then obtain 9 sets of images with resolution differences of 1–9 times by downsampling, named as A.

4.1 Implementation

In the specific implementation process, this paper selects the simple FAST feature extraction operator [15] and BRIEF feature descriptor [16]. And other two cross-resolution image alignment algorithms are compared in this paper. The specific descriptions are as follows. To verify the effect of model estimation in Sect. 3.2, Algorithm 1 only extracts feature points and estimates the alignment model on low-resolution scale. Algorithm 2 is the pyramid based ORB algorithm. Algorithm 3 is the proposed method. Considering the comparability of experimental results, the above three algorithms keep the same parameters in the processes of feature extraction, coarse feature matching, outlier removal and iteration.

In addition, although the real resolution ratio of high-resolution and low-resolution images are mostly decimals, the integer k is always used for upsampling and downsampling in our experiment. This can further save time and space cost in particular, and the parameter k has a certain tolerance and has no significant impact on the final alignment result. As shown in Fig. 3, the resolution ratio of the test image is 5.83 times. When the parameter k is set as 4, 5, 6, 7 and 8, the alignments can still be successful. And the closer the integer k is to the real resolution ratio, the better the alignment effect is, which can be seen from the fused image and the distribution of inlier points.

$k = 4$ $k = 5$ $k = 6$ $k = 7$ $k = 8$

Fig. 3. Influence of approximate ratio k on alignment result

4.2 Results

The results of test experiment No. 1 are shown in Fig. 4 and Table 1. Considering the limited space for this article, Fig. 4 only shows the image alignment results of groups H1 and H5, and Table 1 shows the final projection errors of all five groups.

It can be seen from Fig. 4 that Algorithm 2 and our method both have a better effect in detail than Algorithm 1, such as the outdoor region of the air conditioner, in which Algorithm 1 has obvious artifacts. We know that Algorithm 1 directly performs feature extraction and matching on low-resolution scale, that results in inadequate accuracy of feature points. While the proposed model estimation in high-resolution can fix this problem.

Furthermore, the projection error of Algorithm 1 is much bigger than Algorithm 2 and our method, and our method perform better than Algorithm 2 slightly as shown in Table1. Since our method does not utilize the pyramid structure to extract feature points, it can reduce time and space consumption in feature extraction phase compared with Algorithm 2.

The results of test experiment No. 2 are shown in Fig. 5 and Table 2. Figure 5 only shows the image alignment results of groups D2, F2 and G1, and Table 2 shows the final projection errors of all eight groups.

As shown in Table 2, the projection error of Algorithm 1 increases along with the increase of the resolution ratio, while algorithm 2 and proposed method are not influenced. Again, the proposed method performs best. With the increase of the resolution ratio, the measuring accuracy of feature points extracted by Algorithm 1 becomes more and more insufficient, so the corresponding projection error increases. However, Algorithm 2 handles this problem using complex pyramid structure. And the proposed method estimates the alignment model in high-resolution iteratively, so it succeed in cross-resolution image alignment with different resolution ratio.

10   K. Chen et al.

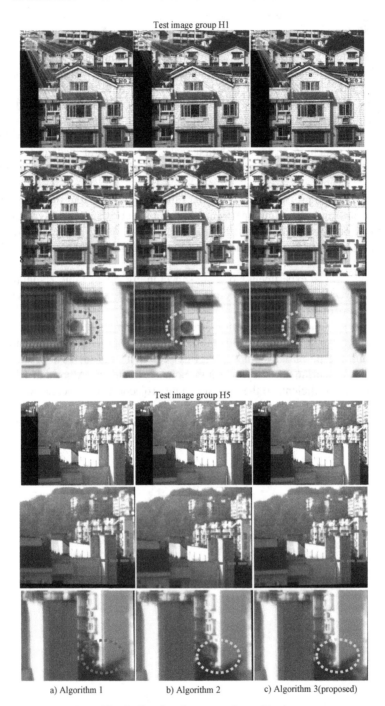

Test image group H1

Test image group H5

a) Algorithm 1   b) Algorithm 2   c) Algorithm 3(proposed)

Fig. 4. Results of test experiment No. 1

Table 1. Projection errors of test experiment No. 1

Resolution ratio	Test group	Algorithm comparison		
		Algorithm 1	Algorithm 2	Algorithm 3 (proposed)
7.4	H1	5.97	2.96	**2.35**
	H2	8.49	**3.33**	3.88
	H3	4.44	2.66	**2.05**
	H4	7.12	3.41	**3.40**
	H5	7.45	2.71	**1.97**

Table 2. Projection errors of test experiment No. 2

Resolution ratio	Test group	Algorithm comparison		
		Algorithm 1	Algorithm 2	Algorithm 3 (proposed)
3.00	D1	2.20	2.37	**1.85**
3.00	D2	4.52	1.82	**1.75**
3.89	E1	2.82	2.20	**1.70**
4.17	E2	4.64	2.64	**2.18**
5.11	F1	4.52	3.09	**2.24**
5.11	F2	5.21	2.67	**1.23**
5.83	G1	6.18	3.05	**1.30**
5.83	G2	6.11	**2.55**	3.37

The results of test experiment No. 3 are shown in Fig. 6. In order to better explore the relationship between the projection error and the resolution magnification, simulation experiments are conducted. Figure 6 shows the registration error results of 9 groups of experiments with the resolution multiplier from 1 to 9 under image A.

As shown in Fig. 6, the abscissa of the figure represents different resolution magnification, and the ordinate represents projection error. It can be clearly seen in the line chart that the projection error of Algorithm 1 presents an upward trend with the improvement of resolution. However, the projection error of Algorithm 2 and the proposed method is not affected by the resolution multiplier. Meanwhile, the projection error line of the proposed method is below the projection error line of Algorithm 2. This is exactly consistent with the results of Experiment No. 2, thus verifying the correctness and effectiveness of our method.

Although the test images have a large difference in spatial resolution, the experimental results show that the proposed method can always obtain a good alignment effect without the complex pyramid structure. Even in some tests, as shown in Fig. 5 and Fig. 6,

Fig. 5. Results of test experiment No. 2

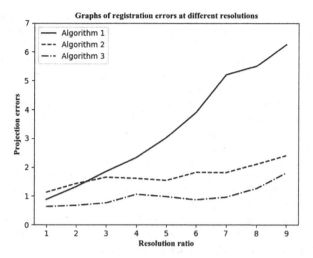

Fig. 6. Results of test experiment No. 3

the proposed method performs better than the pyramid based ORB method. The precondition is getting the approximate resolution ratio of high-resolution and low-resolution image, which is very easy to measure in multi-camera system applications.

5 Conclusion

According to the problem that the current pyramid structure has high time and space complexity and is not applicable to the multi-camera system, this paper proposed a novel cross-resolution image alignment method, including the coarse feature matching in low-resolution and the matching model estimation in high-resolution. Based on our method, combined with artificial intelligence technology, the interesting computational imaging on the multi-camera system like high-quality continuous zooming, wide field-of-view imaging with high-resolution and so on can be realized. However, when the feature points are restored from low-resolution scale to high-resolution, the influence of image texture information can be deeply considered in the future. In addition, for the iterative solution of the optimal alignment model, the perspective of selecting points from high-resolution patch for further speeding up this method can be taken into consideration in the future.

Acknowledgement. The authors thank the financial support from National Natural Science Foundation of China (Grant No. 61905033), and Chongqing Basic and Frontier Research Project (Grant cstc2018jcyjAX0314).

References

1. Yuan, X., Fang, L., Dai, Q., et al.: Multiscale gigapixel video: a cross resolution image matching and warping approach. In: 2017 IEEE International Conference on Computational Photography (ICCP), pp. 1–9. IEEE (2017)

2. Chen, Y., Jiang, G., Yu, M., et al.: Learning stereo high dynamic range imaging from a pair of cameras with different exposure parameters. IEEE Trans. Comput. Imaging **6**, 1044–1058 (2020)
3. Milgrom, B., Avrahamy, R., David, T., et al.: Extended depth-of-field imaging employing integrated binary phase pupil mask and principal component analysis image fusion. Opt. Express **28**(16), 23862–23873 (2020)
4. Cui, J., Zhang, S., Jiang, Z., et al.: Approach of spectral information-based image registration similarity. J. Appl. Remote Sens. **14**(2), 026520 (2020)
5. Ma, J., Jiang, X., Fan, A., et al.: Image matching from handcrafted to deep features: a survey. Int. J. Comput. Vis. **129**(1), 23–79 (2021)
6. Lowe, D.G.: Distinctive image features from scale-invariant keypoints. Int. J. Comput. Vis. **60**(2), 91–110 (2004). https://doi.org/10.1023/B:VISI.0000029664.99615.94
7. Bay, H., Ess, A., Tuytelaars, T., et al.: Speeded-up robust features (SURF). Comput. Vis. Image Underst. **110**(3), 346–359 (2008)
8. Rublee, E., Rabaud, V., Konolige, K., et al.: ORB: an efficient alternative to SIFT or SURF. In: 2011 International Conference on Computer Vision, pp. 2564–2571. IEEE (2011)
9. Fischler, M.A., Bolles, R.C.: Random sample consensus: a paradigm for model fitting with applications to image analysis and automated cartography. Commun. ACM **24**(6), 381–395 (1981)
10. Barath, D., Matas, J., Noskova, J.: MAGSAC: marginalizing sample consensus. In: Proceedings of the IEEE/CVF Conference on Computer Vision and Pattern Recognition, pp. 10197–10205 (2019)
11. Chum, O., Matas, J.: Matching with PROSAC-progressive sample consensus. In: 2005 IEEE Computer Society Conference on Computer Vision and Pattern Recognition (CVPR 2005), vol. 1, pp. 220–226. IEEE (2005)
12. Ono, Y., Trulls, E., Fua, P., et al.: LF-Net: learning local features from images. Adv. Neural Inf. Process. Syst. **31**, 6237–6247 (2018)
13. DeTone, D., Malisiewicz, T., Rabinovich, A.: Superpoint: self-supervised interest point detection and description. In: Proceedings of the IEEE Conference on Computer Vision and Pattern Recognition Workshops, pp. 224–236 (2018)
14. Sarlin, P.E., DeTone, D., Malisiewicz, T., et al.: Superglue: learning feature matching with graph neural networks. In: Proceedings of the IEEE/CVF Conference on Computer Vision and Pattern Recognition, pp. 4938–4947 (2020)
15. Rosten, E., Drummond, T.: Machine learning for high-speed corner detection. In: Leonardis, A., Bischof, H., Pinz, A. (eds.) Computer Vision – ECCV 2006, vol. 3951, pp. 430–443. Springer, Heidelberg (2006). https://doi.org/10.1007/11744023_34
16. Calonder, M., Lepetit, V., Strecha, C., et al.: Brief: binary robust independent elementary features. In: Daniilidis, K., Maragos, P., Paragios, N. (eds.) Computer Vision, vol. 6314, pp. 778–792. Springer, Heidelberg (2010). https://doi.org/10.1007/978-3-642-15561-1_56

IOT Water Meter Reading System Based on Multi-agent and Ah Hoc

Yonghua Wu[1]([⊠]) and Ruijuan Zuo[2]

[1] College of Electronic and Information Science, Fujian Jiangxia University, Fuzhou, Fujian 350108, People's Republic of China
`wuyonghua@fjjxu.edu.cn`
[2] College of Mathematics and Informatics, Fujian Normal University, Fuzhou, Fujian 350117, People's Republic of China

Abstract. Aiming at the shortcomings of traditional wireless meter reading system, such as difficulty in expansion, high deployment cost, and high power consumption during data transmission, this paper designs an IOT water meter reading system based on multi-agent and Ah hoc. The system can be automatically networked between nodes with LoRa, which is easy to expand. The system uses a multi-agent structure, each agent is responsible for different tasks, the complex system is divided into independent small systems, reducing the complexity of the system. In order to ensure the data security of the information in the water meter and transmission process, the Agent hardware design security module based on FMCOS-SE, the key information is encrypted and stored using SM4 algorithm.

Keywords: Wireless meter reading system · Ad hoc · Multi-agent · SM4 · IOT

1 Introduction

Micro-power wireless meter reading has been applied to the hydropower industry since the late 1990s. During more than 10 years of technical development, they have experienced star network, tree network, fixed frequency grid transmission, and have been partially developed to the fourth-generation technology. The fourth-generation technology focus on Ad-Hoc network data transmission mode with automatic frequency hopping and self-organizing network [1]. Ad hoc network applications have received little attention in the meter reading industry. Based on GPRS and ad hoc networks a novel design of a wireless ad hoc network remote meter reading system is proposed [2]. In order to facilitate the advanced measurement system with real-time interaction in smart grid and to satisfy the requirements for power quality management, a wireless ad hoc smart metering system for power quality using Internet of things (IoTs) technology is presented in the paper [3]. Typically, the electric power companies employ a group of power meter readers to collect data on the customers energy consumption. This task is usually carried out manually, which can lead to high cost and errors, causing financial losses, so in the paper [4], propose an architecture to the Automatic Meter Reading

© ICST Institute for Computer Sciences, Social Informatics and Telecommunications Engineering 2022
Published by Springer Nature Switzerland AG 2022. All Rights Reserved
Y. Chenggang et al. (Eds.): MobiMedia 2022, LNICST 451, pp. 15–30, 2022.
https://doi.org/10.1007/978-3-031-23902-1_2

(AMR) system using Unmanned Aerial Vehicles (UAV). These studies mainly focus on reducing the node's transmission power, detecting abnormal nodes, etc. The intelligence and coordination of the node itself are not considered, the receiving sensitivity is not good, and the meter reading speed is slow.

Agent theory and technology originated in the 1980s and are now gradually applied to industries, agriculture, and other fields [5, 6]. A multi-agent architecture is proposed. To exploit the advantages of multi-agent systemsmodelling for WSN services, network topologies and sensor device architectures [7]. These studies mainly focus on the accuracy of the data of the nodes without considering the networking capabilities of the nodes And low power consumption.

At present, the domestic and foreign wireless water meter reading network technologies include WIFI, HomeRF, Bluetooth BLE4.0, Zigbee, GPRS, micro-power wireless network, and low-power wide area network (LPWAN). WIFI, HomeRF, Bluetooth, etc. are not widely used in domestic water meter collection. Zigbee's communication technology is used more internationally [8]. With the rise of the Internet of Things, a low-power wide area network (LPWAN) came into being. NB-IoT and LoRa are among the best [9]. NB-IoT is currently not commercialized, and domestic research is very popular. The LoRa network has been piloted or deployed in many places abroad, but Lora has fewer applications in China and less in the collection of water meters [10].

Based on the current status of technology development at home and abroad, this paper uses the low-power LoRa transmission module currently on the market and integrates the Agent theory into various nodes of the meter reading system to build a self-organizing multi-hop Ad-Hoc network of nodes, which is used in the water meter collection and reading industry. Provide a three-dimensional perception system for the development of smart water services. The system is composed of multiple Agent structures, and each level of Agent can intelligently complete the corresponding tasks of data collection, communication, and summary. Using SX1278 LoRa as a communication module can have a longer communication distance and lower power consumption [11]. The nodes can self-organize to form an Ad-Hoc network. Any node can forward data for other nodes as a route, which has strong scalability and low deployment cost. The security module is embedded in various Agent hardware designs, and the key loaded in the module is used as the cornerstone to ensure the security of data communication, access, and storage. The encryption method uses the domestic SM4 algorithm [12, 13]. By introducing a ministerial key system, a three-level key management method for water meter application is established at the ministerial, project, and user levels.

2 System Model Based on Multi-agent

2.1 System Architecture

Combining the idea of multi-agent system with Ad hoc self-organizing network technology, the wireless meter reading system model (see Fig. 1) is designed. From the topology diagram, the system is divided into three levels, with a collector agent, a concentrator agent, and a management center agent. Three different agents communicate with each other to complete the water meter collection task. The concentrator Agent node is connected to multiple water meter sensors, which can collect the readings of multiple water meters in real time. The concentrator agent is responsible for managing the work of multiple collector agents. It can not only collect the data of the collector agent, but also issue instructions to the collector to control its running state. The management center agent manages multiple concentrator agent nodes, summarizes the data of each concentrator agent node, and can issue commands to the collector agent under it through the concentrator agent node. An Ad hoc network is formed between the Collector Agent and the Concentrator Agent. Although the concentrator agent is the central node of several collector agents logically, it is not necessary for the concentrator agent and collector agent to communicate directly. Any node in the network can forward packets for other nodes. The water meter data collected by the collector agent can be transmitted to the corresponding concentrator agent through multi-hops. Similarly, the control instructions of the concentrator agent can reach a certain collector agent in a multi-hop manner. Therefore, the Collector Agent and Concentrator Agent also have the ability to perceive the network topology and determine the data transmission path. The communication between the concentrator agent and the management center agent is performed via the 4G network using HTTP protocol. When the concentrator agent submits the data request, it will submit the data to the corresponding HTTP API of the management center.

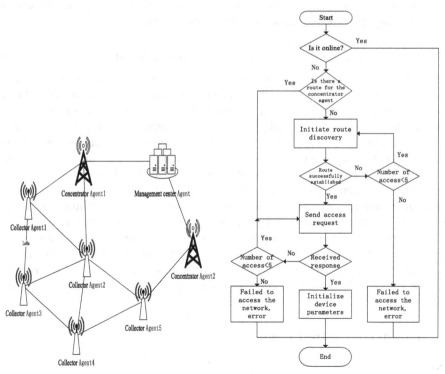

Fig. 1. Wireless meter reading system model

Fig. 2. The unconnected collector agent actively initiates a network access request to the concentrator agent

2.2   Coordination Mechanism Between Agents

2.2.1   Formation of Multi-agent Network

The network formation between the concentrator agent and the collector agent is initiated actively by the collector agent. The unconnected collector agent actively initiates a network access request to the concentrator agent (see Fig. 2).

The request may reach the concentrator node directly, or route through multiple nodes in the network (see Sect. 6 for detailed routing mechanism and protocol) to the concentrator agent. After confirming the network access request, the concentrator Agent sends basic system parameters to it. The parameters include the time and interval assigned to the node to initiate data upload. Different upload time points are used to avoid network congestion caused by multiple collector agents simultaneously uploading, and different time intervals affect the real-time performance and power consumption of data. The shorter the data upload interval, the better the real-time data, but the higher the communication frequency, the higher the average power consumption, the shorter the battery life; on the contrary, the longer the data upload interval, the more real-time data Poor, but the lower the average power consumption, the longer the battery life. After receiving the basic parameters of the system, the collector agent will update the configuration of its own node and respond to the concentrator to complete the network access. The concentrator agent uses the 4G module to access the management center agent to register and obtain the system configuration when it is first started.

2.2.2   Communication Coordination Among Multiple Agents

Most of the time, the communication between the collector agent and the concentrator agent is initiated actively by the collector agent. The collector agent uploads data to the concentrator agent at the determined time interval based on the upload time point determined when accessing the network. The concentrator agent caches the data transmitted by the collector agent in local storage. The communication between the concentrator Agent and the management center Agent has two modes, real-time and non-real-time. In real-time mode, when the concentrator agent receives the data from the collector agent or meets a certain time interval, it will immediately initiate communication with the management center and submit the data to the management center. In non-real-time mode, the concentrator agent initiates communication only at fixed time intervals. When receiving the request from the concentrator agent, the management center agent checks whether there are any tasks not assigned to the agent in the task queue. If so, the corresponding task is delivered in the response. When the concentrator agent receives the task, it will actively contact the collector agent node that should actually execute the task and release the task.

3   System Hardware Design

3.1   Collector Agent

The hardware framework of the collector is mainly composed of PIC single-chip microcomputer, power supply module, LoRa wireless communication module, FMCOS-SE safety module, and pulse metering sensor module (see Fig. 3).

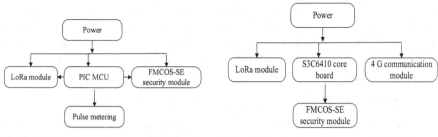

Fig. 3. The hardware framework of the collector agent

Fig. 4. The hardware framework of the concentrator agent

3.1.1 PIC Microcontroller Microcontroller Module

The microcontroller of the collector Agent uses Microchip's PIC24FJ128GA308 16-bit low-power microcontroller. The hardware module is responsible for sensor data reading, control signal output, data storage and communication. The microcontroller has a 16 × 16 hardware multiplier and a 32 × 16 hardware divider, which facilitates the processing of water meter data. At the same time, the current consumption of the microcontroller during sleep is 400 nA, which can run for a long time under battery power.

3.1.2 Power Module

The power supply switching circuit supports DC power supply and dry battery power supply separately. When the DC power supply and the battery are connected at the same time, the DC power supply is preferred. The storage module and the wireless communication module are respectively provided with 3.3 V power input by two separate HT7333 low dropout linear regulators. The on-off of the control circuit is controlled by a MOS field effect switch.

3.1.3 LoRa Wireless Communication Module

Use SX1278 LoRa wireless module from Semtech. The module is a long-distance, low-power wireless communication module that uses spread-spectrum technology, and has the characteristics of long communication distance, high receiving sensitivity, and low power consumption. The typical current consumption during sleep is 0.2 uA, the typical current consumption during reception is 10 mA, and when using 7 dm transmit power transmission, the typical current consumption is 2 mA. The maximum transmission distance in the city is about 3 km, suitable for long-distance low-power data transmission.

3.1.4 FMCOS-SE Security Module

The FMCOS-SE security module is a security module developed based on the FM1280 chip. It uses an ARM 32-bit security CPU and is equipped with a dedicated operating system. The FMSE security module encrypts some sensitive data related to the water meter, such as user password, user ID, card authentication data, ladder water price, water meter reading, valve control status, equipment root key, etc. The encryption algorithm used is SM4 security algorithm. The SM4 algorithm was officially approved by the State Password Administration in 2012. It is the first commercial password algorithm for wireless LAN in my country. It has the characteristics of simple, safe and fast. SM4 is symmetric encryption, and the key length and packet length are both 128 bits.

3.2 Concentrator Agent

Based on the requirements of data processing and protocol conversion, the hardware of the concentrator agent is mainly based on the S3C6410 development board (see Fig. 4). The development board uses a SPI interface and a USB interface wireless communication module to connect to the 4G communication module. The concentrator agent obtains the system information, water meter information, valves, etc. encrypted by the FMCOS-SE transmitted from the collector agent through the LoRa wireless module, and uploads it to the server through the 4G communication module. The server completes the encryption and decryption of the data.

3.2.1 Processor

Use Samsung S3C6410 processor. This is a core based on ARM1176JZF-S, including 16 KB instruction data cache and 16 KB instruction data TCM.

3.2.2 Power Supply

In order to maintain long-term continuous operation, the power supply on the concentrator Agent board is provided by the DC power supply.

3.2.3 LoRa Wireless Communication Module

Use the same SX1278 LoRa wireless module as the collector Agent, and connect to the CPU with SPI interface.

3.2.4 4G Communication Module

This system uses U8300C 4G wireless module, it is a wireless terminal product suitable for TDD-LTE/TD-SCDMA/UMTS/EVDO/EDGE/GPRS/GSM/CDMA multiple network standards and GPS positioning services. While providing high-speed data access and GPS positioning services, the U8300C can provide functions such as SMS and address book, and can be widely used in products such as mobile broadband access, video surveillance, handheld terminals, and car equipment. The system uses the serial port UART of the ARM embedded system S3C6410 to complete the control of the U8300C 4G module. Drive the transistor S8050 through the S3C6410 GPIO pin to reset the 4G module. The concentrator agent remotely transmits user data, channel information, water meter dial data, valve control data and other related data to the background database through the U8300C 4G wireless module, enabling centralized management and monitoring of multiple concentrator agents.

3.2.5 FMCOS-SE Security Module

Use the same FMCOS-SE security module as the collector Agent, and connect with the S3C6410 embedded processor with SPI interface.

4 FMCOS-SE Security Module File Structure Design

The security module is a special security encryption chip designed based on the requirements of the ISO7816 specification, and supports the watch to realize the security protection of sensitive data. The product uses a dedicated domestic cryptographic algorithm chip as a hardware platform and is equipped with a dedicated operating system. The security module has adopted perfect security protection measures during hardware design, such as anti-tampering, anti-attack and other functions, and the operating system has also designed and implemented a perfect software security mechanism, using domestic cryptographic algorithms to meet the storage and storage of key data. Encryption protection. The security module contains the water meter application, and the application directory is MF. The following (see Fig. 5) shows the file structure of the Collector Agent and Concentrator Agent security modules.

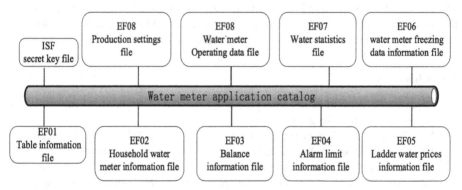

Fig. 5. File structure of the collector agent and concentrator agent security modules

5 Agent Communication Protocol Design

According to the characteristics of LoRa hardware and the actual application scenarios, the communication protocol between collector agent and concentrator agent is designed. The communication between the collector Agent, the concentrator Agent and the server/handheld terminal interacts in the form of data packets. A complete command packet consists of the start identification unit, packet length, command 1, command 2, command 3, command unit and check unit end character, see Table 1.

5.1 Command 1

Represents the source device: 53H (V) represents the server, 57H (W) stands for handheld terminal/Bluetooth, 55H (U) stands for serial debugger, 52H (R) represents the collector, 4DH (M) stands for concentrator.

Table 1. Common format of the information interaction command packet of server, concentrator and collector

Packet header	Packet length	Command 1	Command 2	Command 3	Data	Check code
55 99 2 bytes	1 byte	Source device 1 byte	Terminal device 1 byte	1 byte	JSON format	CRC 2 bytes

5.2 Command 2

On behalf of the terminal equipment: 53H (V) on behalf of the server, 57H (W) stands for handheld terminal/Bluetooth, 55H (U) stands for serial debugger, 52H (R) represents the collector, 4DH (M) stands for concentrator.

5.3 Command 3

The command includes up to 100 commands such as querying the agent information of the collector, serial port setting, water meter information and valve information setting, Ad-Hoc network channel type and frequency setting.

5.4 Check Unit

a) Check the "command data" in the protocol. From the first byte of "Command 1" to the last byte of the data area;

b) A 16-bit CRC check polynomial $x16 + x2 + 1$ (0×8005) is used to generate a 2-byte CRC checksum (high byte in the back, low byte in the front);

c) The sender should generate a two-byte CRC checksum according to the "command unit". After receiving the complete data packet, the receiver should generate a new CRC checksum according to the "command unit";

d) The new CRC checksum is equal to the received checksum, indicating that the data packet is valid.

6 Routing Protocol Design

6.1 Ad Hoc routing protocol

Routing protocol provides the path selection for communication between collector node and concentrator node. Ad Hoc routing protocols are divided into active routing and on-demand routing. Active routing is similar to traditional routing protocols. Each node in the network needs to maintain a routing table to other nodes, Periodically broadcast routing packet information is exchanged and routing table updates are maintained. On-demand routing is the opposite of table-driven routing. Each node makes routing requests only when needed, and instead of establishing and maintaining routing information to other nodes, it creates routing tables temporarily based on communication needs.

In this design, for the acquisition Agent, The data finally flows to the corresponding concentrator Agent. A collector Agent node will not take other collector Agents as the destination node for communication, so there is no need to maintain the routing information to all other nodes in the network, so Table - driven routing protocol should not be used. In addition, the location of collector Agent and concentrator Agent in this design is relatively fixed, so the items in the routing table will not change frequently and the frequent changes of node topology need not be considered. The concentrator Agent can broadcast its routing information and save the routing request cost generated by the node.

6.2   Four Basic Messages Design

In this design, Ad Hoc protocol is designed based on on-demand protocol, and has four basic messages (see Fig. 6): Routing request message, Router response message.

The concentrator agent broadcast message and Routing error message.

The fields of each message are described below:

Version: The version number of the protocol currently in use

Type: Message type

TTL: Time to live, A counter used to limit packet lifetime. Each time the message goes through the route forward, TTL-1, When the TTL decays to 0, the packet is discarded.

Hops: The number of hops a message passes through a router

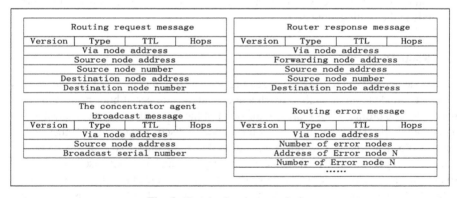

Fig. 6. Four basic messages design

1) The concentrator agent broadcast message

① Via node address: The address of the node through which the broadcast message is currently passing

② Concentrator Agent source node address: Address of the concentrator Agent node issuing the broadcast

③ Broadcast serial number: Broadcast serial number maintained by a source

2) Routing request message

① Via node address: The address of the routing request message currently passing through the node

② Source node address: The address of the routing request originating node

③ Source node number: The sequence number maintained by the source node, indicating the order of the request

④ Destination node address: The address of the destination node

⑤ Destination node number: The sequence number maintained by the destination node, indicating the order of the response

3) Router response message

① Via node address: The address of the current routing response message passing through the node

② Forwarding node address: Specifies the address of the node to forward this message

③ Source node address: The address of the node sending the routing response message

④ Source node number: The sequence number maintained by the source node, indicating the order of the response

⑤ Destination node address: The destination node address of the routing response message

4) Routing error message

① Via node address: The address of the node at which the current routing error message is routed

② Number of error nodes: The number of error nodes contained in the message

③ Address of Error node N: The address of the Nth node at which a connection error occurred

④ Number of Error node N: When an error occurs, the sequence number of the error node in the routing table cache

6.3 Route Discovery

Each node maintains a routing table (see Fig. 7). The routing table contains the address of the next node to go through to reach a node and the number of hops needed to reach that node. The ordinal fields represent the order of the data and are used to route updates and avoid loops. There are three ways for a node to discover the route to other nodes: address broadcast, passive acquisition, and on-demand request. The address broadcast mode can only be initiated by the concentrator Agent, which is mainly used to convey its route to the accessible nodes in the network at the initial stage of network establishment. When address broadcasting is used, the concentrator Agent will broadcast its address to neighboring nodes. The node receiving the broadcast will update its routing table and forward the broadcast packet to its neighboring nodes. In the form of flooding, the routing information of the concentrator Agent will be transmitted to all reachable nodes in the network. After address broadcasting is completed, the initial nodes at the time of network establishment will establish a routing item to the concentrator Agent node. Passive acquisition means that during communication, a node retrieves the route to a node in reverse. Suppose that a newly added collector Agent node A obtains the route to concentrator Agent node C by on-demand request, but node C does not know the route of node A. When node A sends data message to node C via node B routing, node C will add node B to the routing item to node A. Before sending data to a node that is not recorded in the routing table, any node will request a route to a destination to its neighbor node on demand. This is typically used when a newly added node starts communicating with the concentrator agent, when one node has a network unreachable failure and the other nodes need to update the routing table. The following sections describe the detailed steps of address broadcasting and on-demand.

Destination	Next hop	Hops	Destination ID
0x00000001	0x00000004	3	3

Fig. 7. Node routing table

6.3.1 Address Broadcast Mode

(1) Launch of broadcast

The broadcast message initiated by the concentrator Agent contains three elements: < via address, source address, source serial number >. Where, the address of the source address is written to the concentrator Agent, and the source serial number is written to a set of increasing serial Numbers maintained by the concentrator initiating the broadcast to identify the order of the broadcast message. Fill the TTL according to the size of the broadcast and set the hops to 0.

(2) Broadcast reception

After the neighbor node receives the broadcast message of the concentrator Agent, it first checks whether the TTL is greater than 0. If it is greater than 0, it continues to check whether the address of the concentrator Agent node in the broadcast message is equal to the address of the concentrator to which it belongs. If so, it checks whether there is a route to the concentrator node in the routing table. If the routing table meets one of the following conditions: ① The routing table does not contain the node; ② The ID number of the node in the routing table is less than t the ordinal numbe in the message; ③ The ID number of the node in the routing table is equal to the ordinal numbe in the message, and the number of hops is greater than the number of hops in the message, the routing table is updated and the message is forwarded.

(3) Routing table update:

The address and ID of the source node in the received message are filled in destination node field and the serial number field of the destination node, the via node field in the message is filled in the next hop field, and the hops number in the message is added by one to fill in the hops field.

(4) Message forwarding:

When forwarding the message, fill the node address into the via node field, and subtract 1 from TTL and add 1 to the hop number.

The solid node is the concentrator Agent with address D, and the hollow node is the collector Agent with addresses A, B, and C respectively (see Fig. 8). Nodes directly connected by solid lines are neighbor nodes. In the figure, A, B and C are neighbor, C and D are neighbor, while A,B and D are not. Address broadcast is initiated by concentrator Agent node D, and the serial number of broadcast is 1. The arrow in the figure shows the propagation path of the address broadcast. The address broadcast issued by A and B is omitted. When broadcast to all reachable nodes in the network, each node caches the next hop path to D in the routing table. Node C can directly transfer data to Node D, while nodes A and B will transfer data to node C, which will then transfer data to node D. After the broadcast, Node D is not aware of the existence of other nodes. Only when other nodes initiate communication to node D, can node D establish a reverse route by passive acquisition.

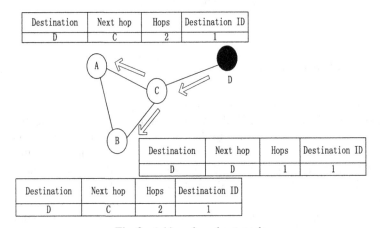

Fig. 8. Address broadcast mode

6.3.2 Request on Demand

(1) Initiate routing request

Routing request message contains five elements: via node address, source node address, source node serial number, destination node address, and destination node serial number. The node that initiates the routing request fills the address of the node into the address field of the source node and the address field of the routing node, fills the address of the destination node into the address field of the destination node, and fills the self-increasing ordinal number maintained by the node into the ordinal number field of the source node. The destination node field fills in the latest serial number of the known destination node. If the destination node has never been found by the node, fill in −1.

(2) Processing of routing requests

The node receiving the routing request message first determines whether the TTL of the message is 0. If not, it continues to determine whether the message is sent by the node itself. If not, detects whether it has received a request containing the same source node address and source node number in a certain time。 if not then check if the nodes in the routing table and orderly, is greater than the packet destination node in the serial number of the record, if any, is issued a response message routing, if not then start the timer, and set up a in the routing table for packet source node as the destination node in routing record, will jump under the node address fill in the address field, will jump Numbers to add 1 in the packet, fill in the jump number, from the source node number fill in the destination node number field. After completing the routing table, the node fills its serial number into the routing field of the received message, and forwards the message after subtracting 1 from TTL and adding 1 to the hops.

(3) Initiate routing response

When a node receives a valid routing request message, if the node is the destination of the request or the routing record of the request node is in the routing table of the node, and the node ordinal number in the record is greater than that in the request message, then the routing response message is issued. The node sending the response fills the destination address and serial number in the request message into the address and serial number fields of the source node in the routing response message, fills the address of the node itself into the address field of the routing node, fills the hopping number into the hopping number section, and fills the address of the originating node in the routing request message into the address field of the destination node. The via node address is filled in the forward node field, the source node address is filled in the destination node address field, and the TTL value is reset.

(4) Processing of routing response

The node receiving the routing response message checks whether the TTL value in the message is 0. If not, it continues to check whether the current node matches the destination node in the message. If it is, and the serial number of the source node in the message is greater than that in the routing table, then the address of the source node, the serial number of the source node, and the address of the routing node in the response message are updated into the address of the destination node, the serial number of the destination node, and the address of the next hop in the routing table respectively, and the number of hops is added by 1 to fill in the hopping number segment. If the destination node address of the received message does not match the address of the current node, check whether the address of the node itself matches the forwarding node field in the message. If so, update the routing table and fill the forwarding node address field with the next-hop node address of the routing item in the routing table. Fill its address into the via node field, subtract 1 from the number of hops and TTL, and then forward the response message.

New node E joins the existing network. Where A, B, C and D are nodes in the existing Agent network (see Fig. 9). After running for A certain time, A, B, C and D have all learned the next hop route to other nodes in the network. Only the routing tables of Nodes A and B that are directly connected to E are listed in the figure. Node E broadcasts routing requests to node D to neighboring nodes. Since node E knows nothing about node D, the destination node in the request message is numbered −1.

Destination	Next hop	Hops	Destination ID
D	C	2	2
B	B	1	2
C	C	1	2

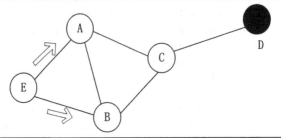

Destination	Next hop	Hops	Destination ID
D	C	2	2
A	A	1	2
C	C	1	2

Fig. 9. Request on demand

Since routing entries to D are in routing tables of A and B, and their Ordinal Numbers are greater than −1, both A and B will issue routing response to E (see Fig. 10). Since the number of hops to D in both A and B routing tables is 2, and the last known Node D saved in the routing table also needs to be the same, node E will update the information in the response message that arrives first into the routing table, ignoring the information in the message that arrives later.

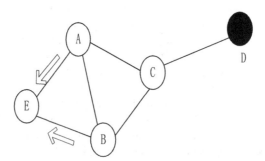

Fig. 10. Node E update routing table

7 Conclusion

This paper combines LoRa wireless networking technology and FMCOS-SE security module into the meter reading system to implement an Ad hoc network water meter collection and reading system based on multi-agent. This system combines the advantages of the current mainstream wireless meter reading technology, and has the characteristics of low deployment cost, low power consumption and strong scalability. This system adopts a highly modular design, which can be widely used for the collection and monitoring of various meter data such as user electric meters, water meters, gas meters, etc. This system provides a basic IoT perception layer for smart water services, provides accurate water data for water management, obtains all available information such as water quality at any time, achieves water saving and energy saving goals, and better manages water supply and drainage facilities throughout, Improve the efficiency of asset operation and maintenance management, promote the modernization of city management, and accelerate the construction of a "smart city".

Acknowledgments. This work was funded by Natural Science Foundation of Fujian Province (Grant Number 2021J011221);

Conflict of Interest. The authors declare that they have no conflict of interest.

References

1. Yin, J., Wei, L., Sun, H., et al.: An incentive mechanism for mobile crowd sensing in vehicular ad hoc networks. J. Transp. Technol. **12**(1), 15 (2022)
2. Shen, X., Li, C., Li, M., Feng, Y.: Design and implementation of wireless ad hoc smart metering system for power quality. Int. J. Sci. **3**(12), 84–90 (2016)
3. Sajan, R.I., Christopher, V.B., Kavitha, M.J., et al.: An energy aware secure three-level weighted trust evaluation and grey wolf optimization based routing in wireless ad hoc sensor network. Wirel. Netw. **28**(4), 1439–1455 (2022). https://doi.org/10.1007/s11276-022-029 17-x
4. Muntean, M.V.: Multi-agent system for intelligent urban traffic management using wireless sensor networks data. Sensors **22**, 208 (2021)
5. Qin, J., Fu, W., Gao, H., et al.: Distributed k-means algorithm for sensor networks based on multi-agent consensus theory. IEEE Trans. Cybern. **47**(3), 772–783 (2017)
6. Alsboui, T., Qin, Y., Hill, R., et al.: An energy efficient multi-mobile agent itinerary planning approach in wireless sensor networks. Computing **103**, 2093–2113 (2021)
7. Xu, B., Lu, M., Zhang, H., et al.: A novel multi-agent model for robustness with component failure and malware propagation in wireless sensor networks. Sensors **21**(14), 4873 (2021)
8. Qi, M., Pan, J., Song, S.: The design of user meter reading system based on ZigBee and GSM. In: 2020 12th International Conference on Measuring Technology and Mechatronics Automation (ICMTMA) (2020)
9. Lil, Y., Yan, X., Zeng, L., Wu, H.: Research on water meter reading system based on LoRa communication. In: IEEE International Conference on Smart Grid and Smart Cities, vol. 248–251 (2017)

10. Kumari, P., Mishra, R., Gupta, H.P., et al.: An energy efficient smart metering system using edge computing in LoRa network. IEEE Trans. Sustain. Comput. **PP**(99), 1 (2021)
11. Wu, Y.H., Zuo, R.J., Jiang, H.: The two-level group network meter reading system based on SX1278. In: Proceedings of SPIE International Conference on Optical Communications and Networks, vol. 11048 (2019)
12. Bai, K., Chuankun, W.: A secure white-box SM4 implementation. Secur. Commun. Netw. **9**(10), 996–1006 (2016)
13. Hu, X., Qin, X., Mou, H.: Secure measuring and controlling methods embedded SM4 algorithm for smart home. In: Deng, Z., Li, H. (eds.) Proceedings of the 2015 Chinese Intelligent Automation Conference, vol. 336, pp. 179–187. Springer, Heidelberg (2015). https://doi.org/10.1007/978-3-662-46469-4_19

The Optimization of Higher Vocational Accounting Curriculum System Under the Background of Intelligentization: A Web Crawler Based Method

Shuangshuang Ying[1]([✉]) [iD] and Tingting He[2] [iD]

[1] Taizhou Vocational and Technical College, Taizhou, Zhejiang, China
yingshuang40@163.com
[2] Zhejiang Industry and Trade Vocational College, Wenzhou, Zhejiang, China

Abstract. Based on the OBE education concept, this paper adopts Python web crawler technology to conduct big data collection and analysis of accounting job recruitment information, sort out market demand for accounting talents' knowledge, ability, and quality, and pays attention to the knowledge structure, post ability and professional quality that students should have in the real work situation, makes clear accounting talent cultivation objectives in the era of intelligence, reverse design and reconstruct the higher vocational accounting curriculum system, which is conducive to enhance the accounting graduates' job adaptability and market competitiveness, and ultimately deepen the reform of talent cultivation mode, effectively improve the actual effect of talent cultivation.

Keywords: OBE education concept · Web crawler technology · Curriculum system · Talent cultivation

1 OBE Education Concept

OBE, also known as outcome-based education, which emphasizes that educators should start from the actual demand of the society for talents, reversely design the ability indicators that students are expected to achieve, and set the teaching objectives, teaching contents, teaching methods and teaching evaluation according to these ability indicators, so as to maximize the consistency of educational objectives and results, therefore to improve the quality of talent cultivation.

The core concepts of OBE education mainly include the following three aspects: (1) Student centered. Focusing on what students "learn" rather than what teachers "teach", curriculum development returns to what students "acquire" and "what they can do"; (2)

This work was supported by the General Research Project of Department of Education of Zhejiang Province through the Project Research on the Optimization of Higher Vocational Accounting Curriculum System under the Background of Intelligentization——Based on Outcomes-based Education (OBE) Educational Concept under Project Y202044760.

Y. Chenggang et al. (Eds.): MobiMedia 2022, LNICST 451, pp. 31–42, 2022.
https://doi.org/10.1007/978-3-031-23902-1_3

Outcome-based philosophy. In accordance with the reverse design principles as "the needs of education stakeholders → objectives of the talent cultivation → graduation requirements → curriculum system", emphasis on students' learning output as the starting point to launch cultivation program design, teaching resources allocation and teaching implementation; (3) Continuous improvement concept. It emphasizes the importance of establishing effective quality supervision and continuous improvement mechanism, which can continuously track the teaching situation, correct students' learning curriculum system, teachers and teaching activities, so as to make the cultivation objectives meet the needs of the society, and finally continuously promote the improvement of professional talent cultivation quality.

2   Problems Existing in Cultivating Accounting Professionals in Higher Vocational Colleges

At present, there is an increasingly obvious gap between the skill structure of accounting graduates and the demands of employers. The main reason is that the traditional accounting education in colleges and universities carries out the subject-oriented talent cultivation mode, pays attention to the breadth and depth of knowledge in teaching, lacks the demand analysis of industries and professions, and does not pay attention to the cultivation of students' post ability and professional quality. As a result, the structural imbalance between the supply and demand of accounting talents becomes increasingly prominent. The Implementation Plan for The Reform of National Vocational Education issued by The State Council (2019) clearly states that: It should take the initiative to align with the trend of scientific and technological development and market demand, cultivate high-quality technical and skilled personnel for regional development, and alleviate the structural employment contradiction. As the cradle of talent cultivation and under the development and reform of information technology such as big data, Internet+ and artificial intelligence, universities have to rethink: the goal of training students to become the traditional data processors can no longer meet the needs of current economic development. In order to bring education up to date, what courses can be set to promote the training of accounting talents required by the era of intelligence, so that we cultivate talents in line with the market demand, conform to the trend of time.

2.1   Market Demand Positioning is Not Accurate

The cultivation and curriculum setting of accounting professionals in higher vocational colleges should closely follow the development of enterprises and technological changes, adhere to the outcome-based education concept, and cultivate students' knowledge ability and accomplishment according to the specific needs of accounting jobs in enterprise. However, the definition of the current demand of talent market is mostly adopts the methods of questionnaire survey, field research in enterprises or inviting experts to school for in-depth interviews and son on. These research methods all need to spend a lot of time, manpower and material resources while the obtained information has problems such as low efficiency, small sample size and one-sided judgment, which leads to incomplete and inaccurate information acquisition of accounting talent market demand in higher vocational colleges, and the market demand positioning is inaccurate.

2.2 Talent Cultivation Target Positioning is Not Clear

College is the cradle of talent cultivation. What kind of talent should accounting major cultivate? What kind of knowledge, ability and quality can represent the value orientation of education? Due to the lack of the support of big data samples, the universities lack a clear goal orientation for talent cultivation, the homogenization of talent cultivation goals among universities is serious, and the positioning of talent cultivation is vague.

2.3 The Setting of Professional Curriculum is Out of Date

Currently, the accounting curriculum of higher vocational colleges in China is still based on traditional courses, one-sided pursuit of the passing rate of the certificate of examination. Curriculum and content are mostly set around the accounting qualification certificate examination, and the awareness of general education is insufficient. At the same time, there is also a lack of courses related to financial strategy, intelligence and financial sharing. The curriculum system in this mode ignores the cultivation of accounting talents' post ability and professional quality, which cannot meet the current market demand for accounting talents.

3   The Market Demand of Accounting Talents' Knowledge, Ability and Accomplishment

Under the OBE education concept, the education side should fully define the knowledge ability and accomplishment level that students should achieve when they graduate, and then construct the corresponding curriculum system to ensure that students achieve these expected goals. In order to ensure that the accounting talents knowledge, ability and quality of the comprehensiveness and accuracy of market demand information, under the background of the era of big data, this paper uses the Python language web crawler technology, from the post requirement information of recruitment website, in 51 job recruitment website, for low, medium and high levels of financial assistant, financial personnel, financial director and chief financial officer position information data capture, collected and screened thousands of useful original recruitment data. Through the collection and analysis of large sample data, the specific market demand for accounting talents' knowledge structure, post ability and professional quality can obtained.

3.1 Accounting Personnel Knowledge Structure Demand Data and Analysis

Through word frequency analysis (as shown in Table 1), this paper summarizes the knowledge structure that accounting personnel should master. There are eight contents in descending order: financial management, financial accounting, information technology, financial analysis, cost accounting and management, laws and regulations, tax, internal control and audit (as shown in Fig. 1).

Table 1. Demand for knowledge structure of accounting talents at different levels

Index post			Financial assistant	Financial personnel	Financial executive	Chief financial officer	Total
Knowledge structure	Financial Accounting	Accounting treatment	2625	1359	5628	3670	13282
		Financial audit	3549	2439	6234	5025	17247
		Assets management	1902	1617	3301	3495	10315
	Financial analysis	Financial analysis	3229	3984	9850	10956	28019
		Statement analysis	917	1241	3681	3271	9110
	Cost accounting and manage	Cost plan	100	1066	806	5314	7286
		Cost accounting	460	1526	1682	3464	7132
		Cost analysis	342	1366	2018	4418	8144
		Cost control	188	1740	2998	4092	9018
	Financial management	Financial management	5666	6461	12444	15086	39657
		Financial budget	253	646	1134	1728	3761
		Capital operation	59	104	208	510	881
	Tax	Tax law	1010	1045	2353	2201	6609
		Tax declaration	1431	736	1650	767	4584
		Tax planning	467	748	3165	5076	9456
	Internal control	Financial regulations	560	664	2851	4242	8317
		Financial monitoring	145	236	721	1567	2669
	Audit	Organize internal audit; Cooperate with external audit	451	1716	2249	4174	8590
	Laws and regulations	Laws and regulations	1178	2529	4039	4969	12715
		Accounting standard	976	1080	2941	2954	7951
	Information technology	OFFICE	2945	1644	2455	1709	8753
		Financial software	6708	3288	7658	5106	22760
		ERP	1288	1395	2249	1893	6825

According to the analysis in Table 1, with the increase of post level, the importance of financial management, financial analysis, cost accounting and management, laws and regulations, taxation, internal control and audit increased significantly, among which the importance of cost accounting and management rose sharply. Among the demands

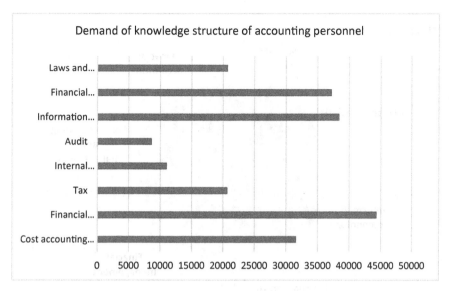

Fig. 1. Demand analysis of knowledge structure of accounting personnel

of knowledge structure, tax declaration and information technology decline with the increase of post level.

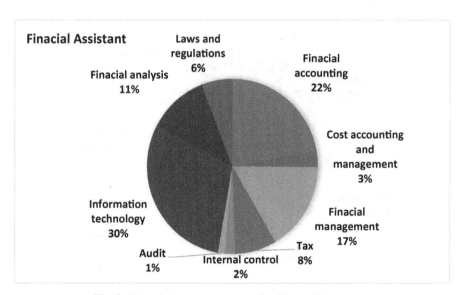

Fig. 2. Knowledge structure analysis of financial assistants

As can be seen from Fig. 2, the financial assistant position has the highest requirements for information technology and financial accounting knowledge, followed by financial management and financial analysis. From Fig. 3, it can be seen that financial

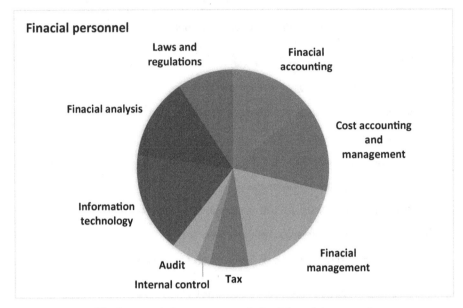

Fig. 3. Knowledge structure analysis of financial personnel

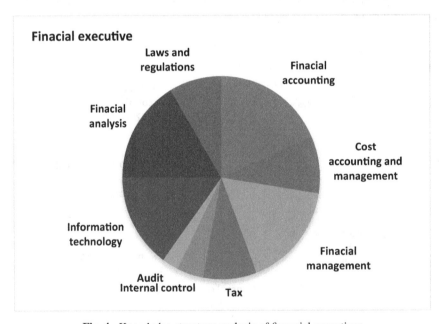

Fig. 4. Knowledge structure analysis of financial executives

personnels have balanced requirements on financial accounting, financial management, cost accounting and management, while information technology, tax, internal control

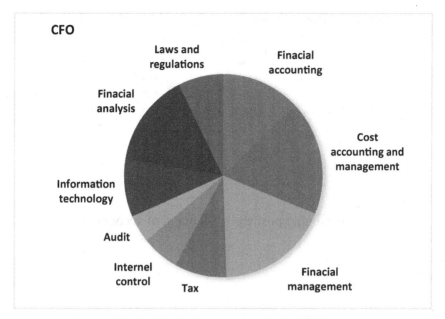

Fig. 5. Knowledge structure analysis of CFO

and audit are less important. Figure 4 shows that the requirements of financial director position on the knowledge structure of accounting talents are basically similar to those of financial personnels. As can be seen from Fig. 5, the position of CFO strengthens the requirements on financial management, cost accounting and management knowledge, and weakens the requirements on information technology.

3.2 Accounting Personnel Post Ability Demand Data and Analysis

By Table 2 Different levels of accounting personnel post ability demand and Fig. 6. Analysis of accounting personnel post ability demand, it can be seen that employers pay particular attention to accounting personnel's interpersonal skills, including communication, coordination and teamwork skills. In addition, they have high requirements on learning ability, language expression ability and English ability. With the upgrade of accounting job, the importance of interpersonal skills, among which the importance of coordination has skyrocketed. Although the employment positions of accounting graduates in higher vocational colleges are mostly basic accounting positions, but while focusing on knowledge learning in personnel cultivation and curriculum setting, more attention should be paid to the cultivation and improvement of students' interpersonal skills, learning skills and language skills, so as to lay a good foundation for the development of their future career.

Table 2. Different levels of accounting personnel post ability demand

Index post			Financial assistant	Financial personnel	Financial executive	Chief financial officer	Total
Post ability	Interpersonal skill	Communication	12832	9339	15378	14975	52524
		Coordinate	4366	5413	9827	12785	32391
		Team work	7236	5644	8583	10241	31704
	Self-learning ability		7193	3847	4760	3232	19032
	language competence		1486	1352	1684	2062	6584
	English ability		1861	1427	1333	1519	6140

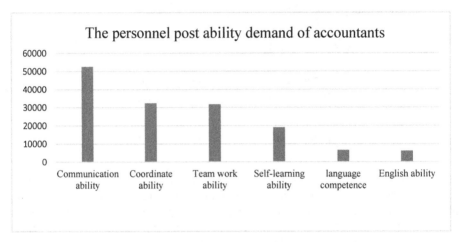

Fig. 6. Analysis of accounting personnel post ability demand

3.3 Accounting Personnel's Professional Literacy Demand Data and Analysis

As can be seen from Fig. 1 and Fig. 1, employers attach particular importance to accounting personnel's sense of responsibility and professional ethics, as well as stress resistance. They hope that accounting personnel should be meticulous, rigorous, practical and have hard-working craftsman spirit. With the upgrade of accounting positions, they have higher and higher requirements for stress resistance. In addition, the employer also has a requirement to the health of accountant personnel and disposition, just the requirement is not outstanding (Table 3 and Fig. 7).

Table 3. Demand for professional quality of accountants at different levels

Index Post		Financial assistant	Financial personnel	Financial executive	Chief financial officer	Total
Professional accomplishment	Conscientiousness	8731	4644	8265	6380	28020
	Professional ethics	5432	3279	6020	6030	20761
	Compressive resistance	2747	2493	4448	4707	14395
	Meticulous and rigorous	6012	2872	4845	4327	18056
	Practical	2275	1128	1482	977	5862
	Hard work and enduring hardship	1765	726	1213	741	4445
	Healthy body	541	602	509	580	2232
	Open personality	1113	493	682	540	2828

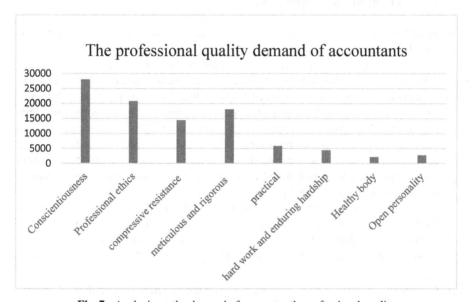

Fig. 7. Analysis on the demand of accountant's professional quality

4   Establishment of Cultivation Objectives for Higher Vocational Accounting Professionals in the Era of Intelligence

Different talent cultivation objectives determine how to cultivate the corresponding professional talents for a major. Based on the collation and analysis of large sample data, this paper defines the knowledge structure, post ability and professional quality of accounting talents in line with market demand. On this basis, the cultivation objectives of higher vocational accounting talents in the intelligent era are set as follows: Cultivating innovative, developmental and compound technical accounting talents with all-round development of morality, intelligence, body, beauty and labor who are oriented to the construction of socialism with Chinese characteristics, adapt to technological change and enterprise development, who master national financial laws and regulations and economic policies, have strong accounting processing ability and certain cost management, tax planning, financial data analysis and decision-making ability; who are good at accounting management and decision-making; who are proficient in using Internet tools and common office software for data retrieval and analysis and daily business processing, familiar with the analysis and processing of commercial data, with the ability to solve problems with big data analytical thinking; who are with strong interpersonal skills and lifelong learning ability, pragmatic cooperation spirit and good professional ethics and accomplishment.

5 Construction of Curriculum System of Higher Vocational Accounting in Intelligent Era

(1) Meet the demands of the accounting industry, reconstruct the traditional professional courses.

As most graduates of accounting major in higher vocational colleges are engaged in basic accounting positions, the construction of accounting major course system mainly relies on the requirements of financial assistant positions, while considering future career development. Specifically, financial management, financial accounting (including basic accounting), financial analysis, cost accounting and management accounting computerization tax calculation and declaration and the application of Excel in accounting should be set as the core courses of accounting major; and Internal control, audit, tax planning, ERP and financial budget can be selected as professional courses.

In addition, in addition to Excel, Word and PPT are also required by employers for the operation of Office software for accountants. During the implementation of each course, students can choose the electronic version of homework submission, so as to improve the operation level of Office software in the process of learning.

(2) Change the traditional education idea, design the integrated curriculum of general education and professional education.

One-sided pursuit of professional education and neglect of general education is not conducive to the cultivation of students' professional quality, as well as the shaping of their outlook on life and values, while, students often lack interest and enthusiasm in learning for the specialized integrated curriculum of general education and professional education. General education and professional education are not exclusive, and they can be coordinated and integrated with each other. Therefore, it is possible to change the traditional educational concept and design the integrated curriculum based on general education and centered on accounting courses. On the one hand, by the form of case teaching and task-driven, professional ethics and financial laws and regulations should be integrated into the teaching of professional courses (such as basic accounting, financial accounting, tax calculation and declaration, etc.) in a planned and targeted way. On the other hand, setting up a series of professional elective courses in the form of special lectures combined with the characteristics of accounting major to strengthen students' psychological quality education such as sense of responsibility and resistance to pressure.

At the same time, the student-centered education idea should be highlighted in the teaching process. On the one hand, various teaching methods and teaching modes should be flexibly used in the classroom teaching process to strengthen students' communication and coordination ability, teamwork ability and independent learning ability. On the other hand, combined with the teaching design, more opportunities to exercise and display should be given to students to cultivate their language expression ability.

(3) Keep up with the development of information technology and increase intelligent accounting courses

With the constant change and development of information technology and financial intelligence, the cultivation of accounting talents in colleges and universities should be forward-looking. Based on the characteristics of the talent cultivating target in higher vocational colleges, combined with the current market demand, students do not need to master computer language and programming related to intelligent accounting, and there is no need to set up a large number of intelligent accounting courses in the course. But on the basis of traditional curriculum system, it can increase big data technology applications (such as Python language introductory course), business data analysis, intelligent accounting courses, such as business financial integration and financial sharing courses to make students familiar with the development direction of future accounting, train students' big data and intelligent thinking, and strengthen the ability of big data analysis to solve practical problems.

6   Conclusion

The main conclusions of this paper are as follows: First, make clear the demand of accounting talent market. Through the analysis of large sample data, define the specific market demand for accounting talents from three aspects: knowledge structure, post ability and professional accomplishment. Second, establish accounting personnel cultivation objectives. Based on the market demand, combined with the background of the current intelligent era, formulating the cultivation objectives of higher vocational accounting talents. It should emphasize the cultivation of accounting talent management and decision-making ability, strengthen the education consciousness of post ability and professional quality, and pay attention to the formation of big data analysis thinking. Third, reconstruct accounting curriculum system. Based on the data analysis and cultivation objectives, the core and elective courses of the major are readjust, the integrated courses of general and specialized are designed, and the intelligent accounting course is added, so as to cultivate accounting talents that meet the market demand in the background of the intelligent era.

References

1. Li, Z.: Outcome based instructional design. China Univ. Teach. (03), 32–39 (2015)
2. Li, L., Meng, Y.: Imbalance between supply and demand of accounting talent skill structure in China: present situation and countermeasures. China Account. Rev. (03), 117–132 (2015)
3. Yan, D.: An approach to instructional design based on outcome-based. J. Zhengzhou Univ. Aeronaut. (06), 132–128 (2018)
4. Cao, Z., Cao, Y., Hao, C., Wang, J., Qu, Q.: Discussion on student cultivation system of mineral processing engineering under the background of engineering education certification -- a case study of Inner Mongolia University of Science and Technology. Univ. Educ. (02), 39–41 (2019)
5. Zhou, S., Tang, D.: Transformation and development of accounting education in intelligent era. Account. Res. (12), 92–94 (2019)
6. Chang, F., Li, Z., Wen, J., Chang, F.: Design and implementation of recruitment data crawler based on Python. Softw. Guide (12), 130–133 (2019)

A Direct Location Algorithm Based on Gauss Newton Iteration

Zhong Gaozhi[1]($\boxtimes$), Xiao Sa[2], Zhang Jie[1], Wu Xiangyu[1], and Hou Changbo[1]

[1] Harbin Engineering University, Harbin, China
2845520623@qq.com, houchangbo@hrbeu.edu.cn
[2] Beijing Institute of Astronautical Systems Engineering, Beijing, China

Abstract. Introduction: With the rise of logistics, navigation, takeout and other industries, location information plays a more and more important role in daily life. It is different from military positioning, which takes high positioning accuracy as the main principle. Due to the need to consider its popularity, civil positioning generally focuses on the principle of economy, and strives to reduce the hardware requirements of the positioning system as much as possible under the condition of reasonable and relaxed positioning accuracy.

Objective: This paper aims to use the received signal strength to locate the emitter signal, and improve the positioning accuracy of the algorithm through continuous iteration and correction, so as to ensure the positioning accuracy on the premise that the positioning method based on RSS does not need additional hardware equipment.

Methods: The algorithm in this paper locates the emitter based on the received signal strength, uses the median weighted filter to collect the emitter power and preliminarily screen out the gross error, then uses the genetic algorithm to select the initial point of the iteration, and uses the improved weighted least squares algorithm based on Gauss Newton iteration to estimate the parameters. Finally, an error correction module is added to further ensure the positioning accuracy.

Keywords: Received signal strength · Median weighted filtering · Direct location algorithm

1 Introduction

Thanks to the vigorous development of deep learning, image processing, computer vision and other technologies, the machine is equipped with eyes that can see the world. Modern life is gradually developing in the direction of intelligence and automation. In people's daily life, many applications, such as automatic driving, automatic storage, machine meal delivery and other services [10], need to obtain the location information of the target. It can be seen that the popularization of positioning information is of key significance for building an interconnected society.

In military affairs, the location of radiation source is an important characteristic information of electromagnetic radiation source, and has a relatively stable state [17]. It is

Y. Chenggang et al. (Eds.): MobiMedia 2022, LNICST 451, pp. 43–56, 2022.
https://doi.org/10.1007/978-3-031-23902-1_4

not only closely related to battlefield situation, mission planning and combat operations, but also an important basis for distinguishing different radiation sources [16, 17]. The location of radiation source is an important work that needs to be processed and used in all kinds of electronic warfare [5]. The distributed communication jamming network based on multiple beacon nodes can obtain the position or distance information of multiple enemy emitter nodes, provide useful state information for target intention recognition, and improve the state perception level of emitter targets.

Document [7] proposes an improved indoor positioning system method based on WiFi triangle. The improved model is based on the test results using Intel Galileo (Gen2) board as the access point. By improving the measurement of received signal strength, the problem of signal blocking caused by obstacles in the building is solved. Document [18] proposes a new uncertainty analysis method of RSSI based distance estimation (uam-rde) to study the uncertainty propagation in RSSI based distance estimation.

In order to improve the positioning accuracy of emitter target positioning based on received signal strength (RSS), this paper first innovates in data preprocessing, abandons the traditional average filter and selects the median weighted filter to reduce the gross error more effectively. Then, the target position is preliminarily estimated by genetic algorithm, and then the modified Gauss Newton iterative algorithm is used for secondary positioning, and the final convergent iterative result is taken as the target position. At the same time, the error correction module is added to iterate the convergence result twice to further improve the positioning accuracy. Simulation results show that the algorithm can save cost and ensure positioning accuracy at the same time.

2   Normal Shadow Fading Model

Commonly used RSSI propagation models include free space propagation model, ground reflection (two ray) model, log distance path loss model and log normal shading model. In practical applications, the situation is much more complex, especially in densely distributed wireless sensor networks. Reflection, multipath propagation, non line of sight, antenna gain and other problems will produce significantly different propagation losses at the same distance. Therefore, the log distance path loss model and log normal shadow model are two path loss estimation models suitable for sensor networks, they all describe the characteristics of the logarithm of path loss. The former is a deterministic model and describes the average characteristics of signal strength, while the latter describes different random shadow effects with the same distance on the propagation path. Lognormal shadow model is often used in the design and analysis of wireless communication system, so as to calculate and simulate the received power at any position. In this paper, the lognormal shadow model is used as the simulation model to verify the reliability of the algorithm. The calculation formula is as follows:

$$PL(d)[dB] = \overline{PL}(d) + X_\sigma = \overline{PL}(d_0) + 10n \log_{10}\left(\frac{d}{d_0}\right) + X_\sigma \tag{1}$$

where: d is the distance between the receiving end and the transmitting end; d_0 Is the reference distance, generally 1 m; $\overline{PL(d)}$ is the received signal power of the receiving end; $\overline{PL(d_0)}$ is the received signal power corresponding to the reference distance point

d_0; X_σ is a Gaussian random variable with a mean value of 0, which reflects the change of received signal power when the distance is fixed; n is the path loss index, which is a value related to the environment

Through the analysis of lognormal shadow model, it can be seen that there is random error in using this method to estimate the distance. In addition, due to the influence of multipath and reflection of wireless channel, there are still errors between the established model and the signal propagation model of actual environment. Therefore, it is not enough to simply use Eq. (1) for ranging. RSSI values shall be measured many times under the same conditions, and these RSSI values shall be screened to discard the RSSI values with large error and leave the RSSI values with small error, so as to improve the ranging accuracy.

3 Methodology

3.1 Data Preprocessing

Based on the strong anti error ability of the median, aiming at the positioning problem in the actual typical environment, this paper first communicates between the two nodes for a period of time, obtains a certain amount of data, finds the median of the signal strength in the signal sequence, then calculates the weight of each signal strength in the signal sequence according to the median, and finally multiplies each signal by the corresponding weight, Then sum the signal value between the two nodes and output it. The distance estimation method based on median weighting proposed in this paper mainly includes four steps: data sampling, obtaining the median of signal sequence, calculating weight and estimating distance, as shown below:

Sampling Measurement
Firstly, the information sent by the unknown node is received at the same location, and the RSSI propagation loss of the signal is calculated automatically. In order to obtain the distribution characteristics between nodes, it is necessary to sample multiple times in a certain time period to obtain RSSI sequence $\{RSSI_1, RSSI_2, RSSI_3, ..., RSSI_n\}$.

Get the Median of Signal Sequence
Take the median of the obtained signal sequence. The median represents the value in the middle when a group of data is arranged in the order of size. Calculate the median of RSSI sequence:

$$Med_{RSSI} = \begin{cases} RSSI_{(n+1)/2}, N \text{ is an odd number} \\ \frac{1}{2}\left(RSSI_{\frac{n+1}{2}} + RSSI_{\frac{n}{2}+1}\right), N \text{ is an even number} \end{cases} \tag{2}$$

Calculate Weight
On the basis of obtaining the median of the signal sequence above, first calculate the variance between each signal value in each RSSI signal sequence and the median of the sequence. The variance is calculated as follows:

$$\textbf{Var}_i = (RSSI_i - Med_{RSSI})^2 \tag{3}$$

Secondly, in order to avoid that there is a RSSI signal in the sequence whose value is the same as the median of the sequence, resulting in zero variance, the non normalized weighting coefficient can be calculated according to the following formula:

$$R_i = 1/(1 + \mathbf{Var}_i) \tag{4}$$

Then, sum and normalize the weighting coefficients obtained by the above formula. The formula is as follows:

$$w_i = R_i/(\sum_{i=1}^{n} R_i) \tag{5}$$

The larger the difference between the RSSI value and the median in the sequence, the smaller the corresponding weighting coefficient. When the RSSI value and are equal, the weighting coefficient is the largest, and the corresponding RSSI value is given the maximum weight at this time. Because the difference between the RSSI value and the median in the sequence is directly used to determine the weight, when the RSSI signal value containing gross error in the sequence is too close to the median value of the sequence, it is possible to give these RSSI signals too large weight, resulting in the decline of algorithm performance. Therefore, we set a threshold. If the variance is greater than the threshold T, the weight is determined by the variance; If the variance is less than the threshold, it is determined by the threshold. Then the weight of each RSSI signal in each sequence can be calculated according to the following formula:

$$\mathbf{w}_i = \frac{1}{\sum_{i=1}^{n} \frac{1}{1 + \max\{T, (RSSI_i - Med_{RSSI})^2\}}} \tag{6}$$

where, T is the mean value of the variance between each signal value and median in the RSSI signal sequence, which is called the threshold, which can be expressed by the following formula:

$$\mathbf{T} = \frac{\sum_{i=1}^{n} (RSSI_i - Med_{RSSI})^2}{n} \tag{7}$$

Among them, $RSSI_i$ is the ith $RSSI$ signal value in the region. It can be seen that the greater the difference between $RSSI_i$ and Med_{RSSI}, the smaller the corresponding weighting coefficient w_i, and T changes with the $RSSI_i$ and sum variance Med_{RSSI}.

Estimated Distance
Use the method in step 3 to obtain the corresponding weight of each signal value in the signal sequence, multiply and sum each signal value in the signal sequence with the corresponding weighting coefficient, that is $RSSI = \sum_{i=1}^{n} w_i \times RSSI_i$, output it as the RSSI signal value between node pairs, and calculate the distance from the signal point to the unknown location node using the RSSI ranging formula.

The advantages of using this processing method are as follows: (1) when calculating the weight based on the median, a very small weight is given to the RSSI value containing the gross error signal, the value with error can be ignored during accumulation, some abnormal points are filtered, and the gross error data is not simply deleted; (2) Accumulation is similar to the use of mean model, which can filter out some random noise; (3) The algorithm is suitable for different complex environments, which increases the applicability of the algorithm.

3.2 Gauss Newton Iterative Algorithm

Advantages of Gauss Newton Iterative Algorithm over Maximum Likelihood Estimation Algorithm

Target position estimation is to determine the approximate position of the target node by using the measured distance, angle and other data and other information. The common methods of position calculation are trilateral method and triangular method. If there is noise in the measurement data, the maximum likelihood method or its improved method can be used to estimate the unknown node coordinates. It only needs the ranging information and does not need the prior information of the position [20].

Maximum likelihood estimation is a statistical method, which takes the maximum probability of the occurrence of the observed value as the quasi measurement. It is considered that the wireless sensor network $\{X_1, X_2, ..., X_n\}$ composed of N nodes $X_i (i = 1, 2, ..., n)$ is deployed in the $d (d = 2, 3)$ dimensional monitoring area. The IDs of the nodes are $1, 2,..., N$, the real coordinates of the nodes X_i are (x_i, y_i), and the distances from them to the unknown node D are d_i respectively, assuming that the coordinates of D are $X = (x, y)$. Then there is a coordinate distance relationship equation between the beacon node and the unknown node, that is

$$\begin{cases} (x - x_1)^2 + (y - y_1)^2 = d_1^2 \\ (x - x_2)^2 + (y - y_2)^2 = d_2^2 \\ \vdots \\ (x - x_n)^2 + (y - y_n)^2 = d_n^2 \end{cases} \tag{8}$$

Among them, if the first to Nth-1 equations are subtracted from the nth equation respectively, the following can be obtained:

$$\begin{cases} 2(x_n - x_1)x + 2(y_n - y_1)y = d_1^2 - d_n^2 + y_n^2 + x_n^2 - y_1^2 - x_1^2 \\ 2(x_n - x_2)x + 2(y_n - y_2)y = d_2^2 - d_n^2 + y_n^2 + x_n^2 - y_2^2 - x_2^2 \\ \vdots \\ 2(x_n - x_n)x + 2(y_n - y_n)y = d_{n-1}^2 - d_n^2 + y_n^2 + x_n^2 - y_{n-1}^2 - x_{n-1}^2 \end{cases} \tag{9}$$

Order

$$A = 2 \times \begin{bmatrix} (x_1 - x_n) & (y_1 - y_n) \\ (x_2 - x_n) & (y_2 - y_n) \\ \vdots & \vdots \\ (x_{n-1} - x_n) & (y_{n-1} - y_n) \end{bmatrix} \tag{10}$$

$$b = \begin{bmatrix} x_1^2 - x_n^2 + y_1^2 - y_n^2 + d_n^2 - d_1^2 \\ x_2^2 - x_n^2 + y_2^2 - y_n^2 + d_n^2 - d_2^2 \\ \vdots \\ x_{n-1}^2 - x_n^2 + y_{n-1}^2 - y_n^2 + d_n^2 - d_{n-1}^2 \end{bmatrix} \tag{11}$$

$$X = \begin{bmatrix} x \\ y \end{bmatrix} \tag{12}$$

The above equations can be transformed into the form of $AX = b$. Although the noise reduction processing is carried out in the ranging process, there is always a certain error in the distance measurement in the actual environment, so the equation can be expressed as:

$$AX = b + \xi \tag{13}$$

In order to obtain the optimal solution of unknown node position, the sum of squares of errors is used as the judgment standard, so there is a loss equation $S(x)$:

$$\begin{aligned} S(\mathbf{x}) &= \|\xi\|^2 = \|\mathbf{Ax} - \mathbf{b}\|^2 \\ &= (\mathbf{Ax} - \mathbf{b})^T (\mathbf{Ax} - \mathbf{b}) = \mathbf{x}^T \mathbf{A}^T \mathbf{Ax} - 2\mathbf{b}^T \mathbf{Ax} + \mathbf{b}^T \mathbf{b} \end{aligned} \tag{14}$$

In order to obtain the optimal solution, the partial derivative of the loss equation is obtained and set equal to 0, and the following is obtained:

$$\partial \|\xi\|^2 / \partial \mathbf{x} = -2\mathbf{A}^T \mathbf{b} + 2\mathbf{A}^T \mathbf{Ax} = 0 \tag{15}$$

Calculation shows that

$$\mathbf{A}^T \mathbf{b} = \mathbf{A}^T \mathbf{Ax} \tag{16}$$

If the beacon point is not on a straight line, when the square array $\mathbf{A}^T \mathbf{A}$ is reversible, the estimated coordinates of the unknown node can be obtained from Eq. (16):

$$\hat{\mathbf{x}} = \left(\mathbf{A}^T \mathbf{A}\right)^{-1} \mathbf{A}^T \mathbf{b} \tag{17}$$

Therefore, it is the whole principle of using the maximum likelihood estimation method to solve the coordinates of unknown points. From the above analysis process, it can be seen that there is a disadvantage of using the maximum likelihood estimation method, that is, in the calculation process, this method uses equation subtraction to eliminate the quadratic term for linearization. This simple coordinate subtraction will have a certain loss of known coordinate information. At the same time, it is considered that the farther away from the unknown node, the greater the ranging error of the beacon node.

The Steps of Gauss Newton Iterative Method

In this project, the weighted least square estimation method based on Gauss Newton iteration is used to estimate the position of unknown targets. Its basic principle is as follows:

Order $f(x, y) = \sqrt{(x - x_i)^2 - (y - y_i)^2}$, The first-order Taylor expansion of the $f(x, y)$ formula at point (x_0, y_0) is obtained:

$$f(x, y) = f(x_0 + h, y_0 + k) = \sqrt{(x_0 - x_i)^2 + (y_0 - y_i)^2}$$
$$+ \frac{(x_0 - x_i)}{\sqrt{(x_0 - x_i)^2 + (y_0 - y_i)^2}} h + \frac{(y_0 - y_i)}{\sqrt{(x_0 - x_i)^2 + (y_0 - y_i)^2}} k \qquad (18)$$

Apply Eq. (18) to equation group (8) to obtain:

$$\begin{cases} \frac{(x_0 - x_1)}{\sqrt{(x_0 - x_1)^2 + (y_0 - y_1)^2}} h + \frac{(y_0 - y_1)}{\sqrt{(x_0 - x_1)^2 + (y_0 - y_1)^2}} k = d_1 - \sqrt{(x_0 - x_1)^2 + (y_0 - y_1)^2} \\ \frac{(x_0 - x_2)}{\sqrt{(x_0 - x_2)^2 + (y_0 - y_2)^2}} h + \frac{(y_0 - y_2)}{\sqrt{(x_0 - x_2)^2 + (y_0 - y_2)^2}} k = d_2 - \sqrt{(x_0 - x_2)^2 + (y_0 - y_2)^2} \\ \vdots \\ \frac{(x_0 - x_n)}{\sqrt{(x_0 - x_n)^2 + (y_0 - y_n)^2}} h + \frac{(y_0 - y_n)}{\sqrt{(x_0 - x_n)^2 + (y_0 - y_n)^2}} k = d_n - \sqrt{(x_0 - x_n)^2 + (y_0 - y_n)^2} \end{cases}$$
$$(19)$$

Then the Gauss Newton iterative method is used to approximate the solution of Eq. (19). The main steps are as follows:

Step one: Initialize (x_0, y_0) and select the midpoint of each beacon node;

Step two: For Eq. (19), the least square method is used to solve h and k;

Step three: Judge whether the h and k solved in step two meet the inequality $\sqrt{h^2 + k^2} < \varepsilon_{th}$. If it is true, stop the calculation; Otherwise, increase the step size of (x_0, y_0), update Eq. (19), continue the cycle from step two until the threshold ε_{th} condition is meet, and stop the calculation;

Step four: The output (x_0, y_0) is the approximate solution of the target coordinate (x, y) to be estimated.

Considering that the distance error between nodes varies with the distance between nodes, if different weighting values are given to each node according to the distance accuracy of each node, that is, in the least squares estimation based on Gauss Newton iterative method mentioned above, different weighting coefficients are added to the decomposed Eq. (19), so as to obtain the weighted least squares method based on Gauss Newton iterative method, The positioning accuracy can be improved.

3.3   Direct Location Algorithm

Principle of Direct Positioning Algorithm

When using RSSI for two-step positioning, first collect the power and convert the distance between each node through the power, that is, there is a functional relationship between the distance and power:

$$P = F(D) \tag{20}$$

Finally, the position parameters are solved through geometric relationship and coordinate system, and the calculated position parameter is set as X, that is, there is also a functional relationship between parameter position and distance:

$$X = G(D) \tag{21}$$

The main idea of direct positioning is to convert the formula into

$$X = G\left(F^{-1}(P)\right) \tag{22}$$

That is, the steps of calculating and storing distance parameters are omitted, and the radiation source is located directly through the data collected by the node.

The Steps of Direct Positioning Method

According to the shadow fading model. Since the reference distance d_0 is usually taken as one meter. It can be obtained by transforming the above formula (1):

$$d = 10^{\left(\frac{pld - pl(d_0) - x}{10n}\right)} \tag{23}$$

According to Taylor expansion:

$$a^x = e^{x \ln a} = 1 + \frac{x \ln a}{1!} + \frac{(x \ln a)^2}{2!} + \frac{(x \ln a)^3}{3!} + \cdots \tag{24}$$

Combining the two formulas can be obtained:

$$d = 10^{\left(\frac{pl(d) - pl(d_0) - x}{10n}\right)} = 1 + \frac{\left(\frac{pl(d) - pl(d_0) - x}{10n}\right) \ln 10}{1!} + \frac{\left(\left(\frac{pl(d) - pl(d_0) - x}{10n}\right) \ln 10\right)^2}{2!} + \frac{\left(\left(\frac{pl(d) - pl(d_0) - x}{10n}\right) \ln 10\right)^3}{3!} \tag{25}$$

Obviously, d can be expressed as:

$$d = A * P \tag{26}$$

where a vector and P vector are respectively:

$$A = \left[1, \frac{\frac{\ln 10}{10n}}{1!}, \frac{\left(\frac{\ln 10}{10n}\right)^2}{2!}, \frac{\left(\frac{\ln 10}{10n}\right)^3}{3!} \cdots \right] \tag{27}$$

$$\mathbf{P} = \left[1, (pl(d) - pl(d_0) - x), (pl(d) - pl(d_0) - x)^2, (pl(d) - pl(d_0) - x)^3, \ldots \right]^T \tag{28}$$

where a vector is a coefficient vector, which is determined by A. since $a = 10$ is a constant value, it is a constant coefficient vector. P is the power vector, which is determined by the power collected by each node in real time. Therefore, $D = F^{-1}(P)$ can be obtained on the basis of retaining the high-order item information.

Combined with Eq. (19) above, We can get the matrix expression:

$$[E] * [h, k]^T + [e] = [A] * [P] \tag{29}$$

The specific expressions of each matrix are:

$$[E] = \left[\begin{array}{cc} \dfrac{x_0 - x_1}{\sqrt{(x_0 - x_1)^2 + (y_0 - y_1)^2}} & \dfrac{y_0 - y_1}{\sqrt{(x_0 - x_1)^2 + (y_0 - y_1)^2}} \\ \dfrac{x_0 - x_2}{\sqrt{(x_0 - x_2)^2 + (y_0 - y_2)^2}} & \dfrac{y_0 - y_2}{\sqrt{(x_0 - x_2)^2 + (y_0 - y_2)^2}} \\ \cdots & \cdots \end{array} \right] \tag{30}$$

$$[e] = \left[\begin{array}{c} \sqrt{(x_0 - x_1)^2 + (y_0 - y_1)^2} \\ \sqrt{(x_0 - x_2)^2 + (y_0 - y_2)^2} \\ \cdots \end{array} \right] \tag{31}$$

$$[A] = \left[\begin{array}{c} \mathbf{A} \\ \cdots \end{array} \right] \tag{31}$$

$$[P] = \left[\begin{array}{c} \mathbf{P}_1 \\ \mathbf{P}_2 \\ \cdots \end{array} \right] \tag{32}$$

[E], [e], [P] are called the characteristic matrix of the anchor node group, where E and e are determined by the position parameters of the iteration initial point and the anchor node itself, and P is determined by the power collected by the anchor node group.

We can obtain the following matrix expression from multiple groups of anchor node groups:

$$[E_1] * [h, k]^T + [e_1] = [A] * [P_1]$$
$$[E_2] * [h, k]^T + [e_2] = [A] * [P_2] \tag{33}$$
$$\cdots$$
$$[E_n] * [h, k]^T + [e_n] = [A] * [P_n]$$

Multiple sets of $[h, k]^T$ values are obtained through the simultaneous constant coefficient matrix $[A]$, so as to realize the direct positioning based on Gauss Newton iteration and improve the positioning accuracy.

3.4 Error Correction

Based on the improved Gauss Newton iterative algorithm, it still needs to calculate the Hessian matrix and select the initial value strictly. If this matrix is ill conditioned, it may lead to iterative failure or output local optimal solution. Therefore, this paper adopts the operation of multiple positioning of the same radiation source after receiving the radiation source power through the node and preprocessing the data. In multiple iterations of the same radiation source, the initial point is selected from the optimal population of the point provided by GA genetic algorithm to ensure that each initial point is different. Because the Heisenberg matrix is ill conditioned only at a specific initial value, it can converge to the global optimal solution for most initial points under the joint action of the improved Gauss Newton iterative algorithm and the direct location algorithm. For very few cases, although a certain initial point can cause the Heisenberg matrix to become an ill conditioned matrix, which will lead to the failure of the iteration and output the local optimal solution, that is, the iteration will bring a large mean square error. However, due to multiple positioning of the same radiation source, a series of positioning results at the same point will be stored. The median weighted output of a series of positioning results can greatly reduce the mean square error caused by matrix ill condition in a certain iteration (Figs. 1 and 2).

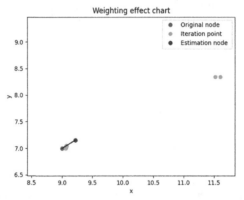

Fig. 1. The figure on the left shows 11 times of positioning for (7, 9), of which the results of two iterations obviously deviate from the expected results. It is found from the final positioning results (blue dots) that the results of these two deviations can be corrected (Color figure online)

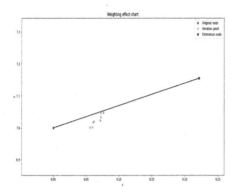

Fig. 2. The upper right figure is the enlarged figure of the left figure near (7, 9). It can be found that most iterative results belong to the normal error range

4   Experimental Results and Conclusions

As can be seen from the above figure, the traditional maximum likelihood estimation method uses equation subtraction to eliminate the quadratic term for linearization in the calculation process. This simple coordinate subtraction will have a certain loss of known coordinate information. Therefore, the mean square error of ML algorithm in most variance scenarios is greater than that of the other two algorithms (Figs. 3 and 4).

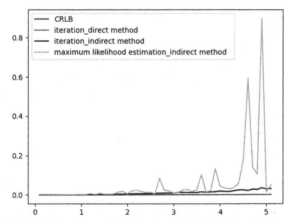

Fig. 3. The above figure is the comparison diagram of positioning mean square error of three kinds of algorithms under different variances. Where x-axis is variance and y-axis is mean square error.

It can be seen from the above figure that under the same other conditions, compared with the two-step positioning algorithm, the direct positioning algorithm can significantly reduce the mean square error of positioning parameter estimation under the high variance power signal (i.e. the power signal is greatly affected by shadow fading at this time) (Fig. 5).

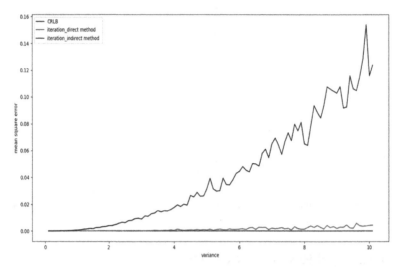

Fig. 4. The above figure shows the comparison of the mean square error of direct positioning algorithm and two-step positioning algorithm under different variance conditions. Where x-axis is variance and y-axis is mean square error.

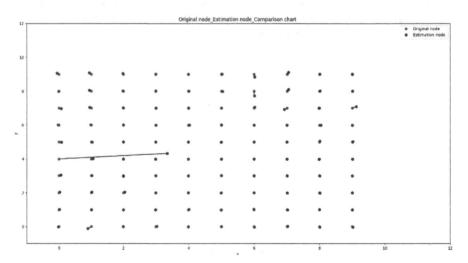

Fig. 5. In the figure above, the red point is the actual point and the blue point is the positioning result output by the algorithm. The higher the coincidence degree of the two points, the better the positioning effect of the point (Color figure online)

This paper explores the emitter location algorithm based on the received signal strength. On the premise of retaining the low cost of RSSI based location algorithm, the location accuracy is improved by integrating the advantages of various algorithms.

The experimental results show that compared with the traditional two-step location algorithm, the direct location algorithm is closer to the lower bound of CRLB under the condition of large noise interference, can better reduce the mean square error of location, and has strong anti-interference ability.

Gauss Newton iterative algorithm can effectively solve the disadvantage that the maximum likelihood estimation algorithm uses equation subtraction to eliminate the quadratic term to linearize in the calculation process, resulting in a certain loss of known coordinate information. Ensure positioning accuracy.

Carry out multiple power acquisition for the same radiation source and preprocess the collected dataThe paragraph starting with "This work is supported by..." has been treated as "Acknowledgment". Kindly check and confirm. After that, the target is located for many times, and the median weighting processing of the positioning results can greatly reduce the impact of the local optimal solution on the positioning results. To some extent, solve the problem that Gauss Newton iterative algorithm will fail due to singular matrix.

Acknowledgment. This work is supported by the National Natural Science Foundation of China (62001137); the Natural Science Foundation of Heilongjiang Province (JJ2019LH2398); the Fundamental Research Funds for the Central Universities (3072021CF0805).

References

1. Ding, X., Dong, S.: Improving positioning algorithm based on RSSI. Wireless Pers. Commun. **110**(4), 1947–1961 (2020). https://doi.org/10.1007/s11277-019-06821-0
2. Liu, C., Yang, J., Wang, F.: Joint TDOA and AOA location algorithm. J. Syst. Eng. Electron. **24**(2), 183–188 (2013)
3. Bishop, A.N., Fidan, B., Dogançay, K., et al.: Exploiting geometry for improved hybrid AOA/TDOA-based localization. Signal Process. **88**(7), 1775–1791 (2008)
4. Yin, J., Wan, Q., Yang, S., et al.: A simple and accurate TDOA-AOA localization method using two stations. IEEE Signal Process. Lett. **23**(1), 144–148 (2015)
5. Wang, Y., Ho, K.: Unified near-field and far-field localization for AOA and hybrid AOA-TDOA positionings. IEEE Trans. Wirel. Commun. **17**(2), 1242–1254 (2017)
6. Rusli, M.E., Ali, M., Jamil, N., et al.: An improved indoor positioning algorithm based on RSSI-trilateration technique for Internet of Things (IOT). In: International Conference on Computer and Communication Engineering. IEEE (2016)
7. Lin, Y., Zhu, X., Zheng, Z., Dou, Z., Zhou, R.: The individual identification method of wireless device based on dimensionality reduction and machine learning. J. Supercomput. **75**(6), 3010–3027 (2019). https://doi.org/10.1007/s11227-017-2216-2
8. Ding, G., Qihui, W., Zhang, L., Lin, Y., Tsiftsis, T.A., Yao, Y.-D.: An amateur drone surveillance system based on the cognitive Internet of Things. IEEE Commun. Mag. **56**(1), 29–35 (2018)
9. Ya, T., Lin, Y., Wang, J., Kim, J.-U.: Semi-supervised learning with generative adversarial networks on digital signal modulation classification. Comput. Mater. Continua. **55**(2), 243–254 (2018)
10. Lin, Y., Ya, T., Dou, Z., Chen, L., Mao, S.: Contour stella image and deep learning for signal recognition in the physical layer. IEEE Trans. Cogn. Commun. Netw. **7**(1), 34–46 (2020)
11. Sun, J., et al.: A data authentication scheme for UAV ad hoc network communication. J. Supercomput. **76**(6), 4041–4056 (2020)
12. Lin, Y., Zhao, H., Ma, X., Ya, T., Wang, M.: Adversarial attacks in modulation recognition with convolutional neural networks. IEEE Trans. Reliab. **70**(1), 389–401 (2020)

13. Wang, M., Lin, Y., Tian, Q., Si, G.: Transfer learning promotes 6G wireless communications: recent advances and future challenges. IEEE Trans. Reliab. **70**, 790–807 (2021)
14. Demirbas, M., Song, Y.: An RSSI-based scheme for Sybil attack detection in wireless sensor networks. In: International Symposium on World of Wireless, Mobile and Multimedia Networks. IEEE (2006)
15. Folkes, S.R., Lahav, O., Maddox, S.J.: An artificial neural network approach to the classification of galaxy spectra. Mon. Not. R. Astron. Soc. **283**(2), 651–665 (2018)
16. Jebadurai, J., Peter, J.D.: SK-SVR: sigmoid kernel support vector regression based in-scale single image super-resolution. Pattern Recogn. Lett. **94**(5), 100–123 (2017)
17. Yan, X., Zhou, P., Luo, Q., et al.: UAM-RDE: an uncertainty analysis method for RSSI-based distance estimation in wireless sensor networks. Neural Comput. Appl. **32**(17), 13701–13714 (2020). https://doi.org/10.1007/s00521-020-04777-y
18. Pennington, J., Schoenholz, S.S., Ganguli, S.: Resurrecting the sigmoid in deep learning through dynamical isometry: theory and practice. **11**(2), 12–20 (2017)
19. Kim, D.Y., Yi, K.Y.: RSSI-based indoor localization method using virtually overlapped visible light. Trans. Korean Inst. Electr. Eng. **63**(12), 1697–1703 (2014)
20. Saadi, M.,Yan, Z., Wuttisittikulkij, L.: Artifical neural network based visible light positioning system employing received signal strength. In: ITC-CSCC: International Technical Conference on Circuits Systems (2015)
21. Wang, H., Wan, J., Liu, R.: A novel ranging method based on RSSI. Energy Procedia **12**(1), 230–235 (2011)

Angle of Arrival Based Signal Classification in Intelligent Reflecting Surface-Aided Wireless Communications

Haolin Tang[1](✉)(iD), Yanxiao Zhao[1](iD), and Wei Wang[2](iD)

[1] Department of Electrical and Computer Engineering, Virginia Commonwealth University, Richmond, VA 23284, USA
{tangh4,yzhao7}@vcu.edu
[2] Department of Computer Science, San Diego State University, San Diego, CA 92115, USA
wwang@sdsu.edu

Abstract. Intelligent Reflecting Surface (IRS) has been recognized as a promising technology for future wireless communications. It can reconfigure the radio signal propagation environment and improve the performance of wireless networks. However, this attractive strength of the IRS is grounded on a commonly perceived assumption that the IRS is able to distinguish the incoming signals so that IRS can be controlled to either improve or reduce the total received signal strength at a receiver. The signal differentiation issue for IRS is overlooked in the literature. To tackle this challenge, this paper proposes a solution that integrates an Angle of Arrival (AoA) algorithm into IRS systems. First, we propose a new idea that IRS can work as smart antenna by a hybrid architecture, i.e., all elements are passive except for a few active sensing elements. The active elements can collaboratively serve as a smart antenna. Second, the MUSIC (MUltiple SIgnal Classification) AoA algorithm is applied to this hybrid IRS architecture to classify the incoming signal directions due to its advantages of simple implementation and high resolution. Last, extensive simulations are conducted to evaluate the classification performance of the proposed method under various scenarios. The simulation results demonstrate the effectiveness and accuracy of our approach.

Keywords: Intelligent reflecting surface · Spectrum sensing · Angle of arrival · MUSIC · Signal classification

1 Introduction

In the last decade, we have witnessed the rapid evolution of wireless communication which has become an essential part of our daily lives than ever before. Academia, industries and governments are continually making every effort to further enhance the performance of Fifth-Generation (5G) and Next Generation

© ICST Institute for Computer Sciences, Social Informatics and Telecommunications Engineering 2022
Published by Springer Nature Switzerland AG 2022. All Rights Reserved
Y. Chenggang et al. (Eds.): MobiMedia 2022, LNICST 451, pp. 57–66, 2022.
https://doi.org/10.1007/978-3-031-23902-1_5

(NextG) wireless networks. Recently, Intelligent Reflecting Surface (IRS) as a new emerging and promising technology has been investigated and adopted for wireless communications due to its capability of reconfiguring wireless communication environment. IRS typically consists of a large number of low-cost passive reflecting elements, which are able to reflect the incident wireless signal with an adjustable phase shift. The reflected signals by IRS can be constructively or destructively added at the receiver by jointly adjusting the phase shifts of all reflecting elements [1–4]. Consequently, the desired signal will be enhanced or the undesired signal (e.g., jamming signal) will be suppressed at the receiver. In recent research of IRS-aided wireless communications, the majority works focus on the optimization of the phase shift coefficient at the IRS taking some constraints (e.g., total transmit power, the existence of eavesdroppers, etc.) into consideration [5–8]. However, these works are based on a strong assumption that the IRS knows the sources of its received signals. For instance, an IRS receives an intended signal or a jamming signal along with some signals from unknown sources. The IRS needs to strengthen the intended signal or mitigate the jamming signal for the legitimate receiver by adjusting the phase shift dynamically. This service essentially depends on the fact that the IRS distinctly knows the sources of each signal in advance.

From the above mentioned, we conclude that it is imperative to develop a new approach to help IRS to determine which signal is to be reflected in order to enhance or suppress accordingly. In this paper, we address this problem and propose a promising classification method based on incoming signal's Angle of Arrivals (AoA) for IRS-aided system. The new idea is to enable IRS as smart antenna by proposing a hybrid IRS architecture, which consists of dominant passive elements, and a small number of active sensing elements, so that it works as a smart antenna array. Consequently, the active sensing elements enable the IRS to detect the arrival angles of all incoming signals. Therefore, if the location information of signal sources is known in advance, the IRS is able to determine whether its received signals are from the known sources or not.

The contributions of this paper can be summarized as follows.

- We propose a new idea that enables IRS to work as a smart antenna in a hybrid architecture where all the elements are passive except for a few active sensing elements, which are linearly arranged. The small number of active elements work collaboratively to act as a linear antenna array.
- The MUSIC (MUltiple SIgnal Classification) AoA algorithm is employed to classify the signals from different sources since it has several advantages, e.g., higher resolution and less implementation cost. MUSIC algorithm plots a spatial spectrum in which the peaks indicate the arrival angles from distinct signal sources.
- Various simulations are conducted for evaluations and the results demonstrate the MUSIC AoA algorithm effects in the most simulation scenarios. The relation between the number of the active elements and the performance is investigated. In addition, the detectable angle difference is discussed.

The remainder of the paper is organized as follows. Section 2 briefly reviews the recent deployments of the IRS in wireless communications and introduce the AoA estimation. Section 3 proposes a new IRS architecture and formulate the MUSIC AoA based signal classification approach. Simulations in different scenarios are conducted to evaluate the classification performance in Sect. 4.

2   Related Works

2.1   Intelligent Reflecting Surface-Aided Wireless Communication

IRS has been proposed to reduce energy consumption and improve the performance of wireless communications [4]. Basically, IRS is a planar surface which is constructed by a large number of reconfigurable reflecting elements and is controlled by a smart controller [9]. The IRS reflecting elements thus can change the phases and/or amplitudes of the incident signals, thereby enhancing desired signals or mitigating undesired signals. IRS is typically used to enhance secrecy rate or Signal-to-Noise Ratio (SNR) of the communication system and hence to protect the quality of wireless communications between legitimate users [7]. [1] presents an IRS-aided wireless communication system for security where an Access Point (AP) sends confidential messages to a user in the presence of a eavesdropper. To improve the secrecy rate of the communication system, an optimization algorithm is proposed by jointly designing the AP's transmit beamforming and the IRS's reflect beamforming. In [5], IRS is used for mitigating inter-cell interference in cellular communication system. They also analyze the IRS placement optimization problem to make the most use of IRS. An IRS assisted Guassian Multiple-Input Multiple-Output (MIMO) wiretap channel is carefully considered in [10]. They propose an alternative joint optimization algorithm to optimize the transmit covariance at transmitter and phase shift coefficient at IRS to maximize the secrecy rate. In short, the majority of recent IRS-related research focuses on optimizing the IRS with some constraints to improve the overall performance of wireless communications. However, there is an overlooked problem in the above deployments of the IRS. In a practical wireless signal propagation environment, the IRS may receive signals not only from the desired transmitter but also from other unknown sources. The successful implementation of the IRS thus depends on whether the IRS is able to identify the source of the incoming signals.

2.2   Angle of Arrival Estimation

AoA estimation methods allow a device to identify the arrival angle of the incident signals by examining the differences in the received signal across the antenna elements [11]. Spectrum sensing-based AoA methods, including Bartlett, MUSIC and Capon methods, have been studied extensively [12–14]. In this paper, the MUSIC AoA based sensing approach is selected to classify the sources of the incoming signals, because MUSIC algorithm provides high precision measurement and measures multiple signals simultaneously [15]. Furthermore, it can achieve real-time processing using high-speed processing technology. The MUSIC algorithm works by conducting characteristic decomposition for the covariance matrix associated with any array output data, resulting in a signal subspace orthogonal to the noise subspace that corresponds to the signal components. Then the two orthogonal subspaces are used to construct a spectrum function to estimate the arrival angle of the incident signals.

3   System Model and Proposed Methodology

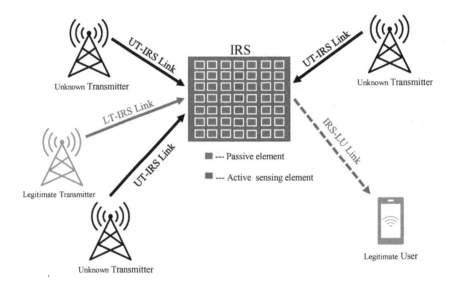

Fig. 1. Illustration of an IRS-aided communication, including a legitimate transmitter and user, and the unknown transmitters. IRS is deployed to improve the communication performance between the legitimate transmitter and user.

3.1   System Model

As discussed previously, we propose to enable IRS to distinguish signals from different sources by measuring their arrival angles. To implement this, we adopt a hybrid IRS architecture which is constructed by dominant passive reflecting elements along with a small number of active sensing elements. In particular, the active elements have two functional modes: (i) spectrum sensing mode where they work as a set of multiple connected adaptive array antennas (i.e., smart antenna), and (ii) reflecting mode where they merely reflect the incoming signals passively. Consider an IRS-aided wireless communication network, as depicted in Fig. 1, including a legitimate transmitter, a legitimate user and the unknown transmitters (e.g., malicious users or attackers). The IRS with the proposed architecture is deployed to improve the communication performance between the legitimate transmitter and user. Specifically, the IRS receives the signal from the legitimate transmitter (via LT-IRS link) and signal from the unknown transmitters (via UT-IRS links). The IRS is required to identify the signal from the legitimate transmitter and then reflect the signal to the legitimate user (via IRS-LU link). We assume all the transmitters are equipped with omini-directional antennas, while the IRS has M active sensing elements which comprise a smart antenna array. The direction or angle information of the legitimate transmitter is assumed available, which can be acquired by many methods. For instance, if the location of the legitimate transmitter is denoted as (x_1, y_1) and the location of the IRS is denoted as (x_2, y_2). It is straightforward to calculate the actual angle observed at the IRS is $\theta = \arctan \frac{|y_1-y_2|}{|x_1-x_2|}$ from the legitimate transmitter. In such a communication system, an AoA based method can be applied to estimate the angle of the incoming signals. Therefore, a decision whether the signal originates from the legitimate transmitter or not can be made by comparing the estimated and actual arrival angles. For instance, if the angle from the legitimate transmitter to the IRS, denoted by θ_i, is given in advance and the estimated angle of an incoming signal is denoted by $\widehat{\theta}_i$. We can determine the incoming signal is from the legitimate transmitter when $|\theta_i - \widehat{\theta}_i| \leq \Delta\phi$ holds, where $\Delta\phi$ indicates the detectable angle difference and will be discussed in Sect. 4.

3.2 AoA Based Signal Classification

With the hybrid architecture described in Fig. 1, IRS is able to behave as smart antenna, so that AoA based spectrum sensing approaches are feasible to estimate the angles of incoming signals [14,16]. This subsection first briefly introduces typical AoA technology, then MUSIC AoA is selected for signal classification in our paper since it provides a higher resolution, less computation, and better robustness.

Assume there are D signal sources from the legitimate transmitter and the unknown transmitters to the IRS, and let $\mathbf{s}(t) = [s_1(t), s_2(t), ..., s_D(t)]^\top$ represents the vector of source signal values from D sources at a discrete time t. At this time, the active elements of the IRS are on the spectrum sensing mode and we assume the M active sensing elements lays on the IRS linearly with equal spacing, denoted by d. Such that the active elements construct a liner antenna array with M identical elements. Each active sensing element receives signals from all D sources along with the noise. At the $i^{th}(i = 1, 2, ..., M)$ element, the received signal thus can be expressed as

$$x_i(t) = \sum_{k=1}^{D} a_{ik}(t)s_k(t) + n_i(t), \tag{1}$$

where $a_{ik}(t)$ is the steering factor from the source k to the active element i and $n_i(t)$ represents the additive white Gaussian noise. We can rewrite this equation into a compact matrix form as

$$\mathbf{x} = \mathbf{A}\mathbf{s} + \mathbf{n}, \tag{2}$$

where $\mathbf{x}(t) = [x_1(t), x_2(t), ..., x_M(t)]^\top$ is an $M \times 1$ vector of the received signal and additive noise. Here $\mathbf{A} = [\mathbf{a}(\theta_1), ..., \mathbf{a}(\theta_k)]$ is an $M \times D$ Vandermonde matrix of steering vectors $\mathbf{a}(\theta_k) = [1, e^{-j2\pi\lambda \sin(\theta_k)/d}, ..., e^{-j2\pi(M-1)\lambda\sin(\theta_k)/d}]^\top$. $\mathbf{n}$ is an $M \times 1$ vector of the channel noise.

Thus, the $M \times M$ array correlation matrix of $\mathbf{x}$ can be expressed as

$$\mathbf{R}_{xx} = \mathbb{E}[\mathbf{x} \cdot \mathbf{x}^H] = \mathbb{E}\left[(\mathbf{As} + \mathbf{n}) \cdot (\mathbf{As} + \mathbf{n})^H\right] = \mathbf{A}\mathbf{R}_{ss}\mathbf{A}^H + \sigma_n^2 \mathbf{I}_D, \qquad (3)$$

where $\mathbf{R}_{ss}$ represents the correlation matrix of the source signal vector $\mathbf{s}$ and σ_n^2 indicates the noise variance. $\mathbf{I}_D$ is a $D \times D$ identity matrix and H indicates the operation of conjugate transpose.

The purpose of the AoA estimation is to construct a function that determines the angles of the incoming signals using Pseudo spectrum, $P(\theta)$. Several off-the-shelf approaches are available to construct $P(\theta)$. We select the MUSIC AoA algorithm due to its advantages in higher resolution, less computation, and better robustness.

Let $\mathbf{u_i}$ be one of the eigenvector of $\mathbf{R}_{xx}$ corresponding to the eigenvalue σ_i^2, where $i = 1, 2, ..., M$. Then,

$$\mathbf{R_{xx}u_i} = \mathbf{A}\mathbf{R}_{ss}\mathbf{A}^H\mathbf{u_i} + \sigma_n^2 \mathbf{I}_D\mathbf{u_i} = \sigma_i^2\mathbf{u_i}. \qquad (4)$$

Here $M > D$ such that $\sigma_i^2 > \sigma_n^2 > 0$ for $i = 1, 2, ..., D$ and $\sigma_i^2 = \sigma_n^2$ for $i = D + 1, ..., M$. Thus, we conclude

$$\mathbf{A}\mathbf{R}_{ss}\mathbf{A}^H = \begin{cases} (\sigma_i^2 - \sigma_n^2)\mathbf{u}_i, & \text{if } i = 1, 2, ..., D \\ 0, & \text{if } i = D + 1, ..., M. \end{cases} \qquad (5)$$

We can split the M-dimensional vector space into two subspaces since $\mathbf{A}\mathbf{R}_{ss}\mathbf{A}^H$ has D positive real eigenvalues and $(M - D)$ zero eigenvalues. The eigenvectors corresponding to the positive eigenvalues span the signal subspace, $\mathbf{U}_s$. The eigenvectors corresponding to the zero eigenvalues are orthogonal to the signal space and span the null subspace, $\mathbf{U}_n$. The MUSIC algorithm searches for all arrival angles θ, and the spatial spectrum over the angle space is given by

$$P_{MUSIC}(\theta) = \frac{1}{\mathbf{a}^H(\theta_k)\mathbf{U}_n}. \qquad (6)$$

Specially, the steering vector $\mathbf{a}(\theta_k)$ is only in the signal space which results in $\mathbf{a}^H(\theta)\mathbf{U}_n = 0$. From the Eq. 6, we can conclude that $P_{MUSIC}(\theta)$ shows a peak when $\theta = \theta_k$. It indicates that a peak should only appear at the angle from which a signal originates. Therefore, finding the estimated arrival angle corresponds to finding the peak in the spatial spectrum. That is, the angle of incoming signal is estimated as

$$\widehat{\theta} = \arg\max_{\theta} P_{MUSIC}(\theta). \qquad (7)$$

Comparing the estimated arrival angle $\widehat{\theta}$ with the angle of legitimate transmitter known in advance, we can classify the signal sources and determine which signal is from the legitimate transmitter or the unknown transmitters. After the signal classification, the active elements of the IRS will be on the reflecting mode and collaborate with the passive elements to reflect the identified signal from the legitimate transmitter to the legitimate user.

4 Numerical Results

This section evaluates the performance of the AoA based signal classification method in two scenarios for IRS-aided wireless communications. The impact of factors such as the number of active sensing elements on the IRS and the angle of signal sources is investigated. The first scenario analyzes the relationship between the classification accuracy and the number of active sensing elements in the MUSIC AoA algorithm. We consider that there are four signal sources, including a legitimate transmitter and three unknown transmitters, in an IRS-aided wireless communication system. The corresponding angles to the IRS are $\theta_1 = -20°, \theta_2 = -10°, \theta_3 = 10°$, and $\theta_4 = 20°$, respectively. In addition, we conduct simulations for 5, 10 and 15 active sensing elements. Figure 2 shows the MUSIC AoA algorithm spectrum results. It shows four peaks (angles of the source signals) exactly at $\theta_1 = -20°, \theta_2 = -10°, \theta_3 = 10°$, and $\theta_4 = 20°$. This demonstrates the MUSIC AoA algorithm can classify the incoming signals successfully with high accuracy. If we know the actual angle from the legitimate

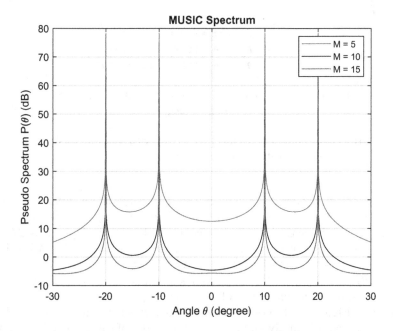

Fig. 2. Illustration of pseudo spectrum $P_{MUSIC}(\theta)$ with 5, 10 and 15 active sensing elements on IRS for four signal sources ($\theta_1 = -20°, \theta_2 = -10°, \theta_3 = 10°$).

transmitter to the IRS is $\theta = 10°$ in advance, the result suggests that the signal from the legitimate transmitter is identified accurately. The IRS can reflect the identified signal accordingly to the legitimate user. Specially, if the direction or angle information of the three unknown transmitters is accessible, the signals from them can also be recognized successfully which indicates the MUSIC AoA algorithm can classify multiple signals simultaneously. Moreover, we can conclude the relation between the classification accuracy and the number of the active sensing elements from the spectrum results. With more active sensing elements, classification accuracy increases.

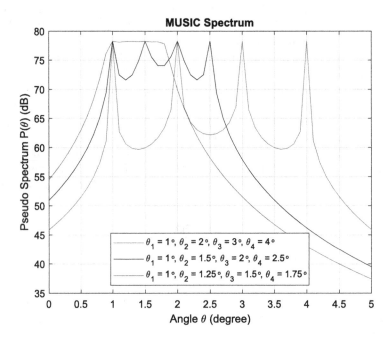

Fig. 3. Illustration of pseudo spectrum $P_{MUSIC}(\theta)$ with 5 active sensing elements on IRS for four signal sources with three angles sets.

In the second scenario, we explore the detectable angle difference $\Delta\phi$ for the MUSIC AoA approach when the signal sources are close to each other. The number of the active sensing elements on IRS is configured as $M = 5$. Similar with the first scenario, four signal sources are considered. We conduct simulations for three sets of angles, i.e. ($\theta_1 = 1°, \theta_2 = 2°, \theta_3 = 3°, \theta_4 = 4°$), ($\theta_1 = 1°, \theta_2 = 1.5°, \theta_3 = 2°, \theta_4 = 2.5°$) and ($\theta_1 = 1°, \theta_2 = 1.25°, \theta_3 = 1.5°$, $\theta_4 = 1.75°$). The angle differences of the three angles sets are $1°, 0.5°$ and $0.25°$, respectively. Figure 3 exhibits the results, from which it can be observed that four peaks appear distinctly and indicates the angles of source signals accurately for the first set. From the results for the second set, it shows that the MUSIC AoA algorithm can still detect all signal sources in spite of the lower resolution.

However, the four signals are detected as the same in the results of the last angles set. The MUSIC AoA algorithm fails to detect the signal sources when the angles become very closer. This failure may lead a threat to the legitimate user. For instance, if a malicious attacker exists closely with the legitimate transmitter, the IRS can not identify the signal sources and thus may reflect the attacking signals to the legitimate user.

Overall, MUSIC AoA based signal classification method can detect and classify multiple signal sources effectively when the signal sources are separated sufficiently far and we suggest the detectable angle difference $\Delta\phi = 1°$.

5   Conclusions

In this paper, we have pointed out an overlooked issue of signal differentiation using IRS in current research of IRS-aided wireless communications. In an IRS-aided environment, the IRS should have the ability to identify the signal sources so that it knows how to control phase shifts of reflecting elements correspondingly. To tackle this challenge, we propose a new idea that enable IRS to perform signal differentiation by adopting a hybrid IRS architecture, which consists of dominant passive elements and a few of active sensing elements. These active elements can serve as a linear antenna array. We then propose to utilize the active sensing elements to help an IRS to classify the signals between the legitimate transmitter and unknown transmitters leveraging an AoA based method. The MUSIC algorithm was selected for the AoA estimation and the performance was tested in two scenarios. The simulation results demonstrated that MUSIC AoA based signal classification is effective in general, except when the angles of sources are highly close to each other.

Acknowledgment. This research is partially supported by Commonwealth Cyber Initiative (CCI) and Virginia Commonwealth University (VCU) Presidential Research Quest Fund (PeRQ) award.

References

1. Cui, M., Zhang, G., Zhang, R.: Secure wireless communication via intelligent reflecting surface. IEEE Wirel. Commun. Lett. **8**(5), 1410–1414 (2019)
2. Shen, H., Wei, X., Gong, S., He, Z., Zhao, C.: Secrecy rate maximization for intelligent reflecting surface assisted multi-antenna communications. IEEE Commun. Lett. **23**(9), 1488–1492 (2019)
3. Sun, Y., An, K., Luo, J., Zhu, Y., Zheng, G., Chatzinotas, S.: Intelligent reflecting surface enhanced secure transmission against both jamming and eavesdropping attacks. IEEE Trans. Veh. Technol. **70**(10), 11017–11022 (2021)
4. Qingqing, W., Zhang, R.: Intelligent reflecting surface enhanced wireless network via joint active and passive beamforming. IEEE Trans. Wireless Commun. **18**(11), 5394–5409 (2019)
5. Hashida, H., Kawamoto, Y., Kato, N.: Intelligent reflecting surface placement optimization in air-ground communication networks toward 6G. IEEE Wirel. Commun. **27**(6), 146–151 (2020)

6. Qingqing, W., Zhang, R.: Towards smart and reconfigurable environment: intelligent reflecting surface aided wireless network. IEEE Commun. Mag. **58**(1), 106–112 (2019)
7. Wu, Q., Zhang, S., Zheng, B., You, C., Zhang, R.: Intelligent reflecting surface-aided wireless communications: a tutorial. IEEE Trans. Commun. **69**, 3313–3351 (2021)
8. Xianghao, Yu., Dongfang, X., Sun, Y., Ng, D.W.K., Schober, R.: Robust and secure wireless communications via intelligent reflecting surfaces. IEEE J. Sel. Areas Commun. **38**(11), 2637–2652 (2020)
9. Zhang, Z., Lv, L., Wu, Q., Deng, H., Chen, J.: Robust and secure communications in intelligent reflecting surface assisted NOMA networks. IEEE Commun. Lett. **25**(3), 739–743 (2020)
10. Dong, L., Wang, H.-M.: Secure MIMO transmission via intelligent reflecting surface. IEEE Wirel. Commun. Lett. **9**(6), 787–790 (2020)
11. Khan, A., Wang, S., Zhu, Z.: Angle-of-arrival estimation using an adaptive machine learning framework. IEEE Commun. Lett. **23**(2), 294–297 (2018)
12. Balanis, C.A.: Antenna Theory: Analysis and Design. John wiley & Sons, Hoboken (2015)
13. Fried, D.L.: Differential angle of arrival: theory, evaluation, and measurement feasibility. Radio Sci. **10**(1), 71–76 (1975)
14. Gross, F. Smart antennas for wireless communications. McGraw-Hill Professional (2005)
15. Xie, J., Fu, Z., Xian, H.: Spectrum sensing based on estimation of direction of arrival. In: International Conference on Computational Problem-solving, pp. 39–42. IEEE (2010)
16. Zhao, Y., Huang, J., Wang, W., Zaman, R.: Detection of primary user's signal in cognitive radio networks: angle of arrival based approach. In: 2014 IEEE Global Communications Conference, pp. 3062–3067. IEEE (2014)

An Efficient Compression and Reconstruction Framework for Electromagnetic Spectrum Data

Dong Xiao, Jiangzhi Fu, Lu Sun, and Yun Lin$^{(\boxtimes)}$

College of Information and Communication, Harbin Engineering
University, Harbin, People's Republic of China
linyun@hrbeu.edu.cn

Abstract. Spectrum monitoring often demands a great quantity of spectrum data, and the massive characteristics of spectrum data make it consume a lot of resources in the process of transmission and storage. At the same time, the compressed acquisition system of spectrum data often has the problem of low reconstruction accuracy of the original data, and the reconstruction accuracy and compression performance cannot be achieved simultaneously. This paper studies the factors affecting the reconstruction error in the process of electromagnetic spectrum data utilization. In this paper, an electromagnetic spectrum compression and reconstruction framework called QRK-SVD is proposed. Aiming at the problems of slow dictionary convergence and low accuracy in dictionary learning, QRK-SVD purposely uses k-means clustering to construct the initial dictionary, which effectively improves the compression accuracy and system robustness. QRK-SVD increases the minimum singular value of sensing matrix through QR decomposition to optimize the problem of low accuracy of random observation matrix in compressed system. We designed a set of spectrum data acquisition and compression system based on QRK-SVD. It can adapt to various collection scenarios, greatly reduce the amount of data transmitted and stored, and has high reconstruction accuracy. The measured data proves that the performance of QRK-SVD is better than the traditional K-SVD framework in different data compression situations.

Keywords: Dictionary learning · QRK-SVD · Electromagnetic spectrum · Data compression

1 Introduce

With the increasing update of information science, wireless network devices can be seen everywhere in daily life, which also leads to the increasing shortage of spectrum resources. The spectrum resources in the electromagnetic space are distributed unevenly, scheduling is uneven, and the electromagnetic environment is facing deterioration. The utilization rate of a large number of spectrum resources is low, and only 15% to 85% of spectrum resources are utilized [1]. Spectrum resources are limited, and the available spectrum resources are difficult to meet the needs of various communication services. Exponential growth of radio services, repeated prohibitions of illegal radio equipment,

Y. Chenggang et al. (Eds.): MobiMedia 2022, LNICST 451, pp. 67–80, 2022.
https://doi.org/10.1007/978-3-031-23902-1_6

ecological deterioration of environmental noise and other factors make it imperative to effectively and reasonably monitor and manage spectrum resources [2]. The management of spectrum utilization inevitably requires a great quantity of spectrum data. Currently, with the development of networking radar, electromagnetic space network, wireless communication and other technologies, a large amount of electromagnetic spectrum data has been collected in various regions. Electromagnetic spectrum data is a kind of electromagnetic big data, which has the characteristics of high dimension, many types, and wide sources. The amount of electromagnetic spectrum data collected for a long time is extremely large, which makes it extremely inconvenient to transmit, store, and use spectrum data in real time [3, 4].

In order to solve the "dimension disaster" caused by massive data, Candes et al. proposed Compressed Sensing (CS) [5]. Compressed sensing is a technology that can effectively reduce the data sampling rate and compress data redundancy. However, most signals do not have sparseness, and the theory of signal sparse representation came into being. Its purpose is to linearly represent a given non-sparse signal using some coefficients. The sparse representation of the signal meets the requirements of compressed sensing technology and can be compressed, transmitted and stored.

For the problem of dictionary learning, authors in [6] proposed the Sparsenet dictionary learning algorithm [7], which uses the sparse coding of images to emergence the receptive field of a single cell. The optimization effect of the algorithm in the literature [6] is not ideal. To further optimize the above algorithm, a method of updating the dictionary by alternating optimization is proposed, namely MOD (Method of optimal directions) [8]. However, MOD requires matrix inversion, which leads to high algorithm complexity. K-SVD [9] is proposed on the basis of MOD by updating dictionary atoms one by one, which does not need to calculate matrix inverse and is more efficient. Dictionary learning under various constraints has been proposed one after another, and online dictionary learning with batch dynamic updates is proposed [10]. In this paper, we study the sparse representation and compression and reconstruction process of electromagnetic spectrum data. Aiming at the acquisition, compression, transmission, storage and reconstruction of electromagnetic spectrum data, the QRK-SVD framework is proposed to promote the compression and reconstruction capability of spectrum data.

2 Dictionary Learning and QRK-SVD

2.1 Dictionary Learning

As shown in Fig. 1, let X be a discrete signal. X satisfies $X = \Psi\theta$ under a specific set of basis (dictionary) Ψ, where θ is sparse, signal X is said to be sparse under basis Ψ, where Ψ is called the sparse basis of signal X, and θ is marked as the sparse representation of signal X under sparse basis Ψ. Different sparse bases are generally not universal. Sparse bases are usually for a specific signal. For example, common natural image signals are sparse under discrete cosine transform basis, discrete wavelet transform basis or discrete fourier transform basis.

Moreover, the performance of general sparse basis can not meet our requirements. Dictionary learning can design a dictionary with less reconstruction error according to the signal. One of the widely used algorithms is K-SVD. It mainly includes two

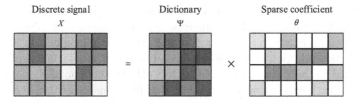

Fig. 1. Signal sparse representation

parts: sparse decomposition and dictionary updating. First, D is generated as the initial dictionary, and the corresponding optimization problem is:

$$\min_{D,\theta}\left\{\|X - D\theta\|_F^2\right\} \quad \text{s.t. } \|\theta_i\|_0 \le s, \forall i. \tag{1}$$

where X is the discrete signal and θ is the sparse coefficient matrix. Then fix dictionary $D^{(t-1)}$ and use OMP algorithm to solve the following optimization problems:

$$\min_{\theta_i}\left\{\left\|x_i - D^{(t-1)}\theta_i\right\|_2^2\right\} \quad \text{s.t. } \|\theta_i\|_0 \le s, \forall i. \tag{2}$$

When K-SVD updates the dictionary, each atom is updated. The error matrix of the signal corresponding to the k-th atom removed is:

$$E_k = X - \sum_{j\neq k} d_j\theta_T^j. \tag{3}$$

where θ_T^j is the j-th row vector of θ. Then perform singular value decomposition on E_k^R, which is a matrix determined by the nonzero-valued indices of θ_T^j:

$$E_k^R = U\Sigma V^T. \tag{4}$$

Update the dictionary $\hat{d}_k = u_1$ and the coefficient $\hat{\theta}_k^R = \Sigma[1, 1]v_1$ at the same time.

2.2 QRK-SVD

We often need to reconstruct a high-dimensional original sparse matrix from a low-dimensional observation matrix, as shown in Eqs. (5) and (6). The most commonly used method is orthogonal matching pursuit. We can linearly transform the signal X to get Y. When reconstructing X from Y, there will be errors in both the matching algorithm and dictionary learning. We propose to choose a more accurate initial dictionary in dictionary learning and improve the sensing matrix to make observations contain more information.

$$Y = \Phi X = \Phi D\theta \tag{5}$$

$$\theta_i^* = \arg\min_{\theta_i^* \in R^m} \|\theta_i\|_0, \; s.t \; \Phi D\theta_i = Y. \tag{6}$$

In dictionary learning, the selection of the initial matrix is very important. For real-time systems, the efficiency of data compression is very important. It is worth thinking about how to achieve a high reconstruction SNR with fewer iterations. In K-SVD, the initial dictionary selection method is to randomly select several columns of X, which is random and has poor performance. In QRK-SVD, each column of X is clustered by k-means, and each cluster center μ_i is selected as the initial dictionary, see Eq. (7). x_i that is not in the initial dictionary can be well represented by its own class center μ_{ji}, as shown in Eq. (8). The overall error of the initial dictionary of QRK-SVD will be smaller than that of K-SVD, see Eq. (9).

$$D_1 = (\mu_1, \mu_2, \ldots, \mu_m) \tag{7}$$

$$x_i \approx D_1 \theta_i^* = (\mu_{1i} \ldots \mu_{ji} \ldots \mu_{mi}) \begin{pmatrix} \theta_{1i}^* \\ \vdots \\ \theta_{ji}^* \\ \vdots \\ \theta_{mi}^* \end{pmatrix} \tag{8}$$

$$\left\| Y - D_1^* \theta^* \right\|_2 \leq \left\| Y - D_1 \theta^* \right\|_2. \tag{9}$$

where D_1^* represents initial dictionary for QRK-SVD, D_1 represents initial dictionary for K-SVD.

In coefficient reconstruction, the selection of the observation matrix is very important, and the observation matrix is generally selected as a Gaussian random matrix. However, it is not easy to generate random numbers in hardware, and the precision of random matrices is not high. Literature research shows that so as to enhance the independence of matrix column vector, it is essential to make its minimum singular value larger. The QR decomposition can increase the minimum singular value of the matrix without changing the original properties of the matrix, so we use QR decomposition to increase the reconstruction accuracy of the sensing matrix. The QRK-SVD data compression and reconstruction framework is shown in Fig. 2.

QR decomposition decomposes the transpose of the sensing matrix Ψ^T into Q matrix and R matrix, as shown in Eq. (10). Perform Then set all elements in R except on the diagonal to zero to obtain matrix $\widehat{R}$, as shown in Eq. (11), matrix I is a unit matrix. The optimized matrix $\widehat{\Psi}$ is obtained by multiplying the matrix Q and $\widehat{R}$, as shown in Eq. (12).

$$\Psi^T = (\Phi D)^T = QR \tag{10}$$

$$\widehat{R} = IR \tag{11}$$

$$\widehat{\Psi} = (Q\widehat{R})^T \tag{12}$$

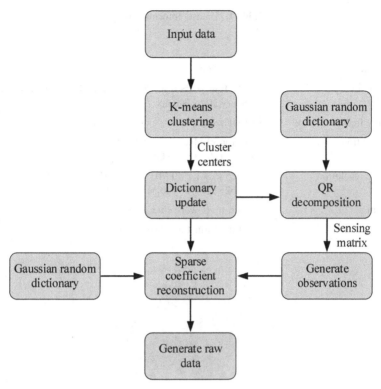

Fig. 2. The QRK-SVD data compression and reconstruction framework

3 Data Set and System Model

3.1 Electromagnetic Spectrum Data Set

The experimental dataset is an open-source measured spectrum dataset from the Broadband Spectrum Observatory of the Wireless Networks and Communications (WiNCom) Research Center of the Illinois Institute of Technology (IIT). The spectrum dataset was collected at a fixed location in Turku, Finland, and included a continuous 8-day spectrum data from January 20 to January 27, 2015 to 2018. The total dataset size is over 900 GB, and the acquisition frequency band is from 30 MHz to 6 GHz. See Table 1 for details.

In most cases, what we want to analyze and study is often a certain frequency band that may have key signals, rather than all frequency bands, so in the experiment, we consider the compression of data in one frequency band. The experimental data set selects the spectrum data of the first frequency band in the data collected in 2018, and the frequency band of the data is 17.93–22.14 MHz. Figure 3 shows the original time-frequency graph of the data from 8:00 am to 9:00 am in the second day.

3.2 System Model

The electromagnetic spectrum data compression storage system is shown in Fig. 4. On the local end, spectrum data collection is mainly implemented, which is divided into nyquist

Table 1. Dataset information

Data information	
Data volume	Over 900 GB
Collecting time	In the four years from 2015 to 2018, there are 32 days from January 20 to January 27
Collecting frequency band	30 MHz~6 GHz
Time resolution	10 s for 30 MHz~130 MHz and 3 s for 130 MHz~6 GHz
Frequency resolution	78.125 kHz for 30 MHz~130 MHz and 3 GHz~6 GHz, 39.0625 kHz for 130 MHz~3 GHz
Data form	Spectrum power value and GPS data
Data format	Mat file format and excel table

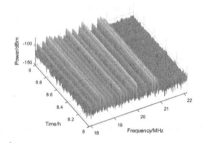

Fig. 3. Time-frequency graph of the second day spectrum

sampling and undersampling. Nyquist sampled data is compressed by CS module and QR decomposition. The compressed value is transmitted over the network to the cloud, where the compressed value is stored in the cloud database. Then the compressed value can generate initial dictionary, and dictionary learning is performed, and the dictionary is fed back to the local end. The sparse coefficients are reconstructed in the cloud using the dictionary and compressed data, and raw spectral data is generated for analysis. The following describes the detailed work on the local side and the cloud.

Local Slide

At the local slide, we use RF spectrum analyzers, acquisition antennas, power supply equipment, transportation equipment, etc. to sample the electromagnetic spectrum. The collection methods of electromagnetic spectrum data are generally divided into Nyquist sampling and Nyquist sampling. We compress the Nyquist sampled data through the CS module, and then go through QR decomposition to improve its reconstruction performance.

Under-nyquist sampling is a collection method based on compressive sensing theory, its process graph is shown in Fig. 5. The RF signal $x(t)$ is divided into m signals, each

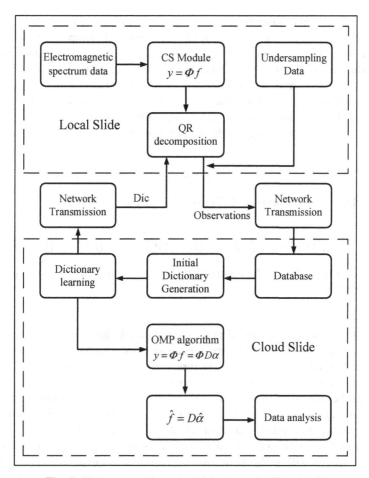

Fig. 4. Electromagnetic spectrum data compression system

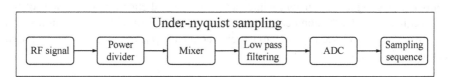

Fig. 5. Under-nyquist sampling process

signal is mixed with a pseudo-random code $p_i(t)$ with a period of T_p, and then passed through a low-pass filter $h(t)$ with a cutoff frequency of $1/(2T_s)$, and finally get the sequence $y[n]$ after sampling, and the discrete-time Fourier transform of $y[n]$ can be denoted by Eq. (13).

$$Y_i\left(e^{j2\pi fT_s}\right) = \sum_{n=-\infty}^{\infty} y_i[n]e^{-j2\pi f_n T_s} = \sum_{l=-L_0}^{L_0} c_{il}X\left(f - lf_p\right), \quad f \in \mathcal{F}_s \qquad (13)$$

where $X(f)$ is the spectrum of $x(t)$, c_{il} is the fourier series coefficient of $p_i(t)$.

The collected electromagnetic spectrum data is generally temporarily stored in the local computer. The current local storage method consumes a lot of storage resources. Cloud storage, cloud computing and other methods are more suitable for the processing of big data. When we transmit the collected electromagnetic data to the cloud server, we also face the problem of a large amount of transmitted data, so we need to compress the collected electromagnetic data in the local computer first. This process uses a matrix with a smaller dimension. Multiplied by the electromagnetic data matrix, the model can be expressed as Eq. (14).

$$Y = [y_1, y_2, \ldots y_n] = \Phi F = \Phi[f_1, f_2, \ldots f_n]. \tag{14}$$

Similarly, we can also express Eq. (13) in this form.

$$\begin{aligned} Y &= \left[Y_i\left(e^{j2\pi fT_s}\right), Y_i\left(e^{j2\pi fT_s}\right), \ldots, Y_i\left(e^{j2\pi fT_s}\right)\right] \\ &= A\left[X\left(f - L_0 f_p\right), X\left(f - (L_0 + 1)f_p\right), \ldots, X\left(f + L_0 f_p\right)\right]. \end{aligned} \tag{15}$$

In the Eq. (14) and (15), the observation value matrix is denoted by Y, Φ and A is the observation matrix.

Cloud Side

After the observations are uploaded to the cloud through the network, we can directly store the observations in the cloud server database. However, the observed values cannot be directly used for data analysis. Before analyzing the electromagnetic spectrum data, we need to obtain the original electromagnetic spectrum data. The known prior condition is the observation matrix Φ, and the electromagnetic spectrum data itself is not sparse, so we cannot reconstruct the original electromagnetic spectrum data with only the observation matrix Φ and the observation value matrix Y.

In the cloud, we also need to train a complete or over-complete dictionary of electromagnetic spectrum data. The dictionary is the sparse domain of the data, and the data is represented by the dictionary in the form of multiplying the dictionary and the sparse coefficient, as shown in Eq. (16). The over complete dictionary includes more dictionary atoms than the signal dimension, while in the complete dictionary, the number of the two is equal. First, let the number of clusters equal the number of dictionary atoms, and minimize the error E, see Eq. (17), to get cluster center $(\mu_1, \mu_2, \ldots \mu_n)$. Let the initial dictionary $D_1 = (\mu_1, \mu_2, \ldots \mu_n)$.

$$f = D\alpha \tag{16}$$

$$E = \sum_{i=1}^{k} \sum_{f \in C_i} \|f - \mu_i\|_2^2 \tag{17}$$

where f is the spectrum data, the dictionary is denoted by D, and the sparse coefficient is denoted by α.

When the dictionary of a certain frequency band is trained in the cloud and the observed values are known, we can use various methods to reconstruct the sparse coefficients, such as greedy algorithm, convex optimization algorithm and so on. In this paper, the most commonly used OMP is selected to construct the sparse coefficients. The OMP ensures the accuracy and efficiency of reconstruction. Through the OMP, we can obtain the estimated value of the sparse coefficient reconstructed from the observation matrix and the dictionary. The estimated value of the signal can be obtained by multiplying the dictionary and the estimated value, and the estimated value of the signal can be sent to the data analysis model for data analysis and data mining.

There are bound to be errors in the entire system model, and there are three main types of errors. One is the acquisition error generated during acquisition, which can be improved by improving the accuracy of the acquisition device. The second type of error is the dictionary error generated when learning the dictionary. Because a dictionary cannot perfectly match all signal sets, there must be a dictionary error. The way to improve this error is to select appropriate system parameters and perform dictionary learning. The third error is the reconstruction error generated when using the OMP. The reason for this error is that the OMP cannot reconstruct a completely accurate sparse coefficient. The selection of observation matrix, sparsity and observation size will affect the reconstruction accuracy. The QRK-SVD framework can effectively reduce the latter two errors and improve the system performance.

4 Experiments

4.1 Evaluation Indicators

Through data acquisition, data compression, data transmission, data decompression and other processes, the estimated value of electromagnetic spectrum data is obtained in the cloud. We measure the accuracy of signal reconstruction by reconstruction SNR, which is defined as:

$$\text{SNR} = 10 \lg \frac{1}{\text{RRMSE}^2} = 10 \lg \frac{\|X\|_2^2}{\left\|X - \hat{X}\right\|_2^2}. \tag{18}$$

Among them, RRMSE is the relative root mean square error, X is the original electromagnetic spectrum data, and the estimated value is denoted by $\hat{X}$.

We define the ratio of the size of the observations to the size of the original sample as the compression ratio (Cr), which is defined as Eq. (19).

$$Cr = \frac{row(Y)}{row(X)} \times 100\%. \tag{19}$$

4.2 Dictionary Error and Reconstruction Error

We select the data from 8:00 am to 9:00 am in the first frequency band on the second day, the fourth day, and the seventh day to study the relationship between the dictionary error and the reconstruction error. We performed 50 iterations with a dictionary sparsity of 0.05, a dictionary size of 380, and the Cr value of 25%. Figure 6 shows the relationship between dictionary error and reconstruction error.

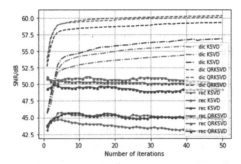

Fig. 6. The reconstruction SNR changes with the number of iterations

As can be seen from Fig. 6, no matter what day the data is, the reconstructed SNR of QRK-SVD is greatly improved than that of K-SVD. When the number of iterations is small, the dictionary error is not much different from the reconstruction error. When the number of iterations is large, the reconstruction performance of the K-SVD method decreases, while the QRK-SVD method still has good reconstruction performance. This is mainly because the selection strategy of the initial dictionary is better and because the QR decomposition reduces the correlation between the observation matrix and the dictionary, QRK-SVD achieves higher reconstruction accuracy.

4.3 Reconstruction Capability with Different Dictionary Sizes

We select the electromagnetic spectrum data from 8:00 to 9:00 in the first frequency band on the second day, the fourth day, and the seventh day to study the reconstruction ability of K-SVD under different dictionary sizes. We let the dictionary size vary from 360 to 400, the dictionary sparsity is 0.05, the number of iterations is 5, and the Cr value is shown in the figure. Figure 7 shows the effect of dictionary size on reconstruction performance under different Cr values.

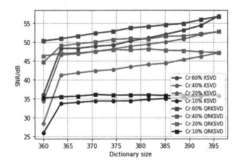

Fig. 7. The reconstruction SNR changes with the size of the dictionary

As can be seen from Fig. 7, no matter what day the data is, under any Cr value, the performance of QRK-SVD is better than that of K-SVD. And as the dictionary size increases, the reconstructed SNR also increases. Since the dictionary size increases, more atoms participate in the sparse representation, and the sparse representation power also increases.

4.4 Reconstruction Capability with Different Sample Sizes

We select the electromagnetic spectrum data from 8:00 to 9:00 in the first frequency band on the second day, the fourth day, and the seventh day to study the reconstruction ability of K-SVD under different sample sizes. The sample size is changed from 36 to 1800, the dictionary sparsity is 0.05, the dictionary size is 380, and the Cr value is 20%. Figure 8 shows the reconstruction SNR curve under the change of sample size.

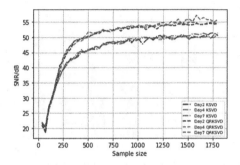

Fig. 8. The reconstruction SNR changes with the size of sample

As can be seen from Fig. 8, QRK-SVD outperforms K-SVD at any sample size. Because in the case of the same Cr value, the larger the spectrum sample size, the more the information content of the observed value. In this way, the reconstruction accuracy that can be obtained based on the orthogonal matching pursuit is also greater. However, it is not wise to choose a large sample size, as this will make the running time of the algorithm become longer and increase of the dictionary size, which reduces the system efficiency.

4.5 The Amount of Data at the Same Reconstruction Accuracy

We study the size of the transmitted data size of the two frameworks under the same reconstructed SNR. The dictionary size is 380, the dictionary sparsity is 0.05, and the number of iterations is 5. When the reconstruction SNR is 35 dB, 40 dB, and 45 dB, the amount of transmitted data of the two frameworks is shown in Fig. 9, 10 and 11.

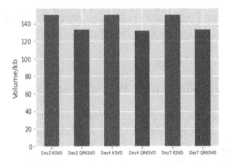

Fig. 9. Comparison of the data volume of the two frameworks at 35 dB

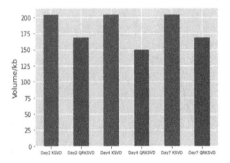

Fig. 10. Comparison of the data volume of the two frameworks at 40 dB

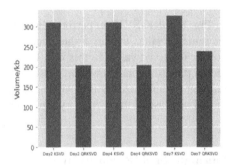

Fig. 11. Comparison of the data volume of the two frameworks at 45 dB

As can be seen from the figure, the amount of data in the QRK-SVD framework under any reconstruction SNR is smaller than that in the K-SVD framework. And when the reconstruction SNR is large, this advantage is more obvious.

5 Summarize

This paper studies the whole process of electromagnetic spectrum data acquisition, compression, transmission and utilization. It is proposed to use dictionary learning to improve the performance of spectral data compression and reduce the storage capacity. The reconstruction error of electromagnetic spectrum data is related to many factors, including the number of algorithm iterations, the sample size, and the size of the dictionary. This paper studies the influence of these factors on the reconstruction error. The electromagnetic spectrum data compression and reconstruction framework of QRK-SVD is proposed, and the reconstruction ability of QRK-SVD under different parameter conditions is analyzed. For different dictionary sizes, the reconstruction ability of the overcomplete dictionary is better than that of the complete dictionary, but the storage space required is also larger. The increase of dictionary size can effectively improve the reconstruction performance. When the sample size increases, the reconstruction ability of QRK-SVD continues to improve, indicating that QRK-SVD can adapt to samples of various sizes, which is very valuable in practical applications, because the size of each compressed sample cannot be guaranteed to be the same in actual spectrum data collection. In the follow-up research, we can think about how to ensure that there is no error in the transmission process and at the same time have a strong real-time transmission capability. Whether a more efficient dictionary can be designed and whether a stronger observation matrix can be designed to meet the requirement reconstruction needs further research and analysis.

References

1. Zheng, X.: Design of spectrum sharing platform based on USRP for heterogeneous wireless network. In: 2021 Asia-Pacific Conference on Communications Technology and Computer Science (ACCTCS). IEEE (2021)
2. Lin, J., et al.: Spectrum resource trading and radio management data sharing based on blockchain. In: 2020 IEEE 3rd International Conference on Information Systems and Computer Aided Education (ICISCAE). IEEE (2020)
3. Sankaran, S., Ehsani, R.: Introduction to the electromagnetic spectrum. In: Manickavasagan, A., Jayasuriya, H. (eds.) Imaging with Electromagnetic Spectrum, pp. 1–15. Springer, Heidelberg (2014). https://doi.org/10.1007/978-3-642-54888-8_1
4. Guo, L., Wang, M., Lin, Y.: Electromagnetic environment portrait based on big data mining. Wirel. Commun. Mob. Comput. **2021**, 1–13 (2021)
5. Donoho, D.L.: Compressed sensing. IEEE Trans. Inf. Theory **52**(4), 1289–1306 (2006)
6. Olshausen, B.A., Field, D.J.: Emergence of simple-cell receptive field properties by learning a sparse code for natural images. Nature **381**(6583), 607–609 (1996)
7. Tošić, I., Frossard, P.: Dictionary learning. IEEE Signal Process. Mag. **28**(2), 27–38 (2011)
8. Engan, K., Aase, S.O., Husoy, J.H.: Method of optimal directions for frame design. In: 1999 IEEE International Conference on Acoustics, Speech, and Signal Processing. Proceedings, ICASSP99 (Cat. No. 99CH36258), vol. 5. IEEE (1999)
9. Aharon, M., Elad, M., Bruckstein, A.: K-SVD: an algorithm for designing overcomplete dictionaries for sparse representation. IEEE Trans. Signal Process. **54**(11), 4311–4322 (2006)
10. Mairal, J., et al.: Online learning for matrix factorization and sparse coding. J. Mach. Learn. Res. **11**(1), 19–60 (2010)
11. Papyan, V., et al.: Theoretical foundations of deep learning via sparse representations: a multilayer sparse model and its connection to convolutional neural networks. IEEE Signal Process. Mag. **35**(4), 72–89 (2018)
12. Lin, Y., et al.: Multisensor fault diagnosis modeling based on the evidence theory. IEEE Trans. Reliab. **67**(2), 513–521 (2018)

13. Lu, Y., Wang, Y.: A physics-constrained dictionary learning approach for compression of vibration signals. Mech. Syst. Signal Process. **153**, 107434 (2021)

14. Wang, M., et al.: Transfer learning promotes 6G wireless communications: recent advances and future challenges. IEEE Trans. Reliab. **70**(2), 790–807 (2021)

15. Duan, L., Yang, X., Li, A.: WSN data compression model based on K-SVD dictionary and compressed sensing. In: Zeng, J., Qin, P., Jing, W., Song, X., Lu, Z. (eds.) ICPCSEE 2021. CCIS, vol. 1451, pp. 429–442. Springer, Singapore (2021). https://doi.org/10.1007/978-981-16-5940-9_33

16. Shen, F., et al.: 3D compressed spectrum mapping with sampling locations optimization in spectrum-heterogeneous environment. IEEE Trans. Wirel. Commun. **21**(1), 326–338 (2021)

17. Liu, J.: Research on power quality signals reconstruction method based on K-SVD dictionary learning. In: 2020 39th Chinese Control Conference (CCC). IEEE (2020)

18. Wang, L., et al.: IK-SVD: dictionary learning for spatial big data via incremental atom update. Comput. Sci. Eng. **16**(4), 41–52 (2014)

A Survey on Intelligent Question and Answer Systems

Xuechao Guo, Bin Zhao, and Bo Ning[(✉)]

School of Information Science and Technology, Dalian Maritime University,
Dalian, China
{xuechao,zhaobin,ningbo}@dlmu.edu.cn

Abstract. With the rapid development of technology in society, people are surrounded by all kinds of data in the information age. So the means to access external information accurately and quickly have become particularly important. Currently, intelligent question and answer systems are a promising area of research in the field of artificial intelligence and natural language processing. As an interactive system, it significantly differs from traditional search engines. When people perform advanced information retrieval, it can accurately understand the natural language questions asked by the user and give the user a corresponding answer using natural language, which meets people's needs for quickly, easily and accurately accessing information. Intelligent question and answer systems are already widely used in people's daily life, such as common intelligent voice interaction, online customer service, knowledge acquisition, emotional chat, etc. Deep learning, a branch of machine learning, is now widely used for various tasks in natural language processing. This paper focuses on the applications of deep learning to intelligent question and answer systems.

Keywords: Intelligent question and answer systems · Information retrieval · Natural language processing · Deep learning

1 Introduction

Traditional search engine systems have many drawbacks, such as a lack of accuracy in the representation of requirements when searching. The search needs of users are often very complex and specific, which cannot be expressed by a simple logical combination of a few keywords. Traditional search engines are not concise enough and return too many results making it extremely difficult for users to locate the information they need quickly and accurately. Lacking the support of semantic processing technology, traditional keyword-based information retrieval remains on the surface of language without containing semantics, making the retrieval effect mediocre. Intelligent question and answer systems based on natural language processing technology are one of the directions in which traditional

Y. Chenggang et al. (Eds.): MobiMedia 2022, LNICST 451, pp. 81–88, 2022.
https://doi.org/10.1007/978-3-031-23902-1_7

search engines are being improved. The query information is used to parse out the user's query intent, then the location of the answer is pinpointed from the document based on the intent, and finally the answer is extracted and returned to the user. Rather than just returning a documented distribution of answers to questions to the user, which is a great improvement both in terms of accuracy and meeting the user's search needs. Deep learning [10], a branch of machine learning, is a class of algorithms that attempt to perform high-level abstractions of data using multi-processing layer computational models that contain complex structures or consist of multiple non-linear transformations. It gradually transforms the initial low-level feature representation into a high-level feature representation through multi-layer processing, and allows complex learning tasks such as classification to be performed with simple models. Deep learning techniques have been used in a wide range of fields such as image recognition, speech recognition and natural language processing. A number of scholars have already applied deep learning to intelligent question and answer systems.

Classified according to the type of domain, intelligent question and answer systems can be divided into limited domain-oriented question and answer systems and open domain oriented question and answer systems. Depending on the implementation method, domain-limited QA systems are divided into Pipeline QA systems and end-to-end QA systems. Open domain QA systems are divided into search-based QA systems, generative-based QA systems and hybrid-based QA systems. The following article will focus on each of these types of QA systems.

2   Qualified Domain Oriented QA Systems

Domain-oriented QA systems, also known as task-based QA systems, are oriented towards vertical domains and aim to help users complete predetermined tasks or actions using as few dialogue rounds as possible. For example, booking tickets, restaurants, hotels, etc. The current mainstream research approach is to study task-based QA systems in three modules: Natural Language Understanding (NLU), Dialogue Management (DM) and Natural Language Generation (NLG) [2]. There are two broad approaches to the study of task-based QA systems, one is the Pipeline task-based QA systems and the other is the end-to-end task-based QA systems.

2.1   Pipelined Task-Based QA Systems

Pipelined task-based QA systems including Natural Language Understanding (NLU) modules, where Kim [8] and Lee [11], et al. use the user's dialogue to perform intention analysis and translate it into pre-defined semantic slots. Next comes the Dialogue State Tracking (DST) module, Williams et al. [26] assess the status of each round of dialogue based on information about the current dialogue and the history of the dialogue. There follows the Policy Learning (POL) module, it will make the next reaction based on the current state of the conversation, i.e. it determines the action of the system. And finally, there is the Natural Language Generation (NLG) module. Wen et al. [25] convert the responses made by the policy learning module into the corresponding natural language responses provided to the user. The Dialogue State Tracking module and the Dialogue Policy Learning module make up the Dialogue Manager (DM), which is the core controller of the task-based QA systems. In some situations, several of these modules can be used in combination, depending on the needs of the task. Budzianowski et al. [1] combine NLU and DST modules and map the user's historical conversation information to the corresponding conversation states. Chen et al. [3] combine POL and NLG modules and map the user's historical discourse and conversation state to the system response. The first joint modelling of intention recognition and slot filling tasks using a GRU-based approach by Zhang et al. [31] After the GRU encodes the sentence the representation of the sentence is obtained by the max- pooling layer for intent recognition. Finally the joint learning of the two tasks is performed through a shared GRU layer to obtain an implicit relationship between them. Liu et al. [15] first used a sequence-to-sequence fusion attention mechanism approach to jointly model intention recognition and slot-filling tasks. Goo et al. [6] first used the slot-gate mechanism to explicitly focus on learning the relationship between slot-filling and intention recognition tasks and to obtain better semantic information through global optimization. Li et al. [12] use the Gate mechanism to use information to guide the slot-filling task, explicitly exploiting information about intentions. They explored the role of self-attention mechanisms on this task for the first time, which achieved good performance.

2.2 End-to-End Task-Based QA Systems

Although pipelined task-based QA systems can achieve good performance on individual tasks with a combination of modules, this modular system has significant drawbacks in deep learning training. When using a multi-step, multi-model to solve a complex task, inconsistency in the training objectives of each module makes it difficult to achieve optimal performance of the trained model. The end-to-end model uses only one model, one objective function and uses back propagation to optimise the parameters, the inherent pitfalls of multiple models are avoided. Recurrent neural networks are mostly used as encoder and decoder modules in end-to-end task-based dialogue systems. Madotto et al. [17] used an end-to-end memory network (MemNN) to address the problem of unstable performance in long sequences of recurrent neural networks as well as high temporal computational overhead. It uses several embedding matrices as external memory and reads the memory repeatedly using query vectors, it is therefore more suitable for storing information from external knowledge bases in task-based conversations. Eric et al. [5] propose a complete end-to-end model where they model conversation context and conversation generation based on an existing sequence-to-sequence architecture. They added an attention-based key-value pair mechanism to the retrieval of knowledge base entries, addressing the issue of how the model could be more smoothly interfaced with the knowledge base. Wu et al. [27] fused memory networks and copy mechanisms to more smoothly embed the knowledge base during sequence generation, allowing for better integration of the knowledge base into task-based dialogue systems. Luo et al. [16] proposed the Profile Model and Preference Model based on the end-to-end memory network model. The former learns personalisation by embedding user profiles and uses global memory to store the conversation context of similar users. The latter is done by establishing a link between the portrait and the knowledge base, thus the best result among the candidate answers can be selected.

3   Open Domain Oriented QA Systems

The Open Domain QA systems differs significantly from the Limited Domain QA system in that it does not target domain-specific questions and complete any task. Instead, they are data-driven [20] and use natural language to mimic human discourse for everyday interactions. Three broad categories of open domain QA systems have been studied, including generative-based QA systems, retrieval-based QA systems and hybrid-based QA systems. The widespread use of deep learning techniques is now leading to breakthroughs in open domain QA systems.

3.1   Retrieval-Based QA Systems

Retrieval-based QA systems usually begin with the construction of a large corpus that can be retrieved by the system. The system identifies the responses from the conversation corpus that most closely resemble the input utterance. For each input statement, the retrieval model selects the statement with the greatest semantic match from the candidate statements as its response. In recent years, some models have taken into account not only current conversations but also rich historical conversations in the selection of responses. The core modules of a retrieval-based QA systems include a candidate answer retrieval module, a question-answer similarity calculation module and a ranking module. The overall step can be considered as a classification prediction of candidate responses. In another way, the question and the candidate responses are fed into a neural network model, and all candidate responses are classified or ranked.

The calculation of question-answer similarity is a key aspect of retrieval-based QA systems. Traditional text similarity calculation methods are based on surface text similarity calculation. The main method is to directly target the unprocessed text and use the degree of match and distance of the characters or strings in it as a criterion of similarity. This method is simple to implement and easy to understand. Kondrak et al. [9] used an n-gram model to calculate the similarity between characters, the main idea being to calculate the ratio of the number of identical N tuples to the total number of N tuples for two texts. Surface text similarity calculations do not take into account the semantic relationship of the text very well. In response to this problem, semantic similarity calculation methods have been proposed, of which neural network-based methods are currently the mainstream research direction. Mikolov et al. [18] proposed the word vector embedding (Word2Vec) approach, which includes the CBOW model that uses context to predict central words and the Skip-gram model that uses central words to predict context. It uses contextual information to transform words into high-dimensional vectors. Shen et al. [22] based on convolutional neural networks to obtain a semantic representation vector of the user's query and the word vector of candidate answers with its fixed length by convolution and pooling operations, and then use the cosine similarity function to measure how well the queries and responses match. The task of simulating image recognition by Pang et al. [14] The matrix is first constructed based on the similarity between word vectors, then the fused information is gradually captured using convolutional and pooling layers, and finally the matching scores are calculated for answer ranking. Kim et al. [7] propose a DRCN model based on the generic framework of DenseRNN, which contains a multilayer recurrent neural network and an attention mechanism. The input to each layer of the neural network is a fusion of the outputs of all previous layers, and the output vector is used as input directly by the pooling layer before semantic fusion, thus alleviating the problem of gradient disappearance caused by the increase in the number of layers of the model. With the creation of the Transformer [24] model, more and more pre-trained models are emerging and performing well on various tasks in natural language processing. For example, the Bidirectional Encoder Representation from Transformers (BERT) [4] model addresses the case where the word2vec model is unable to determine multiple meanings of a word. The Bert model is trained using a large-scale unlabeled corpus, and the text obtained contains rich semantic information.

3.2   Generative-Based QA Systems

The main goal of a generative QA system is to generate responses based on the contextual information of the current conversation. This is usually done by using a deep learning based encoder-decoder architecture. Deep learning-based techniques do not usually rely on specific answer banks or templates, but rather on linguistic competence acquired from a large corpus. Specifically, a recurrent neural network is used to encode the input utterance as a vector representation, while another recurrent neural network is used at the decoding end and an attention mechanism is used to generate the replies one by one.

People do not simply ask one question and answer another in general chat. Answers often refer to the content of contextual chat messages, so contextual information should be introduced into the encoder, which helps the encoder to generate better session response content. Sordoni et al. [23] proposed the use of multilayer feedforward neural networks instead of recurrent neural networks in the encoder part. In this way, both the contextual information and the current conversation to be encoded by a multi-layer feed-forward neural network to generate an intermediate semantic representation of the encoder-decoder architecture, while avoiding the problem of recurrent neural networks being sensitive to excessively long inputs. Li et al. [13] used the idea of adversarial learning to train both a response generator and a response discriminator. Generators are sequence-to-sequence based generative dialogue models. The discriminator is a classification model that completes a binary classification task which classifies the generated responses into two categories, human responses and machine responses, and is used to assess the quality of the responses. The core idea of the model is to motivate generators that can generate discourse in place of human replies. Xu et al. [29] used generative adversarial networks to the task of dialogue generation. They propose to replace the sampled decoding results in the decoder with an approximate embedding layer. It is an end-to-end model overall, allowing discriminators and generators to be trained with simultaneous parameter tuning by back-propagation. Shao et al. [21] connect the decoder head to tail and then use the generated part as part of an attention mechanism with further additions to the existing informativeness for generating long replies with high information content. Wu et al. [28] improved the word mapping at decoding and proposed a sequence-to-sequence model based on a dynamically decoded lexicon. The model makes it possible to have a different lexicon for each decoding step depending on the actual current conversation, in order to remove the interference of irrelevant words, narrow the mapping and speed up decoding.

3.3   Hybrid-Based QA Systems

QA systems based on retrieval-based approaches often respond to discourses that are limited by constructed corpus, and sometimes the retrieved content does not fit well with the contextual content. QA systems based on generative approaches may generate discourse that is more generic, or even output answers that are not relevant to the user's input question. The hybrid-based QA systems integrates both retrieval and generative approaches, providing a clever blend of the two. Qiu et al. [19] generated responses using a sequence-to-sequence model and then scored the responses obtained by the retrieval method using the rerank model. If the score is below the initially set threshold, the response generated by the seq2seq model is used directly as the answer to the user, otherwise the response obtained by retrieval is used as the answer to the user. Liu et al. [30] built a neural network dialogue model that mixes retrieval-based ranking models and generative models, and combines the advantages of retrieval-based and generative QA systems, providing new insights into how to integrate retrieval and generative models to build QA systems.

4   Conclusion

Current intelligent question and answer systems have significant shortcomings in terms of semantics, consistency and interactivity. In terms of semantics, deep learning-based generative models are more likely to generate meaningless universal replies, such as 'I don't know'. The amount of information, appropriateness and logic of the generated content is still inadequate, and there is a long way to go before semantic understanding in the true sense of the word. In terms of consistency, it is easy to create semantic identity and personality conflicts in the interaction. In terms of interactivity, current intelligent QA systems have significant shortcomings in terms of emotional interaction and strategic response. It is not able to adaptively adjust its own strategies to the user's topic status, such as topic strategies, active-passive strategies and emotional expression strategies, and it also makes it impossible to achieve smooth and natural human-computer interaction. With the advancement of technology and media publicity, people are more inclined to think of an intelligent QA system as their life companion rather than a machine that can only be used to perform a task. To meet this expectation of users, the future intelligent QA systems will need to have some emotional intelligence. They can carry out emotional response and interaction, and reflect personality, language style and personality in dialogue and interaction.

References

1. Budzianowski, P., Wen, T.H., Tseng, B.H., Casanueva, I., Gai, M.: MultiwOZ - a large-scale multi-domain wizard-of-OZ dataset for task-oriented dialogue modelling (2018)
2. Chen, H., Liu, X., Yin, D., Tang, J.: A survey on dialogue systems: recent advances and new frontiers. ACM SIGKDD Explor. Newslett. **19**(2), 25–35 (2017)
3. Chen, W., Chen, J., Qin, P., Yan, X., Wang, W.Y.: Semantically conditioned dialog response generation via hierarchical disentangled self-attention (2019)
4. Devlin, J., Chang, M.W., Lee, K., Toutanova, K.: BERT: pre-training of deep bidirectional transformers for language understanding (2018)
5. Eric, M., Manning, C.D.: Key-value retrieval networks for task-oriented dialogue (2017)
6. Goo, C.W., Gao, G., Hsu, Y.K., Huo, C.L., Chen, Y.N.: Slot-gated modeling for joint slot filling and intent prediction. In: Proceedings of the 2018 Conference of the North American Chapter of the Association for Computational Linguistics: Human Language Technologies, Volume 2 (Short Papers) (2018)
7. Kim, S., Kang, I., Kwak, N.: Semantic sentence matching with densely-connected recurrent and co-attentive information (2018)
8. Kim, Y.B., Lee, S., Stratos, K.: OneNet: joint domain, intent, slot prediction for spoken language understanding. Amazon Alexa Brain, Seattle, WA; Microsoft Research, Redmond, WA; Toyota Technological Institute, Chicago, IL
9. Kondrak, G.: N-Gram similarity and distance. In: Consens, M., Navarro, G. (eds.) SPIRE 2005. LNCS, vol. 3772, pp. 115–126. Springer, Heidelberg (2005). https://doi.org/10.1007/11575832_13
10. LeCun, Y., Bengio, Y., Hinton, G.: Deep learning. Nature **521**(7553), 436–444 (2015)
11. Lee, S., et al.: ConvLab: multi-domain end-to-end dialog system platform (2019)
12. Li, C., Li, L., Qi, J.: A self-attentive model with gate mechanism for spoken language understanding. In: Proceedings of the 2018 Conference on Empirical Methods in Natural Language Processing, pp. 3824–3833 (2018)
13. Li, J., Monroe, W., Shi, T., Jean, S., Ritter, A., Jurafsky, D.: Adversarial learning for neural dialogue generation (2017)
14. Liang, P., Lan, Y., Guo, J., Xu, J., Cheng, X.: Text matching as image recognition (2016)
15. Liu, B., Lane, I.: Attention-based recurrent neural network models for joint intent detection and slot filling (2016)

16. Luo, L., Huang, W., Qi, Z., Nie, Z., Xu, S.: Learning personalized end-to-end goal-oriented dialog (2018)
17. Madotto, A., Wu, C.S., Fung, P.: Mem2Seq: effectively incorporating knowledge bases into end-to-end task-oriented dialog systems (2018)
18. Mikolov, T., Chen, K., Corrado, G., Dean, J.: Efficient estimation of word representations in vector space. Comput. Sci. (2013)
19. Qiu, M., et al.: AliMe chat: a sequence to sequence and Rerank based chatbot engine. In: Proceedings of the 55th Annual Meeting of the Association for Computational Linguistics (Volume 2: Short Papers), pp. 498–503. Association for Computational Linguistics, Vancouver, July 2017. https://doi.org/10.18653/v1/P17-2079. https://aclanthology.org/P17-2079
20. Ritter, A., Cherry, C., Dolan, B.: Data-driven response generation in social media. In: Empirical Methods in Natural Language Processing (EMNLP), January 2011. https://www.microsoft.com/en-us/research/publication/data-driven-response-generation-in-social-media/
21. Shao, L., Gouws, S., Britz, D., Goldie, A., Strope, B., Kurzweil, R.: Generating high-quality and informative conversation responses with sequence-to-sequence models (2017)
22. Shen, Y., He, X., Gao, J., Deng, L., Mesnil, G.: Learning semantic representations using convolutional neural network for web search. In: Proceedings WWW, pp. 373–374 (2014)
23. Sordoni, A., et al.: A neural network approach to context-sensitive generation of conversational responses. In: Proceedings of the 2015 Conference of the North American Chapter of the Association for Computational Linguistics: Human Language Technologies, May-Jun 2015
24. Vaswani, A., et al.: Attention is all you need. arXiv (2017)
25. Wen, T.H., Gasic, M., Mrksic, N., Su, P.H., Vandyke, D., Young, S.: Semantically conditioned LSTM-based natural language generation for spoken dialogue systems. Comput. Sci. (2015)
26. Williams, J., Raux, A., Ramachandran, D., Black, A.: The dialog state tracking challenge. In: Proceedings of the SIGDIAL 2013 Conference (2013)
27. Wu, C.S., Socher, R., Xiong, C.: Global-to-local memory pointer networks for task-oriented dialogue (2019)
28. Wu, Y., Wu, W., Yang, D., Xu, C., Li, Z., Zhou, M.: Neural response generation with dynamic vocabularies (2017)
29. Xu, Z., et al.: Neural response generation via GAN with an approximate embedding layer. In: Proceedings of the 2017 Conference on Empirical Methods in Natural Language Processing, pp. 617–626 (2017)
30. Yang, L., et al.: A hybrid retrieval-generation neural conversation model. In: Proceedings of the 28th ACM International Conference on Information and Knowledge Management (2019)
31. Zhang, X., Wang, H.: A joint model of intent determination and slot filling for spoken language understanding (2016)

Cyberspace Security on Cryptography, Privacy Protection, Data Sharing, Access Control and Task Prediction

Privacy-Preserving Decision Tree Classification Protocol Based on Bitwise Comparison

Peihang Yu[1]($\boxtimes$), Baodong Qin[1], and Dong Zheng[2]

[1] School of Cyberspace Security, Xi'an University of Posts and Telecommunications,
Xi'an 710121, China
199910095860163.com, qinbaodong@xupt.edu.cn
[2] School of Computer Qinghai Normal University, Xining 810008, China

Abstract. Decision tree model is widely used in telemedicine, credit evaluation and other fields because of its high efficiency and ease of use. Companies can charge customers who do not have professional knowledge or resources to build pre-diction models to achieve the purpose of profitability. In order to protect the privacy of client data and decision tree model parameters in this scenario, we propose an integer comparison protocol based on distributed bitwise comparison, and further design an efficient privacy-preserving decision tree classification model. Our protocol uses the idea of Beaver triple multiplication combined with secret sharing to replace the ciphertext homomorphic operation in the original comparison protocol. Compared with the comparison protocol relying on the traditional semi-homomorphic encryption scheme, it further im-proves the operation efficiency and compresses the communication cost in ciphertext transmission. Security analysis shows that this scheme achieves the expected privacy for users and model providers. Experimental results on real datasets show that the overall running time of this scheme is about 0.8s for a decision tree of depth 3, and about 5s for a decision tree of depth 17. So, its computational overhead is low and acceptable.

Keywords: Machine learning · Decision tree · Secret sharing · Homomorphic encryption · Privacy-preserving

1 Introduction

With the diversification of Internet technology more and more companies are offering a wide range of remote services to their users. These include machine learning classifiers for data analysis and prediction services such as healthcare, transportation, and image recognition. In actual deployment, typically the classification service provider has a trained model, the user gives an instance as

Y. Chenggang et al. (Eds.): MobiMedia 2022, LNICST 451, pp. 91–104, 2022.
https://doi.org/10.1007/978-3-031-23902-1_8

input, and its output represents the classification label of its output. The classifier is trained by the hospital with human and material resources, which is a trade secret and cannot be disclosed [1]. The user's input includes their own, such as height, weight, heart rate, etc., which are personal privacy which cannot be disclosed. Therefore, privacy protection in the use of machine learning models is crucial. Since Agrawal et al. [2] proposed privacy-preserving data mining techniques, mainstream data mining techniques have emerged successively with solutions to privacy-preserving problems such as neural networks [3], support vector machines [4], decision trees [5] and random forests [6], etc. In this paper, we focus on privacy-preserving issues related to decision tree models, its related work is as follows.

In 2015, Bost et al. [7] were the first to design a privacy-preserving decision tree evaluation scheme using FHE technique, which uses FHE to encrypt the data and process the decision tree as a polynomial, and computes the polynomial by homomorphism to finally obtain the classification result. Subsequently, Wu et al. [8] used a more lightweight additive homomorphic encryption combined with oblivious transfer(OT) [9] instead of fully homomorphic encryption to reduce the computational overhead. Tai et al. [10] proposed to represent the decision tree as multiple linear functions and determine whether a single leaf node contains a classification result by calculating the path cost of that leaf node, which reduces the computational overhead and communication compared to the Wu [8]. In 2019, Zheng et al. [11] proposed to use additive secret sharing technique to divide the decision tree thresholds with user features into two secret shares and outsource to two servers to complete the overall classification process using MSB, but requires a large number of parameters to be prepared in advance by trusted third parties. In 2020, Xue et al. [12] used Paillier encryption scheme to encrypt the data using respective shares to do the difference comparison size. Recently, Cao et al. [13] proposed a multi-key privacy preserving decision tree evaluation scheme based on double trapdoor encryption scheme, the scheme encrypts data using DT-PKC encryption system with additive homomorphic property and uses DGK [14] comparison protocol for node comparison, the overall efficiency of the scheme is low due to the low efficiency of double trapdoor encryption scheme and the per-bit comparison of decision nodes.

Our Contribution. In this paper, we propose a privacy-preserving decision tree classification protocol in the client-server model. The protocol improves the bit-by-bit comparison scheme proposed by Garay et al. [15] to compare user's features with decision nodes bit-by-bit, while ensuring the confidentiality of user input and decision tree thresholds. It uses Beaver multiplicative triples to complete the multiplicative operations in the comparison protocol, and avoids the bit encryption by homomorphic encryption scheme. Hence, it improves the efficiency of the comparison protocol in the decision tree classification protocol. To generate the final classification result, the decision tree is transformed into multiple linear functions and combined with Paillier homomorphic encryption to complete the cipher-text operation and selection of classification results.

The rest of this paper is organized as follows: In Sect. 2, we recall the definition of decision tree classification and some cryptographic tools, including Beaver multiplicative triple and Paillier cryptosystem. In Sect. 3, we introduce the system model and its security model. Our main protocol and its security analysis are given in Sect. 4 and Sect. 5 respectively. We evaluate its performance in Sect. 6. Finally, we conclude this paper in Sect. 7.

2 Preliminaries

2.1 Decision Tree Classification

Assume that the input to the user side of the decision tree model is in the form of an n dimensional feature vector $X = (x_1, \ldots, x_n) \in Z^n$, the number of internal nodes of the decision tree is m, and the node threshold vector is $Y = (y_1, \ldots, y_m) \in Z^m$. We assume that the decision tree is a complete binary tree and each node has 0 or 2 children, as shown in Fig. 1. A complete binary tree with m non-leaf nodes has $m + 1$ leaf nodes and the leaf nodes are denoted by $V = (v_1, v_2, \ldots, v_{m+1})$, then the evaluation function of the decision tree is denoted as $T : Z^n \rightarrow \{v_1, v_2, \ldots, v_{m+1}\}$. The output of the decision tree is denoted as $v = T(X)$, v representing the classification result to which the input X belongs. The decision process of a decision tree starts at the root node, tests the conditions on the current node and descends to the left branch node or right branch node until it reaches some leaf node storing $T(X)$. Usually, each decision point corresponds to a Boolean function $f_k(X) = 1\{x_{i_k} > y_k\}$, where $k \in \{1, 2, \ldots, m\}$ and $i_k \in \{1, 2, \ldots, n\}$. If and only if x_{i_k} is greater than y_k, then $f_k(X)$ equals to 1. When $f_k(X) = 1$, then the next step goes to the left branch of the decision node; Otherwise, it goes to the right branch of the node.

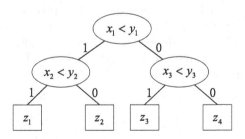

Fig. 1. An example of decision tree.

2.2 Beaver Multiplicative Triple

The Beaver triplet was proposed by Donald Beaver [16] and is mainly applied to multiplication operations in secure multi-party computation protocols. To simplify notation, we use "[·]" denote the secret sharing of "·".

Suppose the communicating parties A and B have the secret sharing of x and y. Party A has share $[x]_A$ and $[y]_A$, and Party B has share $[x]_B$ and $[y]_B$. They satisfy $[x]_A + [x]_B = x$ and $[y]_A + [y]_B = y$. Now, the secret share $[xy]$ can be calculated by Party A and Party B according to the following steps:

1. A trusted third party generates a multiplicative triple (u, g, z), which satisfies $z = u \cdot g$. The triple is kept secret from the two parties in the operation, but each of the two parties has the secret share $[z]$, $[u]$ and $[g]$.
2. Party A and Party B calculate the shares of $\alpha = x - u$ respectively, and made them public, i.e., $[\alpha]_A = [x]_A - [u]_A$ and $[\alpha]_B = [x]_B - [u]_B$.
3. Party A and Party B calculate the shares of $\beta = y - g$ respectively, and made them public, i.e., $[\beta]_A = [y]_A - [g]_A$ and $[\beta]_B = [y]_B - [y]_B$.
4. The two parties reconstruct α and β according to the secret shares.
5. Party A and Party B calculate the shares of η, that is

$$[\eta]_A = [z]_A + \alpha \cdot [g]_A + \beta \cdot [u]_A \text{ and } [\eta]_B = [z]_B + \alpha \cdot [g]_B + \beta \cdot [u]_B + \alpha \cdot \beta.$$

The correctness of above steps to calculate the shares $[xy]$ is showed as follows: Since the shares $[\alpha]$ and $[\beta]$ are public, each party can reconstruct α and β, and hence the above shares $[\eta]_A$ and $[\eta]_B$. So,

$$[\eta]_A + [\eta]_B = [z]_A + \alpha \cdot [g]_A + \beta \cdot [u]_A + [z]_B + \alpha \cdot [g]_B + \beta \cdot [u]_B + \alpha \cdot \beta.$$
$$= u \cdot g + (x - u) \cdot g + (y - g) \cdot u + (x - u) \cdot (y - g)$$
$$= x \cdot y.$$

2.3   Paillier Encryption Algorithm

The Paillier encryption algorithm [16] is a public key encryption scheme based on the composite residuosity problem, proposed by Paillier et al. in 1999. It supports additive homomorphic operations over the message space Z_N and is widely used in various security domains. In this paper, we use $\| \cdot \|$ to denote the encryption of ".", and use $\mathsf{Dec}(\cdot)$ to denote the decryption of C. Assume that m_1 and m_2 are two plaintext messages, and r_1 and r_2 are two random numbers in Z_N^*. (N, g) is the public key of the Paillier encryption algorithm, where N is the product of two large prime numbers p, q and $g = 1 + N$. The Paillier encryption algorithm is additively homomorphic, as it has the following two properties.

1. **Addition:** For any two messages $m_1, m_2 \in Z_N$, it has that

$$\|m_1\| \cdot \|m_2\| = \left(g^{m_1} r_1^N \bmod N^2\right) \cdot \left(g^{m_2} r_2^N \bmod N^2\right)$$
$$= g^{m_1 + m_2} (r_1 r_2)^N \bmod N^2$$
$$= \|m_1 + m_2\|.$$

2. **Scalar Multiplication:** For any integer $k \in Z_N$, it has that

$$\|m_1\|^k = \left(g^{m_1} r_1^N \bmod N^2\right)^k$$
$$= g^{k \cdot m_1} (r_1^k)^N \bmod N^2$$
$$= \|k \cdot m_1\|.$$

3   System Model and Security Model

3.1   System Model

The system involves three main entities: a user, a service provider, and a trusted authority. The specific interactions are shown in the following Fig. 2.

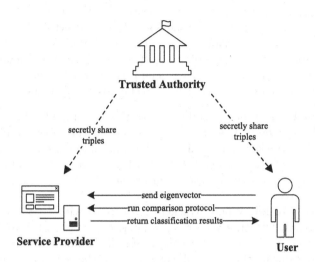

Fig. 2. System model.

- **User (U).** The user has a private input in the form of a feature vector, which contains information about a different attribute of the user, such as height, weight, heart rate etc. During the operation of the protocol, the user wants to use the decision tree model to obtain the classification results corresponding to their input. As the feature vector may contain sensitive personal information, the user will not send data in plain text during the operation of the protocol.
- **Service provider (P).** This entity is the party in the protocol that work the major computational overhead, usually a commercial company, hospital, etc. It holds a decision tree model that has been trained by a decision tree algorithm (e.g. CART, C4.5, etc.) and uses it to provide a classification service to the user. During the classification process, the model parameters should be avoided to be leaked to users during the protocol process while ensuring the decision tree classification function.
- **Trust Authority (TA).** This entity performs the operations related to Beaver tri-ples. At the beginning of the protocol, it first generates the corresponding number of triples and shares them secretly with the user and the classification service pro-vider for the subsequent multiplication of the triples.

3.2   Security Model

Unlike some research on privacy preservation in the training phase [18–20], we mainly focus on the existence of security issues in the process of decision tree.

We use U and P to denote the user and the service provider, respectively. De-note by A an attacker that can collude with either the user or the service provider to obtain the secret information of the other party. Let $X = (x_1, x_2, \ldots, x_m) \in Z^m$ denote the user's feature vector. $Y = (y_1, y_2, \ldots, y_m) \in Z^m$ and $Z = (z_1, z_2, \ldots, z_n)$ denote the node threshold vector and the classification result vector of the decision tree, respectively. Let $U(X) \leftrightarrow P(Y, Z)$ denote the running process of the protocol, and $(U(X) \leftrightarrow P(Y, Z)) = v$ denote the classification results obtained by the user. The privacy of the user and the privacy of the decision tree model can be defined respectively as follows.

- **Privacy of User.** When A colludes with the model holder P, A can obtain the model parameters Y and Z. When a user initiates a protocol $U(X) \leftrightarrow P(Y, Z)$, the attacker can obtain all the information from the user during the execution of the protocol. The attacker should not be able to obtain other information about the user's feature vectors $X = (x_1, x_2, \ldots, x_m)$ and classification results.
- **Privacy of Model.** When attacker A conspires with U, the attacker can choose a different feature vector $X_j = (x_{j,1}, x_{j,2}, \ldots, x_{j,m})$, initiate protocol $U(X_j) \leftrightarrow P(Y, Z)$. The attacker can obtain all the information from the service provider during the protocol execution and the corresponding classification result v_j. Except for the dimensionality of the node threshold vector, the dimensionality of the classification result vector and the classification result v_j, The attacker should not be able to obtain the node threshold vector and other information about the classification result vector.

4   Privacy-Preserving Decision Tree Classification

4.1   Secure Decision Node Comparison

This section focuses on the secure comparison of the values owned by the participating service provider and users of the protocol. It uses additive secret sharing and comparison scheme of [17], and allows the service provider to obtain the encrypted comparison results for each decision node.

Suppose a feature value of the user is represented in bits $c_l \cdots c_2 c_1$, and a node threshold y_p of the decision tree model is represented in bits $p_l \cdots p_2 p_1$. That is $x_c = \sum_{k=1}^{l} c_k 2^{k-1}$ and $y_p = \sum_{k=1}^{l} p_k 2^{k-1}$, where l is the bit length of x_c and y_p. Let t_i denote the result of comparing $\sum_{k=1}^{i} c_k 2^{k-1}$ with $\sum_{k=1}^{i} p_k 2^{k-1}$, i.e., the result of comparing the first i bits of x_c with the first i bits of y_p. When $\sum_{k=1}^{i} c_k 2^{k-1} > \sum_{k=1}^{i} p_k 2^{k-1}$, t_i equals to 1; Otherwise, it is 0. To obtain the result of the comparison between x_c and y_p, it is necessary to compare the iterative formula of the protocol to calculate:

$$t_i = (1 - (c_i - p_i)^2) t_{i-1} + c_i (1 - p_i) \tag{1}$$

where i denotes the number of bits and $1 \leq i \leq l$, $t_0 = 0$. When i equals to l, t_l is the final comparison result. Under the modulo 2 operations, the formula Eq. 1 is further simplified into the following equation:

$$t_i = (1 + c_i + p_i)t_{i-1} + c_i(1 + p_i) \tag{2}$$

As both the provider and the user are honest and curious, both parties can secretly save each other's bits during the iterative computation process of t_l, and thus recover the full threshold and user's feature values. To solve this problem, we use additive secret sharing combined with Beaver triples to solve the multiplication operation in Eq. 2, including $(1 + c_i + p_i)t_{i-1}$ and $c_i(1 + p_i)$.

In detail, for each $i \in 1, 2, \ldots, l$, the user side and the service provider divide each bit of secret sharing x_c with y_p into $[c_i]_0$, $[c_i]_1$, $[p_i]_0$ and $[p_i]_1$, where the subscript 0 indicates the secret share of the user and the subscript 1 indicates the secret share of the service provider. Specifically,

$$[c_i]_0 = c_i, \ [c_i]_1 = 0, \ [p_i]_0 = 0 \text{ and } [p_i]_1 = p_i$$

According to the above approach, the user and the provider can calculate the secret sharing of $1 + c_i + p_i$ and $1 + p_i$ respectively:

$$[1 + c_i + p_i]_0 = 1 + [c_i]_0 + [p_i]_0 \qquad [1 + p_i]_0 = 1 + [p_i]_0$$
$$[1 + c_i + p_i]_1 = [c_i]_1 + [p_i]_1 \qquad\qquad [1 + p_i]_1 = [p_i]_1$$

Initializing the secret sharing of t_0 as $[t_0]_0 = [t_0]_1 = 0$. Using the prepared Beaver triple for multiplication, the user and the provider calculate the secret sharing of t_i respectively. With the help of the Beaver triple, they compute the secret shares of $(1 + c_i + p_i)t_{i-1}$ and $c_i(1 + p_i)$ respectively. Then, the additive secret sharing of t_i is calculated for both parties as:

$$[t_i]_0 = [(1 + c_i + p_i)t_{i-1}]_0 + [c_i(1 + p_i)]_0$$
$$[t_i]_1 = [(1 + c_i + p_i)t_{i-1}]_1 + [c_i(1 + p_i)]_1$$

The process is iterated until i equals to l. Finally, the user encrypts $[t_l]_0$ using the Paillier public key and sends $\|[t_l]_0\|$ to the provider. Then, the provider calculates $\|t_l\|$ based on its own secret sharing:

- If $[t_l]_1 = 0$, then $\|t_l\| = \|[t_l]_0\|$;
- If $[t_l]_1 = 1$, then $\|t_l\| = \|1 - [t_l]_0\|$.

For each threshold y_k in the node threshold vector of the decision tree model $Y = (y_1, y_2, \ldots, y_m)$ and the corresponding feature value x_{i_k} in the feature vector $X = (x_1, y_2, \ldots, x_n)$, the user runs the protocol and the service provider can then calculate the ciphertexts of the comparison results for any decision node $\|B\| = \{\|b_1\|, \|b_2\|, \ldots, \|b_m\|\}$, where $\|b_j\|$ is the ciphertext of the comparison results for the j-th decision node. More details are shown in Protocol 1.

Protocol 1: Secure Decision Node Comparison

Input (U): x_c, pk

Input (P): y_p, pk

Output (P): $\|b\|$

1. U & P:
   - (1) x_c and y_p are represented in bits, i.e., $x_c = c_l \cdots c_1$, $y_p = p_l \cdots p_1$.
   - (2) Define the secret sharing of each bit:
     $$[c_i]_0 = c_i, [p_i]_0 = 0, [c_i]_1 = 0, [p_i]_1 = p_i, i \in \{1, 2, \ldots, l\}$$
   - (3) Define secret sharing according to step (2):
     $$[1 + c_i + p_i]_0 = 1 + [c_i]_0 + [p_i]_0, [1 + p_i]_0 = 1 + [p_i]_0$$
     $$[1 + c_i + p_i]_1 = [c_i]_1 + [p_i]_1, \qquad [1 + p_i]_1 = [p_i]_1$$

2. U & P:
   - (1) Set $[t_0]_0 = [t_0]_1 = 0$, then calculate the value of $1 + c_i + p_i$ and $1 + p_i$ using Beaver triple.
   - (2) Calculate the secret shares of t_i:
     $$[t_i]_0 = [(1 + c_i + p_i)t_{i-1}]_0 + [c_i(1 + p_i)]_0$$
     $$[t_i]_1 = [(1 + c_i + p_i)t_{i-1}]_1 + [c_i(1 + p_i)]_1$$

z (3) Repeat steps (1)(2) until $i = l$.

3. U:

   Encrypt $[t_l]_0$ using pk, then send the ciphertext $\|[t_l]_0\|$ to P.

4. P:

   Calculate the ciphertext $\|t_l\|$ according to $[t_l]_1$:
   $$\|t_l\| = \begin{cases} \|[t_l]_0\| & \text{if } [t_l]_1 = 0 \\ \|1 - [t_l]_0\| = \|1\| \cdot \|[t_l]_0\|^{N-1} & \text{if } [t_l]_1 = 1 \end{cases}$$
   Denote $\|t_l\|$ as the ciphertext of decision node comparison result $\|b\|$.

4.2 Secure Path Evaluation

After running the comparison protocol of the previous section for each node of the decision tree, the classification service provider obtains the encrypted comparison result $\|b_j\|$ for each decision node $Node_j$ and the set of encrypted comparison results are denoted as $\|B\| = \{\|b_1\|, \ldots, \|b_j\|, \ldots, \|b_m\|\}$. In this section, the classification service provider will perform path evaluation using $\|B\|$ to obtain the path cost of all leaf nodes.

In detail, for each decision node $Node_j$ associated with its two branches: the left branch is assigned edge cost $e_{j,left} = b_j$ and the right branch is assigned edge cost $e_{j,right} = 1 - b_j$. The path cost P_k for each leaf node is defined as the sum of all edge costs on the path to that leaf node, and the classification value v_k contained classification result of the decision tree if and only if $P_k = 0$.

Combined with the path cost mechanism in [13], the secure path evaluation of this scheme is shown in Protocol 2. First, the classification service provider sets the left edge cost of each decision node to be $\|e_{j,left}\| = \|b_j\|$. For the right edge cost, it is $\|e_{j,right}\| = \|1\| \cdot \|b_j\|^{N-1}$ using the homomorphic property of Paillier cryptosystem. Finally, the classification service provider multiplies the ciphertext of the edge cost on each leaf node path to obtain the ciphertexts $\|P\| = \{\|P_1\|, \|P_2\|, \ldots, \|P_{m+1}\|\}$ of each leaf node path cost.

Protocol 2: Secure Path Evaluation

Input (P): $\|b_j\|$, pk
Output (P): $\|P_k\|$
1. P:
  For each decision node $Node_j$, set:
$\|e_{j,left}\| = \|b_j\|$ and $\|e_{j,right}\| = \|1 - b_j\| = \|1\| \cdot \|b_j\|^{N-1}$.
2. P:
  Set the path cost of $Leaf_k$: $\|P_k\|$ is the concatenated product of each edge cost $\|e\|$
on that path.

4.3 Secure Classification Result Generation

After the secure path evaluation phase, the service provider obtains the ciphertext of the path cost of each leaf node. In this phase, the provider outputs the
corresponding classification results based on the ciphertext of the path cost of
the leaf nodes and sends them to the user. The user decrypts the ciphertexts to
obtain the final classification results.

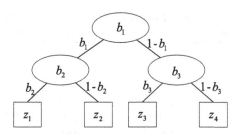

Fig. 3. System model.

Suppose the current decision tree has $m + 1$ leaf nodes, and denote by
$Leaves = \{leaf_1, leaf_2, \ldots, leaf_{m+1}\}$ the set of leaf nodes. Each leaf node has
the corresponding classification result $V = \{v_1, v_2, \ldots, v_{m+1}\}$ and its corresponding path cost $P = \{P_1, P_2, \ldots, P_{m+1}\}$. The protocol first transforms the decision
tree model into $m+1$ linear functions according to equation $h_k = P_k + v_k$, where
$k \in \{1, 2, \ldots, m + 1\}$. When the path cost $P_k = 0$, the value of h_k is the final
classification result, and the user can use this property to recover the correct
classification result v_k. As shown in Fig. 3, the linear function of each leaf node
of the decision tree is defined as follows:

$$P_1 = b_1 + b_2 \qquad\qquad h_1 = P_1 + v_1$$
$$P_2 = b_1 + (1 - b_2) \qquad\qquad h_2 = P_2 + v_2$$
$$P_3 = 1 - b_1 + b_3 \qquad\qquad h_3 = P_3 + v_3$$
$$P_4 = 1 - b_1 + (1 - b_3) \qquad\qquad h_4 = P_4 + v_4$$

In detail, the protocol is shown in Protocol 3 below. First, for each $k \in \{1, 2, \ldots, m+1\}$, it selects a random number $r_k \in Z_P^*$ and multiples it with the path cost P to obtain $P_k^* = \|P_k\|^{r_k}$ by the Paillier encryption homomorphic property. This step is a randomized masking of the path cost and classification values of the leaf nodes. It ensures that the user will only recover the right classification value after receiving them and hence achieves the purpose of hiding the decision tree structure from the user side.

Protocol 3: Secure Classification Result Generation

Input (P): $\|P\| = \{\|P_1\|, \|P_2\|, \ldots, \|P_{m+1}\|\}$, pk
Output (U): v
1. P:
For each leaf node $leaf_k$, where $k \in \{1, 2, \ldots, m+1\}$, do:
    (1) Randomly select $r_k \in Z_P^*$.
    (2) Calculate $P_k^* = \|r_k \cdot P_k\| = \|P_k\|^{r_k}$.
    (3) Encrypt v_k, denoted as $\|v_k\|$.
    (4) Calculate $h_k^* = P_k^* \cdot \|v_k\| = \|r_k \cdot P_k + v_k\|$.
Send $H^* = \{h_1^*, h_2^*, \ldots, h_{m+1}^*\}$ and $\{P_1^*, P_2^*, \ldots, P_{m+1}^*\}$ to U.
2. U:
    (1) For every $k \in \{1, 2, \ldots, m+1\}$, decrypt the P_k^* corresponding to each leaf node.
    (2) If $\mathsf{Dec}(P_k^*) = 0$, decrypt the corresponding h_k^* to be the classification result v.

The service provider then sends to the user these randomized linear functions $H^* = \{h_1^*, h_2^*, \ldots, h_{m+1}^*\}$ and P_k^* corresponding to each h_k^*, where $h_k^* = \|r_k \cdot P_k^* + v_k\|$ and $k \in \{1, 2, \ldots, m+1\}$. The user decrypts these P_k^* using the Paillier private key sk. If $P_k^* = 0$, then the plaintext corresponding h_k^* to is just the final classification result. If $P_k^* \neq 0$, the user only gets the random value $r_k \cdot P_k^* + v_k$, which is the sum of v_k plus the multiplication of the random number r_k with P_k^*.

5 Security Analysis

According to the system model, the privacy preserving decision tree classification protocol should be guaranteed to be secure to the semi-honest service provider and user. In other words, the user will not disclose any information about the feature vectors and classification results during the protocols, and the service provider will not disclose any information about the parameters of the decision tree.

1. **Security for users.** The user owns the full share of the feature vector before the beginning of the protocol. During the process of step 1 in Protocol 1, the server provider owns the secret share of the bits of feature vector, but it cannot recover their value. During the secure multiplication operation via

Beaver triple, the user and the provider operate locally through their respective secret shares. By the property of the Beaver triple, it guarantees that the user and provider compute their own secret shares, i.e. the intermediate and final results of the comparison are completely hidden to each other. Thus, the user's feature data is confidential, during the calculation of the comparison results. In step 3 of the Protocol 1, the user encrypts the shares of the node comparison results via Paillier encryption scheme. As the Paillier cryptosystem is semantically secure, the eavesdropper would still not be able to obtain any information about the comparison results, even he captures the ciphertexts. Therefore, our protocol is secure for the user.

2. **Security for service provider.** The security of the provider is mainly related to Protocol 1 and Protocol 3. In Protocol 1, similar to the security analysis of user data, the secret shares of the intermediate comparison results are kept secret from each other according to the property of the Beaver triple. In step 4 of Protocol 1, as the service provider processes the share of comparison result of each decision node locally, the user does not obtain any information about the comparison results and cannot calculate the threshold value from the comparison results. In step 1 of Protocol 3, the path cost of each leaf node is randomized. The user only gets the classification result corresponding to the path cost with 0 from decryption. Thought the user can decrypt the other path costs and classification results, these values are masked by multi-plying randomness and thus the user cannot get any information about the original path costs and classification results from the decryption results. Thus, the model's thresholds and other classification data are kept confidential from the user or other external attackers.

6   Performance Evaluation

6.1   Complex Analysis

The main difference between this scheme and [10,12] is the way of handling the comparison of decision node threshold and feature value. In [10], the authors use the traditional bit-by-bit encryption, which has higher computational complexity but relatively less communication rounds. Users only need to encrypt their respective feature data bit-by-bit via a homomorphic encryption scheme, and then send them to the service provider. The service provider runs the homomorphic encryption according to the property of DGK comparison protocol. In [12], the authors use Paillier cryptosystem to encrypt data and determines the comparison results by judging between positive and negative difference values.

The comparison of the complexity and communication rounds with ours and [10,12] is shown in the following Table 1. In the table, n is the dimension of the user feature vector, m is the number of decision tree nodes of the provider, d is the depth of the decision tree, and t is the bit length of a feature value and a threshold value. Also, it is defined that the user sends the data and the provider processes the data and returns it to the user for one communication round. According to Table 1, our protocol has low computational complexity compared with the other two schemes. While it requires too many communication rounds, the comparison algorithm of our protocol is under the modulo 2 operations and the communication complexity should not be large.

Table 1. Computational complexity.

Protocols	Complexity		Communication rounds
	User	Provider	
[10]	$O((n+m)t)$	$O((n+m)t)$	2
[12]	$O(n+m)$	$O(m)$	2
Ours	$O(m)$	$O(m)$	t

6.2 Efficiency Analysis

This protocol is evaluated on a laptop with Windows 10 operating system, 2.40GHz Intel i5-10200H processor and 16GB RAM. We used BigInteger in Java to implement our decision tree evaluation protocol, and select three datasets from the UCI database (breast cancer, heart disease and spambase) to test the computation time and communication overhead of this protocol. The evaluation results of our scheme with [10] and [12] are shown in Table 2, where n represents the number of user feature vector dimensions, d denotes the depth of the decision tree, and m denotes the number of decision nodes.

When the decision tree structure is simpler, our scheme has only a small difference in time overhead from [10] and [12]. When the decision tree is more complex, our protocol is more efficient than the other two protocols. The protocol in [10] uses Lifed ElGamal encryption scheme to encrypt data bit by bit, so the user re-quires a large amount of computation.

Table 2. Performance comparison.

Dataset	n	d	m	Protocols	Total time (s)	Bandwidth (KB)
Breast-cancer	9	8	12	[10]	1.491	64.384
				[12]	1.125	6.016
				Ours	0.642	4.768
Heart-disease	13	3	5	[10]	0.855	22.271
				[12]	0.545	3.840
				Ours	0.322	3.320
Spam-base	57	17	58	[10]	17.202	632.922
				[12]	14.911	34.560
				Ours	4.638	28.528

The protocol in [12] uses Paillier encryption scheme to encrypt data and uses the homomorphic property of Paillier encryption to compare the threshold and feature value. It reduces the computational overhead of per-bit comparison in [10], but the user and the provider still need to spend some time overhead and communication overhead to compute the ciphertext homomorphic operation and to transmit ciphertexts.

7   Conclusion

In this paper, a secure and efficient decision tree classification protocol based on an improved per-bit comparison protocol of [17]. In the decision node comparison stage, the original idea of homomorphic multiplication under ciphertext is replaced with Beaver multiplicative triples. In the process of decision tree classification, the Paillier encryption scheme is used to guarantee the privacy of user in-put, classification results and model thresholds. Through experimental analysis and comparison on real datasets, our protocol achieves low computational and communication overhead between user and service provider. We will subsequently optimize the scheme to continue reducing the computational overhead on the user side and extend the model to other machine learning algorithms such as random forests and neural networks.

Acknowledgement. This research is supported by the Basic Research Program of Qinghai Province 2020-ZJ-701.

References

1. Cock, M.D., Dowsley, R., Horst, C.: Efficient and private scoring of decision trees, support vector machines and logistic regression models based on pre-computation. IEEE Trans. Dependable Secure Comput. **16**(2), 217–230 (2019)
2. Agrawal, R., Srikant, R.: Privacy-preserving data mining. In: Proceedings of the 2000 ACM SIGMOD International Conference on Management of Data, pp. 439–450. ACM (2000)
3. Xiong, A., Nguyen, M., So A., Chen, T.: Privacy preserving inference with convolutional neural network ensemble. In: 2020 IEEE 39th International Performance Computing and Communications Conference (IPCCC), pp. 1–6. IEEE, New York (2020)
4. Li, X., Zhu, Y., Wang, J.: On the soundness and security of privacy-preserving SVM for outsourcing data classification. IEEE Trans. Dependable Secure Comput. **15**(5), 906–912 (2018)
5. Qin, B., Li, Y., Yu, P.: Efficient privacy-preserving decision trees evaluation protocol with cloud-assisted computing. J. Xi'an Univ. Posts Telecommun. **27**(1), 1–8 (2022)
6. Hou, J., Li, Q., Meng, S., Ni, Z., Chen, Y., Liu, Y.: DPRF: a differential privacy protection random forest. IEEE Access **7**, 130707–130720 (2019)
7. Bost, R., Popa, R.A., Tu, S., et al.: Machine learning classification over encrypted data. In: Network and Distributed System Security Symposium, pp. 1–34. The Internet Society, San Diego (2015)

8. Wu, D.J., Feng, T., Naehrig, M., et al.: Privately evaluating decision trees and random forests. Proc. Priv. Enh. Technol. **2016**(4), 335–355 (2016)

9. Hsu, J.C., Tso, R., Chen, Y.C., Wu, M.E.: Oblivious transfer protocols based on commutative encryption. In: 2018 9th IFIP International Conference on New Technologies, pp. 1–5. IEEE, Paris (2018)

10. Tai, R.K.H., Ma, J.P.K., Zhao, Y., Chow, S.S.M.: Privacy-preserving decision trees evaluation via linear functions. In: Foley, S.N., Gollmann, D., Snekkenes, E. (eds.) ESORICS 2017. LNCS, vol. 10493, pp. 494–512. Springer, Cham (2017). https://doi.org/10.1007/978-3-319-66399-9_27

11. Zheng, Y., Duan, H., Wang, C.: Towards secure and efficient outsourcing of machine learning classification. In: Sako, K., Schneider, S., Ryan, P.Y.A. (eds.) ESORICS 2019. LNCS, vol. 11735, pp. 22–40. Springer, Cham (2019). https://doi.org/10.1007/978-3-030-29959-0_2

12. Xue, L., Liu, D.X., Huang, C., et al.: Secure and privacy-preserving decision tree classification with lower complexity. J. Commun. Inf. Netw. **5**(1), 16–25 (2020)

13. Cao, L.X., Li, Y.T., Wu, R., Guo, X., et al.: Multi key privacy protection decision tree evaluation scheme. J. Tsinghua Univ. **62**, 862–870 (2021). https://doi.org/10.16511/j.cnki.qhdxxb.2021.21.044

14. Damgard, I., Geisler, M., Krøigaard, M.: A correction to efficient and secure comparison for on-line auctions. Int. J. Adv. Comput. Technol. **1**, 323–324 (2018)

15. Garay, J., Schoenmakers, B., Villegas, J.: Practical and secure solutions for integer comparison. In: Okamoto, T., Wang, X. (eds.) PKC 2007. LNCS, vol. 4450, pp. 330–342. Springer, Heidelberg (2007). https://doi.org/10.1007/978-3-540-71677-8_22

16. Beaver, D.: Efficient multiparty protocols using circuit randomization. In: Feigenbaum, J. (ed.) CRYPTO 1991. LNCS, vol. 576, pp. 420–432. Springer, Heidelberg (1992). https://doi.org/10.1007/3-540-46766-1_34

17. Paillier, P.: Public-key cryptosystems based on composite degree Residuosity classes. In: Stern, J. (ed.) Advances in Cryptology — EUROCRYPT 1999. Lecture Notes in Computer Science, vol. 1592, pp. 223–238. Springer, Heidelberg (1999)

18. Sheela, M.A., Vijayalakshmi, K.: A novel privacy preserving decision tree induction. In: Information & Communication Technologies (ICT), pp. 1075–1079. IEEE, Thuckalay (2013)

19. Sumalatha, L., Sankar, P.U.: Fuzzy random decision tree (FRDT) framework for privacy preserving data mining. In: 2016 SAI Computing Conference (SAI), pp. 195–202. IEEE, London (2016)

20. Dowlin, N., Gilad-Bachrach, R., Laine, K., et al.: CryptoNets: applying neural networks to encrypted data with high throughput and accuracy. In: Proceedings of The 33rd International Conference on Machine Learning, pp. 201–210. PLMR (2016)

A Bi-objective Source Hiding Method for Network Propagation

Tianyang Gao[1], Danni Qu[1], Liqin Hu[1(✉)], and Zhen Wang[1,2]

[1] School of Cyberspace, Hangzhou Dianzi University, Hangzhou 310018, China
{gaotianyang,qudanni,huliqin,wangzhen}@hdu.edu.cn
[2] Zhuoyue Honors College, Hangzhou Dianzi University, Hangzhou 310038, China

Abstract. In many scenarios, sources want to publish information anonymously and allow it to be distributed on a large scale in a short period of time. To this end, we proposed a bi-objective source hiding method to locate the sources with both hiding and propagation capability in the network. Firstly, three heuristic methods are proposed to evaluate the hiding performance of nodes. Secondly, based on the characteristics of network propagation, breadth first search is applied to measure the propagation capability of nodes. Then, a normalization method is proposed to comprehensively evaluate the hiding ability and propagation ability of nodes, and the node with the strongest comprehensive ability is used as the propagation source. Finally, experiments are simulated based on five different source detection methods on multiple network structures, and the experimental results demonstrate the effectiveness of our method.

Keywords: Complex network · Propagation · Source hiding

1 Introduction

In the face of various network risks, such as public opinion, computer viruses and biological viruses, pinpointing the source of propagation in the network is an effective means to control the risks in a timely manner [1, 2]. Therefore, the identification of propagation sources in complex networks has been a hot topic of interest for researchers. However, there are still risks in locating sources using current source detection methods. They usually target infinite networks and randomly select sources to be simulated in simulation experiments. This makes it possible to successfully evade detection.

Propagation sources have an incentive to evade source detection in multiple scenarios to maintain their privacy. For example, anonymous platforms want to guarantee the anonymity of message senders to enable their freedom of expression [3, 4], and publishers of messages in social networks want to deliver messages on a large scale without revealing the personal information of the publishers [5–7]. Therefore, work on their possible hiding strategies from a source hiding perspective can not only be useful in these scenarios to meet the demand, but also be used to help network administrators analyze the strategies and behavior patterns of evaders to facilitate timely and effective

Y. Chenggang et al. (Eds.): MobiMedia 2022, LNICST 451, pp. 105–125, 2022.
https://doi.org/10.1007/978-3-031-23902-1_9

risk containment. In addition, the ability of nodes to efficiently disseminate information is an important factor in measuring their performance, which illustrates the impact of nodes on the dynamic dissemination process. Revealing this property of nodes will help to better optimize the limited resources for information dissemination [8, 9], which can be used, for example, to describe and predict the dynamic characteristics of financial markets [10] or to effectively market products at low cost [11].

Based on this, we propose a bi-objective source hiding method that satisfies the dual requirements of hiding and propagation capability. The main contributions of this paper are summarized as follows:

- Based on the analysis and replication of existing source detection work, we tested the hiddenness of sources at different locations and found that the closer the location is to the network boundary, the stronger the hiding.
- Heuristic methods are proposed to measure source hiding and propagation capabilities. In scenarios where there is a need for anonymity, locating nodes with high hiding in the network to use them as sources is more operable than methods such as setting propagation protocols [12, 13] and changing the network structure [14].
- A bi-objective strategy is proposed to locate sources in the network with both hiding and propagation, and the node with both high hiding and high propagation capability is selected as the source through a comprehensive evaluation of the nodes.
- Evaluation metrics are proposed to measure the effectiveness of detection from multiple perspectives. The evaluation metrics proposed in this paper are not only generalized to measure the detection effectiveness of arbitrary source detection methods, but also applicable to evaluate the propagation capability and hiding performance of arbitrary nodes.

2 Source Hiding Analysis

In real life, networks are bounded. A paper [17] states that the boundaries of the network can affect the effectiveness of source detection methods. This is indeed the case, a simple example of which is shown in Fig. 1. When node 1 is the source and both nodes 2 and 3 are infected, the infected network is shifted towards the subtree with node 4 as the root. If the tracer uses the central method of rumor [1, 2] to locate the propagation source in the network snapshot shown in the figure, node 4 will be detected as the propagation source, while the real source (node 1) is not detected. It can be concluded that the boundary of the network will have a great impact on the detection of the source.

Further, the location of sources in the finite network will affect the detection effectiveness of the source detection method. As shown in Fig. 2, node A is a source in the network of Fig. 2(A) and node B is a source in the network of Fig. 2(B). Obviously, due to the different positions of nodes A and B in the network, their own hiding is also different. If we use the rumor center method [18, 19] to locate the source in snapshot 3, we can accurately locate the source A in Fig. 2(A), but cannot accurately locate the source B in Fig. 2(B). Therefore, the difficulty of locating the source at different locations based on the same source detection method is different.

To verify the above conclusions, we used several classical source detection methods including the rumor centrality (RC) [2] method, the Jordan centrality (JC) [16] method,

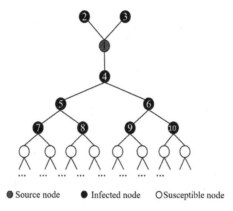

Fig. 1. Example network used to illustrate the impact of network boundaries.

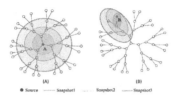

Fig. 2. Example network to illustrate the effect of different location sources on results.

the reverse infection (RI) [20] algorithm, the dynamic age (DA) [21] method and a maximum a posteriori (MAP) estimator [22] for sources at different locations to test the hiding of sources at different locations. First, the underlying network is set as a scale-free network with the number of nodes of 500. Then, the positions of the nodes are described based on the closeness centrality [23] of the nodes. Finally, we use the above method to detect the sources at different locations and calculate the distance between the real source and the detected estimated source, denoted by E. The final test results are shown in Fig. 3.

The horizontal axis of the figure indicates the closeness centrality of the source, and the vertical axis indicates the mean value of the error distance obtained by detecting it M times ($M \geq 500$). The blue scatter points are the actual detection result data points, and the red straight line is the fitted line. It is clear from the figure that the error distance increases with increasing source closeness centrality for any source detection method. This indicates that the effectiveness of the source detection method is directly related to the location of the propagating source, and that sources located at the network boundary have better hiding.

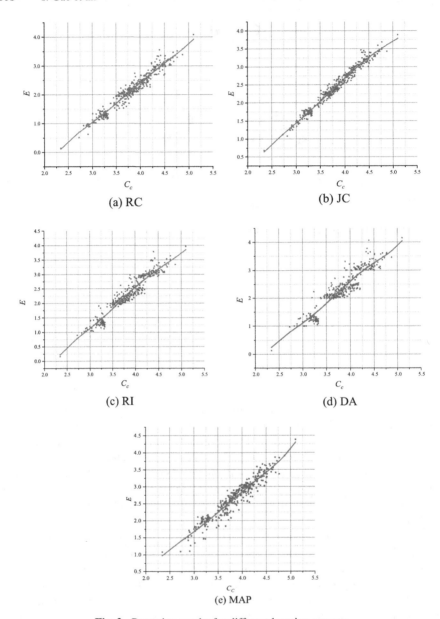

Fig. 3. Detection results for different location sources.

3 Metric and Method

We assume that the propagation process starts at a single source and use an SI model based on the Gillespie algorithm [15] to simulate the propagation process. Table 1 shows some important symbols.

Table 1. Main mathematical symbols and their meanings.

Symbol	Meaning
$G = G(V, E)$	The network structure, V is the set of nodes and E is the set of edges
$G_I = G_I(V_I, E_I)$	An infected subgraph of G
v^*	The real infection source
$\hat{v}$	The detected source
$N(v_i)$	The set of neighbor nodes of node v_i
$N_I(v_i)$	The set of neighbor nodes of node v_i that are in the infected state
$d_G(v_i, v_j)$	The shortest distance between node v_i and v_j
$g_G^{v_i}$	The number of paths through node v_i in graph G

3.1 Metric for Source Hiding

Hiding of Sources Based on Centrality Metric. Through the analysis in Sect. 2, we know that nodes located at the boundary of the network have better hiding. The closeness centrality of a node can indicate the position of the node in the network structure. In a network with N nodes, the closeness centrality of node v_i can be calculated using the following equation.

$$C_C(v_i, G) = \frac{\sum_{v_j \in V} d_G(v_i, v_j)}{N - 1} \tag{1}$$

In addition to this, the betweenness centrality [24] of a node can indicate the intermediary performance of the node in the network. By calculating it can find the endpoint of the shortest path in the network and consider this node more hided compared to other nodes. The formula for the betweenness centrality is as follows.

$$C_B(v_i, G) = \frac{g_G^{v_i}}{\sum_{v_j \in V} g_G^{v_j}} \tag{2}$$

Hiding of Sources Based on Improved K-Shell Algorithm. The K-Shell algorithm is often applied to evaluate the importance of nodes [25]. However, this method is not effective for some networks. As shown in Fig. 4, if the traditional K-Shell algorithm is used to mark the location attributes of nodes in the network, all nodes in Fig. 4(a) will be marked with the same location, and the nodes in Fig. 4(b) are divided into two levels. Obviously, this does not fully confirm the location of the structure where each node is located. In fact, the position of these nodes in the network structure is different. Therefore, we propose an improved K-Shell method for marking the location properties of nodes more efficiently. The specific steps are:

1. Find the nodes in the network with degree 1, mark their position attribute k_{ns} as 1, and then delete these nodes and their connected edges.

2. Step 1 is repeated until the degree of each node in the network is greater than 1. In each round, the k_{ns} values of the marked nodes are added by 1, and then these marked nodes and their connected edges are deleted.
3. Find the node with degree 2 in the network, continue to mark its k_{ns} as the current k_{ns} plus 1, and then delete the marked nodes and their connected edges.
4. Repeat until all nodes in the network are tagged with the corresponding location attributes.

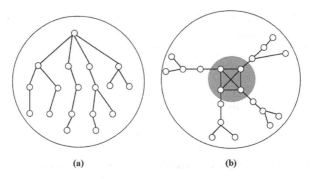

Fig. 4. Example network for which traditional K-Shell methods fail.

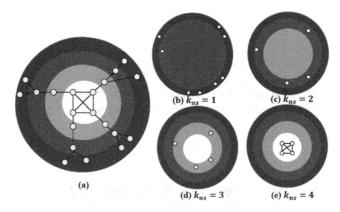

Fig. 5. Results of the improved K-Shell algorithm on the example network.

The node partitioning of our improved K-Shell algorithm for the network shown in Fig. 4(b) is illustrated in Fig. 5. This allows a more efficient description of where the nodes are located in the network structure and thus locates the nodes located at the network boundaries.

Hiding of Sources Based on Network Diameter. The maximum value of the shortest distance between any two nodes in the network is the diameter of the network [26]. As shown in Fig. 6, the shortest path between node 1 and node 7 constitutes diameter 1, and the shortest path from node 8 to node 13 constitutes diameters 2 and 3. This shortest path spans the entire network, and its length indicates the "depth" of the network. Therefore, the node located at the center of the network diameter must be located at the center of the network structure will be called the central node. Accordingly, the nodes located at the diameter boundary must be located at the boundary of the network. It is worth mentioning that there may be multiple diameters in a network, and each diameter will have corresponding central and boundary nodes. The set of central nodes on all diameters is the set of central nodes of the network.

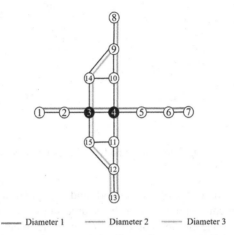

Fig. 6. Example network for illustrating network diameter.

Based on this, we can mark the location attribute l_d of the nodes in the network by the diameter. The larger the value of l_d, the better the node hiding. First, we find all the network diameters and thus the central set of nodes, marking the l_d values of the nodes in the set as 0. Then, the location attributes l_d of other nodes in the network are marked layer by layer according to the central node set. Specifically, the l_d of each non-central node takes the value of its shortest distance from all nodes in the central node set. The l_d values of the nodes of the example network in Fig. 6 are shown in Fig. 7.

3.2 Metric for Source Dissemination Capability

The propagation capability of a source indicates whether it can efficiently disseminate information to other nodes in the network. Therefore, we quantify the propagation capability of a source as the reachable propagation size in a specific time, and apply the breadth-first idea to the metric of node propagation capability. Combining the infection time and infection scale, the propagation capacity of node v_i in the network is denoted as $S(v_i)$, which is defined as follows.

$$S(v_i) = \int_1^{dia} |V_I(v_i, t)| d_t \tag{3}$$

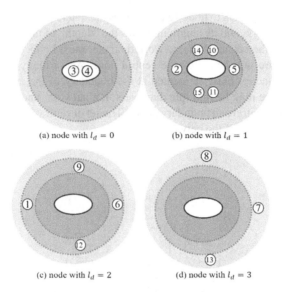

(a) node with $l_d = 0$

(b) node with $l_d = 1$

(c) node with $l_d = 2$

(d) node with $l_d = 3$

Fig. 7. The l_d values of the nodes in the example network.

where *dia* denotes the diameter of the network and $|V_I(v_i, t)|$ denotes the number of infected nodes at moment t with node v_i as the source and propagation probability of 1. Specially, since the propagation probability is set to 1, the infection process is similar to a breadth-first traversal process with v_i as the root. Specifically, $|V_I(v_i, t)|$ can be expressed as

$$\begin{cases} N_t(v_i) = N(N_{t-1}(v_i)) \\ |V_I(v_i, t)| = 1 + \sum_t |N_t(v_i)| \end{cases} \tag{4}$$

where $N_t(v_i)$ denotes the number of infected nodes added at moment t, i.e., the number of neighboring nodes of the infected nodes added at moment $t - 1$, using node v_i as the source.

3.3 Bi-objective Source Hiding Method

We synthesize the above parameters based on the normalization idea to locate the nodes with both hiding and propagation ability. First, the above evaluation metrics are divided into two categories of node hiding evaluation metrics ($C_C(v_i)$, $C_B(v_i)$, $k_{ns}(v_i)$, $l_d(v_i)$) and node propagation ability evaluation metrics ($S(v_i)$), which are normalized separately. The combined calculation of hiding metrics is shown in Eq. (5) and Eq. (6).

In Eq. (5), $C_{C_{min}}$ and $C_{C_{max}}$ denote the minimum and maximum values of closeness centrality in the network, respectively, and $\widetilde{C_C}$ denotes the normalized result of closeness centrality values. Other hiding metrics have the same meaning as closeness centrality.

$$\begin{cases} \widetilde{C_C(v_i)} = \frac{1}{4} \times \frac{C_C(v_i)-C_{C_{min}}}{C_{C_{max}}-C_{C_{min}}} \\ \widetilde{C_B(v_i)} = \frac{1}{4} \times \frac{C_B(v_i)-C_{B_{min}}}{C_{B_{max}}-C_{B_{min}}} \\ \widetilde{k_{ns}(v_i)} = \frac{1}{4} \times \frac{k_{ns}(v_i)-k_{ns_{min}}}{k_{ns_{max}}-k_{ns_{min}}} \\ \widetilde{l_d(v_i)} = \frac{1}{4} \times \frac{l_d(v_i)-l_{dmin}}{l_{dmax}-l_{dmin}} \end{cases} \tag{5}$$

$$\widetilde{E(v_i)} = \widetilde{C_C(v_i)} + \widetilde{l_d(v_i)} - \widetilde{k_{ns}(v_i)} - \widetilde{C_B(v_i)} \tag{6}$$

In Eq. (6), all the node hiding metrics are combined to obtain $\widetilde{E(v_i)}$. The higher its value is, the better the node is hidden. The normalization of the node dissemination capability metrics is as follows.

$$\widetilde{S(v_i)} = \frac{S(v_i) - S_{min}(v_i)}{S_{max}(v_i) - S_{min}(v_i)} \tag{7}$$

where $S_{min}(v_i)$ and $S_{max}(v_i)$ denote the minimum and maximum quantitative values of node propagation capacity, respectively. $\widetilde{S(v_i)}$ is the normalization of the propagation capacity, and the higher its value the stronger the propagation capacity of the node.

Finally, we combine the parameters $\widetilde{E(v_i)}$ and $\widetilde{S(v_i)}$ to locate the nodes in the network. Since the normalized parameters $\widetilde{E(v_i)}$ and $\widetilde{S(v_i)}$ both take values in the range of 0 to 1, and the larger their values, the stronger the corresponding characteristics. Therefore, we construct a two-dimensional plane based on these two parameters to describe each node in the network. In this plane, the limit optimal value (1, 1) is taken as the center. The five points with the closest distance to the center are the target points with both hiding and propagation ability. Where the calculation of the distance $D(v_i)$ can be expressed as

$$D(v_i) = \sqrt{\left(1 - \widetilde{E(v_i)}\right)^2 + \left(1 - \widetilde{S(v_i)}\right)^2} \tag{8}$$

4 Experiment

4.1 Dataset

To verify the effectiveness of our proposed method, we conducted simulation experiments on two types of generative networks (small-world network and scale-free network) and two types of real networks (E-mail network and Facebook network), respectively.

1. Small-world network: The Watts-Strogatz model was used in the experiments to reconnect each edge on the network with a probability of 0.03, resulting in a small-world phenomenon.
2. Scale-free network: A scale-free network is generated in the experiments based on the Barabasi-Albert model, and its scale-free property is ensured by continuously adding new nodes and preferentially connecting height nodes.

3. E-mail network: This network contains the communication data of about 500,000 E-mails. The addresses of the E-mails are derived as nodes in the network, and an undirected edge will be established between the sender and the receiver of the E-mails [27].
4. Facebook network: contains information about users who registered to the Facebook social platform. The nodes in the network represent users of the Facebook platform, and the edges represent the interactions between users [28].

The specific network parameters used in the experiments are shown in Table 2.

Table 2. Network parameters.

Network	Number of nodes	Number of sides	Average degree	Average clustering coefficient	Network diameter
Small-world	500	5,000	20	0.614	10
Scale-free	500	1,994	7.976	0.246	7
E-mail	1,005	25,571	25.444	0.473	7
Facebook	4,039	88,234	18.816	0.635	7

4.2 Evaluation Metrics

In this paper, the following parameters are applied to evaluate the detection results of source detection methods.

1. $e(v^*, k)$: the distance between the detected true propagation source v^* and the estimated source detected by the source detection method when the infection size is k. It is called the error distance, abbreviated as e. It is usually expressed in terms of hop count, which is obtained by calculating the number of edges passed by the shortest path between two points.
2. $E(v^*, k)$: the mean value of the distance between the real source v^* and the estimated source located by the source detection method, abbreviated as E, when the infection size is k, and the infection and detection process is executed M times with node v^* as the real source. The calculation formula is as follows.

$$E\left(v^*, k\right) = \frac{\sum_{i=1}^{M} e_i(v^*, k)}{M} \tag{9}$$

3. $t(v^*, k)$: the time required to reach the infection size k with node v^* as the source, abbreviated as t.

4. $T(v^*, k)$: the average value of the time required to execute the infection and detection process M times with node v^* as the source, abbreviated as T, and calculated as follows.

$$T(v^*, k) = \frac{\sum_{i=1}^{M} t_i(v^*, k)}{M} \tag{10}$$

5. $\overline{T}$: the mean value of the time required to traverse each node in the network as a source and reach a fixed infection size k, calculated as follows.

$$\overline{T} = \frac{\sum_{v^* \in V} T(v^*, k)}{|V|} \tag{11}$$

6. $\overline{Error}$: the mean value of the error distance obtained by traversing each node in the network as a source when the infection size k is fixed, which will be abbreviated as $\overline{E}$ in the later section and calculated as follows.

$$\overline{Error} = \frac{\sum_{v^* \in V} E(v^*, k)}{|V|} \tag{12}$$

It is worth mentioning that the detection result obtained when the number of randomizations is large enough will be the same as the result of traversing the source, so we traverse the source to obtain this value in our experiments.

7. $P_e(v^*, k)$: the probability that the error distance in the detection result is e when the node v^* is set as the source and the infection size is k, which will be abbreviated as P_e in the later section and calculated as follows.

$$P_e(v^*, k) = P(e(v^*, k) = e|v^*) \tag{13}$$

4.3 Experimental Results on Scale-Free Network

In the scale-free network, we rate the nodes in the network based on their hiding and propagation capabilities, and the top five nodes are shown in Table 3, and the nodes shown in the table are used as sources in turn for the experiments.

Table 3. Information about nodes in scale-free network.

Source ID	S	k_{ns}	l_d	C_C	C_B	D
255	2,514	4	3	3.980	0.703	0.720
370	2,479	4	3	4.050	0.505	0.724
352	2,462	4	3	4.084	0.549	0.726
473	2,418	4	3	4.172	0.364	0.731
468	2,404	4	3	4.200	0.260	0.733

To test the source hiding, we use the five algorithms described in Sect. 2 to locate the propagation source respectively, and the experimental results are shown in Fig. 8.

The horizontal axis in the figure indicates the infection size, and the vertical axis indicates the error distance between a specific source and a randomly selected source

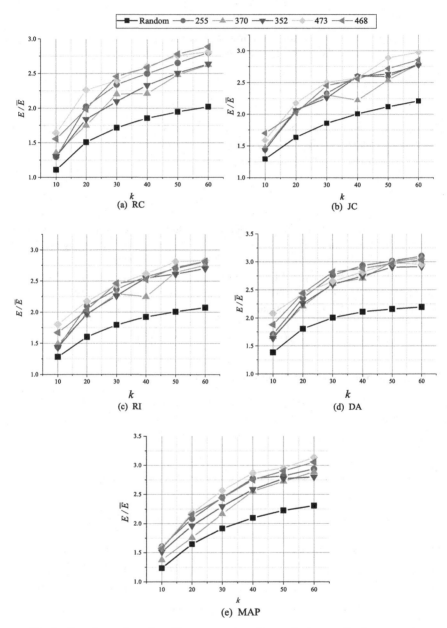

Fig. 8. Experimental results of five source detection methods on scale-free network.

in the detection results. It can be clearly seen that the selection of sources based on the method described in this paper will improve the error distance of the detection results compared to the random selection of sources. This not only shows that sources taken for the experiments have strong hiding, but also demonstrates that our proposed heuristic method can effectively measure the hiding of nodes and thus locate the nodes with strong hiding.

To test the propagation ability of the source, we compare the propagation efficiency of a randomly selected source and a source selected with heuristics at different infection sizes. Specifically, the propagation efficiency is expressed as the time required to propagate to a specified size with the node as the source. A shorter time required indicates a higher propagation efficiency and a higher propagation capability of the source. Similarly, traversing the nodes in the network as sources, the mean value of the infection time is calculated and denoted as $\overline{T}$ and the infection time of other source-specific nodes is denoted as T. The experimental results are shown in Fig. 9. Compared with the randomly selected source, the source selected based on the composite scoring method has a stronger propagation capability, and it can quickly infect the specified number of nodes to reach the expected infection scale.

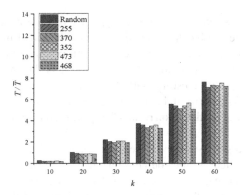

Fig. 9. Source propagation capacity comparison on scale-free network.

Table 4 shows sources selected for this policy for a number of 60 infected nodes. Sources in the table are ranked according to their overall scores.

From the experimental data, it can be seen that the best propagation source for strategy selection is the node with the strongest overall capability. For example, source 255 is not the most well hidden, but its propagation ability is higher than other nodes. Overall, the sources selected by the source hiding strategy have higher hiding and propagation capabilities than the randomly selected sources. In addition, the results in the table show that the detection effect is different when different source detection methods are used with the same node as the source. For the sources selected by the strategy, the JC method is less effective in detecting them compared to other source detection methods. However, the JC method is not the worst performer when looking at the detection results of all nodes in the network. This indicates that the detection results of the JC method are more

Table 4. Comprehensive comparison of experimental results on scale-free networks

Source ID	$T/\overline{T}$	$E/\overline{E}$				
		RC	JC	RI	DA	MAP
255	7.122	2.800	3.105	2.795	2.810	2.937
370	7.320	2.625	3.070	2.790	2.750	2.887
352	7.279	2.635	2.910	2.770	2.700	2.800
473	7.521	2.810	2.955	2.975	2.830	3.137
468	7.220	2.885	3.030	2.855	2.815	3.057
Random	10.878	2.021	2.196	2.209	2.073	2.308

correlated with the source location and its detection is more susceptible to the influence of the source location.

4.4 Experimental Results on Small-World Network

In the small-world network, the integrated capability of each node in the network is measured based on the bi-objective source hiding method, and the node with strong integrated capability is selected as the source. The information of the top five nodes in the comprehensive ability score in the calculation results is shown in Table 5.

The experimental results of testing source hiding using five source detection methods are shown in Fig. 10. The horizontal axis in the figure indicates the infection scale, and the vertical axis indicates the detection results for specific sources and randomly selected sources.

In this case, the larger the value of the error distance, the worse the detection and the better the hiding effect on the source. Obviously, compared to randomly selected sources, the error distance of the detection results of policy-selected sources is greater and the detection is worse. This shows that sources based on the composite scoring method in small-world network can still select sources with high hiding, successfully avoid detection, and ensure the anonymity of the sources.

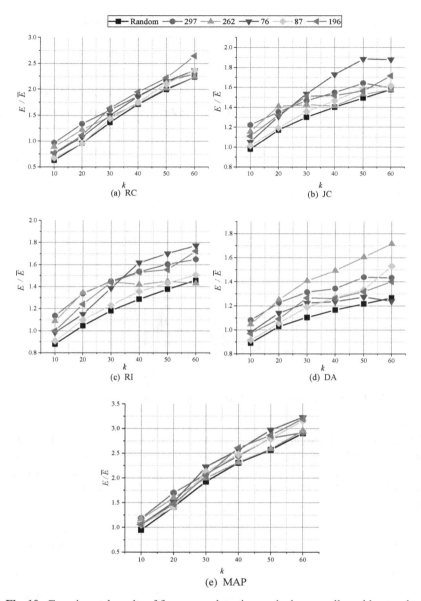

Fig. 10. Experimental results of five source detection methods on small-world network.

The results of testing the propagation capability of the sources selected by the strategy at different infection sizes are shown in Fig. 11. The experimental results vary at different scales, and the detection effect for different sources at the same scale also differs. For example, node 297 and node 262 lags behind other nodes in terms of propagation capability, while nodes 87 and 196 are consistently higher than randomly selected sources.

Table 5. Information about nodes in small-world network.

Source ID	S	k_{ns}	l_d	C_C	C_B	D
297	1,880	16	2	5.251	2.201	0.840
262	1,965	16	1	5.080	19.660	0.914
76	1,775	18	3	5.461	1.707	0.932
87	1,681	18	3	5.649	2.101	0.935
196	1,659	18	3	5.693	0.862	0.939

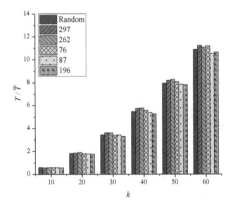

Fig. 11. Source propagation capacity comparison on small-world network.

This is because there are more connected edges between nodes in a small-world, and nodes located at different locations in the network have similar propagation capabilities.

The experimental results of the policy-selected source and the random-selected source in the small-world network when setting the infection size to 60 are shown in Table 6.

Table 6. Comprehensive comparison of experimental results on small-world network.

Source ID	$T/\overline{T}$	$E/\overline{E}$				
		RC	JC	RI	DA	MAP
297	11.233	2.298	1.434	1.596	1.648	2.917
262	11.075	2.235	1.716	1.587	1.466	2.950
76	11.193	2.364	1.238	1.880	1.772	3.227
87	10.530	2.364	1.532	1.616	1.508	3.160
196	10.649	2.644	1.400	1.714	1.722	3.197
Random	10.878	2.234	1.266	1.576	1.457	2.943

The results show that the policy-selected sources have similar propagation ability to the randomly selected sources, but the hiding is higher than that of the randomly selected sources. This is because compared to scale-free network, small-world networks have higher clustering properties and smaller average shortest distance between nodes, making the size of the infected networks generated in the same time similar when different nodes are sources.

4.5 Experimental Results on Real Network

The effectiveness of the source selection method is demonstrated by comparison in the simulations of small-world network and scale-free network. On this basis, we tested the integrated node scoring method in real E-mail networks and Facebook networks. The information of the top five nodes in both networks is shown in Table 7 and Table 8, respectively. The number of nodes in the E-mail network and the Facebook network are 1005 and 4039, the number of edges are 25571 and 88234, respectively.

The number of infected nodes is set to 100 and 300 in the experiments of E-mail network and Facebook network, respectively. The propagation traceability process is then executed 500 times. The results of the different source detection methods are shown in Table 9 and Table 10.

Table 7. Information about nodes in the E-mail network.

Source ID	S	k_{ns}	l_d	C_C	C_B	D
625	6,020	6	2	20,080,761.58	0	0.853
988	5,855	2	2	20,080,761.75	0	0.854
911	5,972	3	2	20,080,761.63	0	0.846
773	5,892	1	2	20,080,761.71	0	0.847
780	5,886	1	2	20,080,761.71	0	0.848

Table 8. Information about nodes in the Facebook network.

Source ID	S	k_{ns}	l_d	C_C	C_B	D
2,814	23,145	2	4	3.270	0	0.744
2,838	23,158	4	4	3.267	0	0.748
2,885	23,158	4	4	3.267	0	0.748
3,003	23,158	4	4	3.267	0	0.748
2,704	22,406	2	4	3.453	0	0.757

The probability of successful detection is 0 for all source detection methods we tested on the E-mail network. There is a high probability that the error distance will

Table 9. Average detection time, average error distance, and the probability (%) of each error distance on the E-mail network.

Source ID	T	Method	E	P_0	P_1	P_2	P_3	P_4
625	0.882	RC	2.028	0.00	1.75	93.75	4.50	0.00
		JC	2.088	0.00	3.00	85.25	11.75	0.00
		DA	1.985	0.00	3.75	94.00	2.25	0.00
		RI	1.993	0.00	2.50	95.75	1.75	0.00
		MAP	2.043	0.00	2.25	91.50	6.00	0.25
988	0.864	RC	2.758	0.00	0.25	24.00	75.50	0.25
		JC	2.425	0.00	0.75	56.00	43.25	0.00
		DA	2.705	0.00	0.00	29.50	70.50	0.00
		RI	2.475	0.00	0.00	52.50	47.50	0.00
		MAP	2.720	0.00	0.25	28.25	70.75	0.75
911	0.888	RC	2.055	0.00	0.75	93.00	6.25	0.00
		JC	2.168	0.00	1.25	80.75	18.00	0.00
		DA	2.013	0.00	0.00	98.75	1.25	0.00
		RI	2.003	0.00	0.25	99.25	0.50	0.00
		MAP	2.105	0.00	0.75	88.00	11.25	0.00
773	0.906	RC	2.15	0.00	0.75	83.50	15.75	0.00
		JC	2.128	0.00	1.75	83.75	14.50	0.00
		DA	2.1	0.00	0.25	89.50	10.25	0.00
		RI	2.013	0.00	1.00	96.75	2.25	0.00
		MAP	2.198	0.00	0.25	80.00	19.50	0.25
780	0.869	RC	2.005	0.00	3.00	93.50	3.50	0.00
		JC	2.148	0.00	0.25	84.75	15.00	0.00
		DA	2.013	0.00	0.00	98.75	1.25	0.00
		RI	2.005	0.00	0.00	99.50	0.50	0.00
		MAP	2.028	0.00	5.75	85.75	8.50	0.00

be 2 or 3. And on the Facebook network, in rare cases the real source can be detected with a very small probability. In the vast majority of cases, the error distance is 1 or 2. The maximum error distance can even reach 5. This shows that the sources selected according to our proposed method are highly hidden and can effectively evade tracking by multiple source detection methods.

Table 10. Average detection time, average error distance, and the probability (%) of each error distance on the Facebook network.

Source ID	T	Method	E	P_0	P_1	P_2	P_3	P_4	P_5
2,814	33.941	RC	1.245	0.00	77.25	21.50	0.75	0.50	0.00
		JC	1.625	0.50	48.50	39.50	11.00	0.50	0.00
		DA	1.333	0.00	69.00	29.75	0.50	0.50	0.25
		RI	1.388	0.00	64.50	32.25	3.25	0.00	0.00
		MAP	1.245	0.00	78.25	20.00	1.00	0.50	0.25
2,838	36.193	RC	1.393	0.00	65.75	31.25	1.00	2.00	0.00
		JC	1.693	0.75	45.75	38.00	14.50	1.00	0.00
		DA	1.535	0.00	53.00	43.00	1.50	2.50	0.00
		RI	1.478	0.00	56.50	39.25	4.25	0.00	0.00
		MAP	1.388	0.00	68.25	27.00	2.50	2.25	0.00
2,885	36.158	RC	1.370	0.00	68.25	27.75	2.75	1.25	0.00
		JC	1.663	0.50	45.00	42.25	12.25	0.00	0.00
		DA	1.510	0.00	55.25	40.25	2.75	1.75	0.00
		RI	1.473	0.00	57.00	38.75	4.25	0.00	0.00
		MAP	1.380	0.00	69.25	25.00	4.25	1.50	0.00
3,003	36.494	RC	1.328	0.00	70.75	27.00	1.00	1.25	0.00
		JC	1.653	1.75	43.75	42.25	12.00	0.25	0.00
		DA	1.488	0.00	56.75	39.75	1.50	2.00	0.00
		RI	1.465	0.00	58.00	38.00	3.50	0.50	0.00
		MAP	1.345	0.00	71.00	24.75	3.00	1.25	0.00
2,704	34.458	RC	1.433	0.00	65.75	28.00	3.50	2.75	0.00
		JC	1.798	1.75	36.00	44.50	16.25	1.50	0.00
		DA	1.570	0.00	58.00	32.50	4.25	5.00	0.25
		RI	1.538	0.00	53.00	40.50	6.25	0.25	0.00
		MAP	1.450	0.00	67.25	24.00	5.25	3.50	0.00

5 Conclusion

In this paper, we propose a bi-objective source hiding method that takes into account both source hiding and propagation capability based on the propagation characteristics of the network. In addition, this paper defines a variety of evaluation metrics for testing the propagation capability and hiding of nodes in different types of network structures. Experiments are conducted in small-world network, scale-free network, E-mail network and Facebook network. The results show that the policy-selected sources have higher propagation capacity compared to randomly selected sources. We also use a variety of source detection methods to detect the source, and the results show that the source selected by the policy can successfully evade detection.

References

1. Shah, D., Zaman, T.: Detecting sources of computer viruses in networks: theory and experiment. In: Proceedings of the ACM SIGMETRICS International Conference on Measurement and Modeling of Computer Systems, pp. 203–214 (2010)
2. Shah, D., Zaman, T.: Rumors in a network: who's the culprit? IEEE Trans. Inf. Theory **57**(8), 5163–5181 (2011)
3. Wikipedia. Wickr. [EB/OL] (5 February 2022). https://www.wickr.com/
4. Wikipedia. FireChat. [EB/OL] (5 February 2022). http://opengarden.com/firechat/
5. Chen, J., Chen, L., Chen, Y., et al.: GA-based Q-attack on community detection. IEEE Trans. Comput. Soc. Syst. **6**(3), 491–503 (2019)
6. Fionda, V., Pirro, G.: Community deception or: how to stop fearing community detection algorithms. IEEE Trans. Knowl. Data Eng. **30**(4), 660–673 (2017)
7. Waniek, M., Michalak, T.P., Wooldridge, M.J., et al.: Hiding individuals and communities in a social network. Nat. Hum. Behav. **2**(2), 139–147 (2018)
8. Lü, L., Zhou, T., Zhang, Q.M., et al.: The H-index of a network node and its relation to degree and coreness. Nat. Commun. **7**(1), 1–7 (2016)
9. Morone, F., Makse, H.A.: Influence maximization in complex networks through optimal percolation. Nature **524**(7563), 65–68 (2015)
10. Kenett, D.Y., Preis, T., Gur-Gershgoren, G., et al.: Dependency network and node influence: application to the study of financial markets. Int. J. Bifurc. Chaos **22**(07), 1250181 (2012)
11. Conitzer, V., Panigrahi, D., Zhang, H.: Learning opinions in social networks. In: International Conference on Machine Learning, pp. 2122–2132 (2020)
12. Fanti, G., Kairouz, P., Oh, S., et al.: Metadata-conscious anonymous messaging. IEEE Trans. Signal Inf. Process. Over Netw. **2**(4), 582–594 (2016)
13. Fanti, G., Kairouz, P., Oh, S., et al.: Rumor source obfuscation on irregular trees. ACM SIGMETRICS Perform. Eval. Rev. **44**(1), 153–164 (2016)
14. Luo, W., Tay, W.P., Leng, M.: Infection spreading and source identification: a hide and seek game. IEEE Trans. Signal Process. **64**(16), 4228–4243 (2016)
15. Luo, W., Tay, W.P., Leng, M.: On the universality of Jordan centers for estimating infection sources in tree networks. IEEE Trans. Inf. Theory **63**(7), 4634–4657 (2017)
16. Zhou, H., Jagmohan, A., Varshney, LR.: Generalized Jordan center: a source localization heuristic for noisy and incomplete observations. In: 2019 IEEE Data Science Workshop (DSW), pp. 243–247 (2019)
17. Yu, P.D., Tan, C.W., Fu, H.L.: Rumor source detection in finite graphs with boundary effects by message-passing algorithms. In: IEEE/ACM International Conference on Advances in Social Networks Analysis and Mining, pp. 175–192 (2018)
18. Brzozowski, M.J., Adams, P., Chi, E.H.: Google+ communities as plazas and topic boards. In: Proceedings of the 33rd Annual ACM Conference on Human Factors in Computing Systems, pp. 3779–3788 (2015)
19. Anderson, M., Caumont, A.: How social media is reshaping news. Pew Research Center, vol. 24 (2014)
20. Zhu, K., Ying, L.: Information source detection in the SIR model: a sample-path-based approach. IEEE/ACM Trans. Netw. **24**(1), 408–421 (2014)
21. Fioriti, V., Chinnici, M., Palomo, J.: Predicting the sources of an outbreak with a spectral technique. Appl. Math. Sci. **8**(135), 6775–6782 (2014)

22. Chang, B., Chen, E., Zhu, F., et al.: Maximum a posteriori estimation for information source detection. IEEE Trans. Syst. Man Cybern.: Syst. **50**(6), 2242–2256 (2018)
23. Albert, R.: Scale-free networks in cell biology. J. Cell Sci. **118**(21), 4947–4957 (2005)
24. Luo, W., Tay, W.P., Leng, M.: Identifying infection sources and regions in large networks. IEEE Trans. Signal Process. **61**(11), 2850–2865 (2013)
25. Namtirtha, A., Dutta, A., Dutta, B.: Weighted kshell degree neighborhood: a new method for identifying the influential spreaders from a variety of complex network connectivity structures. Expert Syst. Appl. **139**, 112859 (2020)
26. Chen, B., Zhu, W.X., Liu, Y.: Algorithm for complex network diameter based on distance matrix. J. Syst. Eng. Electron. **29**(2), 336–342 (2018)
27. Jure Leskovec. http://snap.stanford.edu/data/E-mail-Enron.html. Accessed 5 Jan 2021
28. Jure Leskovec. https://snap.stanford.edu/data/egonets-Facebook.html. Accessed 5 Jan 2021

Proof of Storage with Corruption Identification and Recovery for Dynamic Group Users

Tao Jiang[1,4], Hang Xu[1], Qiong Cheng[2], and Wenjuan Meng[3(✉)]

[1] School of Cyber Engineering, Xidian University, Xi'an, China
`taojiang@xidian.edu.cn, hangxu@stu.xidian.edu.cn`
[2] Guangzhou Institute of Technology, Xidian University, Guangzhou, China
`qcheng2020@stu.xidian.edu.cn`
[3] College of Information Engineering, Northwest A&F University, Yangling, China
`wjmeng2000@gmail.com`
[4] Guangxi Key Laboratory of Cryptography and Information Security, Guilin, China

Abstract. With the widespread deployment of cloud storage, protecting the security and privacy of outsourced data becomes increasingly important. In the last decade, provable data possession/retrievability schemes with different flavors, such as public variability, efficient update, user revocation, protecting privacy, have been designed to protect the rights and interests of cloud users. Although extensive research have been conducted in protecting the security and privacy of group cloud users, there is still a lack of a way to efficiently identify the destroyed data and actualize cloud disaster recovery. In response to these problems, a publicly verifiable proof of storage scheme is proposed for group cloud users in this paper. We provide the construction details, where invalid files can be efficiently identificated and even recovered after being detected by a trusted third-party auditor. Further analysis indicate that the designed scheme is secure for dynamic group user data sharing.

Keywords: Cloud storage · Data sharing · Corruption identification · Proof of retrievability · Dynamic group

1 Introduction

With the rapid development of the Internet of Things, cloud computing, big data and other digital technologies, cloud storage services are widely used from all walks of life around the world. In cloud storage, users can access their data whenever and wherever [17], and even further reduce the storage cost by sharing their data with a group of users. However, in the outsourcing storage mode, users lose control of their data, and the cloud service provider may not be fully trusted [20]. Thus users may lose their data for a variety of reasons. For instance, Amazon has admitted that a small fraction of their customers' data was permanently lost

© ICST Institute for Computer Sciences, Social Informatics and Telecommunications Engineering 2022
Published by Springer Nature Switzerland AG 2022. All Rights Reserved
Y. Chenggang et al. (Eds.): MobiMedia 2022, LNICST 451, pp. 126–141, 2022.
https://doi.org/10.1007/978-3-031-23902-1_10

due to several days' electricity outages caused by lightning strikes [3]. Also, cloud data may be destroyed due to hardware/software failure [18] or misoperations [10]. In fact, when data is outsourced, it is difficult for users to verify that their data is corrupted without inuring serious communication cost. This security problem makes people reluctant to storage their data to the cloud.

To address this concern, various interactive data integrity/recoverability auditing schemes, e.g., provable data possession (PDP) [1] and proofs of retrievability (PoR) [7,12], are designed. Later, PDP and PoR are extended to support efficient and privacy-preserving auditing for shared cloud data [4–6,8,13,21]. Although the above auditing schemes can attest the availability of outsourced data, they can not quickly identify the invalid files/blocks among the data and recover them after the failure. The reason lies in that, a single destroyed file/block can cause the audit to fail when an integrity audit is performed on large-scale data stored on the server. After the failure of data integrity auditing, searching for the location of invalid files/blocks brings a lot of computation and communication overhead, which seriously affects the efficiency of the scheme. To solve the above challenge, the invalid files/blocks identification schemes based on different signature/tag failure identification technologies have been published, such as pruned search tree [9] or binary tree with shared randomizers [2], Exponents Test Based Search (ETBS) [14]. Also, there are many schemes proposed for recovering damaged data, such as extended POR [11] which erasures coding technique [22]. However, the above schemes are mainly designed for single client scenario and have a single function. More precisely, the auditing tags from multiple users are computed with different private keys, which makes it difficult and inefficient in aggregating the authentication tags and identifying the files/blocks in one challenge. Therefore, it is still challenging to design an auditing scheme to efficiently support location of the failed files/blocks and recovery them for dynamic group users with user revocation.

In this paper, we address these problems and propose a new solution for fast locating and recovering data of invalid files for dynamic group users. It enables users to efficiently identify the availability of all outsourced data from valid group users without multiple attestations. Notably, in our scheme, users need to process/upload their original files and corresponding tags only once irrespective of the group users' revocation. Especially, our scheme leverages rapid location and recovery techniques for corrupted data to impose significantly. By doing so, our scheme could efficiently identify the corruption files/blocks from different cloud users at one attestation.

Contribution. In summary, the paper makes the following contributions:

- We figure out that designing storage proof with efficient identifications of corrupt files and recovery for dynamic group users is still an unsolved problem. And on this basis, a corruption identification and recovery scheme dubbed CIRG is proposed in this paper.
- We provide concrete construction for CIRG, which transforms and accumulates data integrity audit results through association calculation and accumulation calculation, reducing the number of calculations for locating damaged

data. Aiming at the problem of recovery of damaged data of group users, the RS erasure code technology and the idea of shared coding are combined to achieve reliable recovery of damaged data, so that damaged data belonging to existing users of the group or revoked users can be effectively recovered.
- We prove the security of CIRG under its threat model, which indicates that the designed scheme is secure in the auditing of data integrity and efficient in the recovery of the corrupt files.

1.1 Related Work

In recent years, various cloud storage data integrity audit verification schemes have been proposed. For example, Ateniese et al. proposed the concept of "provable data ownership" PDP for the first time in [1], and constructed homomorphic verification tags using RSA scheme and discrete logarithms, which saved the retrieval and download of files and protected data privacy. Shacham et al. [12], based on Ateniese et al.'s idea about homomorphic tags, used the BLS short message signature mechanism to construct the Homomorphic verification tag, which had reduced the communication overhead in the verification stage. Jules et al. [7] first considered how to recover the damaged data, and proposed a sensor-based POR scheme, which could not only conduct data integrity audit, but also recover the failure data to a certain extent. However, this scheme is only suitable for individual users. Matt et al. [9] proposed a pairing based signature scheme to identify multiple invalid files after batch audit failure, which substantially reduced the pairing computation cost by leveraging "divide-and-conquer" with pruning the search tree. Bernstein et al. [2] proposed a scheme for locating failure files after the batch audit of elliptic curve signatures, which could effectively reduce the cost of elliptic curve failure signature recognition based on binary tree with shared randomizer. Shin et al. [14] proposed the Exponents Test Based Search (ETBS), which identified the location of the failed files/blocks by comparing the validation values with and without exponents. ETBS, however, only applies to invalidation scenarios for individual files. This method has a large limitation, which is not suitable for the location of multiple failure files. Wang et al. [16] proposed a batch audit method to support fast query of invalid files. The characteristic of this method is that it can resist "invalid file" attack effectively and ensure the availability and efficiency of batch audit scheme.

Data sharing is one of the most widely used services provided by cloud storage. With data sharing services, users can share their data with a group of users on the cloud, reducing the burden of local data storage. When a group user acts improperly or leaves the group, the user shall be revoked from the group, and the data of the revoked user shall be managed by a legal user designated by the group administrator. With the rapid development of group information sharing, related technologies of group user cloud storage have been applied accordingly. Jiang et al. [6] proposed an audit scheme of user revocation of shared data integrity based on group signature, but the efficiency was slow. Recently, Zhang et al. [21] proposed an efficient user revocation data integrity audit scheme, which effectively improved the audit efficiency of user revocation. However, these schemes only focus on the efficiency of data audit and do not consider the failure of data audit. In fact, data integrity audit fails means the data stored on the cloud server is damaged and no longer available, which is a direct cost to users. Therefore, it is very important to design a method that can efficiently locate and recover invalid files.

2 Models and Goals

This section firstly describes the system model and the threat model. Then, the design goals of the system is listed.

2.1 System Model

In our system, as shown in Fig. 1, there are five entities: multiple group users, a group manager, a Cloud Service Provider (CSP), a Private Key Generator ($\mathcal{PKG}$), and a trusted Third Party Auditor (TPA). Following, we introduce the functionalities of different entities in our solution.

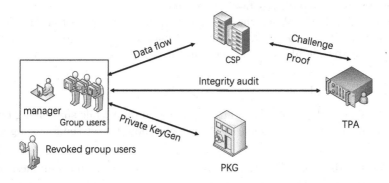

Fig. 1. The system model.

1. Multiple group users: Group users are the data owners, which share the data stored at the cloud server. They encode the files and tag each block of the files for integrity auditing and destroy recovery before outsourcing them to the cloud server. Users may join or leave a group because of personal or group management reasons. We assume that the group users are honest and will not share the private information with any illegal parity, including the revoked group users.
2. Group manager: The group manager is an administrator of a group, which manages the revocation or registration of users when group users leave or new users join the group. It also give assistance to private key generation.
3. CSP: The CSP stores the outsourced file from cloud users and allows group users to enjoy the data sharing service.

4. $\mathcal{PKG}$: The $\mathcal{PKG}$ is a trusted entity. It is responsible for generating the public parameters and keys through the group's identity (UI).
5. TPA: The TPA is responsible for auditing the integrity of cloud data on behalf of group users. Also, it assists the group users or CSP to efficiently locate the invalid file and recover the destroyed file(s) once the data integrity audit fails. The TPA cannot get the real data from the blinded ones of users in the phase of data uploading, nor can it derive the real data from the cloud's response in the phase of auditing.

2.2 Threat Model

This paper further considers the issue of remediation after a failed audit of data integrity. Specifically, once the data integrity audit fails, TPA is able to efficiently locate damaged files. It returns a list of damaged files to the user (or CSP), and then restores the corresponding invalid files based on those locations.

1. File corruption: The files outsourced by a group of cloud users may be corrupted or deleted due to server hardware failure, malicious server or human error. To avoid damage to the server and its reputation, CSP does not tell the user that the data has been corrupted.
2. File irretrievability: When the attestation from TPA reveals that the files are corrupted, the group users and the CSP may not be able to recover the file without a specific file recovery mechanism.

2.3 Design Goals

To ensure secure cloud storage auditing for shared data while supporting invalid files locating and recover efficiently, our scheme should meet the following goals:

Security Goals. For security, we consider the correctness and soundness of the designed scheme. *Correctness* requires that if the outsourced files are intact, the CSP can always pass the data integrity audit. When the destroyed file blocks are under a specific threshold, any group user or the CSP can always recover these blocks. *Soundness* means that if the files from the group users are not stored, less stored or wrongly stored, the CSP can pass the data integrity audit with a negligible probability. If there are invalid files in an attestation, the probability that the TPA cannot locate the destroyed locations is negligible.

Efficiency Goals. Efficiency goals consist of the computing, communication and storage efficiency of our scheme. In our design, we consider efficient file recovery and public auditing. The former means that when the data stored in the cloud server is damaged or lost due to physical disk damage, failure and other reasons, the proposed scheme ensures that users can effectively recover the failed files by calculating valid blocks of the damaged data. The latter means that TPA, on behalf of a group of users, is able to verify the integrity of stored data without accessing shared data stored in the cloud server.

3 Preliminaries and Definitions

This section firstly describes the cryptographic tools as preliminaries. Then, the definition of data encoding and decoding are listed.

3.1 Preliminaries

Bilinear Map. A bilinear map is a map $e : G_1 \times G_1 \to G_2$, where G_1 is a Gap Diffie-Hellman (GDH) group and G_2 is another multiplicative cyclic group of prime order p with the following three properties: 1) *Bilinear:* for all $P, Q \in G_1$ and $a, b \in Z_p$, $e(P^a, Q^b) = e(P, Q)^{ab}$. 2) *Non-Degenerate:* $e(P, Q) \neq 1$, where P, Q are generators of G_1. 3) *Computable:* there exists an efficiently computable algorithm for computing e.

Hash Function of Cryptography. Set three different cryptographic hash functions. Let $H_1 : \{0,1\}^* \times G_1 \to Z_q^*$ be a hash function computing a number in Z_q^* with an input bit string of arbitrary length and Elements in G_1, $H_2 : \{0,1\}^* \times G_1 \times \{0,1\}^* \to Z_q^*$ be a hash function computing a number in Z_q^* with two input bit strings of arbitrary length and Elements in G_1, and $h : \{0,1\}^* \to G_1$ be a BLS hash. All of these hashes are modeled as random oracles and selected randomly in this paper by $\mathcal{PKG}$.

Recovery of Damaged Data of Group Users. This paper provides efficient recovery of damaged data through erasure coding techniques. RS erasure code firstly implements redundant coding on the original data F. Redundant coding is the expansion of F. The data obtained after the extended calculation is called encoded data E. Obviously, E has a larger size than F. We call this increase in E as redundancy *red*. E is finally outsourced to the cloud server. In the following, we define the encode and decode algorithms of RS erasure code:

Definition 1. *Encode*$(m_1, m_2, \cdots, m_k) \to (\omega_1, \omega_2, \cdots, \omega_n)$: *On input a message* $F = m_1, m_2, \cdots, m_k$, *return the encode data* $E = \omega_1, \omega_2, \cdots, \omega_n$ *where* $m_i, \omega_j \in Z_q^*, i \in [1, k], j \in [1, n], n = red + k$.

Definition 2. *Decode*$(\omega_1', \omega_2', \cdots, \omega_k') \to (m_1, m_2, \cdots, m_k)$: *On input an arbitrary selection of k valid data blocks from the corrupted data* $E' = \omega_1', \omega_2', \cdots, \omega_k'$, *return the message* $F = m_1, m_2, \cdots, m_k$ *where* $m_i, \omega_i' \in Z_q^*, i \in [1, k]$.

3.2 Definitions

We target at designing a proof of storage scheme, called CIRG for short, which can efficiently identify the corruption files/blocks and support their recovery for dynamic group users. CIRG defines six algorithms: Setup, KeyGen, TagGen, Challenge, Prove and Recover, which behave as follows:

1. Setup *algorithm*: the setup algorithm is run by the $\mathcal{PKG}$. It takes as input a security parameter κ and outputs a secret key sk, a public key pk and the system public parameters *tuple*.

2. KeyGen *algorithm*: the private key generation algorithm is run by the group users, group manager and $\mathcal{PKG}$ to generate keys for data labels.
3. TagGen *algorithm*: the algorithm is run by the group users. Group users encode the data uploaded to the cloud server as shown in Fig. 2. It takes as inputs the encoded file E and σ, and generates a tag *tag* for each block. The encoded data and *tag* are then uploaded to the cloud server for storage.
4. Challenge *algorithm*: the challenge algorithm is run by the TPA. It takes as input the file information for the challenge and returns challenge chal to the CSP.
5. Prove *algorithm*: the proof generation algorithm is run by the CSP. It takes as inputs batch file $F_1, F_2, \cdots, F_N$, a set of the corresponding authenticators and auditing challenge chal, and generates a proof P which is used to prove the cloud accurately stores $F_1, F_2, \cdots, F_N$.
6. Recover *algorithm*: the proof verification algorithm is run by the TPA. It takes as inputs a proof P and system public parameters, and returns "success" if the proof is valid. Otherwise, returns "failure", which means that the stored file is damaged. At this point, RDI accumulation method is called to quickly locate the damaged file. Then, the user recovers invalid files according to the RS erasure code.

4   CIRG Scheme

In this section, we provide the construction details of CIRG scheme. Notably a high-level explanation of the proposed scheme is given before describing the details of each algorithm.

4.1   High-Level Explanation

The solution in [21] effectively solves the problem of data integrity audit when group users cancel. However, it fails for data integrity audit which means that there are invalid files in the audited data. In fact, querying and recovering invalid files require a lot of communication and computing resources. To address the challenge, we apply RS erasure codes to the data, as shown in Fig. 2. The user encodes the data before storing it on the cloud server. When a file auditing fails, the invalid data can be recovered effectively according to the RS erasure code. In the proposed CIRG structure, we start with a batch file audit. When it fails, the RDI is called to quickly locate the failed files. Then the RS erasure code is used to recover the damaged files. Specifically, after a failure of batch audit, the RDI algorithm is used to correlate the left and right sub-tree audit values of batch audit. This method can reduce the computation amount and effectively improve the efficiency of querying invalid files. After the location of the failed file is determined, the data of the failed file will be effectively recovered by RS erasure code. In this way, the user only needs to recover the invalid data according to RS erasure code. This solution effectively guarantees the security of the data stored by group users on the cloud and improves the solution for users to store and share data in the cloud.

Fig. 2. Data encode.

4.2   Data Encoding of Group Users

As shown in Fig. 2, the file F is divided into $F = m_1, m_2, \cdots, m_k$, and then the data blocks $m_1, m_2, \cdots, m_k$ are coded according to RS erasure code. First of all, the group administrator selects a set of vectors $x_1, x_2, \cdots, x_k$ that are linearly independent and publishes them in the group. Then, F is encoded as $E = \omega_1, \omega_2, \cdots, \omega_n$, where $n = red + k$ and red is the redundancy of RS erasure code. Notably $E = x \times F^{\mathrm{T}}$, where x is a matrix of k linearly independent vectors of length n, x_i is in the finite domain 2^w and w must be large enough that $n \leq 2^w + 1$. The calculation is provided as follow:

$$
E = x \times F^{\mathrm{T}} =
\begin{bmatrix}
vm_{1,1} & vm_{1,2} & \cdots & vm_{1,k} \\
 & & \ddots & \\
vm_{k,1} & vm_{k,2} & \cdots & vm_{k,k} \\
vm_{k+1,1} & vm_{k+1,2} & \cdots & vm_{k+1,k} \\
 & & \ddots & \\
vm_{n,1} & vm_{n,2} & \cdots & vm_{n,k}
\end{bmatrix}
\times
\begin{bmatrix}
m_1 \\
m_2 \\
\vdots \\
m_k
\end{bmatrix}
=
\begin{bmatrix}
\omega_1 \\
\omega_2 \\
\vdots \\
\omega_k \\
\vdots \\
\omega_n
\end{bmatrix}
$$

4.3   Description of CIRD Scheme

In previous cloud storage audit schemes [8,15,19,21], the efficiency of user data integrity audit is mainly addressed. However, this article mainly deals with the situation when the data stored by group users on the cloud server is corrupted. That is, the damaged files can be quickly located and effectively recovered. In addition, for the overall perfection, efficiency and security of the scheme, Schnorr signature [21] is selected in this paper to generate the label key of user data, so as to have an efficient audit for dynamic group users. Our scheme continues to use UI and ssk as the group identity corresponding to $SSig$ and secret key [21]. Further more, we continue to adopt the feature of ID-based digital signature $SSig$ and use it to ensure the integrity of file identifier names, user retract numbers and verification values. As applied in the scenario, RN is the key to update the data label key. Finally, the dedicated description of our scheme is described as follows.

1. Setup *algorithm*: In this algorithm, the $\mathcal{PKG}$ generates its own public keys, secret keys and some system parameters.
    - The $\mathcal{PKG}$ chooses the master secret key $\gamma \in Z_q^*$ and master partial key $\beta \in Z_q^*$. Then, the $\mathcal{PKG}$ computes two public values $Y_1 = g^\gamma$ and $Y_2 = g^\beta$.

The $\mathcal{PKG}$ holds the master secret key itself for generating the group user's identity key and sends the master partial key to group manager for generating the partial key.

- The $\mathcal{PKG}$ arbitrarily selects and publishes *tuple* as the system public parameters, where g and u are arbitrarily selected from G_1 by $\mathcal{PKG}$, e is a bilinear mapping $e : G_1 \times G_1 \rightarrow G_2$, q is the prime order of a group and $tuple = \{G_1, G_2, e, q, g, u, Y_1, Y_2, H_1, H_2, h\}$.

2. KeyGen *algorithm*: The well-known Schnorr signature [21] is utilized to compute the identity key and the partial key. This signature enables dynamic group users to audit efficiently. In this algorithm the $\mathcal{PKG}$ generates the identity key, the group manager generates the partial key and group users generate their private keys using the identity key and the partial key. The calculation of this key are described as follows:

   - The $\mathcal{PKG}$ runs $\{UI, r_{UI}\} \rightarrow \{UIK_{UI}\}$. When $\mathcal{PKG}$ receives the group's identity UI, it chooses a random number $r_{UI} \in Z_q^*$, and computes $R_{UI} = g^{r_{UI}}$ and $\sigma_{UI} = r_{UI} + \gamma H_1(UI, R_{UI}) \bmod q$. Then, the $\mathcal{PKG}$ sends the identity key $UIK_{UI} = (R_{UI}, \sigma_{UI})$ to group users.
   - The group users run $\{UIK_{UI}\} \rightarrow \{0, 1\}$. After receiving the identity key, the group users verify the correctness of the UIK_{UI}. If $g^{\sigma_{UI}} = R_{UI} \cdot Y_1^{H_1(UI, R_{UI})}$, the group users accept the identity key UIK_{UI}; otherwise they refuse it.
   - The group manager runs $\{RN, r_{RN}, UI\} \rightarrow \{TK_{UI,RN}\}$. First, we default the group to start with no one leaving. The group manager sets the number of user revocations $RN = 0$, then sends it to group users and cloud. Later, the group manager chooses a random number $r_{RN} \in Z_q^*$, and computes $R_{RN} = g^{r_{RN}}$ and $\sigma_{RN} = r_{RN} + \beta H_2(UI, R_{RN}, RN) \bmod q$. The group manager sends the partial key $TK_{UI,RN} = (R_{RN}, \sigma_{RN})$ to the group users, where RN is initially set to 0, and when one user leaves the group, $RN = RN + 1$. As long as any user leaves the group, the partial key $TK_{UI,RN}$ is updated as RN changes.
   - The group users run $\{TK_{UI,RN}\} \rightarrow \{0, 1\}$. After receiving the partial key, the group users verify the correctness of the $TK_{UI,RN}$. If $g^{\sigma_{RN}} = R_{RN} \cdot Y_2^{H_2(UI, R_{RN}, RN)}$, the group users accept the partial key $TK_{UI,RN}$; otherwise, refuse it.
   - The group users run $\{UIK_{UI}, TK_{UI,RN}\} \rightarrow \{SK_{UI,RN}\}$. Then, they calculate the private keys based on the identity key $UIK_{UI} = (R_{UI}, \sigma_{UI})$ and the partial key $TK_{UI,RN} = (R_{RN}, \sigma_{RN})$(Here $RN = 0$). Finally, $\sigma = (\sigma_{UI} + \sigma_{RN}) \bmod q$ is computed and the private keys $SK_{UI,RN}$ turns to be (R_{UI}, R_{RN}, σ).

3. TagGen *algorithm*: This algorithm is run by the group user. As shown in Fig. 2, the user first encodes the file F as E. Then, the user computes $t_{ij} = (h(FID\|i_j\|RN) \cdot u^{\omega_{ij}})^\sigma$, $i \in [1, N], j \in [1, n]$, where FID is the file identifier, i is the ith user, j is the data block index, u is the random value and $u \in G_1$, RN is the number of user revocations. The group user computes the file tag $Ftag = FID\|RN\|R_{UI}\|R_{RN}\|\tau$, where $\tau = SSig_{ssk}(FID\|RN\|R_{UI}\|R_{RN})$,

ssk is a file tag private key. Notably, calculation of the key is referenced from [15].

4. **Challenge** *algorithm*: In this algorithm, the TPA generates an auditing challenge for the cloud. The calculation of this chal are described as follows:
   - Randomly pick a set I with $N \cdot s$ elements, where $s \in [1, n]$, N represents the number of the audit users and $I = \{1_1, \cdots, 1_s, \cdots, N_1, \cdots, N_s\}$.
   - Generate a random value $v_{i_s} \in Z_q^*$ for each $i_s \in I, i \in [1, N]$.
   - Send the auditing challenge chal $= \{C_1, C_2, \cdots, C_N\}$ to the CSP, where $C_i = \{i_j, v_{i_j}\}, i \in [1, N], j \in [1, s]$.

5. **Prove** *algorithm*: In this algorithm, after receiving the chal of TPA, the CSP generates a corresponding proof to demonstrate its ownership of the intact cloud data. The calculation of this proof are described as follows:
   - Compute $T = \{T_1, \cdots, T_N\}$, where $T_i = \prod_{j=1}^{s} t_{i_j}^{v_{i_j}}$. $\mu = \{\mu_1, \cdots, \mu_N\}, i \in [1, N]$ and $\mu_i = \sum_{j=1}^{s} v_{i_j} \cdot \omega_{i_j}$. Then computes P where $P = (T, \mu)$.
   - Send P along with the file tag to the TPA as the proof.

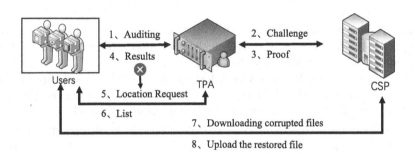

Fig. 3. Procedure of failed file identification and recovery scheme

6. **Recover** *algorithm*:

   As shown in Fig. 3, there may be two situations when the TPA verifies the integrity of the data: data integrity verification passes/fails. As mentioned earlier, the failure of the integrity verification means that the files stored by the user in the CSP are damaged and no longer available. In view of this situation, the CIRG scheme designed in this paper can efficiently locate the damaged file and restore it.

   The TPA first retrieves the file tag $Ftag$, and verifies the validity of the file tag by checking whether τ is a valid signature via UI. If it is, the TPA receives the data possession evidence set P returned by the server and verifies whether the server has correctly stored the client's files in the form of batch processing. The TPA runs $\{P, V\} \rightarrow \{0, 1\}$. As shown in Fig. 4, the TPA verifies the correctness of the proof P by checking whether the following equation holds:

$$\prod_{i=1}^{i=N} e(T_i, g) \stackrel{?}{=} \prod_{i=1}^{i=N} e(\prod_{j=1}^{s} h(FID\|i_j\|RN)^{v_{ij}} \cdot u^{\mu_i}, \mathsf{v}), \tag{1}$$

where $\mathsf{v} = R_{UI} \cdot R_{RN} \cdot Y_1^{H_1(UI, R_{UI})} \cdot Y_2^{H_2(UI, R_{RN}, RN)}$.

TPA   Cloud

1: Generate chal; $\mathsf{chal} = \{C_1, C_2, \cdots, C_N\}$
                    $\xrightarrow{\hspace{4cm}}$

                                2: Compute $T_i = \prod_{j=1}^{s} t_{ij}^{v_{ij}}$, $\mu_i = \sum_{j=1}^{s} v_{ij} \cdot \omega_{ij}$;

                    $\xleftarrow{\hspace{2cm} P \hspace{2cm}}$ Then, set $P = (T, \mu)$;

2: Verifies the correctness of P.

Fig. 4. The protocol of data integrity verification.

If this equation holds, it indicates that all files are intact, and returns 1; otherwise, it indicates that at least one invalid file exists, and returns 0. Next, we elaborate on how to locate corrupted data.

After inputing the challenged file information, the TPA uses the query algorithm to identify all the invalid files and outputs the corresponding list. First, the calculation of RDI is given. We denoted the audit result of Eq. (1) as "$\mathsf{Le} = \mathsf{Re}$". Then, set $\mathsf{RDI}(\cdot)$ and $\mathsf{RDI}(\cdot) \to (\mathsf{Le} - \mathsf{Re} \stackrel{?}{=} 0)$. Thus this RDI converts audit formula (1) to a value 0 judgment: $IFN_{\mathsf{RDI}} = \mathsf{Le} - \mathsf{Re}$. The detail of this calculation is shown as follows:

$$IFN_{\mathsf{RDI}} \stackrel{?}{=} e(T_i, g) - e(\theta_i, \mathsf{v}), \tag{2}$$

where $\theta_i = \prod_{j=1}^{s} h(FID\|i_j\|RN)^{v_{ij}} \cdot u^{\mu_i}$, v is the same as Eq. (1).

We associate Le with Re in terms of moving positions. Then, the audit results of multiple user files are associated with the added method. And the intermediate value of the audit results is used to reduce the calculation and improve the efficiency of the query damage file. For the files of N users, the RDI batch audit formula is:

$$IFN_{\mathsf{RDI}}^{[1,N]} \stackrel{?}{=} \sum_{i=1}^{N} e(T_i, g) - \sum_{i=1}^{N} e(\theta_i, \mathsf{v}), \tag{3}$$

where θ_i and v are the same as above.

If $IFN_{\mathsf{RDI}}^{[1,N]} = 0$, the batch audit is passed, indicating that the files are complete; If $IFN_{\mathsf{RDI}}^{[1,N]} \neq 0$, there is at least one invalid file. According to the above formula, we set $X_{[1,N]}$ to represent the file audit of N users. As shown in Fig. 5, the validation value of the parent node in the binary search tree is equal to the sum of the validation values of the left and right child nodes. In the following formula, by comparing the verification values of the parent node and the left child node, the validity of the right child node can be directly determined without performing batch auditing.

$$IFN_{RDI}^{[N/2+1,N]} = IFN_{RDI}^{[1,N]} - IFN_{RDI}^{[1,N/2]} \tag{4}$$

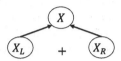

Fig. 5. Schematic diagram of the relational dichotomy

Next, we present a general algorithm for querying multiple corrupted files. The algorithm provides an N-bit string $(b_1, b_2, \ldots, b_N)$ as output. With overwhelming probability $b_i = 1$ if and only if file i is valid. The details of this algorithm are shown as follows:

(a) First, compute $IFN_{RDI}^{[1,N]}$, if $IFN_{RDI}^{[1,N]} = 0$, output N bits $(1, 1, \ldots, 1)$ and stop; otherwise, the TPA does the following steps.
(b) Assuming $X_{[1,N]}$ is the root node, calculate the left child node $X_{L=N/2}$, set $IFN_{RDI}^{[1,N/2]}$.
(c) Calculate the verification value for the right child. If $IFN_{RDI}^{[1,N/2]} = 0$, set $IFN_{RDI}^{[N/2+1,N]} = IFN_{RDI}^{[1,N]}$; If $IFN_{RDI}^{[1,N/2]} = IFN_{RDI}^{[1,N]}$, set $IFN_{RDI}^{[N/2+1,N]} = 0$; Otherwise compute $IFN_{RDI}^{[N/2+1,N]} = IFN_{RDI}^{[1,N]} - IFN_{RDI}^{[1,N/2]}$.
(d) Apply the same algorithm recursively to left sub-tree and right sub-tree. Finally find all the damage files and output $(b_1, b_2, \ldots, b_N)$.

According to the above analysis, the RDI method based on value 0 eliminates the batch audit process of the right child node, thus reduces the number of batch audits. With this method, the location of all the invalid files can be found. Similarly, we can then apply RDI again to locate the specific failed data block of the failed file.

Next, the corrupted data recovery method is instantiated. Notably that for multiple corrupted data recovery cases only the instantiation method needs to be extended. For the sake of description, damaged file E_1 is taken as an example to explain how to restore it. We get k valid data blocks $E'_1 = \omega'_{1_1}, \omega'_{1_2}, \cdots, \omega'_{1_k}$ from E_1 and the sub-matrix B from x (Details in Sect. 4.2) in terms of E'_1. This B and E'_1 correspond one to one. The data recovery is carried out according to the formula: $B^{-1} * E'_1 = F_1^T$, where B^{-1} is the inverse of the k by k matrix consisting of the B. Thus, the original data F_1 can be restored. The details of this calculation are shown as follows:

$$B = \begin{bmatrix} b_{1,1} & b_{1,2} & \cdots & b_{1,k} \\ b_{2,1} & b_{2,2} & \cdots & b_{2,k} \\ & & \ddots & \\ b_{k,1} & b_{k,2} & \cdots & b_{k,k} \end{bmatrix} \quad B^{-1} = \begin{bmatrix} b'_{1,1} & b'_{1,2} & \cdots & b'_{1,k} \\ b'_{2,1} & b'_{2,2} & \cdots & b'_{2,k} \\ & & \ddots & \\ b'_{k,1} & b'_{k,2} & \cdots & b'_{k,k} \end{bmatrix} \quad F_1^{\mathrm{T}} = B^{-1} \times \begin{bmatrix} \omega'_{1_1} \\ \omega'_{1_2} \\ \vdots \\ \omega'_{1_k} \end{bmatrix}$$

4.4 Dynamic Group Users and Data Recovery

The CIRG scheme in this paper supports dynamic group users environment, that is, the case of user cancellation. When a user leaves the group, the label key in the group needs to be updated, thus the value of RN is increased by 1. Meanwhile the partial key $TK_{UI,RN}$ of the user is updated [21], so that the label key in the group is updated. Once a user leaves the group, his data will be managed by legitimate members of the group. CIRG supports dynamic group users environments, which adopts a unified algorithm to encode data. That is, the data uploaded to the cloud server by a group of users adopts this data encoding algorithm. Once the user has not uploaded all the data before leaving the group, the data he shares in the group will be corrupted. At this point, the legitimate user being charged of managing his data can still recover the failed shared data through the encoding algorithm exposed by the group administrator.

5   Security Analysis

Theorem 1 (The Correctness and Security of Batch Audit). *If the group users, group manager, CSP and TPA can perform calculations correctly, the proposed CIRG scheme is both correct and secure in the batch audit of shared files among multiple users.*

Proof. Since this article adopts the label key feature, all users in the group use this key. Therefore, using batch auditing can simultaneously audit different files of multiple users. In order to prove the security of batch audit, consider the following batch auditing. According to the formula of integrity audit, we set the number of stored files of the user as 1 for the convenience of description. The following uses the data integrity audit of users A, B, and C as an example. First, if RN is equal, these three user label keys are the same, so they can be audited simultaneously. The details of this formula are shown as follows:

$$\begin{aligned} \text{left} = \prod_{i=1}^{i=3} e(T_i, g) &= \prod_{i=1}^{i=3} e(\prod_{j=1}^{j=s} (h(FID\|i_j\|RN) \cdot u^{\omega_{i_j}})^{\sigma \cdot v_{i_j}}, g) \\ &= \prod_{i=1}^{i=3} e(\prod_{j=1}^{j=s} (h(FID\|i_j\|RN)^{v_{i_j}} \cdot u^{\mu_i}, g^{\sigma_{UI} + \sigma_{RN}}) \qquad (5) \\ &= \prod_{i=1}^{i=3} e(\prod_{j=1}^{j=s} (h(FID\|i_j\|RN)^{v_{i_j}} \cdot u^{\mu_i}, \mathsf{v}) \end{aligned}$$

$$\text{right} = \prod_{i=1}^{i=3} e(\prod_{j=1}^{j=s} h(FID\|i_j\|RN)^{v_{ij}} \cdot u^{\mu_i}, \mathsf{v}) \tag{6}$$

where $\mathsf{v} = R_{UI} \cdot R_{RN} \cdot Y_1^{H_1(UI,R_{UI})} \cdot Y_2^{H_2(UI,R_{RN},RN)}$.

If a malicious CSP stored incorrect or invalid user data, it must have a private key (σ in equation (5)) to ensure that the left is equal to the right in order to pass the audit. Since a malicious CSP cannot obtain the private key, it cannot generate the correct storage proof, let alone forge the correct data signature. In other words, if the above equation left is equal to right, if and only if the files of A, B and C respectively pass the audit, so only if the CSP has to store the correct data to pass the audit. Obviously, if CIRG is executed correctly, the left is equal to the right,which ensures that batch auditing is correct and secure. On the contrary, the label key will be different while the three RN users are not equal. Therefore, A, B and C perform data integrity audit, respectively. The same as the situation when RN is equal.

Theorem 2 (The Security and efficiency of Data Recovery). *In our scheme, CIRG can effectively recover original data when the group user's data stored on the cloud server is corrupted.*

Proof. The possibility of data recovery in this paper depends on the relationship between the number of damaged data blocks dd and the redundancy red. When $dd \leq red$, damaged data can be recovered. First, the sub-matrix $B_{k \times k}$ of the x-matrix is correctly calculated, according to k uncorrupted data $E_1' = \omega_{1_1}', \omega_{1_2}', \cdots, \omega_{1_k}'$, where E_1' has k valid blocks of data for this file and B is the linearly independent vector corresponding to E_1'. And then, since x is invertible, the inverse of the B-matrix can be correctly figured out. Therefore, the data recovery formula is: $B^{-1} * E_1' = F_1^{\mathrm{T}}$. Finally, the original data F_1 can be restored. When $dd > red$, we can obtain less than k valid data E_1' and calculate the corresponding sub-matrix B. Obviously, the number of columns of B is not equal to the number of rows of E_1', which does not satisfy the mathematical calculation of the matrix. Therefore, the data cannot be recovered.

Next, the efficiency of corrupt data recovery is briefly discussed. This article focuses on the implementation of functions and does not consider the optimal data recovery technique. Therefore, RS erasure code technology, which is easily described in [22], is selected as the coding tool in our scheme. Variety of techniques to improve the computing efficiency of erasure codes were mentioned in [22], such as optimized bit matrix design and optimized computing scheduling, reducing common XOR operations, caching management techniques and vectorization techniques. These techniques can also be similarly applied to our scheme to improve coding efficiency.

6   Conclusion

In this paper, we propose an audit scheme that supports fast location and recovery of corrupted data in the environment of dynamic group users. With our solution, group users can audit the integrity of data stored on the cloud server. Once the data uploading is corrupted, users can efficiently identify the corrupted files and recover them. Finally, the designed scheme is theoretically proved to be secure under the defined threat model.

Acknowledgment. This work was supported by National Natural Science Foundation of China (No. 61702402), Doctoral Research Funds for Northwest A&F University (No. Z1090121092), Fundamental Research Funds for the Central Universities (No. XJS211502), and Guangxi Key Laboratory of Cryptography and Information Security (No. GCIS201716).

References

1. Ateniese, G., et al.: Provable data possession at untrusted stores. In: Ning, P., di Vimercati, S.D.C., Syverson, P.F. (eds.) Proceedings of the 2007 ACM Conference on Computer and Communications Security, CCS 2007, Alexandria, Virginia, USA, 28–31 October 2007, pp. 598–609. ACM (2007)
2. Bernstein, D.J., Doumen, J., Lange, T., Oosterwijk, J.-J.: Faster batch forgery identification. In: Galbraith, S., Nandi, M. (eds.) INDOCRYPT 2012. LNCS, vol. 7668, pp. 454–473. Springer, Heidelberg (2012). https://doi.org/10.1007/978-3-642-34931-7_26
3. Gumaste, P.: Amazon AWS outage (2019). https://www.whizlabs.com/blog/amazon-aws-outage/
4. Guo, H., Zhang, Z., Xu, J., An, N., Lan, X.: Accountable proxy re-encryption for secure data sharing. IEEE Trans. Dependable Secur. Comput. **18**(1), 145–159 (2021)
5. Huo, H., Jiang, T., Tan, S., Tao, X.: Efficient public integrity auditing with secure deduplication in cloud computing. Int. J. Embed. Syst. **11**(6), 764–777 (2019). https://doi.org/10.1504/IJES.2019.103995
6. Jiang, T., Chen, X., Ma, J.: Public integrity auditing for shared dynamic cloud data with group user revocation. IEEE Trans. Computers **65**(8), 2363–2373 (2016)
7. Juels, A., Jr., B.S.K.: PORs: proofs of retrievability for large files. In: Ning, P., di Vimercati, S.D.C., Syverson, P.F. (eds.) Proceedings of the 2007 ACM Conference on Computer and Communications Security, CCS 2007, Alexandria, Virginia, USA, 28–31 October 2007, pp. 584–597. ACM (2007)
8. Li, Y., Yu, Y., Min, G., Susilo, W., Ni, J., Choo, K.R.: Fuzzy identity-based data integrity auditing for reliable cloud storage systems. IEEE Trans. Dependable Secur. Comput. **16**(1), 72–83 (2019)
9. Matt, B.J.: Identification of multiple invalid signatures in pairing-based batched signatures. In: Jarecki, S., Tsudik, G. (eds.) PKC 2009. LNCS, vol. 5443, pp. 337–356. Springer, Heidelberg (2009). https://doi.org/10.1007/978-3-642-00468-1_19
10. Pan, Y., Hu, N.: Research on dependability of cloud computing systems. In: 2014 10th International Conference on Reliability, Maintainability and Safety (ICRMS), pp. 435–439 (2014)
11. Ren, Z., Wang, L., Wang, Q., Xu, M.: Dynamic proofs of retrievability for coded cloud storage systems. IEEE Trans. Serv. Comput. **11**(4), 685–698 (2018)
12. Shacham, H., Waters, B.: Compact proofs of retrievability. In: Pieprzyk, J. (ed.) ASIACRYPT 2008. LNCS, vol. 5350, pp. 90–107. Springer, Heidelberg (2008). https://doi.org/10.1007/978-3-540-89255-7_7

13. Shen, J., Zhou, T., He, D., Zhang, Y., Sun, X., Xiang, Y.: Block design-based key agreement for group data sharing in cloud computing. IEEE Trans. Dependable Secur. Comput. **16**(6), 996–1010 (2019)

14. Shin, S., Kim, S., Kwon, T.: Identification of corrupted cloud storage in batch auditing. In: Khalil, I., Neuhold, E., Tjoa, A.M., Da Xu, L., You, I. (eds.) ICT-EurAsia 2015. LNCS, vol. 9357, pp. 221–225. Springer, Cham (2015). https://doi.org/10.1007/978-3-319-24315-3_22

15. Wang, C., Chow, S.S.M., Wang, Q., Ren, K., Lou, W.: Privacy-preserving public auditing for secure cloud storage. IEEE Trans. Comput. **62**(2), 362–375 (2013)

16. Wang, H.F., Li, Z.H., Zhang, X., Sun, J., Zhao, X.N.: Batch auditing supporting fast searching invalid files in cloud storage. Chin. J. Comput. **40**(418), 144–157 (2017)

17. Weikai, W., Lihong, R., Lei, C., Yongsheng, D.: Intrusion detection and security calculation in industrial cloud storage based on an improved dynamic immune algorithm. Inf. Sci. **501**, 543–557 (2019)

18. Wu, D., Xia, Y., Sun, X.S., Huang, X.S., Dzinamarira, S., Ng, T.S.E.: Masking failures from application performance in data center networks with shareable backup. In: Proceedings of the 2018 Conference of the ACM Special Interest Group on Data Communication, SIGCOMM 2018, Budapest, Hungary, 20–25 August 2018, pp. 176–190. ACM (2018)

19. Yu, J., Ren, K., Wang, C., Varadharajan, V.: Enabling cloud storage auditing with key-exposure resistance. IEEE Trans. Inf. Forensics Secur. **10**(6), 1167–1179 (2015)

20. Zafar, F., et al.: A survey of cloud computing data integrity schemes: design challenges, taxonomy and future trends. Comput. Secur. **65**, 29–49 (2017)

21. Zhang, Y., Yu, J., Hao, R., Wang, C., Ren, K.: Enabling efficient user revocation in identity-based cloud storage auditing for shared big data. IEEE Trans. Dependable Secur. Comput. **17**(3), 608–619 (2020)

22. Zhou, T., Tian, C.: Fast erasure coding for data storage: a comprehensive study of the acceleration techniques. In: Merchant, A., Weatherspoon, H. (eds.) 17th USENIX Conference on File and Storage Technologies, FAST 2019, Boston, MA, 25–28 February 2019, pp. 317–329. USENIX Association (2019)

A Coding Management System for Traceability of Chinese Agricultural Products Based on Blockchain

Li-Xian Jiao[1,5], Yan-Dong Yu[1,5(✉)], Yin-Bo Liu[1,5], Da An[1,5], Yu-Ge Yao[1,5], Zhu-qing Lan[2,5], Guo-jie Xie[3,5], Ting Wu[4,5], and Xiao-han Jia[1,5]

[1] Jining Normal University, Inner Mongolia 012000, China
cfssyyd@163.com
[2] Beijing Zhongsheng Huaan Information Technology Co., Ltd., Beijing 100089, China
[3] Zhejiang Key Laboratory of Open Data, Hangzhou 310000, China
[4] Hangzhou Innovation Institute, Beihang University, Hangzhou 310051, China
[5] National Engineering Laboratory for E-Commerce Transaction Technology, Baotou Big Data Research Institute, Inner Mongolia 014014, China

Abstract. In recent years, food safety has become an increasingly serious topic around the world. Problems such as pesticides, heavy metal pollution, and chemical additives in various agricultural products have attracted widespread attention. Therefore, reliable green agricultural products are urgently demanded by consumers. To this end, this paper uses item coding technology and a new generation of information technology such as blockchain to analyze the key data of the entire life cycle of green agricultural products (especially Ulanqab potatoes, oats and other geographical indication products) from growth to harvest to circulation. Blockchain trusted certificate. Through a complete traceability supervision system, product safety and quality will be improved, the market's visibility and recognition of agricultural products in the region will be enhanced, and the "quality and efficiency" of agricultural economic development will be achieved, thereby promoting the construction of smart agricultural big data projects.

Keywords: Food safety · Food traceability · Blockchain · Smart agriculture

1 Introduction

1.1 A Subsection Sample

IN recent years, with the rapid economic development and the continuous improvement of people's living standards, the quality and safety of agricultural products has become increasingly serious and has developed into a worldwide problem. For example, the "mad cow disease" incident in the UK, the "dioxin" incident in Belgium, the "poisonous cucumber" incident in Germany, the "trichloramine" incident in China. These food safety incidents made people feel worried. roughly, the causes of problems can be divided into

Y. Chenggang et al. (Eds.): MobiMedia 2022, LNICST 451, pp. 142–155, 2022.
https://doi.org/10.1007/978-3-031-23902-1_11

the following categories: 1) Chemical fertilizers, pesticides and other substances are commonly used in some vegetables and fruits; 2) Heavy metal pollution in food; 3) The use of inferior raw materials in food manufacturing and processing it poses a great risk to food safety; 4) Excessive use of food additives and other chemical products in food processing, etc. If these problems with potential safety hazards are not solved in time, they may evolve into food safety accidents that endanger consumers' health and bring irreversible consequences to consumers.

Iit is worth noting that, as a major agricultural country in the world, China's annual demand for fruits and vegetables is about 730 million tons. However, in reality, due to the backward agri-food logistics system, the annual loss rate of agri-food in china is as high as 25%–30%. The advantages of agricultural development gradually decreased. At present, although China's agricultural product supply chain system has developed rapidly in recent years, it is still in its infancy on the whole, and there are still many problems, such as the shortage of modern equipment and funds, the low level of informatization, the chaotic supervision system, and the lack of a traceable system that can be monitored. It is for these reasons that the frequent and large-scale outbreaks of food safety incidents in China make consumers a vulnerable group in the market.

At present, a variety of effective methods or standards for food safety control have been proposed, such as ISO9000 certification, GMP (Good Manufacturing Practice), SSOP (Sanitation Standard Operating Procedure), HACCP (Hazard Analysis and Critical Point Analysis System) and so on. However, these standards are for specific links, and they lack the technical means or specifications to connect the supply chain. When there is a problem in a certain link in the middle, if you want to find the source of the problem or the product information related to the problem, the above methods are not perfect.

Based on the above reasons, the main purpose of this paper is to establish a supply chain traceability system for green agricultural products (especially Ulanqab potatoes, oats and other geographical indication products) based on blockchain technology to help the agricultural product market improve food safety and quality. The rest of the paper is organized as follows. In Sect. 2, we review the relevant literature on the application of blockchain technology in agricultural supply chains in recent years. Section 3 explains the technical background of the method used in this paper. The detailed process of the proposed agricultural product supply chain traceability system is described in Sect. 4. Finally, discussions and future work appear in Sect. 5.

2 Related Work

In recent years, agri-food supply chains have been extensively studied. For example, Li et al. developed a dynamic programming model for perishable food supply chains. This method attempts to minimize the loss of agricultural products and maximize the profits of the members of the agricultural supply chain by means of the real-time product quality information of the RFID system. In order to improve the delivery system of perishable products, Wang et al. proposed a rule-based decision support system for real-time monitoring and online decision-making during the distribution of agricultural products. The system includes radio frequency identification (RFID), a sensor network and a decision rule base.

As research progresses, food traceability management has been gaining attention, as traceable food can ensure food safety for consumers. Li et al. proposed a new product tracking model and traceability method based on radio frequency identification (RFID) semantic events for the needs of product tracking and tracing in the supply chain. At the same time, they define five types of RFID business events and extensible Markup Language elements to describe the logistics status of products. In addition, the method is applied to the winery management system to improve the anti-counterfeiting and anti-change performance of products, as well as inventory management. Interest in blockchain technology has surged, especially as it is being applied to agriculture. Tian F proposes an agricultural product supply chain tracking system that utilizes RFID and blockchain technologies. By collecting, transmitting, and sharing real data on agricultural products in production, processing, warehousing, distribution, and sales, the authors bring the traceability of trusted information into the entire agricultural supply chain to ensure food safety. Kamath R looked at the case of Walmart, which used blockchain technology to address food safety issues in the supply chain in response to food contamination scandals around the world. This case study highlights the implementation of blockchain solutions in the global food ecosystem to improve safety and reduce waste. Ciccio C D et al. leveraged new opportunities to run business processes in a supply chain environment on a blockchain infrastructure to provide full traceability to their runtime formulation. Their approach retrieves information only from transactions written on-chain to track the execution of process instances. They present their findings through a realized software prototype and report challenging context of the pharmaceutical supply chain through a case study. A fully decentralized, blockchain-based traceability solution for agrofood supply chain management, called agriculture, for management, is proposed by Caro et al. the solution enables seamless integration of IoT devices that produce and consume digital data along the supply chain. They define the classic farm-to-fork case, in a given vertical, in order to effectively evaluate AgriBlockIoT. Finally, they evaluated and compared the performance of the two deployments, including latency, CPU, and network usage.

Food safety issues have attracted an increasing attention from society. In order to effectively detect and prevent food safety problems and hold them accountable, it is essential to establish a reliable traceability system. Accurately recording, sharing and tracing specific data throughout the food supply chain, including production, processing, warehousing, transportation and retailing, is one of the government's key responsibilities. Lin Q et al. proposed a food safety traceability system based on blockchain and EPC information services, and developed a prototype system. At the same time, they proposed a management framework for on-chain and off-chain data, and the data explosion problem of the IoT blockchain can be alleviated through the traceability system. In addition, enterprise-level smart contracts are designed to prevent data tampering and sensitive information leakage during information interaction between participants. The final results demonstrate the effectiveness of the method. Yuan H et al. analyzed the process of supply chain management information system and the key technologies of blockchain, and proposed a supply chain management information system collaboration mechanism from the perspective of blockchain, including process and consensus collaborative management mechanism, optimized transactions process management and blockchain system consensus, accounting, etc. On this basis, the platform architecture of the supply chain management information system under the collaborative mechanism is designed, which provides a reference path for the performance improvement and platform architecture design of the blockchain-based data transaction system. To address the problem of no access to blockchain data when private keys are lost, Ra et al. have proposed that public blockchain users can use the wallet program to recover their keys. And there are requirements on the server, which should simply recover and store the key and be resistant to malicious attacks. A password-protected secret sharing (PPSS) key recovery system is proposed by the authors, protected by a secure password from a malicious key storage server from a permissioned blockchain PBC. The reconfiguration of long-standing blockchains and byzantine fault-tolerant (BFT) systems poses fundamental security challenges. In the case of state-of-the-art proof-of-stake (PoS) blockchains, stake reconfiguration enables so-called remote attacks, which can lead to forks. Also, often BFT-based permissioned blockchain systems are reconfigured internally, making them vulnerable to similar "i'm still working here" attacks. To this end, Steinhoff S et al. proposed BMS (Blockchain/BFT Membership Service) to provide secure and dynamic reconfiguration services for BFT and blockchain systems, preventing remote and similar attacks.

Among these previous studies, the method of applying blockchain technology to achieve the traceability of different product information has received the most attention. However, few researchers have considered the importance of government regulators in product traceability mechanisms, especially for Chinese agriculture.

3   Technical Background

This section will precise discuss the key techniques covered in this paper.

3.1   The Blockchain Technology

The essence of blockchain is a technical solution for a reliable database, which is centrally maintained in a decentralized and trustless manner. This technical solution can use cryptography to create blocks through any number of nodes in the system. It's just like the name says: a blockchain. Each block contains data for all transactions in the system over a period of time, and it can create a digital format print that verifies the validity of the information and connects to the next block. There may be a large number of such blocks in the blockchain. The blocks are linked to each other in a linear (chain-like) time order, with each block containing the hash of the previous block.

Blockchain technology is a reliable database model composed of technologies such as a comprehensive consensus mechanism, cryptography principles, and smart contracts. It has security features such as decentralization, non-tampering, and traceability. It can eliminate the interference of human factors and realize the openness of the circulation process. It is transparent and targeted to solve various trust problems existing in the current traceability system, which is very suitable for the traceability of agricultural product quality. Therefore, the application of blockchain technology to the agricultural product quality traceability system mainly has the advantages of information security, information sharing, and information traceability. Applying blockchain technology to agricultural product quality traceability can give full play to the advantages of the technology, promote the stable operation of the agricultural product quality traceability system, effectively prevent human tampering and network attacks, and effectively solve the current problems in the system.

Blockchain technology combined with the Internet of Things can provide greater transparency and efficient supply chains. At present, many blockchain architectures suitable for the Internet of Things have been proposed. Based on blockchain technology, a general, scalable, and easy-to-manage IoT distributed access control system architecture is implemented. The blockchain is used to store and distribute access control information. The management center node connects multiple constraint networks to the blockchain network, solves the access expansion problem of billions of restricted devices on the Internet of Things, and effectively improves the ability to handle load. Some scholars have proposed a multi-layer secure IoT network model based on blockchain technology. By dividing the IoT into a multi-level decentralized network, and adopting blockchain technology at all levels of the network, it reduces the cost of blockchain, while retaining the high security and credibility of the blockchain.

The integration of blockchain and network improves the reliability, security and transparency of the system, but with the rapid increase in the number of IoT devices, data transmission and data calculation, the system has an increasing requirement for transmission bandwidth, calculation and response speed. As the future progresses, the scalability, storage capacity, and security issues of the system need to be further improved.

3.2 Item Coding Technology

Under normal circumstances, the so-called item code is mainly used in the creation of the relationship between an item object and a code, and when the item object is represented by a code, the code is called an identification code, and if a code is representing a certain type of item, the code is called a classification code, and if the code has a unique attribute to a certain item, the type of code is called an attribute code. In practical application, relevant units and personnel need to strengthen strict control over the application of item coding to avoid the occurrence of certain undesirable problems, and provide sufficient foundation and guarantee for the improvement of the overall economic level of the country and society.

With the emergence and popularization and application of item coding, all walks of life in China have conducted in-depth research on it. In order to meet the development needs of all walks of life, the number of coding types is also increasing. After investigating a large number of item codes, it is found that in the process of general classification of products, it is mainly based on United Nations statistics, allocating enough professional managers, and providing them with goods, services and economic activities. At the same time, with the application of the CPC, a scientific and reasonable comparison between international statistics and economics can also be made. In addition, in order to ensure the level and quality of item coding, the relevant departments have also formulated the "Commodity Name and Coding Coordination System" for establishing a commodity classification and coding system to manage import and export.

Due to technical barriers and other reasons, there are many standards for item coding and identification, a lack of uniformity, and there are very few open coding systems, among which the GS1 system is the most widely used. The China Article Numbering Center uses the GS1 system, which originated in the United States and provides accurate codes for identifying goods, services, assets and locations worldwide. These codes can be represented by barcode symbols for electronic reading required for business processes. The system overcomes the limitations of manufacturers and organizations using their coding systems or some special coding systems, and improves trade efficiency and responsiveness to customers. The GS1 system uses the Global Trade Item Code, which is also the most widely used identification code in the coding system.

4 Detailed Description of System Functions

The item coding management system realizes one item, one code, one person, one code, corresponding to the information collection of the whole process of planting from the sowing period to the fertilization period to the final harvest period of the relevant agricultural products planted by the farmer and the farmer, and realizes the coding of agricultural products set up. In terms of product coding, the information coding of geographic location, farmer and crops are set in the system, and a batch-to-coding method is adopted for crops. In the system, set up coding packages corresponding to countries, provinces, cities, farmers, agricultural products, etc., and input the information of farmers and agricultural products to generate corresponding codes for easy traceability.

4.1 System Implementation Functions and Requirements

The functional structure diagram of the item code management system is shown in Fig. 1.

In terms of product coding, the information coding of geographic location, farmer and crops is set in the system, and a batch-to-coding method is adopted for crops. In the system, set up coding packages corresponding to countries, provinces, cities, farmers, agricultural products, etc., and input the information of farmers and agricultural products to generate corresponding codes for easy traceability.

The information collection of the planting process realizes the registration of seed/seedling information, the information registration of the seeds/seedlings purchased by the farmer, and the registration of the fertilizer information used. Planting information registration realizes the registration of planting data in the growth process of farmland/greenhouse, sowing, watering, fertilization, loosening, insecticide, weeding, etc., including the registration of time, category, quantity, etc. Harvest information registration realizes the registration of the quantity and time of harvesting batches of agricultural products during the harvest period.

The farmer management realizes the farmer's real-name authentication and information maintenance, and sets the farmer's code rules and checks the types of agricultural products grown by the farmer.

4.2 Detailed Description of Functional Requirements

The system involves the following roles: 1) Farmer: Responsible for the analysis of the farm's business decisions, the management of all the farm personnel, and the tracking and management of the entire process of planting products on the farm. 2) Growers:

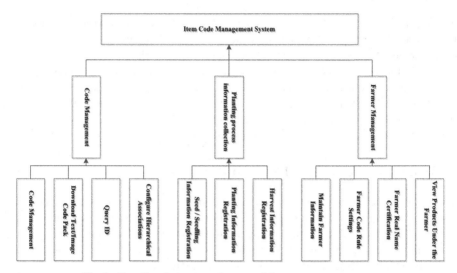

Fig. 1. Functional structure diagram of the management system

responsible for the selection, planting, irrigation and fertilization of agricultural products. 3) System administrator: responsible for system coding rule management, farm/farmer management and information maintenance, basic data maintenance (seed/seedling information registration, statistics) 4) Ordinary users: Ordinary users can log in to the system, scan the code to identify the product through the "traceability interface", and display information such as planting, fertilization, pest control, and harvesting of the product. A detailed introduction is given below.

(1) Farmer Functional Requirements

Farmer management realizes the farmer's real-name authentication and information maintenance, sets the farmer's rules, checks the types of agricultural products grown by the farmer, and collects planting process information. Among them, the maintenance of the farmer information realizes the addition of the basic information of the farmer. The real-name authentication of the farmer realizes the setting and maintenance of the basic information of the farmer's personnel. The farmer coding rule setting realizes the setting and viewing of the basic codes of the farmer's personnel, regions, and commodities.

The information collection of the planting process realizes the registration of seed/seedling information, the information registration of the seeds/seedlings purchased by the farmer, and the registration of the fertilizer information used. Planting information registration realizes the registration of planting data in the growth process of farmland/greenhouse, sowing, watering, fertilization, loosening, insecticide, weeding, etc., including the registration of time, category, quantity, etc. Harvest information registration realizes the registration of the quantity and time of harvesting batches of agricultural products during the harvest period.

The detailed management introduction is given below: 1) Base information management: Click on the plot data in the system to view the information about the crop growing plot, which can include the plot name, province, person in charge, contact number, area (mu), floor plan and other information. 2) Land preparation information: record the land preparation time, land preparation method, person in charge and other information. 3) Seedling management: Seedlings and seedlings mainly involve information on the sources of seeds produced by plants, breeding methods and sources of seedlings produced by animals. The main information includes the following: seed name, seed source, seed status, breeding method, whether it is genetic engineering, whether it has undergone chemical and radiation treatment. 4) Fertilization management: Fertilizer is an important part of agricultural production. Fertilizer management mainly collects fertilizer-related information, including fertilizer type, fertilization time, fertilized crops, fertilization amount, fertilization person and other information. 5) Irrigation management: Water is an important factor in the process of plant growth. Irrigation is one of the important processes in the planting process of agricultural products, providing sufficient water for plants. The information collected during plant irrigation includes date, duration, and person in charge, irrigation period, irrigation method, and etc. 6) Flower and fruit management: Flower and fruit management is a commonly used fruit tree management method in the growth process of fruit trees. The management measures for fruit tree flowers and fruits ensure high yield, stable yield and high quality of fruit trees, such as thinning flowers and fruits, fruit coloring, etc. Information on flowers and fruits can be collected, including specific measures, time, operators, etc. 7) Pruning and pruning: During the growth of fruit trees, pruning is performed in order to increase product yield or maintain tree shape, such as topping and topping of cotton. Collect pruning information, such as pruning date, operator, pruning method, and pruning area. 8) Pest control: Information on pest control mainly involves disease control measures for plant production and animal production, as well as drug use and management information, including the name of pests and diseases, time of occurrence, control methods, control measures, and whether chemical products are used. 9) Picking management: Picking management is mainly to determine the picking time, quantity, method (manual or mechanical) and other information in the picking process, so as to ensure that the picking information of the product can be queried in the process of product traceability. Figure 2 shows the commodity viewing interface under the farmer.

(2) Growers' Functional Requirements

The role of the grower is the role of the actual operation of the product seedlings. After the seedlings are sown, fertilized, pest and disease control, and the agricultural products are harvested, they need to log in to the system and record and register the specific operations so that people in need can view them. The role of the grower needs to log in to the system and bind it to operate. After actually operating the agricultural products at different stages in reality, enter the "scan code operation interface" to record the operation behavior.

The detailed discussion is as follows: 1) The sowing record information includes: crop code, variety name, sowing method, sowing plot number, and input of sowing method information. 2) The fertilization record information includes: crop code, fertilization time, fertilization amount, fertilizer number, fertilizer type, and the input of operator information. 3) Pest control information includes: crop

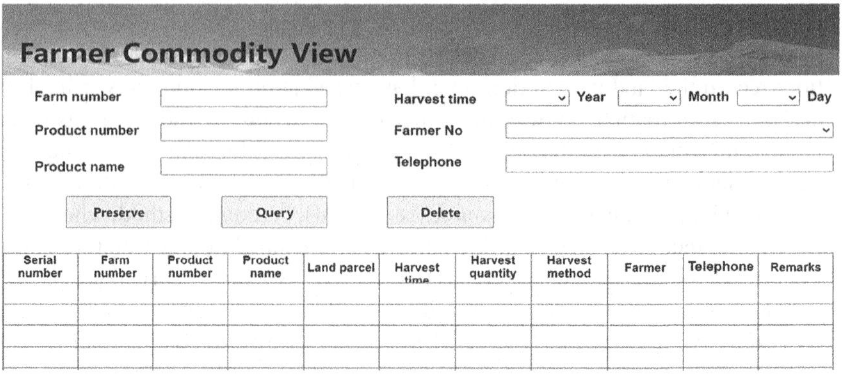

Farmer Commodity View

Farm number		Harvest time	⌄ Year	⌄ Month	⌄ Day
Product number		Farmer No			⌄
Product name		Telephone			

[Preserve]   [Query]   [Delete]

Serial number	Farm number	Product number	Product name	Land parcel	Harvest time	Harvest quantity	Harvest method	Farmer	Telephone	Remarks

Fig. 2. The farmer's commodity viewing interface

code, time, name of pests and diseases, control methods, control measures, whether drugs are used, drug number, quantity used, and input of operator information. 4) Harvest record information includes: crop code, crop name, farm, plot, harvest time, harvest batch, and harvest method. Figure 3 shows the summary page of planting process information collection.

Planting Process Information Collection

| Crop code | | Harvest time | ⌄ Year | ⌄ Month | ⌄ Day | [Query] |
| Lot No | | Product category No | | | | |

Serial No	Crop code	Crop name	Base No	Parcel name	Positi on	Land prepar ation	Land prepar ation metho d	Crop type	Seed categ ory	Warni ng sign	Transge ne marker	Breedi ng mode	Fertiliz ation metho d	Irrigati on metho d	Flower and fruit manage ment	Prune or not	Pest contro l metho ds	Wheth er chemi cals are used	Harvest quantity	Harve st meth od	Operat or	Teleph one	Remar ks

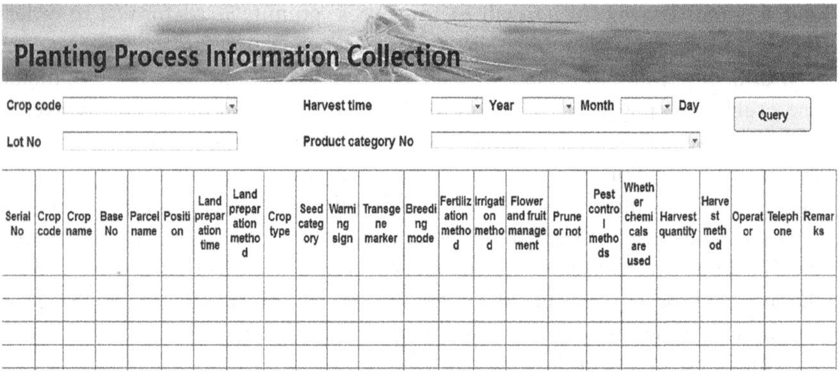

Fig. 3. Summary of planting process information collection.

(3) Administrator Functional Requirements

The general administrator role mainly has three functions: 1) The source code traceability management function can realize source code traceability type management and source code traceability group management. The traceable source code type management function can add, modify and delete different types of traceable source code according to user needs; the traceable source code group management function can check the coding rules, names, number of operations and creation time. 2) The traceability process management function can realize the management of information such as adding and modifying the traceability process. 3) Rights management functions are divided into role management and user management. The role management implements the addition, deletion, modification and query of roles, and displays the operation times, status and creation time of different roles. User management realizes user additions, deletions, changes, and permissions allocation.

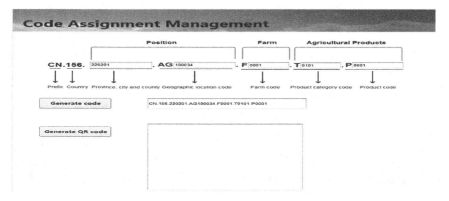

Fig. 4. Assignment management interface.

(4) System Administrator Functional Requirements

System administrators need to maintain the bottom layer of the system, and manage and maintain coding rules, farm/master information and basic data. The system administrator has three modules: coding management, farm/master management, and basic data management. The coding management module mainly completes the functions of coding rule setting, code assignment management and coding analysis. Coding rule setting mainly completes the design and definition of different types of coding rules. Code assignment management is a summary of different types of code sets. Different data combinations can generate different codes and QR codes, as shown in the Fig. 4 shown. The code analysis uses the "code analysis interface" (as shown in the Fig. 5) to scan and identify the QR code, and displays the code through the "code analysis result interface" (as shown in the Fig. 6), and parses the code in the form of text.

The farm/master management module mainly completes the maintenance and statistics of farm information and farmer information data. The farm information maintenance function realizes the maintenance of farm information data, mainly including the modification and deletion of the farm name, farm number, farm owner name, contact address, planting crop types and planting area information; the farm information list is a list display module for farm information. The farm information in the system can be displayed more intuitively and quickly; the farmer's real-name authentication function is to record the farmer's personal information, mainly including the farmer's name, contact information, contact address, ID number and other information.

The basic data management module realizes the management and maintenance of basic data. It mainly includes the management and maintenance of seed/seedling information, land identification information, drug information, and fertilizer information. The seed/seedling information registration interface can add, delete, and

Fig. 5. Code analysis interface.

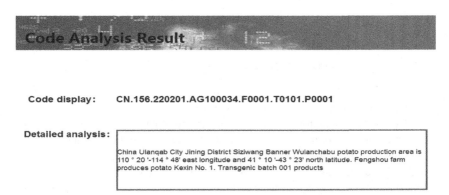

Fig. 6. Code analysis result interface.

modify information such as product type number, seed number, seed category number, etc. The seed/seedling information statistics interface is a list display module for seed/seedling information, and you can also directly query certain information through this module. Specific seed/seedling information; the land information registration interface can add, delete, or modify information such as land number, plot name, province, city, etc. The land information statistics interface is a list display module for land information, and you can also use this module Directly query a specific land information; the drug information registration interface can add, delete, or modify information such as drug number, drug name, functional category, and technical registration. The drug information statistics interface is a list display module for drug information, which can also be Directly query a specific drug information; the fertilizer information registration interface can add, delete, or modify information such as fertilizer number, fertilizer name, nutrient type, and character. The fertilizer information statistics interface is a list display module for fertilizer information, and you can directly Inquire about a specific fertilizer information.

(5) Code Management

Coding management implements coding application management and review and release management. Coding application management includes manual application and automatic application. The main function of manual code management to realize the manual application code is that when the user is familiar with the code, the user can directly fill in the content of the first seven digits of the code, and the system automatically extracts the company code from the registration form. After the code is obtained, the system will automatically parse the obtained code, so that the user can know whether the code he entered meets the code he needs. When saving the code, the system will also prompt whether to fill in the attributes of the code. After entering the seven-digit code (only seven digits are allowed in the input box), you must press the Enter key to end, so as to trigger the operation of the system. After getting the code, the user is not allowed to modify it. If you want to modify it, you must click the clear button and then re-fill it. Users can only fill in the codes assigned to their own rules. If they are not within the scope of their own rules, the system will pop up a dialog box indicating that the applied codes exceed the assigned rules. If the entered code does not conform to the encoding rules, a dialog box will pop up to prompt the user that the entered code is incorrect and the code cannot be parsed correctly. Please re-enter a new code. Figure 7 shows the interface of encoding rule setting. Automatic code generation management requires selecting code rules, filling in the corresponding code information, and the system automatically obtains the number corresponding to the code package, thereby generating a new code.

Code review enables code managers to manage the codes that designers have submitted for applications, including review and release. First, make a logical judgment on the coding that has been applied for. The logical judgment is only to judge whether the coding conforms to the rules according to the coding rules. For the coding that conforms to the coding rules through logical judgment, the system will fill in "Y" in the column of "Pass", otherwise Is empty. For codes that conform to the coding rules and the coding administrator thinks that they cannot be applied for, the system will pop up a dialog box to ask for the reason for not applying, and the

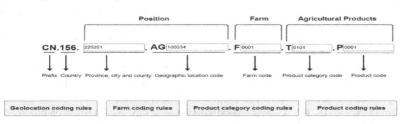

Fig. 7. Setting of encoding rules.

system will automatically return the codes to the applicant for processing. If there is no problem with the coding, right-click and click to go to the review status in the pop-up menu, then these codes have passed the review and are waiting to be published. For a code that has been released, the system does not allow deletion of the code, but can only be abolished.

5 Conclusion

This paper shows that blockchain technology can help us build a verified and trusted environment for transparent and more sustainable food production and distribution that integrates key stakeholders into the supply chain. However, there are still many problems and challenges. Therefore, the government is advised to lead by example and promote the digitalization of public administration. In the future, more enabling technologies in the agri-food chain should be encouraged and popularized so that the agri-food supply chain remains sustainable and well-competitive.

References

1. Lin, J., Shen, Z., Zhang, A., et al.: Blockchain and IoT based food traceability for smart agriculture. In: Proceedings of the 3rd International Conference on Crowd Science and Engineering, pp. 1–6 (2018)
2. Qin, Y.M., Kong, D.L., Li, S.: China cold-chain logistics development report, p. 116ll7. China Fortune Press, Beijing (2014)
3. Tian, F.: An agri-food supply chain traceability system for China based on RFID & blockchain technology. In: 2016 13th International Conference on Service Systems and Service Management (ICSSSM), pp. 1–6. IEEE (2016)
4. Li, D., Kehoe, D., Drake, P.: Dynamic planning with a wireless product identification technology in food supply chains. Int. J. Adv. Manuf. Technol. **30**(9), 938–944 (2006)
5. Wang, L., Kwok, S.K., Lp, W.H.: A radio frequency identification and sensor-based system for the transportation of food. J. Food Eng. **1**(01), 120–129 (2010)
6. Li, M.B., Jin, Z.X., Chen, C.: Application of RFID on products tracking and tracing system. Comput. Integr. Manuf. Syst. **16**(1), 202–208 (2010)
7. Tian, F.: A supply chain traceability system for food safety based on HACCP, blockchain & Internet of Things. In: 2017 International Conference on Service Systems and Service Management, pp. 1–6. IEEE (2017)
8. Kamath, R.: Food traceability on blockchain: Walmart's pork and mango pilots with IBM. J. Br. Blockchain Assoc. **1**(1), 3712 (2018)
9. Di Ciccio, C., et al.: Blockchain-based traceability of inter-organisational business processes. In: Shishkov, B. (eds.) Business Modeling and Software Design. BMSD 2018. Lecture Notes in Business Information Processing, vol. 319. Springer, Cham (2018). https://doi.org/10.1007/978-3-319-94214-8_4
10. Caro, M.P., Ali, M.S., Vecchio, M., et al.: Blockchain-based traceability in agri-food supply chain management: a practical implementation. In: 2018 IoT Vertical and Topical Summit on Agriculture-Tuscany (IOT Tuscany), pp. 1–4. IEEE (2018)
11. Lin, Q., Wang, H., Pei, X., et al.: Food safety traceability system based on blockchain and EPCIS. IEEE Access **7**, 20698–20707 (2019)

12. Yuan, H., Qiu, H., Bi, Y., et al.: Analysis of coordination mechanism of supply chain management information system from the perspective of block chain. IseB **18**(4), 681–703 (2020)
13. Ra, G.J., Roh, C.H., Lee, I.Y.: A key recovery system based on password-protected secret sharing in a permissioned blockchain. Comput. Mater. Contin. **65**(1), 153–170 (2020)
14. Steinhoff, S., Stathakopoulou, C., Pavlovic, M., et al.: BMS: secure decentralized reconfiguration for blockchain and BFT Systems. arXiv preprint arXiv:2109.03913 (2021)
15. Ding, Q., Gao, S., Zhu, J., et al.: Permissioned blockchain-based double-layer framework for product traceability system. IEEE Access **8**, 6209–6225 (2019)
16. Maroufi, M., Abdolee, R., Tazekand, B.M.: On the convergence of blockchain and Internet of Things (IoT) technologies. arXiv preprint arXiv:1904.01936 (2019)
17. Hua, J., Wang, X., Kang, M., et al.: Blockchain based provenance for agricultural products: a distributed platform with duplicated and shared bookkeeping. In: 2018 IEEE Intelligent Vehicles Symposium (IV), pp. 97–101. IEEE (2018)

Blockchain Traceability Platform Based on Green Agricultural Products

Xiao Tian[1], Yu-Ge Yao[1]([⊠]), Hui-Tong Xu[1], Ying-Jie Xie[1], Li-Jie Wei[2], Guo-jie Xie[3], Ting Wu[4], and Yan-Wei Gao[1]

[1] Jining Normal University, Ulanqab 012000, Inner Mongolia, China
yaoyuge@163.com
[2] Baotou Big Data Research Institute, National Engineering Laboratory for E-Commerce Transaction Technology, Baotou 014014, Inner Mongolia, China
[3] Zhejiang Key Laboratory of Open Data, Hangzhou 310000, China
[4] Hangzhou Innovation Institute, Beihang University, Hangzhou 310051, China

Abstract. This paper designs and completes a blockchain traceability platform based on green agricultural products. Using item coding technology, cryptography technology, blockchain, big data and other new generation information technologies, green agricultural products (especially Ulanqab potatoes, oats and other geographical indication products) from growth to harvest to circulation throughout the life cycle. The key data can be trusted and stored in the blockchain, providing consumers with real-time agricultural product traceability query services, and providing agricultural and animal husbandry departments with effective agricultural product quality and safety supervision and management mechanisms and means. With the help of QR code as the mobile Internet entrance, link online and offline, design O2O e-commerce transaction system, form a closed loop of planting, traceability and sales, digitally control the quality of authentic agricultural products, and empower the brand value of agricultural products. Realize the whole chain supervision of green products from planting source to circulation through a perfect traceability system, improve product safety and quality, enhance the market's popularity and recognition of agricultural products in the region, form effective protection of agricultural product geographical indication products, and achieve agricultural economic development "Increase quality and efficiency", and then promote the construction of smart agricultural big data projects.

Keywords: BlockChain · Software platform · Big data technology · Smart agriculture

1   Research and Development

This project has designed and completed a blockchain traceability software platform based on green agricultural products. Use big data technology to complete the intelligent collection and convenient sharing of agricultural data in stages, and then promote the construction of smart agricultural data projects. With the help of item coding technology,

Y. Chenggang et al. (Eds.): MobiMedia 2022, LNICST 451, pp. 156–164, 2022.
https://doi.org/10.1007/978-3-031-23902-1_12

each agricultural product is given a unique label to record the key data information about the whole process of green agricultural products from planting, harvesting, processing, packaging, circulation, warehousing and retailing. At the same time, consumers can check and verify products by scanning the code. The whole process of traceability information, a comprehensive understanding of product information, to achieve peace of mind consumption. And the design of the O2O e-commerce transaction system solves the problem of unsalable agricultural products, creates a brand marketing strategy for green agricultural products, and expands marketing channels. Realize digital control of the quality of authentic agricultural products; empower the brand value of agricultural products.

Specifically include the following:

1. Item code management system. Through the code management of people, places and things, the end-to-end one-code communication is realized, and the brand of origin and the reputation of products are escorted.
2. Item traceability management system. Define the key data in the planting and circulation links, and perform trusted storage and query in the blockchain distributed ledger.
3. O2O e-commerce transaction system. Realize the e-commerce transaction of agricultural products and the scanning and tracing of the products by customers. From the in-depth development of "Internet + agriculture", the origin and sales of agricultural products are closely linked, which not only shortens the supply chain and saves the logistics costs of farmers and e-commerce enterprises, but also achieves information sharing, which is beneficial for the people involved in the transaction. Information can be exchanged. As an important entrance to the mobile Internet, QR code links online and offline, which can help the rapid promotion of agricultural products, and a perfect traceability system can realize the whole chain supervision of products from the source of planting to sales, channels, warehousing, logistics, etc., effectively Improve safety and quality. Brand + quality double promotion can better enhance the market's recognition of agricultural products and achieve rapid sales.

2 Technical Route

2.1 Platform Design Ideas

The system adopts a general and mature software framework, has many successful application cases and provides flexible customization functions, which can be set to meet most personalized needs in data management, data analysis, visualization, etc.; the system should also have high The reliability of the system ensures the correctness of the data and the stability of the system operation, without data loss, software errors and system crashes.

The system adopts a micro-service architecture design, which can easily expand and upgrade the system. As long as a simple operation is performed, new functional modules can be easily added to the software interface. When a module has an upgraded version, the module can be replaced by itself. Yes, it does not affect the normal use of other functions.

2.2 Platform Design Principles

Platform Openness and Practicality. In the system construction, the principle of openness should be fully considered, and various corresponding software and hardware interfaces should be supported to make them flexible and extensible. The system should be an open and flexible platform, with various data collection and conversion methods, flexible index analysis model construction, allowing multiple data sources and data sharing and exchange.

The system should strive to meet the actual work needs to the greatest extent, fully consider the practicability of data processing at each business level and each management link, and consider satisfying the user's work and management business as the first element. It enables administrators to maintain some roles and organizations involved in the system, and supports a multi-level administrator management mechanism. Users can regularly and irregularly maintain their passwords. The whole project starts from the practical point of view, provides services according to the actual needs of users, and focuses on the practicality of the business.

On the premise of ensuring the practicability of the system, the security, upgradeability, platform independence and scalability of the system are maximized. The software and hardware systems selected in the project construction can be easily integrated, so that the application system can reduce the difficulty and requirements of system maintenance, and it is also convenient for users to apply and manage in the future.

Functional Scalability and Compatibility. Taking into account the increase of users and business expansion, the expansion of the system scale, the protection of investment and the specific situation of step-by-step implementation, the system design should take into account the use of current existing resources, and consider the subsequent expansion and maintenance requirements. The system can not only meet current needs, but also meet future development.

Adopt systems and products that follow international standards to facilitate interconnection and expansion with third-party systems, and easy migration to future advanced technologies. An advanced and mature big data architecture generally adopts a component-based and object-oriented design, encapsulates each functional module as a service in layers, reflects the characteristics of a loosely coupled architecture, and ensures the expansion and upgrade of the system in the future. Good scalability often adopts a three-tier architecture. With the gradual improvement of the application and the gradual increase in the amount of information, it is continuously expanded, and the entire system can smoothly transition to the new upgraded system to achieve continuous data scale. Accumulation, continuous upgrade of services and continuous expansion of application scale. Compatibility and scalability are mutually reinforcing. For example, for the models and versions of different browsers on the market (including multi-core browsers such as IE kernel, Chrome kernel, Firefox, firefox), as well as projector resolutions as small as 4k screen resolutions, use the window ratio as the unit The interface layout, when stretching and shrinking, realizes full-scale scaling. This interface-independent technology is an important basis for compatibility and scalability.

System Stability and Security. The software and information resources in the system must meet the reliability design requirements, adopt stable and reliable mature technology, improve the ability of error prevention and error resistance, and ensure that the platform software should have stability, reliability and fault tolerance. The system has a reliable backup and recovery mechanism to ensure rapid recovery of system operation in the event of a system failure.

The security function design adopts hierarchical authorization, data hierarchical and hierarchical management, and pays attention to data security. At the same time, fully consider the security requirements of the network, operating system, database, application, etc. When the system is designed, there are sufficient security measures, such as strict authority management for information access and use, unified identity management, technically providing a login authentication method combined with digital certificates, and supporting the combination with security authentication to ensure the entire system. Safe and reliable. System security is ensured by means of authority classification, SMS verification, and encryption of important information.

User Operability and Maintainability. Ease of operation is reflected in zero requirements for the technical foundation of business personnel. The system has a good man-machine interface, implements the principle of facing the end user, and establishes a friendly user interface. The application interface design on the Web and mobile device App clients conforms to a flat and minimalist style, and the operation is simple, intuitive, flexible, and easy to learn., Easy to use and easy to maintain. The interface style and operation process of all business functions are consistent, in line with business process requirements and usage habits.

Maintainability is reflected in intelligent, visualized, and remote maintenance capabilities. The maintenance terminal has a system configuration interface, which reduces the need to manually modify the code in the background, adopts the technology that can be repaired in time to avoid system restart, uses the system log record to provide effective error reporting and positioning information, supports the addition of new modules during the maintenance period, and provides friendly to other related systems. Interface, etc.

2.3   Development Language Selection

Select Java and Go as the development language, and Node.js as the runtime environment. Java is an object-oriented programming language.

Therefore, the Java language has two characteristics: powerful functions and simplicity and ease of use. Java has the characteristics of simplicity, object orientation, distribution, robustness, security, platform independence and portability, multithreading, and dynamism. Java can write desktop applications, web applications, distributed systems and embedded system applications. Go (also known as Golang) is a statically strongly typed, compiled language developed by Robert Griesemer, Rob Pike, and Ken Thompson of Google.

Go language syntax is similar to C, but the functions include: memory safety, GC (garbage collection), structural form and CSP-style concurrent computing. Node.js is a

JavaScript runtime environment based on the Chrome V8 engine. Node.js uses an event-driven, non-blocking I/O model, making it lightweight and efficient. Npm, the package manager for Node.js, is the world's largest ecosystem of open source libraries.

2.4 Database Selection

This project adopts an application based on the Redis + MySQL + MongoDB storage architecture. The technical architecture of Redis + MySQL + MongoDB fulfills the requirements of big data storage and real-time cloud computing in this project. Using the horizontal dynamic addition of MongoDB slices can ensure the query speed and cloud computing performance after expansion without interrupting the platform business system; index slices according to slice keys, and perform calculations independently in each slice, making real-time analysis under big data a reality. Reality. The data that is frequently accessed is placed in Redis, which reduces disk I/O, makes the business system more agile, and meets the high demand of application services under high concurrency.

2.5 System Functional Structure

The blockchain traceability platform based on green agricultural products includes three subsystems: item coding management system, item traceability management system, and O2O e-commerce transaction system. The functional structure diagram of the system is shown in Fig. 1.

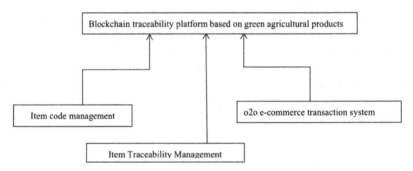

Fig. 1. System main function structure diagram.

Item Code Management System. The functional structure diagram of the item code management system is shown in Fig. 2 and Fig. 3. The item coding management system realizes one item, one code, one person, the code, corresponding to the information collection of the whole process of planting from the sowing period to the fertilization period to the final harvest period of the relevant agricultural products planted by the farmer and the farmer, and realizes the coding of agricultural products. Set up. Set two user roles of administrator and farmer.

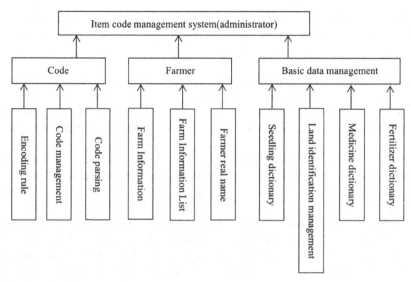

Fig. 2. Functional structure diagram of the item code management subsystem (administrator).

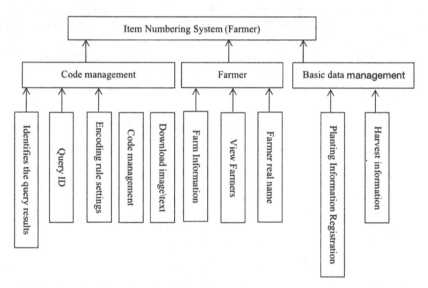

Fig. 3. Functional structure diagram of item code management subsystem (farmer).

Coding management implements coding rule setting, code assignment management and coding analysis management. And realize the identification query display and the download management of the code package.

Farm/owner management realizes the maintenance of farm and farmer information, and realizes the real-name authentication of the farmer. The basic data management function enables administrators to maintain dictionaries such as seeds/seedlings, land identification, medicines, fertilizers And realize the registration of planting information and harvesting information by farmers. The registration of harvest information means the registration of relevant information on the harvest of agricultural products.

Item Traceability Management System. Item traceability management realizes customer scan code traceability and traceability service management. In this system, a distributed ledger and a blockchain browser are designed to complete the traceability management of items. The implementation of the traditional agricultural product traceability system relies on centralized storage, and the data is opaque and easy to be tampered with. However, the existing blockchain traceability system is segregate with the demand for traceability of agricultural products, and the management and query of large-scale traceability information are relatively low. In this project, the blockchain traceability scheme of agricultural products alliance is based on the Hyperledger Fabric framework, on the basis of ensuring the credibility of traceability, according to the characteristics of agricultural product traceability process and alliance blockchain technology, the system architecture and chain operation method are designed to improve large-scale data. The speed of uploading and querying makes it meet the needs of agricultural product traceability applications.

O2O e-Commerce Transaction System. Design O2O e-commerce transaction function and coding query function. The O2O e-commerce transaction function realizes the function of opening a mall for farmers/farmers or enterprises, can maintain the information of agricultural products, and realize the online and offline of the products, and can realize the management of e-commerce transaction orders and the tracking of warehousing and logistics. Customers can scan the code to trace agricultural products, manage

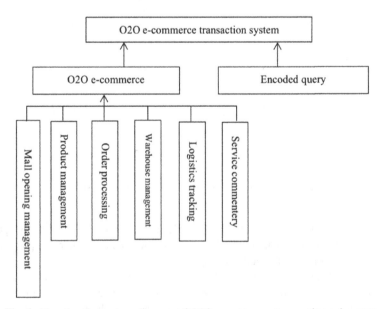

Fig. 4. Functional structure diagram of O2O e-commerce transaction subsystem.

the entire supply chain cycle from sowing to harvesting to warehousing, ordering trans-actions and logistics tracking. The functional structure diagram of the system is shown in Fig. 4.

3 Key Points and Innovation Points

The blockchain traceability platform based on green agricultural products includes three subsystems: item coding management system, item traceability management system, and O2O e-commerce transaction system, which can help agricultural customers realize the informatization of all aspects of production, sales, management, and government monitoring. Improve management level and improve efficiency.

1. Realize the traceability of agricultural product information. Agricultural product traceability can track agricultural products, from the origin to the consumer, all the way to trace the product life track. Just through a corresponding traceable source code, consumers can take out their mobile phones to scan, and then they can obtain the relevant information about the agricultural products, so that consumers can rest assured.
2. To achieve efficient supply chain management. In the past, circulation of agricultural products, due to the opaqueness of information, inventory often accumulated, which led to quality problems of agricultural products over a long period of time. Through the agricultural product traceability system, we can clearly understand the process of agricultural product circulation, run supply chain management, and avoid the occurrence of agricultural product inventory. Accumulation or deficiency occurs.
3. Use coding technology to achieve end-to-end one-code communication. To solve the identification of "people", "land" and "things" that cannot be tampered with, the key growth information of crops is collected through two-dimensional codes in the production process, and the credible and stored data are verified through two-dimensional codes in the circulation process.

4 Summarize

This paper uses the following technologies, blockchain technology. The use of blockchain technology stores the data or information in it have the characteristics of "unforgeable", "full traces", "traceable", "open and transparent" and "collective main-tenance". Item code management system. Through the code management of people, places and objects, the end-to-end one-code communication can be realized, and the information collection, upload and query of agricultural products can be realized by scanning. Item traceability management system. The links required for traceability and the level of detail of the information of each link can be defined according to different crop types and the actual needs of local traceability. The key data is stored in the dis-tributed ledger, which can be verified by the transaction hash in the blockchain browser. O2O e-commerce transaction system.It covers e-commerce modules such as agricultural product category management, commodity management, order management, payment management, and comment management.

Through the demonstration application of this project, agricultural production institutions can create a closed loop of green agricultural products from planting to sales. The key data is stored through the features of blockchain decentralization and non-tampering, so as to reduce the harm caused by fake agricultural products on the market and shoddy products to the planting industry in Ulanqab, and form the protection of geographical indications of agricultural products in the region. Increase economic benefits through direct brand purchases of specific consumer groups on e-commerce platforms.

Use big data technology to complete the intelligent collection and convenient sharing of agricultural data in stages, and then promote the construction of smart agricultural big data projects. Using two-dimensional code technology and blockchain authentication technology, timely collection and upload of agricultural product quality data from growth to sales of agricultural products, providing consumers with timely agricultural product quality and safety traceability query services, and providing agricultural and animal husbandry departments with effective agricultural products Quality and safety supervision and management mechanisms and means. Build an O2O e-commerce transaction system, increase the trading channels of green agricultural products, enhance the market's recognition of agricultural products, realize the rapid sales of the products, and realize digital control of the quality of authentic agricultural products; empower the brand value of the products.

References

1. Christidis, K., Devetsikiotis, M.: Blockchains and smart contracts for the internet of things. Journal. IEEE Access **4**, 2292–2303 (2016)
2. Marc, P.: Blockchain Technology: Principles and Applications. Journal. Post-Print (2016)
3. Yermack, D.: Corporate Governance and Blockchains. Journal. Social Science Electronic Publishing **21**(1), 7–31 (2015)
4. Catalini, C., Gans, J.S.: Some simple economics of the Blockchain. Journal. SSRN Electronic Journal (2016)
5. Underwood, S.: Blockchain beyond Bitcoin. Journal. Communications of the ACM **59**(11), 15–17 (2016)
6. Cachin, C., Vukoli, M.: Blockchain Consensus Protocols in the Wild (Keynote Talk). Journal. (2017)
7. Ouaddah, A., et al.: FairAccess: a new Blockchain-based access control framework for the Internet of Things. Journal. Security and Communication Networks 9(18) (2017)
8. Zhu, K.: Assumption of E-commerce Platform of Agricultural Products Based on F2C2B Mode. Journal. 2022(4)

FPPNet: Fast Privacy-Preserving Neural Network via Three-Party Arithmetic Secret Sharing

Renwan Bi[1] , Jinbo Xiong[1(✉)] , Qi Li[2,3] , Ximeng Liu[4] ,
and Youliang Tian[5]

[1] Fujian Provincial Key Laboratory of Network Security and Cryptology, College of
Computer and Cyber Security, Fujian Normal University, Fuzhou 350117, China
jbxiong@fjnu.edu.cn

[2] School of Computer Science, Nanjing University of Posts and Telecommunications,
Nanjing 210023, China
liqics@njupt.edu.cn

[3] Key Laboratory of Cryptography of Zhejiang Province, Hangzhou Normal
University, Hangzhou 311121, China

[4] Key Laboratory of Information Security of Network Systems, College of
Mathematics and Computer Science, Fuzhou University, Fuzhou 350108, China

[5] State Key Laboratory of Public Big Data, College of Computer Science and
Technology, Guizhou University, Guiyang 550025, China

Abstract. Jointing multi-source data for model training can improve
the accuracy of neural network. To solve the raising privacy concerns
caused by data sharing, data are generally encrypted and outsourced to
a group of cloud servers for computing and processing. In this client-cloud
architecture, we propose FPPNet, a fast and privacy-preserving neural
network for secure inference on sensitive data. FPPNet is deployed in
three cloud servers, who collaboratively execute privacy computing via
three-party arithmetic secret sharing. We develop the secure conversion
method between additive shares and multiplicative shares, and propose
three secure protocols to calculate non-linear functions, such as comparison, exponent and division that are superior to prior three-party works.
Some secure modules for running convolutional, ReLU, max-pooling and
Sigmoid layers are designed to implement FPPNet. We theoretically analyze the security and complexity of the proposed protocols. With MNIST
dataset and two types of neural networks, experimental results validate
that our FPPNet is faster than the related works, and the accuracy is
the same as that of plaintext neural network.

Keywords: Privacy-preserving · Neural network · Secure computing ·
Arithmetic secret sharing · Privacy computing

1 Introduction

In recent years, machine learning (ML) research has made continuous breakthroughs, such as neural network (NN) model, and has been widely used in

Y. Chenggang et al. (Eds.): MobiMedia 2022, LNICST 451, pp. 165–178, 2022.
https://doi.org/10.1007/978-3-031-23902-1_13

intelligent Internet of Things, medical care, connected autonomous vehicles [1] and other scenarios, profoundly changing the life style of people. For example, the model trained from a large amount of medical data can provide valuable predictive services to assist physicians in making more accurate diagnosis. Although advances in technologies such as cloud computing have made big data processing and model training more efficient, jointing multi-source data remains a major challenge. The data with characteristic of sensitivity and confidentiality are important assets of clients or organizations. Data sharing and union in the plaintext environment raise privacy concerns among data owners [2].

Privacy-preserving neural network based on secure multi-party computing (MPC) offers a promising solution [3]. Each independent client encrypted and outsourced their data to a group of cloud servers, who collaboratively execute neural network computing and process on joint data view, without disclosing any information beyond the results [4]. Outsourced cloud computing can effectively alleviate the clients' resource bottleneck. However, how to realize the correct and efficient computing over encrypted data is faced with great challenges [5]. At present, researchers combine cloud computing and MPC primitives, such as garbled circuit (GC), oblivious transfer (OT), secret sharing (SS), to construct some privacy-preserving schemes, mainly consisting of two types of two-party and multi-party settings. These schemes have achieved pretty great effect in the aspects of security, accuracy and overhead. It is worth mentioning that recent FALCON [6] is several orders of magnitude faster than the SecureML [3]. This is a favorable trend, whereas, the existing MPC protocol is still difficult to be deployed in large-scale applications with the reason of high-level computational and communication complexity. Therefore, we further devote to improving the efficiency of privacy computing without compromising security.

The motivations mainly include the following three parts. (i) On the two-party setting, the secure multiplication protocol using beaver triple [7] requires vast memory space, and the computational cost linearly increases with input data size. In contrast, the multiplication calculation no longer requires pre-computing triples and interaction when extended to the three-party setting [8]. (ii) The conversions among arithmetic, boolean and Yao shares require extra overhead in ABY3 [8], and inspired by FALCON [6], adopting only arithmetic secret sharing (ASS) can realize secure and efficient computing protocols. (iii) The secure design of non-linear functions, such as division and exponent, is frequently approximated by low-order polynomials and lacks a general non-linear calculation method [6,9].

On the basis of the above observations, the contributions of this paper are summarized as follows.

- We propose FPPNet, that clients randomly split their data into three shares and outsource them to a group of severs, and severs collaboratively execute neural network inference without compromising the privacy of uploaded data and intermediate results.
- We develop a general non-linear computing method by switching between additive and multiplicative shares, and design secure comparison, secure expo-

nent and secure division protocols, as well as securely realize ReLU, max-pooling and Sigmoid layers embedded in neural network.
– We analyze the security of the proposed secure computing protocols, and the computational and communication complexity are superior to the prior three-party works. Experimental results with MNIST dataset, validate that the runtime of our FPPNet is faster than the related works, and the accuracy is the same as that of the plaintext neural network.

The rest of this paper is organized as follows. In Sect. 2, we introduce the related works. The server-aided model and security model are presented in Sect. 4. Next, we discuss the design of basic secure computing protocols and the implementation of FPPNet in Sects. 3 and 5. Theoretical analysis and experimental results are described in Sects. 6 and 7 respectively. Lastly, we conclude the main work in Sect. 8.

2   Related Work

Privacy-preserving neural network based on MPC has been the hot research issues, including two-party and multi-party schemes.

Two-Party Schemes. Mohasse *et al.* [3] first proposed a privacy-preserving neural network SecureML scheme based on 2PC protocol [10], using beaver triple [7] and OT to perform multiplication and comparison operations, respectively. DeepSecure [11] adopted GC to compute and inference over encrypted data. MiniONN [12] removed some overhead to the offline phase, effectively improving the performance of DeepSecure. Additionally, some mixed-protocol frameworks executed in two non-collusive servers setting have been proposed, such as Chameleon [13], GAZELLE [14], DELPHI [15]. However, they are not easy to expand, because of the existence of computation-intensive cryptographic primitives. Huang *et al.* [16] proposed a lightweight privacy-preserving CNN feature extraction framework leveraging the additive SS, and obtained the good effect in terms of efficiency.

Multi-party Schemes. In order to overcome the offline storage problem of beaver triple, ABY3 [8] adopted $(2, 3)$-sharing, that each party possesses two shares of three shares, to design a non-interactive multiplication protocol. Also, ABY3 realized the secure conversion between Cleartexts and three types of arithmetic, boolean, and Yao sharing, so as to compute using the suitable sharing type. SecureNN [9] designed an effective and secure comparison protocol, which transformed the most significant bit (MSB) in even ring into the least significant bit (LSB) in odd ring. ASTRA [17] is a 3PC scheme with semi-honest security, which abandons some expensive GC protocol and prefix adder in works [3,8]. On the basis, BLAZE [18] has the stronger guarantee of fairness, and tolerates one of the three parties being malicious. Wagh *et al.* [6] proposed FALCON, an honest-majority secure 3PC framework supporting privacy-preserving deep neural network training, which realize the non-linear operation just using ASS instead of the sharing conversion. Furthermore, FLASH [19] and Trident [20] introduce the fourth party to evaluate the behavior of each participant in the protocols, aiming to resist the potential attacks.

Inspired by ABY3 [8] and FALCON [6], we design a fast privacy-preserving neural network (FPPNet) leveraging only the three-party ASS, and devolop a general non-linear computing method by switching between additive shares and multiplicative shares.

3 Problem Statement

We consider a server-aided setting where the clients Us outsource the computation to three honest but curious (HbC) servers S_1, S_2 and S_3, so as to realize privacy-preserving neural network on outsourced data. It contains the following steps.

Setting. Us secretly share their data based on ASS and upload them to S_1, S_2 and S_3. No assumptions are made about the distribution of data, and we only split each value (e.g., the pixels of image data) into three shares in an addition manner.

Computing. Using the trained model, S_1, S_2 and S_3 collaboratively execute secure protocols and model inference over the received data shares. The real inference results can be recovered through simply adding three shares.

Also, we consider that dividing the power of cloud into three parts and allocating to three non-collusive servers. Similar to the semi-trusted model in FALCON [6], we assume an adversary $\mathcal{A}$ who can corrupt at most one of S_1, S_2 and S_3 and obtain the corresponding information. The raw data and intermediate results are private to Us and cannot be known by S_1, S_2 or S_3; while the trained model is private to servers [21]. Our goal is to realize correct privacy-preserving neural network inference while satisfying the privacy constraints of each entity.

4 Basic Protocols

4.1 Concepts and Descriptions

ASS is the addition and multiplication calculation in the form of shares. Due to the advantage of 3PC multiplication in ABY3 [8], we adopt 2-out-of-3 ASS (i.e., $(2,3)$-share) to split data. A secret u is randomly split into three shares $[u]_1$, $[u]_2$ and $[u]_3$ such that $u = [u]_1 + [u]_2 + [u]_3$, each server S_i $(i \in \{1,2,3\})$ holds 2-out-of-3 shares $([u]_i, [u]_{i+1})$. Note that, if $i = 3$, then $i + 1 = (i + 1)$ mod $3 = 1$; and if $i = 1$, then $i - 1 = (i - 1)$ mod $3 = 3$. In other word, any two servers (e.g., S_1 and S_2) can recover the real secret u. Except of additive shares $[u]_i$, we define the multiplicative shares $\langle v \rangle_i$, such that $v = \langle v \rangle_1 \cdot \langle v \rangle_2 \cdot \langle v \rangle_3$. Next, we introduce some preliminary protocols [6], as follows.

$\Pi_{Zeroshare}$: Random 3-out-of-3 additive shares $[\alpha]_1$, $[\alpha]_2$, and $[\alpha]_3$ such that $[\alpha]_1 + [\alpha]_2 + [\alpha]_3 = 0$, S_i holds $[\alpha]_i$. The random shares are generated by psuedo-random function (PRF).

$\Pi_{Oneshare}$: Random 3-out-of-3 multiplicative shares $\langle\beta\rangle_1$, $\langle\beta\rangle_2$, and $\langle\beta\rangle_3$ such that $\langle\beta\rangle_1 \cdot \langle\beta\rangle_2 \cdot \langle\beta\rangle_3 = 1$, S_i holds $\langle\beta\rangle_i$.

Π_{Mul}: To calculate $f = u \cdot v$, such that $u = [u]_1+[u]_2+[u]_3$, $v = [v]_1+[v]_2+[v]_3$ and $f = [f]_1 + [f]_2 + [f]_3$, S_i locally calculates 3-out-of-3 additive share $[f]_i \leftarrow [u]_i \cdot [v]_i + [u]_{i+1} \cdot [v]_i + [u]_i \cdot [v]_{i+1}$. To strengthen the randomness of output, invoking one time of $\Pi_{Zeroshare}$, S_i locally calculates $[f]_i \leftarrow [f]_i + [\alpha]_i$. Then, S_i obtains 2-out-of-3 shares $([f]_i, [f]_{i+1})$ by receiving $[f]_{i+1}$ from party S_{i+1}.

Additionally, all data is represented as double-precision float-point format deployed in IEEE 754–2008 [22], which consists of the sign, mantissa and exponent bits. The fixed mantissa bits can be encoded into integer through the enlargement method, i.e., $\lfloor u \cdot 10^q \rfloor$ from $\mathbb{Z}_n$, where q represents the decimal places.

4.2 Secure Conversion Protocols

Through investigation, the switch between additive and multiplicative shares can help S_i split and share secret, then saving communication rounds. Hence, we design a group of secure protocols Π_{M2A} and Π_{A2M} using $\Pi_{Zeroshare}$, $\Pi_{Oneshare}$ and Π_{Mul} protocols, as illustrated in Protocol 1 and 2, respectively. In Π_{M2A}, given the multiplicative shares $\langle u\rangle_i$, S_1, S_2 and S_3 jointly calculate $[d]_1 + [d]_2 + [d]_3 = \langle u\rangle_1 \cdot \langle u\rangle_2$ and $[f]_1 + [f]_2 + [f]_3 = \langle u\rangle_1 \cdot \langle u\rangle_2 \cdot \langle u\rangle_3$. Similarly given the additive shares $[u]_i$, Π_{A2M} obtains $\langle f\rangle_1 \cdot \langle f\rangle_2 \cdot \langle f\rangle_3 = [u]_1 + [u]_2 + [u]_3$. S_i sets the relationship of $[\alpha]_1 + [\alpha]_2 + [\alpha]_3 + \Delta = \langle\beta\rangle_1 \cdot \langle\beta\rangle_2 \cdot \langle\beta\rangle_3 \cdot \Delta$ (i.e., equals Δ). Since $g = [g]_1 + [g]_2 + [g]_3 = \Delta \cdot ([u]_1 + [u]_2 + [u]_3)$, S_i can obtain multiplicative share $\langle h\rangle_i$ through re-constructing g executed by S_1 (or S_2). Note that g cannot be known by S_3, otherwise S_3 can infer the real value of $[u]_1 + [u]_2 + [u]_3$. The new $\langle\beta\rangle_i^\dagger$ is used to randomize $\langle h\rangle_i$ and re-share $\langle f\rangle_i$.

Protocol 1: Additive to Multiplicative Shares Protocol (Π_{M2A})

Input: S_i ($i \in \{1,2,3\}$) holds $\langle u\rangle_i$.
Output: S_i outputs $[f]_i$.
1 S_1, S_2 and S_3 calculate $[d]_1, [d]_2, [d]_3 \leftarrow \Pi_{Mul}(\langle u\rangle_1, 0, 0; 0, \langle u\rangle_2, 0)$;
2 S_1, S_2 and S_3 calculate $[f]_1, [f]_2, [f]_3 \leftarrow \Pi_{Mul}([d]_1, [d]_2, [d]_3; 0, 0, \langle u\rangle_3)$;
3 S_i returns $([f]_i, [f]_{i+1})$.

---

5 The Construction of FPPNet

In this section, we discuss the implementation details of FPPNet, consisting of secure linear, ReLU, max-pooling and sigmoid layers.

5.1 Secure Linear Layer

In a neural network, the linear full-connected layers connect the relationship between sample feature and category using the trained weight and bias

---

Protocol 2: Multiplicative to Additive Shares Protocol (Π_{A2M})

Input: S_i ($i \in \{1, 2, 3\}$) holds $[u]_i$.

Output: S_i outputs $\langle f \rangle_i$.

1 S_i gets $[\alpha]_i$ and $\langle \beta \rangle_i$ through $\Pi_{Zeroshare}$ and $\Pi_{Oneshare}$;

2 S_3 randomly generates Δ, calculates $[\alpha]_3 \leftarrow [\alpha]_3 + \Delta$ and $\langle \beta \rangle_3 \leftarrow \langle \beta \rangle_3 \cdot \Delta$;

3 S_i calculates $[g]_i \leftarrow [\alpha]_i \cdot [u]_i + [\alpha]_i \cdot [u]_{i+1} + [\alpha]_{i+1} \cdot [u]_i$;

4 S_2 sends $[g]_2$ to S_1, S_3 sends $[g]_3$ to S_1;

5 S_1 calculates $\langle h \rangle_1 \leftarrow ([g]_1 + [g]_2 + [g]_3)/\langle \beta \rangle_1$, S_2 calculates $\langle h \rangle_2 \leftarrow 1/\langle \beta \rangle_2$, S_3 calculates $\langle h \rangle_3 \leftarrow 1/\langle \beta \rangle_3$;

6 S_i gets new $\langle \beta \rangle_i^{\dagger}$ through $\Pi_{Oneshare}$;

7 S_i calculates $\langle f \rangle_i \leftarrow \langle h \rangle_i \cdot \langle \beta \rangle_i^{\dagger}$, and sends $\langle f \rangle_i$ to S_{i-1};

8 S_i returns $(\langle f \rangle_i, \langle f \rangle_{i+1})$.

---

parameters (w, b). The expression is $y = w \cdot x + b$, where x and y are the input and output of this layer. For the data privacy, each data is randomly split into the three-party shares $[x]_1$, $[x]_2$ and $[x]_3$, and single S_i ($i \in \{1, 2, 3\}$) can locally calculates $[y]_i = w \cdot [x]_i + b/3$. Obviously, the sum of all shares $[y]_i$ equals $[y]$. Likewise, S_1, S_2 and S_3 can realize the convolutional layer through locally calculating the linear combination between input share and convolutional kernel parameters.

5.2 Secure ReLU and Max-Pooling Layers

The ReLU layer performs the operation $\text{ReLU}(x) = \max(x, 0)$ over each neuron with the corresponding input x. Each neuron is activated or suppressed by comparing the relationship between x and 0. Instead of using GC in previous work [3,8], we design an efficient and secure comparison protocol Π_{Comp} adopting only ASS. As illustrated in Protocol 3, given $[u]_i$ and $[v]_i$, Π_{Comp} aims to obtain the comparison shares $[f]_i$ between u and v, such that $u = [u]_1 + [u]_2 + [u]_3$ and $v = [v]_1 + [v]_2 + [v]_3$. If $[f]_1 + [f]_2 + [f]_3 = 0$, then $u \geq v$; otherwise ($[f]_1 + [f]_2 + [f]_3 = 1$), $u < v$. In line 2, the additive share $[p]_i$ of the difference of $u - v$ are converted into multiplicative share $\langle r \rangle_i$, The exclusive-or (XOR) result of MSB of $\langle r \rangle_i$ determines whether $u \geq v$ or $u < v$. In line 7–8, the XOR operation of single bit can be converted into arithmetic operation, i.e., $\langle s \rangle_1 \oplus \langle s \rangle_2 \oplus \langle s \rangle_3 = \langle s \rangle_1 + \langle s \rangle_2 + \langle s \rangle_3 - 2 \cdot \langle s \rangle_1 \cdot \langle s \rangle_2 - 2 \cdot \langle s \rangle_2 \cdot \langle s \rangle_3 - 2 \cdot \langle s \rangle_1 \cdot \langle s \rangle_3 + 4 \cdot \langle s \rangle_1 \cdot \langle s \rangle_2 \cdot \langle s \rangle_3 = [f]_1 + [f]_2 + [f]_3$.

On the basis, the secure realization of ReLU layer is executed by Π_{ReLU} protocol. Given the input feature shares $[x]_1$, $[x]_2$, and $[x]_3$, Π_{ReLU} obtains $y = x$ if $x \geq 0$ or $y = 0$ if $x < 0$. In fact, it satisfies $y = x \cdot (1 - \eta)$, where η (i.e., $[\eta]_1 + [\eta]_2 + [\eta]_3$) is the MSB of x.

Π_{ReLU}: To calculate $y = \max(x, 0)$, such that $x = [x]_1 + [x]_2 + [x]_3$ and $y = [y]_1 + [y]_2 + [y]_3$, S_1, S_2 and S_3 jointly calculate $[\eta]_1, [\eta]_2, [\eta]_3 \leftarrow \Pi_{Comp}([x]_1, [x]_2, [x]_3; 0, 0, 0)$ and $[y]_1, [y]_2, [y]_3 \leftarrow \Pi_{Mul}(1 - [\eta]_1, -[\eta]_2, -[\eta]_3; [x]_1, [x]_2, [x]_3)$. Then, S_i obtains 2-out-of-3 shares $([y]_i, [y]_{i+1})$.

Protocol 3: Secure Comparison Protocol (Π_{Comp})

Input: S_i ($i \in \{1,2,3\}$) holds $[u]_i$ and $[v]_i$.

Output: S_i outputs $[f]_i$.

1   S_i calculates $[p]_i \leftarrow [u]_i - [v]_i$;

2   S_1, S_2 and S_3 calculate $\langle r \rangle_1, \langle r \rangle_2, \langle r \rangle_3 \leftarrow \Pi_{A2M}([p]_1, [p]_2, [p]_3)$;

3   **if** $\langle r \rangle_i \geq 0$ **then**

4 | S_i assigns $\langle s \rangle_i \leftarrow 0$;

5   **else**

6 | S_i assigns $\langle s \rangle_i \leftarrow 1$;

7   S_1, S_2 and S_3 calculate $[t]_1, [t]_2, [t]_3 \leftarrow \Pi_{M2A}(\langle s \rangle_1, \langle s \rangle_2, \langle s \rangle_3)$;

8   S_i calculates $[f]_i \leftarrow \langle s \rangle_i - 2 \cdot \langle s \rangle_i \cdot \langle s \rangle_{i+1} + 4 \cdot [t]_i$;

9   S_i sends $[f]_i$ to S_{i-1}, and returns $([f]_i, [f]_{i+1})$.

The max-pooling layer divides the feature map into some pooling regions with the same size (e.g., 2×2) evenly, and selects the maximum feature element from each pooling region. Here, we design a secure max-pooling protocol $\Pi_{Maxpool}$ adopting the designed Π_{Comp} protocol. For each pooling region, given the input feature shares $[\boldsymbol{x}]_1$, $[\boldsymbol{x}]_2$, and $[\boldsymbol{x}]_3$, $\Pi_{Maxpool}$ obtains the maximum feature $y = \max(\boldsymbol{x})$ by executing Π_{Comp} and Π_{Mul} for $\mu^2 - 1$ times. Draw the idea of work [21], we can load the feature with the same position in each pooling region into a block, that is, the entire feature map are turned into μ^2 blocks. Then, we perform $\Pi_{Maxpool}$ over these block in parallel, and obtain the max-pooling output eventually.

$\Pi_{Maxpool}$: For the shares $[\boldsymbol{x}_{j,k}]_i, j = (1, 2, \cdots, \mu), k = (1, 2, \cdots, \mu)$ of each pooling region with size $\mu \times \mu$ in entire feature map, it calculates the maximum feature $y = \max(\boldsymbol{x})$, such that $\boldsymbol{x}_{j,k} = [\boldsymbol{x}_{j,k}]_1 + [\boldsymbol{x}_{j,k}]_2 + [\boldsymbol{x}_{j,k}]_3$ and $y = [y]_1 + [y]_2 + [y]_3$. S_1, S_2 and S_3 jointly calculate $[\delta]_1, [\delta]_2, [\delta]_3 \leftarrow \Pi_{Comp}([\boldsymbol{x}_{1,1}]_1, [\boldsymbol{x}_{1,1}]_2, [\boldsymbol{x}_{1,1}]_3; [\boldsymbol{x}_{1,2}]_1, [\boldsymbol{x}_{1,2}]_2, [\boldsymbol{x}_{1,2}]_3)$ and $[y]'_1, [y]'_2, [y]'_3 \leftarrow \Pi_{Mul}([\delta]_1, [\delta]_2, [\delta]_3; [\boldsymbol{x}_{1,2}]_1 - [\boldsymbol{x}_{1,1}]_1, [\boldsymbol{x}_{1,2}]_2 - [\boldsymbol{x}_{1,1}]_2, [\boldsymbol{x}_{1,2}]_3 - [\boldsymbol{x}_{1,1}]_3)$. S_i obtains the larger feature share $[y]_i \leftarrow [y]'_i + [\boldsymbol{x}_{1,1}]_i$ between $\boldsymbol{x}_{1,1}$ and $\boldsymbol{x}_{1,2}$. Then, S_1, S_2 and S_3 compare y with the remaining $\mu^2 - 2$ features, and obtain the maximum feature share $[y]_i$. Finally, S_i obtains 2-out-of-3 shares $([y]_i, [y]_{i+1})$.

5.3 Secure Sigmoid Layer

Sigmoid function is used to map the classification score to the interval of $(0, 1)$, so as to obtain the predicted probability of each category. The expression for this function is $\text{sigmoid}(x) = 1/(1 + e^{-x})$. To protect the privacy of Sigmoid operation, we design secure exponent and division protocols (i.e., Π_{Exp} and Π_{Div}). Unlike the previous FALCON [6], we only adopt the conversion between additive and multiplicative shares, instead of extra polynomial approximation method. With the help of Π_{Exp} and Π_{Div}, the secure realization $\Pi_{Sigmoid}$ of Sigmoid operation can be finished.

Π_{Exp}: To calculate $f = e^u$, such that $u = [u]_1 + [u]_2 + [u]_3$ and $f = [f]_1 + [f]_2 + [f]_3$, S_1, S_2 and S_3 jointly calculate $[f]_1, [f]_2, [f]_3 \leftarrow \Pi_{M2A}(e^{[u]_1}, e^{[u]_2}, e^{[u]_3})$. Then, S_i obtains 2-out-of-3 shares $([f]_i, [f]_{i+1})$.

Π_{Div}: To calculate $f = u/v$, such that $u = [u]_1 + [u]_2 + [u]_3$, $v = [v]_1 + [v]_2 + [v]_3$ and $f = [f]_1 + [f]_2 + [f]_3$, S_1, S_2 and S_3 jointly calculate $\langle\lambda\rangle_1, \langle\lambda\rangle_2, \langle\lambda\rangle_3 \leftarrow \Pi_{A2M}([u]_1, [u]_2, [u]_3)$, $\langle\gamma\rangle_1, \langle\gamma\rangle_2, \langle\gamma\rangle_3 \leftarrow \Pi_{A2M}([v]_1, [v]_2, [v]_3)$ and $[f]_1, [f]_2, [f]_3 \leftarrow \Pi_{M2A}(\langle\lambda\rangle_1/\langle\gamma\rangle_1, \langle\lambda\rangle_2/\langle\gamma\rangle_2, \langle\lambda\rangle_3/\langle\gamma\rangle_3)$. Then, S_i obtains 2-out-of-3 shares $([f]_i, [f]_{i+1})$.

$\Pi_{Sigmoid}$: To calculate $\text{sigmoid}(x) = 1/(1 + e^{-x})$, such that $x = [x]_1 + [x]_2 + [x]_3$ and $y = [y]_1 + [y]_2 + [y]_3$, S_1, S_2 and S_3 jointly calculate $[\phi]_1, [\phi]_2, [\phi]_3 \leftarrow \Pi_{Exp}(e^{-[x]_1}, e^{-[x]_2}, e^{-[x]_3})$ and $[y]_1, [y]_2, [y]_3 \leftarrow \Pi_{Div}(1, 0, 0; 1 + [\phi]_1, [\phi]_2, [\phi]_3)$. Then, S_i obtains 2-out-of-3 shares $([y]_i, [y]_{i+1})$.

6   Theoretical Analysis

6.1   Security Analysis

The non-collusion assumption can guarantee that each S_i ($i \in \{1, 2, 3\}$) cannot recover the real information from three-party shares. The security of FPPNet depends on the proposed protocols, we provide the security proof using universal composition (UC) framework [23]. We assume that there is a probabilistic polynomial time (PPT) simulator $\mathcal{M}$ which can generate a set of simulatable view $View_{sim}$ for adversary $\mathcal{A}$. In a certain protocol Π, if $View_{sim}$ cannot be computationally distinguished from the real view $View_{real}$ of a physical entity (e.g., S_i), then Π is considered secure. The security proof relies on the following lemmas [24] and theorems.

Lemma 1. *A protocol is perfectly simulatable if all its sub-protocols are perfectly simulatable.*

Lemma 2. *If a random element a is uniformly distributed on $\mathbb{Z}_n$ and independent from any variable $b \in \mathbb{Z}_n$, then $a \pm b$ is also uniformly random and independent from b.*

Theorem 1. *The proposed protocols are secure in the HbC model.*

Proof. For Π_{M2A} protocol, the $View_{real}$ of S_i ($i \in \{1, 2, 3\}$) is $\{\langle u\rangle_i, [d]_i, [f]_i\}$, where $\langle u\rangle_i$ is the input. According to Lemma 2, $[d]_i$ and $[f]_i$ are random. Since Π_{Mul} has been proved to be secure and simulatable in FALCON [6], Π_{M2A} is also simulatable on the grounds of Lemma 1. $\mathcal{M}$ can generate the $View_{sim}$ of S_i, and $\mathcal{A}$ cannot distinguish between $View_{real}$ and $View_{sim}$ computationally. For Π_{A2M} protocol, the $View_{real}$ of S_1 is $\{[u]_1, [\alpha]_1, \langle\beta\rangle_1, [g]_1, g, \langle h\rangle_1, \langle f\rangle_1\}$. S_1 can re-construct $g = u \cdot \Delta$, but not predict real u without knowing Δ. Inversely, although S_3 knows Δ, but not g. Both g and Δ are unknown to S_2. In this way, the data possessed by S_i ($i \in \{1, 2, 3\}$) are random according to Lemma 2. $\mathcal{A}$ cannot computationally distinguish between $View_{real}$ and $View_{sim}$ of S_i. Thus, Π_{M2A} and Π_{A2M} protocols are considered secure in the HbC model. Since

Table 1. Computational complexity of proposed protocols.

Protocols	Input sizes	Plaintext	FPPNet (ours)
Π_{A2M}	n	–	$O(n)$
Π_{M2A}	n	–	$O(n)$
Π_{Comp}	n	$O(n)$	$O(n)$
Π_{Exp}	n	$O(n)$	$O(n)$
Π_{Div}	n	$O(n)$	$O(n)$
Π_{ReLU}	n	$O(n)$	$O(n)$
$\Pi_{Maxpool}$	$n, (\mu, \mu)$	$O(n(\mu^2 - 1)/\mu^2)$	$O(n(\mu^2 - 1)/\mu^2)$
$\Pi_{Sigmoid}$	n	$O(n)$	$O(n)$

Table 2. Communication complexity of proposed protocols.

Protocols	SecureNN [9]		FALCON [6]		FPPNet (ours)	
	Rounds	Message sizes	Rounds	Message sizes	Rounds	Message sizes
Π_{M2A}	–	–	–	–	2	$6nl$
Π_{A2M}	–	–	–	–	2	$5nl$
Π_{Comp}	5	$n(4l \log p + 13l)$	$\log p + 2$	$2nl$	4	$11nl$
Π_{Exp}	–	–	–	–	2	$6nl$
Π_{Div}	$10l_D$	$n(8l \log p + 24l)l_D$	$p \log p + 5p + 7$	$nl(4p + 7)$	4	$16nl$
Π_{ReLU}	10	$n(8l \log p + 24l)$	$\log p + 5$	$4nl$	5	$14nl$
$\Pi_{Maxpool}$	$9(n - 1)$	$(n - 1)(8l \log p + 29l)$	$(\mu^2 - 1)(\log p + 7)$	$n(\mu^2 + 5l)/\mu^2$	$5(\mu^2 - 1)$	$14n(\mu^2 - 1)l/\mu^2$
$\Pi_{Sigmoid}$	–	–	–	–	6	$22nl$

the remaining Π_{Comp}, Π_{Exp}, Π_{Div}, Π_{ReLU}, $\Pi_{Maxpool}$ and $\Pi_{Sigmoid}$ protocols is designed on the basis of Π_{Mul}, Π_{M2A} and Π_{A2M} protocols, likewise, these protocols can be proved to be secure in the HbC model.

Theorem 2. *FPPNet is secure in the HbC model.*

Proof. Since Π_{ReLU}, $\Pi_{Maxpool}$ and $\Pi_{Sigmoid}$ protocols have been proved to be secure in Theorem 1, the outputs of these protocols are random. According to Lemma 1, FPPNet is also simulatable. The $View_{real}$ of FPPNet and $View_{sim}$ generated by $\mathcal{M}$ are computationally indistinguishable for $\mathcal{A}$. Therefore, FPPNet is secure in the HbC model.

6.2 Complexity Analysis

In this section, we analyze the computational and communication complexity of the proposed protocols. As illustrated in Table 1, we assume that n denotes the size of the vector in vectorized implementation, (μ, μ) is the size of pooling region. The secure conversion Protocols Π_{M2A} and Π_{A2M} are designed by only three-party ASS, that cost is $O(n)$. The remaining protocols are on the basis of the Π_{M2A} and Π_{A2M}. In the $\Pi_{Maxpool}$ protocol, it performs Π_{Comp} for $\mu^2 - 1$

times. Clearly, the computational complexity of our protocols is linear, and is the same order as that in plaintext environment.

Compared with the previous works [6,9], Table 2 gives the communication complexity results. l denotes the bit-width, l_D denotes the precision of bits, and p denotes the logarithm of the ring size. For Π_{Comp} protocol, SecureNN [9] transforms MSB in even ring into LSB in odd ring, removing the dependence of communication rounds on l. FALCON [6] adopts (2, 3)-sharing instead of (2, 2)-sharing using in SecureNN, and further reduces the size of ring structure (i.e., $\mathbb{Z}_{2^p}$). By contrast, our Π_{Comp} only uses arithmetic addition and multiplication. Although the communication overhead is higher than FALCON, it greatly compresses the communication rounds and is independent of l and p. For Π_{Div} protocol, we do not require any extra polynomial iteration compared with SecureNN and FALCON. Additionally, we design Π_{Exp} and $\Pi_{Sigmoid}$ protocols, which does not requires to be approximated using ReLU. Overall, our protocol can realize constant rounds for communication, regardless of the size of the input data.

7   Experimental Results

Experiments are performed on a 64-bit personal computer with 1.80 GHz CPU and 20 GB RAM. We implement FPPNet using PyTorch 1.6 deep learning framework and Python 3 language. The tensor package is used as a multidimensional container of numbers to execute the calculation in parallel. We use MNIST dataset to conduct experiments, which consists of 60,000 images for training and 10,000 images for inference. Each image is a 28 × 28 pixel image of a hand-written digit along with a label between 0 and 9. Similar to the previous works [6,8,9], we evaluate the performance of FPPNet by using MNIST dataset and adopting two different networks (i.e., NN-3 and LeNet) in terms of efficiency and accuracy. NN-3 is a three-layer full-connected network with ReLU activation after each layer, which has around 118K parameters. LeNet is a standard convolutional neural network, which contains two convolutional layers, two max-pooling layers, three full-connected layers and five ReLU layers with 431K parameters.

The efficiency of FPPNet depends on the designed protocols. We firstly analyze the runtime of various layers in a certain network, as shown in Table 3. Since we adopt the single computer to simulate the running of three servers, the runtime of secure linear convolutional and full-connected layers are around 3× times than plaintext LeNet. Adopting Π_{Comp} and Π_{Mul} protocols, the secure realization cost of ReLU layer is around 55× to 72× times than the original activation function. Max-pooling and Sigmoid layers have the similar trend, and the runtime linearly increases with the input size. Over all, the runtime of each layer can be maintained in microseconds.

Next, we discuss the performance of FPPNet from the aspect of efficiency and accuracy. Table 4 gives the inference efficiency comparison result between our FPPNet and the existing three-party schemes [6,8,9]. The single number is

Table 3. Comparison of runtime of various layers for FPPNet and plaintext LeNet. All runtimes are reported in microsecond (μs).

Layers	Input sizes	LeNet	FPPNet	Multiple
Convolution	$(1, 28, 28)$	26.7	80.7	3.02×
	$(6, 12, 12)$	27.2	61.2	2.25×
ReLU	$(6, 24, 24)$	29.0	1601.1	55.21×
	$(16, 8, 8)$	6.9	498.0	72.17×
Max-pooling	$(6, 24, 24)$	45.7	1615.0	35.34×
	$(16, 8, 8)$	12.9	460.7	35.71×
Full-connected	$(1, 256)$	1.0	2.2	2.20×
	$(1, 120)$	0.4	1.2	3.0×
	$(1, 84)$	0.1	0.3	3.0×
Sigmoid	$(1, 10)$	0.2	5.4	27.0×

Table 4. Comparison of inference efficiency of various schemes for single image from MNIST dataset. All runtimes are reported in second (s) and communication in MB.

Schemes	NN-3		LeNet	
	Runtime	Communication	Runtime	Communication
ABY3 [8]	0.008	0.5	–	–
SecureNN [9]	0.043	2.10	0.23	18.94
FALCON [6]	0.011	0.012	0.047	0.74
FPPNet (ours)	0.007	0.030	0.031	0.862
Plaintext	0.001	–	0.004	–

stored as fixed 64-bit data type. FALCON [6] combines the advantages of ABY3 [8] and SecureNN [9], and adopt $(2, 3)$-sharing method to perform the end-to-end privacy-preserving inference in a small ring. To pursue the higher performance gains, different from FALCON, our FPPNet transforms the calculation over boolean ring into pure arithmetic calculation, and realizes the non-linear functions by adopting the designed secure conversion protocols. Inevitably, the communication overhead of FPPNet is slightly higher than that of FALCON, but it is acceptable. More importantly, FPPNet is able to achieve faster inference efficiency due to the fewer rounds of communication between servers. In other word, FPPNet further narrows the generation gap between ciphertext and plaintext inference.

Additionally, the inference accuracy is an important factor to evaluate the effectiveness of FPPNet. We set the learning rate as 0.1 and the batch size as 128 in training. After 40 iterations, as shown in Table 5, the inference accuracy of NN-3 and LeNet can achieve 98.09% and 99.03% in plaintext environment, respectively. Clearly, the accuracy of FALCON has low loss. This is because

Table 5. Comparison of inference accuracy for batch size 128 with MNIST dataset.

Networks	Plaintext	FALCON [6]	FPPNet (ours)
NN-3	98.09%	97.42%	98.09%
LeNet	99.03%	96.85%	99.03%

the fixed-point 32-bit algorithm in FALCON is still slightly different from high-precision 64-bit computing. By contrast, we adopt the fixed-point 64-bit data type to ensure that our FPPNet can achieve the consistent accuracy as that of plaintext network as long as multiplicative results do not overflow.

8   Conclusion

In this paper, we proposed a fast and privacy-preserving neural network, referred to FPPNet, leveraging only three-party arithmetic secret sharing. Specifically, we design a group of secure conversion protocols for switching additive and multiplicative shares, and develop a series of secure computing protocols to realize each layer of FPPNet. Three non-collusive servers can collaboratively perform the secure inference while not disclosing the intermediate calculation results. Experimental results indicated that with MNIST dataset, our FPPNet is faster than FALCON, and can achieve the same accuracy as that of plaintext neural network, having the stronger practicality. In the future work, we further try to applied FPPNet to more large-scale deep neural network, and explore the end-to-end privacy-preserving training using the designed secure conversion protocols.

Acknowledgment. This work was supported in part by the National Natural Science Foundation of China under Grant 61872088, Grant U1905211, Grant 62072109, and Grant U1804263; in part by the Guangxi Key Laboratory of Cryptography and Information Security under Grant GCIS202105; in part by the Science and Technology Major Support Program of Guizhou Province under Grant 20183001; in part by the Science and Technology Program of Guizhou Province under Grant 20191098; in part by the Project of High-level Innovative Talents of Guizhou Province under Grant 20206008; and in part by the Open Research Fund of Key Laboratory of Cryptography of Zhejiang Province under Grant ZCL21015.

References

1. Xiong, J., Bi, R., Chen, Q., et al.: Towards edge-collaborative, lightweight and secure region proposal network. J. Commun. **41**(10), 188–201 (2020)
2. Xiong, J., Bi, R., Zhao, M., et al.: Edge-assisted privacy-preserving raw data sharing framework for connected autonomous vehicles. IEEE Wirel. Commun. **27**(3), 24–30 (2020)
3. Mohassel, P., Zhang, Y.: SecureML: a system for scalable privacy-preserving machine learning. In: IEEE Symposium on Security and Privacy (SP), USA, pp. 19–38 (2017)

4. Bi, R., Chen, Q., Xiong, J., et al.: Design method of secure computing protocol for deep neural network. Chin. J. Netw. Inf. Secur. **6**(4), 130–139 (2020)
5. Xiong, J., Zhou, Y., Bi, R., et al.: Towards edge-collaborative, lightweight and privacy-preserving classification framework. J. Commun. **43**(1), 127–137 (2022)
6. Wagh, S., Tople, S., Benhamouda, F., et al.: FALCON: honest-majority maliciously secure framework for private deep learning. Proc. Priv. Enhancing Technol. **1**, 188–208 (2021)
7. Beaver, D.: Efficient multiparty protocols using circuit randomization. In: Feigenbaum, J. (ed.) CRYPTO 1991. LNCS, vol. 576, pp. 420–432. Springer, Heidelberg (1992). https://doi.org/10.1007/3-540-46766-1_34
8. Mohassel, P., Rindal, P.: ABY3: a mixed protocol framework for machine learning, In: Proceedings of the ACM SIGSAC Conference on Computer and Communications Security (CCS), Los Angeles, USA, pp. 35–52 (2018)
9. Wagh, S., Gupta, D., Chandran, N.: SecureNN: 3-party secure computation for neural network training. Proc. Priv. Enhancing Technol. **2019**(3), 26–49 (2019)
10. Demmler, D., Schneider, T., Zohner, M.: ABY-A framework for efficient mixed-protocol secure two-party computation. In: Proceedings of the Network and Distributed System Security Symposium (NDSS), San Diego, USA, pp. 1–15 (2015)
11. Rouhani, B.D., Riazi, M.S., Koushanfar, F.: DeepSecure: scalable provably-secure deep learning. In: Proceedings of the 55th Annual Design Automation Conference (DAC), San Francisco, USA, pp. 1–6 (2018)
12. Liu, J., Juuti, M., Lu, Y., et al.: Oblivious neural network predictions via MiniONN transformations. In: Proceedings of the ACM SIGSAC Conference on Computer and Communications Security (CCS), Los Angeles, USA, pp. 619–631 (2017)
13. Riazi, M.S., Weinert, C., Tkachenko, O., et al.: Chameleon: a hybrid secure computation framework for machine learning applications. In: Proceedings of the 2018 on Asia Conference on Computer and Communications Security (ASIACCS), New York, USA, pp. 707–721 (2018)
14. Juvekar, C., Vaikuntanathan, V., Chandrakasan, A.: GAZELLE: a low latency framework for secure neural network inference. In: 27th USENIX Security Symposium (USENIX Security), Berkeley, USA, pp. 1651–1669 (2018)
15. Mishra, P., Lehmkuhl, R., Srinivasan, A., et al.: DELPHI: a cryptographic inference service for neural networks. In: 29th USENIX Security Symposium (USENIX Security), Boston, USA, pp. 2505–2522 (2020)
16. Huang, K., Liu, X., Fu, S., et al.: A lightweight privacy-preserving CNN feature extraction framework for mobile sensing. IEEE Trans. Dependable Secure Comput. **18**(3), 1441–1455 (2021)
17. Chaudhari, H., Choudhury, A., Patra, A., et al.: ASTRA: high throughput 3PC over rings with application to secure prediction. In: Proceedings of the ACM SIGSAC Conference on Cloud Computing Security Workshop (CCSW), Los Angeles, USA, pp. 81–92 (2019)
18. Patra, A., Suresh, A.: BLAZE: blazing fast privacy-preserving machine learning. In: 27th Annual Network and Distributed System Security Symposium (NDSS), San Diego, USA, pp. 1–18 (2020)
19. Byali, M., Chaudhari, H., Patra, A., et al.: FLASH: fast and robust framework for privacy-preserving machine learning. Proc. Priv. Enhancing Technol. **2**, 459–480 (2020)
20. Chaudhari, H., Rachuri, R., Suresh, A.: Trident: efficient 4PC framework for privacy preserving machine learning. In: Proceedings of the Network and Distributed System Security Symposium (NDSS), San Diego, USA, pp. 1–18 (2020)

21. Xiong, J., Bi, R., Tian, Y., et al.: Towards lightweight, privacy-preserving cooperative object classification for connected autonomous vehicles. IEEE Internet Things J. **9**(4), 2787–2801 (2022)
22. Markstein, P.: The new IEEE-754 standard for floating point arithmetic. In: Dagstuhl Seminar Proceedings, pp. 1–3 (2008)
23. Damgård, I., Fitzi, M., Kiltz, E., et al.: Unconditionally secure constant-rounds multi-party computation for equality, comparison, bits and exponentiation. In: Theory of Cryptography Conference (TCC), New York, USA, pp. 285–304 (2006)
24. Bogdanov, D., Laur, S., Willemson, J.: Sharemind: a framework for fast privacy-preserving computations. In: Jajodia, S., Lopez, J. (eds.) ESORICS 2008. LNCS, vol. 5283, pp. 192–206. Springer, Heidelberg (2008). https://doi.org/10.1007/978-3-540-88313-5_13

Broadband Long-Term Spectrum Prediction Based on Trend Based SAX

Han Zhang, Lu Sun, and Yun Lin[✉]

College of Information and Communication, Harbin Engineering University, Harbin 150001,
People's Republic of China
linyun@hrbeu.edu.cn

Abstract. With the development of communication technology and the growth of equipment, spectrum prediction technology has received more and more attention because of its wide application in spectrum resource management. However, due to the high burst of spectrum usage, there are still some difficulties in spectrum prediction. This paper proposes a new algorithmic framework (TrSAX-seq2seq) for the difficult problem of broadband and long-term prediction in the spectrum prediction problem. In this paper, a trend based symbolic aggregate approximation (TrSAX) method is used to reduce the dimension and represent the historical spectrum observation data, and then perform hierarchical clustering on the symbol sequence after dimension reduction to achieve the purpose of dividing the wide frequency band into multiple narrow frequency bands. Then, we use the LSTM network of seq2seq architecture to predict the spectrum occupation. We validate our method on a real spectrum monitoring dataset. The experimental results show that the method proposed in this paper can effectively improve the prediction accuracy compared with other methods.

Keywords: Broadband spectrum prediction · Long term prediction · Trend based symbolic aggregate approximation · Seq2seq

1 Introduction

The rapid development of communication technology and the sharp increase in the number of communication terminal equipment make the limited electromagnetic spectrum resources more scarce. Therefore, researchers pay more and more attention to the research of spectrum prediction technology, because the spectrum of a specific area can be dynamically allocated in hours or tens of hours based on the prediction of the future state of the spectrum [1]. However, the us-age of many spectrums is dynamic and highly bursty, and the spectrum usage rules of different frequency bands are very different because of their different services and users [2]. At the same time, we always want to predict as far into the future as possible so that dynamic spectrum allocation can be done earlier. These problems bring enormous challenges to spectrum prediction and lead us to con-sider new algorithmic frameworks to achieve long-term spectrum prediction in broadband scenarios.

Y. Chenggang et al. (Eds.): MobiMedia 2022, LNICST 451, pp. 179–189, 2022.
https://doi.org/10.1007/978-3-031-23902-1_14

At present, scholars have proposed many methods for spectrum prediction. In the traditional method, the ARMA algorithm is used more [3]. Among machine learning based methods, algorithms such as Support Vector Machine (SVM) [4], Long Short Term Memory (LSTM) [5], Convolutional Long Short Term Memory (ConvLSTM) [6], CNN + LSTM [14] are also applied to spectrum prediction. For the ISM frequency band with high burstiness, some people propose a clustering method based on statistical features to cut the spectrum and predict based on LSTM respectively [5]. Most of the above methods are used to predict the short-term busy and idle state of the spectrum [7]. The wide-band and long-term prediction problems mentioned above are still not well solved.

The problem of spectrum prediction is essentially a time series prediction problem. An effective idea is to cluster large sequences into multiple smaller sequences to improve prediction accuracy. But considering the long dimension of spectrum monitoring data, we must consider a dimensionality reduction method to ensure the effect of clustering. On the problem of long-term prediction of spectrum, we believe that the seq2seq architecture is more potential than the traditional LSTM network. Based on the above discussion, this paper uses a trend based symbolic aggregate approximation (TrSAX) method combined with a seq2seq network for spectrum prediction, and tests it on a real open source dataset. The main contributions of this paper are as follows:

1. This paper uses a trend based symbolic aggregate approximation method to represent and reduce the dimension of electromagnetic spectrum data. Then, multiple prediction models are constructed based on hierarchical clustering, and the wide-band spectrum prediction problem is transformed into multiple narrow-band prediction problems.
2. Apply the seq2seq network architecture to the spectrum prediction problem to improve the prediction performance in long-term prediction.
3. Validate the proposed method using real open-source spectrum monitoring data and demonstrate its superior performance.

The rest of this paper is outlined below. Section 2 introduces the trend based symbolic aggregate approximation method. Section 3 introduces the seq2seq architecture for spectrum prediction. Section 4 is the experimental part of this paper. Section 5 is the conclusion.

2 Trend Based Symbolic Aggregate Approximation Method

For spectrum monitoring data, due to its large data volume and high dimension, the effect of traditional data mining and clustering methods is affected. In recent years, academia has proposed many representation methods that have outstanding performance in time series, which are characterized by the ability to achieve dimensionality reduction without losing important features [8]. In this paper, a relatively new trend based symbolic aggregate approximation (TrSAX) method is used to reduce the dimension of spectrum monitoring data, and the numerical value and changing trend characteristics of the data are preserved [9]. The broadband electromagnetic spectrum data is then divided into multiple narrow frequency bands using hierarchical clustering.

2.1 Monitoring Data Autocorrelation Analysis

There have been many research results showing that there is widespread correlation between different channels [10]. The correlation of channels can be divided into positive correlation and negative correlation. This paper defines positive correlation as when one channel is busy (idle), the other channel is also in a busy (idle) state. A negative correlation is the opposite. In this paper, the channel correlation factor (CCF) is used to represent the degree of correlation between channels, and its calculation method is shown in formula (1). Where ρ is the correlation coefficient of the two channels, which is the value of CCF; M is the total number of channels, C_i^m is the state of channel i at time m, $I\{A\}$ is the index function, when A is true, $I\{A\} = 1$, otherwise $I\{A\} = 0$. The numerator of formula (1) is the same number of two channel states, and the denominator is the total number of channel states within the monitoring time.

$$\rho = \frac{\sum_{m=1}^{M} I\{C_i^m = C_j^m\}}{\sum_{m=1}^{M} I\{C_i^m = C_j^m\} + \sum_{m=1}^{M} I\{C_i^m \neq C_j^m\}} \tag{1}$$

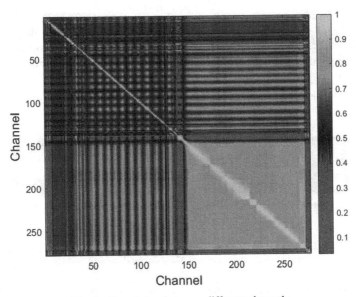

Fig. 1. Correlation between different channels.

Figure 1 is the correlation diagram of all channels in the experimental data in Chapter 4 of this paper. It can be seen that the correlation between channels is ubiquitous, and the CCF value between most channels is above 0.4. The CCF value between some channels is close to 1, which indicates that the evolution laws of these channels are highly correlated. Therefore, it is a feasible method to study a clustering method to find channels with similar laws and train prediction models separately.

2.2 Trend Based Symbolic Aggregate Approximation (TrSAX)

Based on the piecewise aggregation approximation (PAA) method, scholars further developed the symbolic aggregation approximation (SAX) and the trend based symbolic aggregation approximation (TrSAX) method used in this paper.

The TrSAX method assumes that the original time series data approximately obey the normal distribution, divides the original data into several time periods, and uses two symbols to represent the mean and slope of the time periods respectively, so as to achieve the purpose of dimension reduction. The specific process is as follows: first, the original time series data needs to be normalized to data with standard deviation of 1 and average value of 0. Then the original time series is divided into several time periods by using PAA method, and the average value of each time period is obtained. Then, the average value of each segment is compared with the breakpoint of the equal probability partition space under the Gaussian curve, and then mapped to the corresponding characters. Let the length of the time series $X = \{x_1, ..., x_n\}$ be n. Represent it by a vector $\overline{X}$ of length N, the ith element of $\overline{X}$ is defined as:

$$\overline{X}_i = \frac{N}{n} \sum_{j=(n(i-1)+1)/N}^{ni/N} x_j \qquad (2)$$

In this way, the symbolic representation of the original time series data is realized, and the fast and effective dimensionality reduction of the time series is realized. After dimensionality reduction, the overall change of time series can still be reflected. Figure 2 is a schematic diagram of a symbol mapping method.

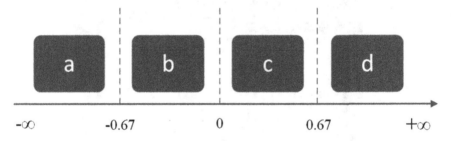

Fig. 2. Schematic diagram of the TrSAX symbol mapping method with word size 4.

The trsax method further adds the trend change information to the symbol coding. The method additionally calculates the slope between each time period. The main improvement of the method is to use two symbols in each time period. Where the first symbol is the segment average value in the original Sax method, and the second symbol is the segment slope value. In this article, lower case letters represent the segment average value, and upper case letters represent the segment slope value. The schematic diagram of segment slope mapping is shown in Fig. 3.

The segment slope value k is estimated by the least squares method:

$$k = \frac{\sum_{i=1}^{n} x_i y_i - n\overline{xy}}{\sum_{i=1}^{n} x_i^2 - n\overline{x}^2} \qquad (3)$$

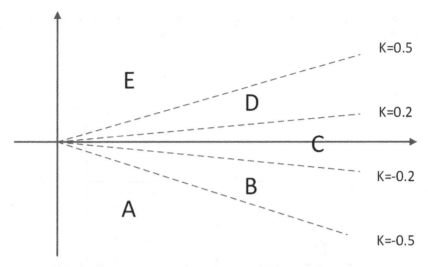

Fig. 3. Schematic diagram of segment slope mapping in the TrSAX method

This method retains the numerical change characteristics and trend information of the original data, which is more conducive to the accurate clustering and grouping of spectrum monitoring data. This method retains the numerical change characteristics and trend information of the original data, which is more conducive to the accurate clustering and grouping of spectrum monitoring data.

3 Spectrum Prediction Based on Seq2seq

Seq2seq model is a typical encoder decoder architecture, which is usually composed of RNN, GRU and LSTM. The encoder encodes the variable length sequence data into a fixed length intermediate vector, and then the decoder decodes the fixed length intermediate vector as the prediction output, realizing that the input sequence of any length can be mapped to the output sequence of any length. Researchers first applied the model to machine translation in the field of NLP. Later, due to its good performance in multi-step prediction, it was also widely used in time series prediction tasks such as transportation [11] and power load [12].

3.1 Long Short-Term Memory Network (LSTM)

Long Short-Term Memory (LSTM) is a widely used temporal recurrent network. LSTM is a gated RNN. The cleverness of LSTM is that the weight of the self-loop is changed by increasing the input threshold, forgetting threshold and output threshold. When the model parameters are fixed, the integration scale at different times can be dynamically changed, thus avoiding the problem of gradient disappearance or gradient explosion when the general RNN is dealing with long-term dependencies (nodes that are far away in the time series). The LSTM cell is shown in Fig. 4.

As shown in Fig. 4, the forget gate determines which information needs to be discarded from the cell. The calculation process is shown in formula (4):

$$\mathbf{f}_t = \sigma(W_f * [\mathbf{h}_{t-1}, x_t] + b_f) \tag{4}$$

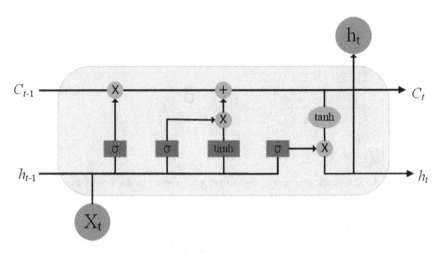

Fig. 4. LSTM cell.

W_f is the weight matrix of the forget gate, where the matrix from cell to gate is diagonal and the rest are non-diagonal. b_f is the offset term of the forget gate and σ is the sigmoid function. The input gate determines what information should be stored. First determine what value needs to be passed through the sigmoid function. The second part is to create a new vector through tanh function, which will be added to the state C_t. The function of the output gate is to determine the content of the output. The gate processes the cell state through tanh to get a value between -1 and 1 and multiplies it with the output of the sigmoid layer, and then determines the output part.

Based on the long-term spectrum prediction problem, the LSTM network with long-term memory is obviously very attractive. But at the same time, we also note that the basic LSTM network capability will also decline significantly in the multi output scenario, so the seq2seq architecture has also been introduced into our work.

3.2 Spectrum Prediction Based on Seq2seq

The network architecture of seq2seq based on LSTM used in this paper is shown in Fig. 5. Among them, $X = \{x_1, ..., x_n\}$ represents the historical monitoring data with step n, and $Y = \{y_1, ..., y_m\}$ represents the output prediction result with step m. The hidden state h_t at each moment in the encoder is jointly determined by the input data x_t at the current moment, the hidden state h_{t-1} and the cell state c_{t-1} at the previous moment:

$$h_t = f(x_t, h_{t-1}, c_{t-1}) \tag{5}$$

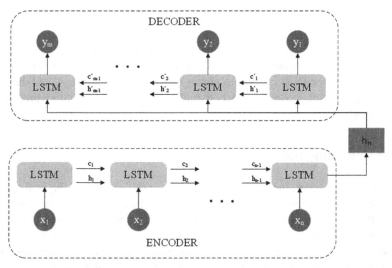

Fig. 5. Network architecture of seq2seq based on LSTM.

The encoder is updated for n time steps, and the input sequence is encoded as the hidden state h_n at the final time step. Due to the long-term memory function of the recurrent neural network, h_n theoretically contains the complete information of the input sequence.

The decoder accepts the final state h_n of the encoder as the initial input value. The hidden state h'_t of the decoder at each moment is updated by the input h_n at the current moment, the hidden state h'_{t-1} and the cell state c'_{t-1} at the previous moment, and its expression is as follows:

$$h'_t = f(h_n, h'_{t-1}, c'_{t-1}) \tag{6}$$

After step-by-step decoding, the final output sequence $Y = \{y_1, ..., y_m\}$ is formed.

Algorithm: The TrSAX-seq2seq based Spectrum Prediction
Input: Broadband historical monitoring data
Output: Multiple narrowband spectrum prediction models
Begin
1. Normalize the historical observation data of each channel;
2. Divide the data into N segments of equal length and calculate the mean and slope;
3. Construct the symbol sequence for each channel using the TrSAX method;
4. Hierarchical clustering based on symbol sequence to get n channel groupings;
5. Construct a dataset according to channel grouping and train it to get n seq2seq prediction models
End

The pseudocode of the complete flow of this method is given. In short, this paper constructs the feature sequence of the channel based on the trend symbol clustering approximation method and clusters to obtain multiple channel groups, and then trains the seq2seq prediction model separately to realize the long-term spectrum prediction of the wide band.

4 Experimental and Results

In the experimental part, the clustering performance of TrSAX and the final spectrum prediction results are compared and analyzed. In the comparison of clustering, we mainly compare the traditional agglomerative hierarchical clustering methods. In the experiment of spectrum prediction, we compared it with some common methods in the field of spectrum prediction, such as LSTM, CNN and attention mechanism, according to the previous literature. It should be noted that most of these literatures do not disclose their data sets and hyperparameters, so this paper may not perfectly restore their performance, but after enough comparisons, it is enough to illustrate the superiority of our method.

4.1 Datasets and Preprocessing

The data set of the experiment in this paper comes from the open-source spectrum measurement data of Aachen university of technology in Germany [13]. The dataset contains 30 MHz-6 GHz spectrum monitoring data collected from three monitoring sites in Aachen and Maastricht. The frequency resolution is 200 kHz, and the acquisition time interval is about 1.8 s. This paper selects the 1500-3000 MHz monitoring results collected at the third-floor balcony of a residential area in Aachen for about 14 days as the data set of this experiment.

In this paper, the spectrum occupancy sequence is predicted, and the monitoring data is processed into an occupancy sequence with an interval of 15 min according to the technical specifications recommended by ITU. At the same time, in order to avoid the influence of a large number of long-term unused or long-term used channels, the above-mentioned channels are excluded from the experiments in this paper. Because the prediction of these channels is easy and meaningless, it will affect the evaluation of algorithm performance. In the prediction experiment in this paper, we use the historical data of the past two days to predict the outcome of the next day. That is, the input sequence length of our prediction model is 192, and the output result length is 96.

4.2 Analysis of Results

We first explore the impact of the TrSAX method on the clustering effect of spectrum monitoring data. The clustering evaluation index used in this paper is the silhouette coefficient. This index is an evaluation method of clustering effect, which combines two factors: cohesion and separation. It can be used to evaluate the impact of different algorithms or different operating modes of algorithms on the clustering results on the basis of the same original data. The results are shown in Fig. 6. We mainly focus on the comparison of the highest points between the curves, that is, the best performance of the two clustering methods under the optimal number of clusters. It can be seen that the best performance of the TrSAX method occurs when the number of clusters is 5, and its silhouette coefficient is much higher than the result of directly clustering the original sequence under all the number of clusters. In contrast, the best performance for clustering using the original sequence occurs when the number of clusters is 2. Obviously, the result of clustering into 2 clusters does not group the data very well, which shows that the clustering results using the original sequence are far from ideal. In the subsequent comparative experiments, the number of clusters used in this paper is uniformly 5.

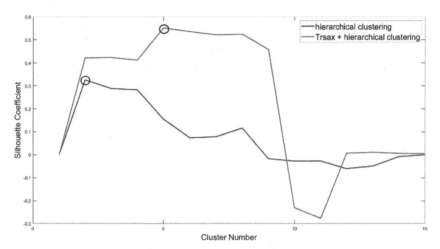

Fig. 6. Performance based on TrSAX clustering.

Then, we compare the performance of spectrum prediction. In this experiment, we uniformly use three layers of LSTM, and the number of hidden units in each layer of LSTM is 128. Experiments were carried out on five clusters based on TrSAX and hierarchical clustering. The experimental results are shown in Fig. 7. It can be seen that the RMSE of multiple networks in the first two clusters are almost the same, and the clustering based method in the last three clusters has achieved obvious advantages, of which our method has more obvious advantages. It can be predicted that this advantage will become more obvious as the predicted spectrum bandwidth increases. Therefore, we believe that clustering grouping is a simple and effective method to improve the performance of broadband prediction involving multiple services.

Finally, we compared the performance of different methods on all prediction steps, as shown in Fig. 8. As shown in the blue curve in the figure, the trsax-seq2seq method used in this paper achieves the overall minimum root mean square error, and the error is relatively stable in all steps. The performance of other clustering based methods is second. The performance of non clustering method is average. We believe that, in the case of the broadband data set used in this paper, even if the clustering method is not

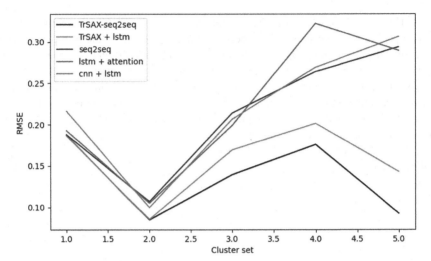

Fig. 7. RMSE performance comparison of different models in five groups

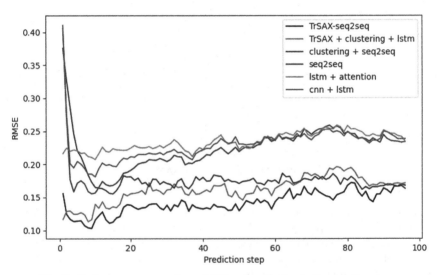

Fig. 8. Performance comparison of different methods on all prediction steps.

ideal, its performance index has been significantly improved. It further shows that our method is effective in this broadband prediction scenario.

5   Conclusion

In this paper, the problem of long-term spectral prediction over broadband is investigated. Based on the difficulties faced by this problem, a clustering and grouping method of spectral data based on TrSAX expression was developed and combined with the seq2seq network to improve the accuracy of prediction. Experiments are carried out on a real open source spectrum monitoring dataset, and the experimental results demonstrate the effectiveness of the method proposed in this paper. We expect to introduce a more advanced encoder-decoder structure model Transformer applied to this problem in the future to further improve the prediction performance.

Acknowledgment. This work is supported by the National Natural Science Foundation of China (61771154) and the Fundamental Research Funds for the Central Universities (3072021CF0801).

This work is also supported by Key Laboratory of Advanced Marine Communication and Information Technology, Ministry of Industry and Information Technology, Harbin Engineering University, Harbin, China.

References

1. Lin, Y., Wang, C., Wang, J., Dou, Z.: A novel dynamic spectrum access framework based on reinforcement learning for cognitive radio sensor networks. Sensors **16**(10), 1675 (2016)
2. Guo, L., Wang, M., Lin, Y.: Electromagnetic environment portrait based on big data mining. Wireless Communications and Mobile Computing (2021)
3. Mosavat-Jahromi, H., Li, Y., Cai, L., Pan, J.: Prediction and modeling of spectrum occupancy for dynamic spectrum access systems. IEEE Transactions on Cognitive Communications and Networking **7**(3), 715–728 (2021)
4. Wang, Y., Zhang, Z., Ma, L., Chen, J.: SVM-based spectrum mobility prediction scheme in mobile cognitive radio networks. The Scientific World Journal (2014)
5. Wang, X., Peng, T., Zuo, P., Wang, X.: Spectrum Prediction Method for ISM Bands Based on LSTM. In: 2020 5th International Conference on Computer and Communication Systems (ICCCS), pp. 580–584. IEEE (2020 May)
6. Shawel, B.S., Woldegebreal, D.H., Pollin, S.: Convolutional LSTM-based long-term spectrum prediction for dynamic spectrum access. In: 2019 27th European Signal Processing Conference (EUSIPCO), pp. 1–5. IEEE (2019 September)
7. Shi, C., Dou, Z., Lin, Y., Li, W.: Dynamic threshold-setting for RF-powered cognitive radio networks in non-Gaussian noise. Physical Communication **27**, 99–105 (2018)
8. Yu, Y., Zhu, Y., Wan, D., Liu, H., Zhao, Q.: A novel symbolic aggregate approximation for time series. In: Lee, S., Ismail, R., Choo, H. (eds.) IMCOM 2019. AISC, vol. 935, pp. 805–822. Springer, Cham (2019). https://doi.org/10.1007/978-3-030-19063-7_65
9. Yahyaoui, H., Al-Daihani, R.: A novel trend based SAX reduction technique for time series. Expert Syst. Appl. **130**, 113–123 (2019)
10. Sun, J., Wang, J., Chen, J., Ding, G., Lin, F.: Clustering analysis for internet of spectrum devices: real-world data analytics and applications. IEEE Internet Things J. **7**(5), 4485–4496 (2020)
11. Zhang, Z., Li, M., Lin, X., Wang, Y., He, F.: Multistep speed prediction on traffic networks: A deep learning approach considering spatio-temporal dependencies. Transportation research part C: emerging technologies **105**, 297–322 (2019)
12. Gong, G., An, X., Mahato, N.K., Sun, S., Chen, S., Wen, Y.: Research on short-term load prediction based on Seq2seq model. Energies **12**(16), 3199 (2019)
13. Wellens, M., Mähönen, P.: Lessons learned from an extensive spectrum occupancy measurement campaign and a stochastic duty cycle model. Mobile networks and applications **15**(3), 461–474 (2010)
14. Zhang, L., Jia, M.: Accurate Spectrum Prediction Based on Joint LSTM with CNN toward Spectrum Sharing. In: 2021 IEEE Global Communications Conference (GLOBECOM), pp. 1–6. IEEE (2021 December)

A Joint Weighted Nonnegative Matrix Factorization Model via Fusing Attribute Information for Link Prediction

Minghu Tang[(✉)]

School of Computer Science, Qinghai Minzu University, Xining 810007, China
mhtang@tju.edu.cn

Abstract. Link prediction is a widely studied problem and receives considerable attention in data mining and machine learning fields. How to efficiently predict missing or hidden edges in the network is a problem that link prediction needs to solve. Traditional link prediction only focuses on the information of network topology and ignores some non-topological information, which makes the prediction performance of algorithm decline rapidly when encountering extremely sparse network. To compensate for this deficiency, this paper proposes a joint weighted nonnegative matrix factorization model for link prediction via incorporates attribute information. By designing a weighted matrix to process the attribute information of each node, both the structure and attribute information fused into the nonnegative matrix factorization framework can fully play a guiding role in the link prediction task, thus solving the problem of structure sparsity and improving the prediction performance of the algorithm. Extensive experiments on five attribute networks demonstrate that the proposed model has better prediction performance than the dozen benchmark methods and the state-of-the-art link prediction algorithms.

Keywords: Link prediction · Nonnegative matrix factorization · Attribute networks

1 Introduction

Link prediction is a widely studied problem and receives considerable attention in data mining and machine learning in the past decades. It aims to infer a link which is not observed in current network or will arise in the future network [1–8]. The network object of link prediction research is a complex topology structure abstracted from real-world physical systems. In general, people observe the interactive system in the real-world, extract the entities in the system as the vertices, and the interaction relationship between entities as the edges, and construct a topological graph corresponding to the physical system, namely complex network model. Then, the network model is taken as the research object to explore some laws underlying the physical interaction system and simulate their evolution mechanism. However, due to the complexity of the real physical system, the extractive network models are often structurally incomplete. That is, there is

© ICST Institute for Computer Sciences, Social Informatics and Telecommunications Engineering 2022
Published by Springer Nature Switzerland AG 2022. All Rights Reserved
Y. Chenggang et al. (Eds.): MobiMedia 2022, LNICST 451, pp. 190–205, 2022.
https://doi.org/10.1007/978-3-031-23902-1_15

always a missing situation of real information about the system in the complex network obtained through observation. The purpose of link prediction is to infer the missing or possible relationships in the future through this abstract complex network model, and to further study the evolution mechanism of real physical systems [9].

Because the research of link prediction problem is of great significance for the development of economy and society, its results are widely used in all walks of life in the real society [3, 4]. For example, analyze the evolution mechanism of the network [9], study the drug targeting relationship in the field of bioinformatics [10], realize the personalized recommendation of scenic spots or recommend new friends in social network [4, 11], and identify criminals in the field of public security [12–15].

At present, with the development of mobile Internet network, the amount of social information increases rapidly. When this real interaction system is abstracted into complex networks, the corresponding number of vertices becomes extremely large. However, the interaction relationship between the nodes did not grow significantly with the node scale. This phenomenon leads to exist many vertices in the extracted complex networks, but the edges between them appear extremely sparse. The phenomenon that the number of links known in the network is much less than the number of no links is called the structural sparsity problem. This problem has a very large impact on the performance of the link prediction [16, 17]. Therefore, how to solve the problem of declining prediction performance due to structural sparsity in large-scale networks becomes a challenge for link prediction. The motivation of this paper is to study the fusion problem of node attributes, so as to dig out the auxiliary information that can compensate for the sparsity of network structure, and build a multi-source information integration mode to realize the improvement of link prediction performance.

Recently, Social platforms based on mobile Internet networks are very frequently used, many network datasets appear with both the topology and node attribute information. For example, a webpage (i.e., vertex) can be associated with other webpages via hyperlinks, and it may have some inherent attributes of itself, like the text description in the webpage. Such type of networks is known as attributed networks. Some studies have shown that the degradation of the link prediction performance due to the sparse structure can be alleviated to some extent by using the node attribute information [17]. Recently, some link prediction methods are proposed based on attribute networks [18–22]. However, due to the diversity and heterogeneity of information and the variability of fusion methods, these algorithms either have poor overall prediction, or lack sufficient migration and robustness, or have too high computational complexity to adapt to large-scale networks. Therefore, the problem of how to reasonably integrate the structure and node attribute information has largely not been successfully solved.

Non-negative matrix factorization (NMF) is an important technique in the field of machine learning [23]. It can integrate heterogeneous information and promote each factor information to play a potential role [24]. In general, for a given matrix $X \in R_+^{n \times m}$, the NMF algorithm tries to find two non-negative factor matrices $B \in R_+^{n \times k}$ and $C \in R_+^{k \times m}$, make $X = X' \approx BC$. Where the k is called internal rank or hidden space, it satisfies $(m + n)k \ll m$. The solution of NMF usually transforms into an optimization problem of finding $min_{B \geq 0, C \geq 0} L(X, BC)$, and the symbol $L(., .)$ represents a certain loss function, such as Euclidean distance, KL divergence, or IS divergence. Given the Euclidean distance, the above optimization method can be converted to $min_{B,C}||X - BC||_F^2$, and the $B \geq 0, C \geq 0$. Symbols $|| \cdot ||_F$ indicate the Frobenius norm. The F-norm of a general matrix is usually defined as $||X||_F = \sqrt{\sum_{ij} |x_{ij}|^2} = \sqrt{tr(X^T X)}$.

Considering the advantages of NMF models when incorporating multi-source information. In this paper, we introduce a *Joint Weighted Nonnegative Matrix Factorization* method for link prediction on attributed networks, namely JWNMF. For a given attributed network, our method presents a mechanism by using joint-NMF to integrate the structural and attribute information. Specifically, we design two matrix factorization terms. One is modeling the topology structure and the other is for attributes. Meanwhile, we modify the NMF by introducing a weighting variable for each attribute, which can be automatically updated and determined in each iteration.

Experiments are performed on five real-world attribute network datasets. The results show the advantages of performance of JWNMF model comparison with the benchmark methods and advanced algorithms.

The rest article develops as follows. Section 2 shows the related works. Section 3 is the network description and the problem definition. Section 4 is about the establishment of the proposed model and its optimization. Section 5 is experimental design and results analysis. The last part contains our conclusions and prospects.

2 Related Work

As a research hotspot in the field of complex network science, link prediction has been widely concerned by researchers in recent years. However, there are not much studies to fuse non-topological information like node attributes with network topological information and then realize link prediction, especially the framework based on NMF. Han et al. [16] used the configuration files of online social-contact users and other non-topological information, such as workplace and school to compute the attribute similarity, for counting the number of attributes the users all possess and the geographic distance between the users. Then, they proposed a prediction model based on support vector machines. Wang et al. [17] extracted topological and non-topological information by an implicit feature representation model, then proposed a link prediction method for missing link. Li et al. [18] proposed a link prediction for dynamic attributed networks. Moreover, for attribute networks with isolated nodes, the literature [17, 19–22] makes full use of attribute information to achieve link prediction on semi-structured networks.

However, it is difficult to integrate multi-source heterogeneous information and make them work in experimental prediction tasks. In this respect, the method based on matrix factorization is widely used [23, 24]. Menon et al. [25] proposed a link prediction algorithm based on the matrix factorization. Pech et al. [26] proposed a matrix filling-based link prediction method using the matrix filling principle in the field of recommendation systems. For the network topology sparsity, Chen et al. [27] proposed a link prediction model of robust NMF by using manifold regularization and sparse learning. To make full use of the node attribute information, Chen et al. [28] proposed a link prediction model incorporating node attribute information based on NMF, but the time complexity of their algorithm is high. Jiao et al. [29] proposed a Link predication model based on matrix factorization. This model fused multi class organizations information of network. They take advantage of the auxiliary information beyond the node attributes. Chen et al. [30] proposed a novel link prediction model based on deep NMF, which elegantly fuses topology and sparsity-constrained to perform link prediction tasks. Inspired by the matrix perturbation principle, Wang et al. [31] proposed a perturbation-based model for NMF link prediction. Moreover, there are also some NMF-based prediction models, they are used in dynamic time-varying networks [32, 33].

3 Preliminary

In this section, we introduce the formalized description of the problem of link prediction, and the network definition.

3.1 Network Representation

Given an undirected attribute network $G(V, E, A)$ with n nodes, where $V = \{v_1, v_2, \cdots v_n\}$ is the set of nodes and $E = \{(v_i, v_j), 1 \leq i \leq n, 1 \leq j \leq n, i \neq j\}$ is the set of edges. The A is the set of attributes of all nodes in network. For the network G with n vertex, there are m attributes value for each vertex. These attributes are available to be represented by a matrix $A_{n \times m}$. Each row of the matrix $A_{n \times m}$ represents an attribute vector of the corresponding node v_i. If the node v_i has the k-th attribute value, then $A_{ik} = 1$, otherwise $A_{ik} = 0$. The topology structure of the attribute network is represented by an adjacency matrix $S_{n \times n}$. The element of the ith row and the jth column in the matrix correspond to the link between nodes v_i and v_j in the network, where $S_{ij} = 1$ if there is a link from v_i to v_j and $S_{ij} = 0$ otherwise. Multiple edges between two nodes and back edges on single nodes are not allowed.

3.2 Link Prediction Problem

The purpose of link prediction is to infer the probability P_{ij} of the existence of an edge between any two nodes v_i and v_j by using the known information in the network. In general, based on the sociological principle that "the more similar people are more likely to be connected", the P_{ij} is treated as some similarity between nodes v_i and v_j. The higher P_{ij}, the more similar v_i and v_j are, and the more likely v_i is to form a link with v_j. For a given observation network G, the P_{ij} probability of forming edges between unconnected nodes is inferred through the model proposed. The predicted values are then arranged in descending order, and the pairs of nodes at the top are considered the most likely to form connections. In this paper, we compute the score P_{xy} based on JWNMF model.

4 Proposed Method

In this section, we will introduce our proposed method in detail, which aims to fuse the attribute information of the nodes into the link prediction process.

4.1 Link Prediction Model: JWNMF

Excavating the available information and constructing a reasonable information fusion mode are the main ideas to solve the problem of network topology sparsity, and realize the link prediction task. Therefore, the basic framework of NMF is used to fully integrate the node attributes and network structure information to compensate for the defects of incomplete topological information, to realize the link prediction task and improve the performance in this paper. First, based on the basic principle of NMF, the adjacency matrix S representing the network topology is decomposed into the product of two non-negative factor matrices, namely $S \approx VV^T$, and the matrix A representing the node attribute information decomposed into $A \approx ZU^T$. However, the aim of this paper is to address information integration. Therefore, in order to enable the network structure and node attribute information to fully integrate and play a leading role in the link prediction, we need to attach certain constraint rules to their decomposed factor matrix. Inspired by the methods described in ref [24], which often delivers promising results for graph clustering, we apply the idea for attributed graph link prediction. Here, the hidden space V after the network structure information S is decomposed is approximately equal to the hidden space Z of the node attribute information, so that it can remain the same in the process of model learning, so as to achieve the purpose of mutual fusion and constraining the network structure and node attribute information. Therefore, the partial information of the attribute A is decomposed into the hidden space V of the structure information, namely $A \approx VU^T$. When the two-source information is integrated in a unified framework and uses Euclidean distance as a loss function, the overall model framework for the link prediction task is expressed as follows:

$$L = min_{V,U}||S - VV^T||_F^2 + \lambda||A - VU^T||_F^2 s.t. V \geq 0, U \geq 0, \qquad (1)$$

where $S \in R_+^{n \times n}$, $A \in R_+^{n \times m}$, the factor matrix $U \in R_+^{m \times k}$ and $V \in R_+^{n \times k}$ represent the hidden space that integrates topological structure and node attribute information, R_+ represents non-negative real number sets. The parameter $\lambda > 0$ balance the availability of structure and attribute information.

Since the node attributes in the network are easy to mix with noise, in order to further reduce the impact of the noise on the prediction results, and promote the guiding role of the attribute information in predicting the network structure information, we also introduce a matrix W to assign a weight for each attribute. At this point, the decomposition form can be expressed as $AW \approx VU^T$. By assigning a weight information to each node attribute with the matrix W, the effect of similarity between the node attributes can be uniformly integrated into the structure information to provide a promotion for the final results of link prediction. The weight matrix W is set to a diagonal matrix, which satisfies $\sum_{i=1}^{m} W_{i,i} = 1$. After introducing the weight matrix W, the complete objective function is expressed as follows:

$$L = min_{V,U}||S - VV^T||_F^2 + \lambda||AW - VU^T||_F^2 s.t. V \geq 0, U \geq 0, \qquad (2)$$

where, the weight matrix $W \epsilon R_+^{m \times m}$. To ensure that the W weights are assigned to a rule space, update operations need to be normalized to:

$$W = \frac{W}{\sum_{i=1}^{m} W_{i,i}}, \tag{3}$$

4.2 Update Rules

The solution of model L is difficult to obtain the global optimal solution, but the local optimal solution can be realized by the multiplicative iterative method. Therefore, for V, U and W three factor matrices, introduce their corresponding non-negative Lagrangian multiplier α, β, γ, thus replacing the objective function Eq. (2) with an unconstrained loss function form:

$$L = \frac{1}{2}\left(||S - VV^T||_F^2 + \lambda||AW - VU^T||_F^2\right) + Tr\left(\alpha^T V\right) + Tr\left(\beta^T U\right) + Tr\left(\gamma^T W\right), \tag{4}$$

Simplified the Eq. (4) and take the partial differentiations of L for V, U, W respectively, then

$$\frac{\partial L}{\partial V} = -\left(SV + S^T V + \lambda AWU\right) + 2VV^T V + \lambda VU^T U + \alpha, \tag{5}$$

$$\frac{\partial L}{\partial U} = -\lambda WA^T V + \lambda UV^T V + \beta, \tag{6}$$

$$\frac{\partial L}{\partial W} = -\lambda A^T VU^T + \lambda A^T AW + \gamma, \tag{7}$$

In this regard, according to complementary relaxation condition of the Karush-Kuhn-Tucker (KKT), we have $\alpha V = 0, \beta U = 0, \gamma W = 0$. Set $\frac{\partial L}{\partial V} = 0, \frac{\partial L}{\partial U} = 0, \frac{\partial L}{\partial W} = 0$, then the update rule for V, U, W is obtained.

$$V \leftarrow V \frac{SV + S^T V + \lambda AWU}{2VV^T V + \lambda VU^T U}, \tag{8}$$

$$U \leftarrow U \frac{WA^T V}{UV^T V}, \tag{9}$$

$$W \leftarrow W \frac{A^T VU^T}{A^T AW}, \tag{10}$$

The above update rules Eq. (8) - Eq. (10) can be solved by element value or by matrix form as a whole. During the model learning training, the three-factor matrix V, U, W is obtained based on the convergence condition of the objective function. Then, the approximate solution of original network topology structure is solved by using the decomposition formula $V \times V^T$. That is, after learning the matrix V through model training, we can obtain the similarity score between any two nodes in the network, or the probability P_{ij} of exist edge between two nodes, and finally realize the link prediction task.

In general, in the learning process, the model will seek the local optimal solutions of V, U, W using the update rules. However, before implementing the update operation, the adjacency matrix S and the attribute matrix A need to be preprocessed and given an initial value.

$$S = \frac{S}{\sum_{i=1}^{n} \sum_{j=1}^{n} S_{i,j}}, \quad (11)$$

$$A = \frac{A}{\sum_{i=1}^{n} \sum_{j=1}^{m} A_{i,j}}, \quad (12)$$

Note that updates the weight matrix W use Eq. (3).

The model JWNMF integrates the network structure and node attribute information through the NMF framework, and assigns a weight constraint information to each node attribute through the introduced diagonal matrix W, so that the network structure and node attributes can maximize their respective roles in the model training and learning process to serve the final prediction results. A schematic diagram of the principle of the model JWNMF is shown in Fig. 1.

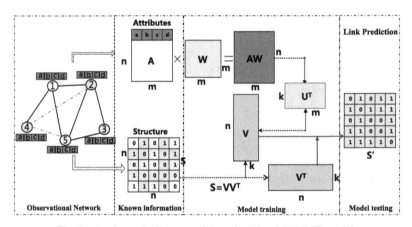

Fig. 1. A schematic diagram of the principle of JWNMF model.

In conclusion, according to the basic principles of the proposed JWNMF model, the pseudo-code description of the algorithm is designed as follows (shown in Table 1).

The experimental environment of this paper is based on the operating system of windows10 of x86 computer, and then the simulation experiment of link prediction is implemented with Matlab tool programming. Here, the computational complexity is discussed. The computational complexity of JWNMF algorithm comes mainly from the time cost when iteratively updating the matrix V, U, W. For a given network $G(V, E)$, the number of vertices V is n, and each vertex has m attributes. When updating V, U and W, to reduce the time overhead, we utilize the objective relative error as the stopping criterion and set to less than 10^{-6} in experiment. Moreover, the dimension

Table 1. Pseudo-code description of JWNMF algorithm

Algorithm Name: JWNMF

Input: S: the adjacency matrix of the given network, A: the auxiliary information matrix,
  k: number of features, λ: parameters.

Output: the approximate matrix of the network S

1: divide S into S^{train}, S^{test}

2: Initialize S and A by using Eq. (11) and Eq. (12).

3: Initialize V, U and W randomly.

4: do while

5:     update V, U and W by means of Eq. (8) – Eq. (10).

6:     get V after until object function convergence

7: end while

8: output VV^T

---

k after the matrix decomposition is a constant. Supposing the algorithm stops after t iterations, the overall cost for Symmetric NMF is $O(n^2 kt)$. As the objective function adds one more linear matrix factorization term, the overall cost for updating rules is $O((n^2 k + m^2 k + mnk)t)$. According to the analysis rules of the time complexity of computer algorithms, when the scale n tends to infinity, the worst case of the time complexity of the model can be approximated by $O(n^2)$.

5   Experiment

This section mainly shows and analyzes the model prediction performance. Next, we will describe the datasets, comparison methods, evaluation metrics, and discussion of experimental results.

5.1   Datasets

This subsection mainly describes the basic topology of the datasets used in this paper, and the method of dividing training set and testing set.

To verify the model prediction performance, five real-world attribute network datasets widely used in the link prediction field were selected.

The basic topological properties of these network datasets are listed in Table 2. Where the symbol N represents the total number of network nodes, E represents the total number of existing links, $< K >$ is the network average degree, $< d >$ is the average shortest distance, C is the clustering coefficient, and *#attributes* represent dimension of node attributes. These network datasets used for the experiment can be downloaded from the following web sites. http://vladowiki.fmf.uni-lj.si/doku.php?id=pajek: data:urls:index; http://snap.stanford.edu/data/. For a detailed description of the data set, please also see the above website introduction.

Table 2. Topological information of the network datasets

Network	N	E	$<K>$	$<d>$	C	#attributes
Lazega	71	378	10.8	2.104	0.3853	7
Facebook	228	3419	29.991	1.868	0.6162	56
Cornell	195	286	2.903	3.2	0.1568	1703
Texas	187	298	3.027	3.036	0.1937	1703
Washington	230	366	3.373	2.995	0.1974	1703

5.2   Datasets Division Method

When comparing the prediction performance of the algorithm, the given network dataset needs to be divided according to the basic principles of machine learning. It is divided into training set and test set. There are many methods to divide data sets, and k-fold cross validation is used in this paper. The sample dataset was randomly divided into k parts, one of which was selected as test set and the remaining as training set, and then a prediction accuracy was calculated, so repeated k times. The prediction accuracy of the algorithm on the entire network dataset is the average of k prediction accuracies. In practical partitioning, k-taking 10 is a common method.

5.3   Evaluation Metrics

Like many existing link prediction studies, in our work adopts also the most frequently-used metrics AUC (area under the ROC curve) and the Precision to measure the performance of algorithm proposed. These metrics are viewed as a robust measure in the presence of data imbalance, which are also one of the most popular indices of evaluation link prediction. For more details on these two evaluation methods, readers can refer to the literature [1–4].

5.4   Baseline Methods

To validate the predictive performance of the newly designed algorithms, people usually select some benchmark methods and those representative up-to-date algorithms from the literature as the reference objects for comparative analysis. Generally, in order to reflect the fairness of comparison, the design principle of the comparison method selected is usually similar to the algorithm proposed. Therefore, in the experiment, several state-of-the-art algorithms based on NMF framework design often used in the link prediction research field are selected as reference objects. The benchmark methods are mainly structural similarity based classical algorithms.

We list four types of link prediction methods as the benchmark methods, including eleven local similarity indices based on the number of common neighbours between pairs of nodes (CN, AA, RA, PA, Salton, Jaccard, Sorenson, HPI, HDI, LHN and TSCN), four random walk methods (ACT, CosPlus, LRW, SRW), three local path methods (LocalP, Katz, LHN-II) and four other similarity algorithms (MFI, LNBCN, LNBAA, LNBRA).

The mathematical expressions of these methods and their definitions can be found in ref. [1–4].

In addition, four state-of-the-art NMF-based link prediction algorithms were used as comparison methods in the experiment. They are the original NMF method [23], matrix fill method (MC) [26], the attribute-based NMF method (NMF_LP) [28] and the NMF method based on the perturbation principle (SPM_NMF) [31] respectively.

5.5 Experimental Results and Analysis

This section provides a comprehensive analysis of the predictive performance of JWNMF model. Experiments were performed on five real-world network datasets. The prediction performance of various algorithms is fairly judged by two evaluation indicators, Precision and AUC, and show the final evaluation results. In experiment, the datasets were divided into test set E^{test} and training set E^{train} in different proportions. The results of experimental simulation are analyzed by taking the overall average at each proportion. Typically, the value of average prediction accuracy obtained from 100 independent simulations via Precision or AUC are taken as the final performance results.

5.6 Model Parameter Setting

To adjust the prediction performance of the JWNMF model to the optimum, the parameter λ in the model was analyzed before the start of the experiment. Figure 2 shows the predictive performance of the model when its parameter values are in the range from 0 to 3. Through the comparative analysis, the local optimum of the parameters λ is finally determined. In experiment, the parameter λ of JWNMF model takes a value of 0.09.

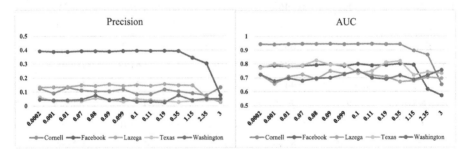

Fig.2. Analysis parameter λ of JWNMF model

5.7 Performance Analysis

According to the conventional way in the field of link prediction research, each experimental data set is first divided by the ratio of 20% to 90%, and the step size is 10, with a total of 8 proportions. Assuming that the total number of existent edges are $|E|=m$ in the

Table 3. Predictive results via AUC metrics on five network datasets

AUC	Texas	Cornell	Washington	Lazega	Facebook
CN	0.5449	0.5620	0.5637	0.6675	0.8863
AA	0.5596	0.5770	0.5695	0.6816	0.9017
RA	0.5562	0.5804	0.5698	0.6808	**0.9102**
PA	0.6970	0.7770	**0.7680**	0.6440	0.8350
Salton	0.5348	0.5435	0.5544	0.6562	0.8431
Jaccard	0.5283	0.5447	0.5518	0.6575	0.8579
Sorens	0.5280	0.5560	0.5150	0.6430	0.8280
HPI	0.5330	0.5670	0.5130	0.6490	0.7870
HDI	0.5270	0.5370	0.5220	0.6580	0.8230
LHN	0.5470	0.5370	0.5270	0.6350	0.7300
TSCN	0.5390	0.5530	0.5060	0.6800	0.4300
ACT	0.5977	0.5713	0.5983	0.6295	0.8476
CosPlus	0.5080	0.5540	0.4860	0.6660	0.9020
LRW_4	0.6500	0.6580	0.6720	0.7640	0.9100
SRW_3	0.6460	0.6250	0.6220	0.7200	0.9080
LocalP	0.5870	0.6110	0.6090	0.6600	0.9020
Katz	0.6539	0.6567	0.6935	0.7093	0.4389
LHNII.9	0.5017	0.5133	0.4910	0.5093	0.6380
MFI	0.6190	0.6720	0.6100	0.7040	0.8980
LNBCN	0.6070	0.6460	0.6290	0.6930	0.8730
LNBAA	0.5940	0.6680	0.6070	0.6730	0.9060
LNBRA	0.6230	0.6300	0.5900	0.6870	0.9090
NMF	0.5521	0.4950	0.4962	0.6783	0.8290
MC	0.5235	0.4470	0.4432	0.5000	0.5005
SPM_NMF	0.6260	0.7095	0.6362	0.7223	0.8745
NMF_LP	0.6421	0.7398	0.6705	0.7551	0.7795
JWNMF	**0.7080**	**0.8100**	0.7170	**0.7811**	0.8880

network. It indicates that 20% of the m are used for the training set when the partition ratio is 20%, while the remaining 80% is used as the test set.

The JWNMF model was trained on this training set together with the benchmark and contrast methods. To judge their prediction performance, the test set is then used to measure the effect. Each experiment needs to be run at least 100 times independently and then averaged as the result. Although the many results generated by experiments, considering the universality and representativeness, Table 3 only shows the overall prediction effect of each method in the data set divided by 50%, the training set and the test set are in half each. The predictions values are shown in Table 3 by using AUC as the evaluation criterion.

From the numerical results presented in Table 3, The JWNMF method led the prediction performance on three datasets: Texas, Cornell and Lazega, but performed poorly on the Washington and Facebook datasets. As the overall analysis, the proposed JWNMF model showed good prediction performance on five datasets of attribute networks. This also shows that when implementing the link prediction, it can mine the external information such as the attributes of the nodes as an auxiliary, which can significantly improve the performance of the link prediction algorithm. This is significantly better effective than simply using structural information. Moreover, for networks with extremely sparse structure, using this external auxiliary information is more helpful to compensate for the insufficient performance problem caused by the sparse topological structure. Of course, the question of how to mine this auxiliary information and which external auxiliary information works better for the prediction is still under discussion. In order to show the overall predictive performance of the various methods more deeply, Fig. 3 shows the prediction effect when the data set is partitioned at 50% with Precision as the evaluation criterion.

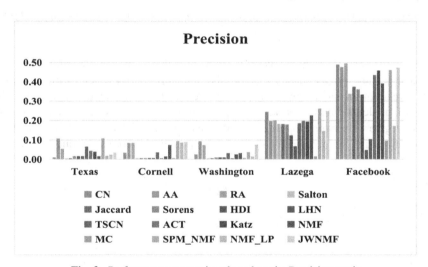

Fig. 3. Performance comparison based on the Precision metic

Above, we briefly mention that the network topology sparsity has obvious effects on the prediction performance of the algorithm. To demonstrate this problem more specifically, many experiments were deliberately designed and completed during the study. In these experiments, the network dataset was divided from dense to sparse in a ratio of 90% to 20%, and under each division scheme, the prediction performance of each algorithm is verified by Precision and AUC standards, to test the impact of network topology on the prediction results of each algorithm. Moreover, it is also used to verify the adaptability and robustness of each algorithm under the different degrees of sparsity at network topology.

Taking the Facebook dataset as an example, the AUC values of each algorithm after the different partition proportions are shown in Table 4.

Table 4. The AUC value under different partitioning of Facebook dataset

AUC	0.9	0.8	0.7	0.6	0.5	0.4	0.3	0.2
CN	0.9243	0.9237	0.9191	0.9069	0.8863	0.8642	0.8100	0.7041
AA	0.9355	0.9329	0.9267	0.9208	0.9017	0.8755	0.8227	0.7175
Salton	0.9260	0.9089	0.8954	0.8727	0.8431	0.8095	0.7620	0.6821
Jaccard	0.9067	0.9048	0.8927	0.8821	0.8579	0.8234	0.7674	0.6912
ACT	0.8468	0.8450	0.8462	0.8532	0.8476	0.8434	0.8344	0.8233
Katz	0.3394	0.3879	0.4147	0.3550	0.4389	0.4697	0.4002	0.2557
MC	0.8326	0.7954	0.7377	0.6458	0.5005	0.5000	0.5000	0.5000
NMF	0.9086	0.8879	0.8642	0.8527	0.8290	0.8004	0.7726	0.7419
SPM_NMF	0.9294	0.9158	0.9050	0.8907	0.8745	0.8575	0.8391	0.8059
JWNMF	0.9445	0.9369	0.9196	0.9073	0.8880	0.8614	0.8354	0.7853

From the analysis of these values, it can be seen that as the topology of the network gradually changes from dense to sparse, the prediction performance of the algorithm will have a significant downward trend. However, the prediction algorithm based on the JWNMF model still performs well at all proportions. This shows when facing different sparse degree of network topology, it can make full use of various external auxiliary information and compensate for the lack of topological information due to structure

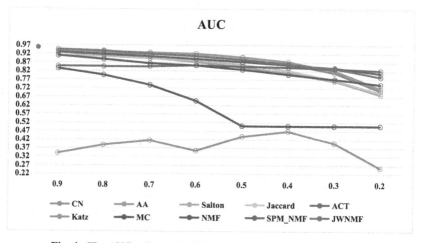

Fig. 4. The AUC value under different partition of Facebook dataset

sparsity. Thus, it basically ensures the prediction performance of the algorithm in abnormal cases, and improves the adaptability and robustness of the algorithm. Figure 4 shows this result more visually.

Similarly, with Precision as the evaluation criterion, we also compared the prediction performance of the various algorithms at different proportions of Facebook dataset (in Fig. 5). Although the model JWNMF is not the best under each partitioning scheme, it still shows a good prediction effect.

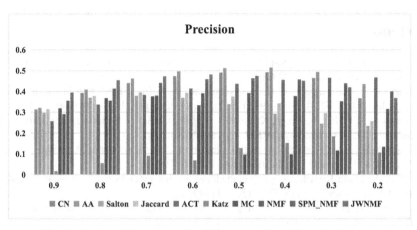

Fig. 5. The Precision value under different partition of Facebook dataset

6   Conclusion

In recent years, link prediction based on network topology has been one of the research hotspots in the field of data mining. However, in many cases, those algorithms that use only the information of network topology do not provide the accuracy required for link prediction, when the network topology is in an extremely sparse state. Furthermore, real-world networks are often sparse and contain noise, which makes the predictive performance of the algorithm very strongly correlated with the properties of the network itself. For these extremely sparse and noisy networks, the ultimate effect is not ideal if only the structural information is used to complete the prediction task. At present, with the development of mobile Internet, it is more and more convenient to obtain the non-topological information of network. This provides a hope for link prediction research.

In this paper, considering the advantages of NMF that is interpretability, nonnegative, and information fusion, we propose a link prediction model of weighted NMF. By designing a weighted matrix w to process the attribute information of each node, both the structure and attribute information fused into the NMF framework can fully play a guiding role in the link prediction task, thus solving the problem of structure sparsity and improving the prediction performance of the algorithm. Although our method can significantly improve the performance of link prediction on sparse networks, its temporal complexity is relatively high. This is also a direction that we need to improve in the future. In addition, we also consider the cold-start link prediction of complex network in a semi-structured state as another target for future studies.

Acknowledgments. We would like to thank the anonymous reviewers for their contributions. This research was supported by the Teaching Reform Research Project of Qinghai Minzu University, China (2021-JYYB-009).

References

1. Martinez, V., Berzal, F., Cubero, J.C.: A survey of link prediction in complex networks. ACM Comput. Surv. **49**(4), 69–102 (2017)
2. Haghani, S., Keyvanpour, M.R.: A systemic analysis of link prediction in social network. Artif. Intell. Rev. **52**(3), 1961–1995 (2017). https://doi.org/10.1007/s10462-017-9590-2
3. Kumar, A., Singh, S.S., Singh, K., Biswas, B.: Link prediction techniques, applications, and performance: A survey. Phys. A **553**, 124289 (2020)
4. Daud, N.N., et al.: Applications of link prediction in social networks: A review. Journal of Network and Computer Applications **166**, 102716 (2020)
5. Rossi, A., et al.: Knowledge graph embedding for link prediction: A comparative analysis. ACM Trans. Knowl. Discov. Data **15**(2), 14–49 (2021)
6. Zhang, H.-F., et al.: Predicting missing links in complex networks via an extended local naïve Bayes model. EPL (Europhysics Letters) **130**(3), 38002 (2020)
7. Cai, L., et al.: Line graph neural networks for link prediction. IEEE Transactions on Pattern Analysis and Machine Intelligence (2021)
8. Singh, S.S., et al.: CLP-ID: Community-based link prediction using information diffusion. Inf. Sci. **514**, 402–433 (2020)
9. Zhang, Q.M., et al.: Measuring multiple evolution mechanisms of complex networks. Sci. Rep. **5**(1), 10350 (2015)
10. Nasiri, E., et al.: A novel link prediction algorithm for protein-protein interaction networks by attributed graph embedding. Computers in Biology and Medicine **137**, 104772 (2021)
11. Li, S., et al.: Friend recommendation for cross marketing in online brand community based on intelligent attention allocation link prediction algorithm. Expert Systems with Applications **139**(2020), 112839 (2020)
12. Bohannon, J.: Counterterrorism's new tool: "metanetwork" analysis. Science **325**(5939), 409–411 (2009)
13. Tayebi, M.A., Glässer, U.: Social network analysis in predictive policing: concepts, models and methods, pp. 7–14. Springer International Publishing (2016)
14. Assouli, N., Benahmed, K., Gasbaoui, B.: How to predict crime — informatics-inspired approach from link prediction. Physica A: Statistical Mechanics and its Applications, 570–125795 (2021)
15. Pang, G., et al. Deep learning for anomaly detection: A review. Association for Computing Machinery **54**(2) (2021)
16. Han, X., et al.: Link prediction for new users in social networks. IEEE International Conference on Communications (ICC), pp. 1250–1255 (2015)
17. Wang, Z., et al.: An Approach to Cold-start link prediction: establishing connections between non-topological and topological information. IEEE Trans. Knowl. Data Eng. **28**(11), 2857–2870 (2016)

18. Li, J., et al.: Streaming link prediction on dynamic attributed networks. Proceedings of the Eleventh ACM International Conference on Web Search and Data Mining, pp. 369–377 (2018)

19. Hao, Y., et al.: Inductive link prediction for nodes having only attribute information. Proceedings of the Twenty-Ninth International Joint Conference on Artificial Intelligence (IJCAI-20), pp. 1209–1215 (2020)

20. Berahmand, K., Nasiri, E., Rostami, M., Forouzandeh, S.: A modified DeepWalk method for link prediction in attributed social network. Computing **103**(10), 2227–2249 (2021). https://doi.org/10.1007/s00607-021-00982-2

21. Shuo, Y., et al.: Inductive link prediction with interactive structure learning on attributed graph. ECML PKDD 2021: Machine Learning and Knowledge Discovery in Databases. Research Track, pp. 383–398 (2021)

22. Zhang, J.W., Kong, X.N., Yu, P.S.: Predicting social links for new users across aligned heterogeneous social networks. 2013 IEEE 13th International Conference on Data Mining (Icdm), pp. 1289–1294 (2013)

23. Gan, J., et al.: Non-negative matrix factorization: a survey. Comput. J. **64**(7), 1080–1092 (2021)

24. Kim, J., Shim, K., Cao, L., Lee, J.-G., Lin, X., Moon, Y.-S. (eds.): PAKDD 2017. LNCS (LNAI), vol. 10234. Springer, Cham (2017). https://doi.org/10.1007/978-3-319-57454-7

25. Menon, A.K., Elkan, C.: Link prediction via matrix factorization. Joint European Conference on Machine Learning and Knowledge Discovery in Databases, pp. 437–452. Springer (2011)

26. Pech, R., et al.: Link prediction via matrix completion. EPL (Europhysics Letters) **117**(3), 38002 (2017)

27. Chen, G., et al.: Robust non-negative matrix factorization for link prediction in complex networks using manifold regularization and sparse learning. Phys. A **539**, 122882 (2020)

28. Chen, B., et al.: Link prediction based on non-negative matrix factorization. PLoS ONE **12**(8), e0182968 (2017)

29. Jiao, P., Cai, F., Feng, Y., Wang, W.: Link predication based on matrix factorization by fusion of multi class organizations of the network. Scientific Reports **7**(1), 8937 (2017)

30. Chen, G., et al.: Link prediction by deep non-negative matrix factorization. Expert Systems with Applications **188**, 115991 (2022)

31. Wang, W., et al.: A perturbation-based framework for link prediction via non-negative matrix factorization. Scientific Reports **6**(10), 38938 (2016)

32. Zhang, T., et al.: Semi-supervised link prediction based on non-negative matrix factorization for temporal networks. Chaos, Solitons Fractals **145**, 110769 (2021)

33. Zhang, J., et al.: Temporal link prediction for cancer networks using structural consistency regularized non-negative matrix factorization. IEEE International Conference on Bioinformatics and Biomedicine (BIBM), pp. 280–283 (2021)

Neural Networks and Feature Learning

Research on Music Genre Classification Based on Residual Network

Zhongwei Xu[1], Yuan Feng[1(✉)], Shengyu Song[1], Yuanxiang Xu[1], Ruiying Wang[2], Lan Zhang[1], and Jiahao Liu[1]

[1] College of Information Science and Engineering, Ocean University of China, Qingdao 266005, China
`fengyuan@ouc.edu.cn`, `{Songshengyu,liujiahao6266}@stu.ouc.edu.cn`
[2] Teaching Center of Fundamental Courses, Ocean University of China, Qingdao 266005, China

Abstract. With the rapid development of information technology, the number of songs is exploding, so the classification of music genres is a very challenging task, and at this stage, the implementation of automated classification of music genres is also a relatively popular scientific research topic. Mobile devices are all over people's lives and have brought great convenience to people's life and work, making it possible to work anywhere and anytime. However, the special characteristics of mobile devices require high model requirements, which are difficult to be realized by traditional models. We hope to use deep learning to automatically identify and classify music, and use the Mobilenet model to achieve lightweight music classification on mobile and improve the classification accuracy. In this paper, we mainly use Free Music Archive dataset for experiments, based on resnet101 network model and MobileNet model for music genre classification, mainly use Short Time Fourier Transform (STFT) and Mel Frequency Cepstrum Coefficient (MFCC) for music feature extraction, improve the data pre-processing, and compare with other model methods were compared, and the accuracy rate was about 7% higher than the traditional CRNN method, and better results were achieved. On the implementation of the lightweight model for mobile, the size of the parameters of the model trained by MobileNet is only 4% of the best model in this paper, and has a high accuracy rate.

Keywords: Residual Network (ResNet) · MobileNet · Depth learning · Short Fourier Transform (STFT) · Mel Frequency Cepstral Coefficient (MFCC)

1 Introduction

In the age of information technology, audio is everywhere. The gym may be playing a powerful DJ; the bookstore is playing beautiful light music; the concert hall is playing a rhythmic concerto; and there is a lullaby before bed...... Different scenes apply different types of music, and different genres of music are loved by different people. Nowadays, due to the rapid development of science and technology, the production of music has become easier and there are a large number of music lovers who are engaged in music,

Y. Chenggang et al. (Eds.): MobiMedia 2022, LNICST 451, pp. 209–223, 2022.
https://doi.org/10.1007/978-3-031-23902-1_16

and with it, the number of music tracks has skyrocketed. There are various music playing software, and the classification of music genres is more refined, and even personalized song list is pushed according to individual listening habits, but it is a great challenge for backend workers to classify music genres manually. Combined with the popularity of mobile devices and the increasing speed of computing, many lightweight tasks can already be done on mobile. However, traditional neural network training parameters and computing volume are relatively large, which is difficult to implement in mobile.

In this paper, we mainly use different feature extraction methods and different models to classify music genres. Different music genres have their unique musical melodies, but some music has a certain degree of similarity and is still difficult to distinguish, for example, pop is interspersed with other types of rhythms, so it is also more difficult to achieve in this dataset classification. Some music has more obvious features, and the classification effect is better (for example, hip-hop instruments are easier to distinguish). At present, MFCC and STFT are more commonly used music feature extraction methods, and have been more widely used in music classification, and have also achieved better results.

We have studied the way of music processing based on MFCC and STFT feature extraction. The traditional method is to feature extract the whole music and then input to the model for training and learning, but some of the audio is long and there may be a lot of data loss if made into feature images for learning (the size of the image display is limited), and the size of the images that can be input to most models for training is also limited. There is no continuity between different audios in music genre classification, so the training effect is not very good. In this paper, the original audio is re-sliced into 4s segments and each segment is overlapped by 50%, and then each segment is subjected to feature extraction to reduce data loss and make the audio segments have some continuity and relevance.

In the use of training models, we selected popular classification method models (ResNet, GoogleNet, MobileNet, etc.) for the unsliced audio to select different feature extraction methods for training and learning, and initially judged which model corresponding to which feature could achieve relatively good results, and we found that STFT was able to have a good accuracy rate in each model training. And using the Resnet101 model and STFT feature extraction method, the best results in training can be achieved with 71.8% accuracy after training with sliced data. And we used MobileNet network to achieve the feasibility of music genre classification in mobile, using two data processing methods achieved better results accuracy reached 58.2% and 60.9%, and the final model parameter size is only about 4% of the traditional model parameters.

1.1 Related Work

In recent years, the classification of music genres is a relatively important topic, and more and more people are devoted to related research fields. Audio feature extraction methods mainly include STFT, MFCC, MEL, etc., whose feature extraction methods also play an important role in different research fields Tao et al. (2020) [1] and Liu et al. (2019) [2]. With the development of information technology, the classification methods of music genres have been continuously pushed from using traditional classical classifiers Basili et al. (2004) [3]; Kostrzewa et al. (2018) [4] and Silla, C.N (2008) [5] to the field of deep learning Choi, K et al. (2017) [6]; Kereliuk et al. (2015) [7] and Oramas et al. (2017) [8], and the current ones are more popular are convolutional neural networks Kim et al. (2018) [9]; Lee et al. (2017) [10] and Lim et al. (2018) [11] and convolutional recurrent neural networks Choi et al. (2017) [12] and Gunawan et al. (2019) [13]. There are also combined methods of different neural networks to explore for music genre classification, such as CNN + LSTM and VGG16 + LSTM [14]. There are also many results on music genre classification using different audio feature extraction methods and combining different deep learning methods. Our previous explorations using models such as deep learning [15] and convolutional neural networks [16] found that the related models have some effect on music genre classification, and the sensitivity of different models to audio features is not the same.

Different datasets have different numbers of music categories, some with different lengths of music, and different criteria and conditions, and the trained results are not always reliable. In this paper, we use a standardized dataset with equal time for each song and compare the best possible effect with the experimental results of other works.

1.2 Contribution and Thesis Structure of the Paper

The main contribution of this paper is that firstly, we select different feature extraction methods for unsliced audio from popular classification models (Resnet, AlexNet, GoogleNet, MobileNet, etc.) and compare the experimental results with other methods to select the best model and feature extraction method. Secondly, the audio is fragmented and each adjacent segment is stacked by 50% on top of the best model and feature extraction method. Finally, the relevant parameters of the model are adjusted and a regularization optimization method is added to the model to prevent overfitting and an attention mechanism is added to improve the model training effect. In this paper, the MobileNet model is used to achieve a lightweight mobile music genre classification with good results.

The datasets and related settings used in this paper are described in Sect. 2; the main methods and depth models used are presented in Sect. 3; the experimental content and related analyses are presented in Sect. 4; and Sect. 5 concludes and outlooks.

2 Data

2.1 Data Sets and Hardware Settings

The Free Music Archive Dataset (FMA) has three main categories of varying sizes (small, medium, and large), and we choose the small dataset. The small subset of the FMA dataset contains 8000 tracks, each 30 s long, divided into 8 top categories each with 1000 audio is a balanced dataset, and the main categories are hip-hop, folk, experimental, international, instrumental, electronic, pop, and rock [17]. Each audio sample type is 44100 Hz dual-channel.

All experiments were conducted on a desktop computer with the following hardware configurations: CPU - Intel Core(TM) i7-9700K, RAM - 32GB RAM, GPU - NVIDIA GeForce GTX 2080 SUPER 8GB GDDR5.

2.2 Additional Settings

Data Normalization

As Eq. 1 shows the normalization method of data to channels:

$$O_{normalized} = (I - mean)/std \qquad (1)$$

I is the input STFT spectrogram, mean is taken as [0.485, 0.456, 0.406], std is taken as [0.229, 0.224, 0.225] normalization can speed up further calculations to an order of magnitude and reduce the error rate [18].

Computer deep learning is indeed powerful in classification, but sometimes it is often prone to overfitting in order to achieve the expected or better results, especially when we set the relevant audio clips to overlap by 50%, so here we use the L2 regularization method when calling the resnet101 model, and we choose the Adam optimizer to set the parameter weight_decay = 0.001, i.e., the weight of the regularization is set to lambda = 0.001.

Data Pretreatment

The audio was read at a sampling frequency of 44100 Hz. The audio was segmented into audio clips of 4-s duration. To make each audio clip relevant and have continuity, we segmented the audio in such a way that each clip took the last 50% of the previous clip and accounted for the first 50% of the latter clip. This data processing both increases the amount of data and achieves strong correlation of the clip audio and enables more features to be learned, which facilitates computer recognition to improve learning efficiency.

Feature Extraction

We mainly extract two different features for each post-slice audio: Short Time Fourier Transform (STFT) and Mel-frequency spectral coefficients, and call different models to compare their accuracy, and then to determine which feature extraction and corresponding model are highly accurate.

3 Method

3.1 Short-Time Fourier Transform (STFT)

As shown in Fig. 1, the vein diagram of STFT image spectrum feature extraction is shown. Short-time Fourier transform is widely used in the field of music classification, and can better reflect the features of different music types. In the figure, the original audio is first binned (50% overlapping between adjacent segments), and the STFT features are extracted from the binned audio to generate the picture. We set n_fft: i.e., FFT window size to 1024 and hop_length: i.e., frame shift, to 512 here.

3.2 Mel-Frequency Spectrum Factor

A schematic diagram of the pulse of MFCC picture spectrum feature extraction is shown in Fig. 2. (MFCC) is a further extension of Mel spectrogram, Mel-Frequency cepstrum coefficients [19] is another representative method after audio clip spectrum compression. In the figure, the original audio is first binned (50% overlapping between adjacent clips), and the feature extraction of the binned audio is performed to generate the image.

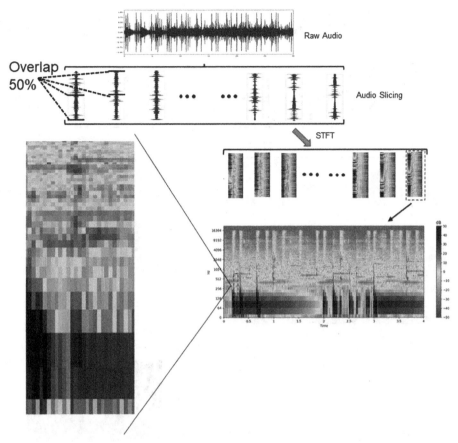

Fig. 1. STFT blue picture for 4 s segmentation middle 50% overlay

3.3 Deep Learning Models

As shown in Fig. 3, it is a network architecture of the ResNet 101 model. In the experiment, you can enter the MFCC or STFT feature to extract the generated picture, first pass through a convolution layer Stride 2, and then pass one 3 × 3 maximum sample layer Stride 2, followed by four residual blocks, and finally the average sample The layer and the full connecting layer are used as the output, as well as SoftMax processing.

The letters of the parameters accumulated below Layer1-Layer4 in Resnet101, we adjusted the number of layers of different Layers on the basis of the original parameters, respectively, and did the following sets of experiments, the audio feature used is STFT, we added and deleted the number of layers of different Layers respectively. As shown in the table below, the variation of the number of layers has a certain influence on the training accuracy, which does not mean that the more the number of layers is, the better the effect is, and the implementation of serial number 9 and 10 is better in comparison (Table 1).

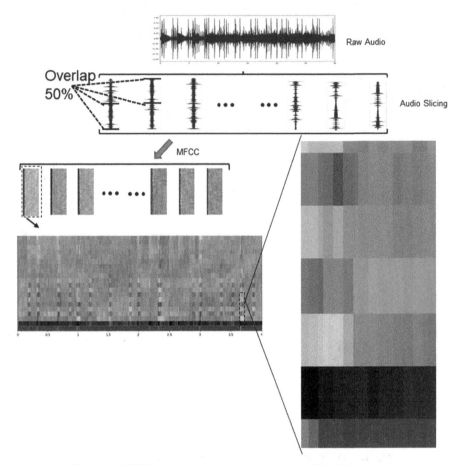

Fig. 2. MFCC blue picture for 4 s segmentation middle 50% overlay

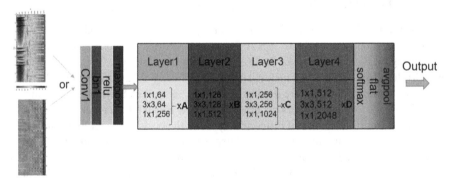

Fig. 3. ResNet

Table 1. Experimental results of Resnet101 parameter adjustment

No	A	B	C	D	Layers	Accuracy (%)
1	3	8	23	3	113	62.8
2	6	4	23	3	110	61.5
3	3	4	32	3	128	61.7
4	4	6	25	6	125	63.4
5	5	6	26	5	128	62.1
6	4	5	24	4	113	61.7
7	4	6	25	6	125	57.3
8	3	4	20	3	92	64.2
9	2	3	22	2	89	68.4
10	3	4	23	3	101	71.8

The following figure shows the comparison of the training accuracy with 10 parameter settings, the overall accuracy does not change much with the increase of the number of layers, and the accuracy is better with 89 and 101 layers.

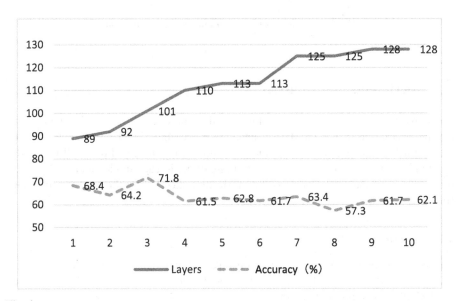

Fig. 4.

The MobileNet model is designed to achieve lightweight and high accuracy in mobile devices, which brings great convenience to life and work nowadays. Compared with the traditional convolutional neural network, MobileNet network has greatly reduced the model parameters and the amount of operations, but only a small decrease in accuracy.

As shown in Fig. 5, the size of MobileNet model is only 16.2MB, which is about 4% of the size of resnet101 model, and the training accuracy of MobileNet model is good compared with other models as shown in Table 6, which is better to achieve light weight.

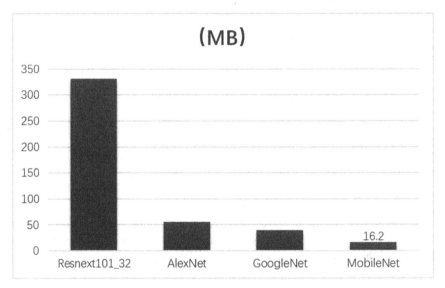

Fig. 5. Best results model parameter size comparison

4 Experiments and Analysis

As shown in Fig. 4 as the flow structure of this experiment, it is mainly divided into two processes, the first is the dataset unsliced processing, direct feature extraction of the original audio data, and then random division of the data, and then call the model for training and learning, save the best training effect in each model, and finally is the prediction and results; the other is the music first slice before the related processing (Fig. 6).

4.1 Quantification Results

The data is divided into three parts: training data, validation data and test data, which are divided into 80% training data, 10% validation data and 10% test data. The data pieces can be called randomly for training.

Before the images were binned, we performed feature extraction and processed to generate STFT images, MFCC images, chromaticity images, and power spectrograms, as shown in Table 2 The accuracy rate trained by extracting STFT features was high, so we trained the images extracted by STFT features using Resnext101_32x8d and MobileNet models, respectively, as shown in the table The accuracy rate was between 63.5% and 58.2%, and the F1 scores are 57.9% and 63%, respectively.

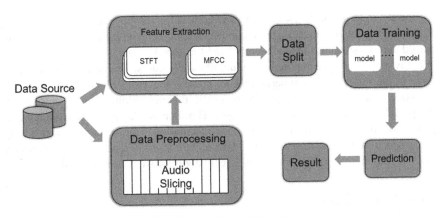

Fig. 6. Experimental flow chart

Table 2. Fma_small unsliced STFT feature learning

Model	Accuracy [%]	Precision [%]	Recall [%]	F1 Score [%]
Resnext101_32x8d	63.5	62.5	63.5	63
MobileNet	58.2	57.6	58.2	57.9

The audio after slicing and editing was also made into these three types of images, and the images extracted by STFT features were trained using Resnext101_32x8d and MobileNet models with accuracy at 71.8% and 60.9% with F1 scores of 71.8% and 60.8%, respectively. The accuracy of the classification effect after slicing the data was improved better (Table 3).

Table 3. Fma_small STFT feature learning after binning

Model	Accuracy [%]	Precision [%]	Recall [%]	F1 Score [%]
MobileNet	60.9	60.8	60.8	60.8
Resnext101_32x8d	71.8	71.6	72	71.8

Here you can see that the best model has an accuracy of 71.8% indeed has better results.

From here, we can see that there is a big gap between the two experimental results. Firstly, on the same feature extraction method, there is a big difference in the amount of data used by the two experiments. The total data volume without slicing is only 8000, the single category data volume is 1000, and the training set for each category is 900 validation set is 100; while the total data volume after slicing is 84183, the single category data volume is 11700, and the training set for each category is 10530 validation set is 1170, the experimental data volume difference is more than 10 times.

Secondly, in terms of data continuity and correlation, binning according to 50% of the front-to-back overlay makes a large number of data sets with large correlation, while unbinned audio each audio independently has little correlation.

Finally there is a large gap in the amount of data features. The model has a limit on the size of the input training images, and we process the audio according to the same image size, which inevitably results in the unsliced audio features being compressed, leading to a large loss of relevant data features. The slice overlay processing, which cuts the long audio into short audio, can show more information in the same size image during feature extraction, maximizing the use of data, and the overlay processing can eliminate the loss of data edge features, which can effectively improve the training efficiency.

4.2 Qualitative Results

As shown in Fig. 7 for the confusion matrix best model classification effect, the number of predicted correct results if they are all concentrated on the diagonal line, indicating the higher the accuracy, which is the best effect shown in the experiments, there is still a large difference in the music classification effect of different genre categories. The amount of validation data for each category is about 1170, and the number of validation sets for each category accounts for 20% of the total data for a single category, here

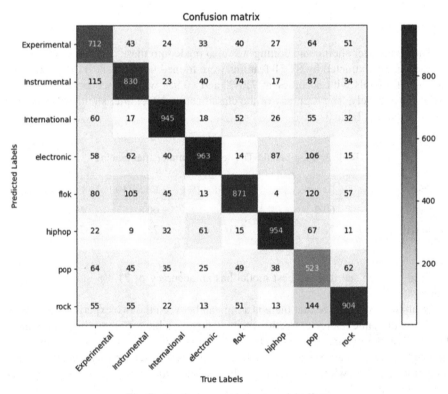

Fig. 7. Confusion matrix best model effect

we call the best training model for the validation set to generate the confusion matrix for testing, as shown in the diagonal line with the darkest color, the number of each category being predicted correctly is concentrated in the squares on the diagonal line, International, electronic and International, electronic and hip-hop are the best in terms of accuracy, pop is relatively poor because pop is more similar to other music, but overall the prediction accuracy is better.

As shown in Table 4 are the training effects of the best model in each genre category. Among them, hip-hop, international, electronic and rock achieved more than 80% accuracy, folk, experimental and instrumental also achieved between 60% and 80%, the worst result is pop only 44.7%, because pop is more special and complex, an audio contains features of almost other genres of music, it is the most difficult to classify, but compared to the paper [17] around 20% we have a large improvement.

Table 4. Best model for each genre of music training effect

	Exp	Ins	Int	Ele	Flok	Hiphop	Pop	Rock
Acc	60.9%	70.9%	80.8%	82.3%	74.4%	81.5%	44.7%	77.3%

As shown in Table 5 for the best model in each genre of music training effect, hiphop accuracy is the best at 81.5%, and all other genres except POP accuracy is above 65%.

Table 5. Best model for each genre of music training effect

Precision		Recall	Specificity
Experimental	0.716	0.611	0.965
Instrumental	0.68	0.712	0.952
International	0.784	0.81	0.968
Electronic	0.716	0.826	0.953
Flok	0.673	0.747	0.948
Hiphop	0.815	0.818	0.973
Pop	0.622	0.449	0.961
Rock	0.719	0.775	0.957

4.3 Comparison of Results

The table below shows a comparison with the relevant models in other Wang et al. (2019) [20]; Yi et al. (2019) [21]; Zhang et al. (2019) [22] and Kostrzewa et al. (2021) [17] papers and shows the relevant results and the best results of this study in black bolded part at the bottom, compared with other models the models and methods used in this paper achieve better results and have a better overall improvement.

Table 6. Compare the different model learning results of Fma_small with their own results. All values are expressed in %.

No	Model	Accuracy	Recall	F1-Score	Remarks
1	K-Nearest Neighbors [22]	36.4	–	–	
2	Logistic regression [22]	42.3	–	–	
3	Multilayer perceptron [22]	44.9	–	–	
4	Support vector machine [22]	46.4	–	–	
5	Original spectrogram [21]	49.4	–	–	
6	Harmonic spectrogram [21]	43.4	–	–	
7	Percussive spectrogram [21]	50.9	–	–	
8	Modulation spectrogram [21]	55.6	–	–	
9	FCN [20]	63.9	43	40.3	
10	TimbreCNN [20]	61.7	36.4	35	
11	End-to-end [20]	61.4	38.4	34.5	
12	CRNN [20]	63.4	40.7	40.2	
13	CRNN-TF [20]	64.7	43.5	42.3	
14	Ensemble 1 – vote [17]	56.4	54.8	54.9	
15	**Resnext101_32x8d**	**63.2**	–	–	**Power spectrum unsecured**
16	**Resnext101_32x8d**	**50.4**	–	–	**Chromaticity map is not separated**
17	**Resnext101_32x8d**	**47.9**	–	–	**MFCC unsliced**
18	**AlexNet**	**61.7**	–	–	**STFT unsliced**
19	**Resnext101_32x8d**	**63.5**	**63.5**	**63**	**STFT unsliced**
20	**MobileNet**	**58.2**	**58.2**	**57.9**	**STFT unsliced**
21	**MobileNet**	**60.9**	**60.8**	**60.8**	**STFT Sliced**
22	**Resnext101_32x8d**	**71.8**	**72**	**71.8**	**STFT Sliced**

The analysis of Table 6 allows us to conclude that, in general, the values of the results of this paper are similar to those of other studies. Rows 1–4 (Table 6) show the values obtained by the classical classification method [22], which are 25–35% lower compared to the values obtained by our best results. Rows 5–8 show the results for

CNN provided by different spectral maps, and rows 9–13 show the quantitative results of full 64 D. Kostrzewa et al. for convolutional neural networks, timbre CNNs, end-to-end music auto-labeling methods, CRNNs, and CRNNs with temporal and frequency dimensions [20], with 7–10% lower accuracy compared to the best results in this paper and with recall and F1 scores are much lower than the current study reaching about 29%. Summarizing all the results, it can be seen that the results achieved in this paper study are 7% higher than the state-of-the-art solution, and better scores are achieved for other parameters. The accuracy of the MobileNet model is also among the better model accuracy as shown in Fig. The effect of the data slicing and stacking process is improved and the model parameter size is smaller.

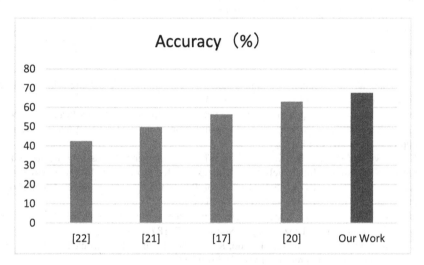

Fig. 8. Comparison of the average accuracy of the best models in the citation and this paper

As shown in Fig. 8, the average accuracy of the citations Kostrzewa et al. (2021) [17]; Wang et al. (2019) [20]; Yi et al. (2019) [21] and Zhang et al. (2019) [22] and the best model in this paper are compared, the blue part is the average of the citation model effect accuracy, and the red part is the average of the best model effect accuracy in our work, and the model in this paper is best in comparison.

5   Conclusion

We used different data processing methods for slicing and overlaying the data to increase the relevance and continuity of the data, and experimentally compared the selection of appropriate classification models and feature extraction methods. The quantitative and qualitative studies show that the obtained experimental results have a large improvement compared to the state-of-the-art methods. In addition, the best feature extraction method (STFT) and the best model (Resnet101) were screened in this study, and the Resnet model was studied and improved, and the classification quality was also improved better by using the STFT feature extraction method. In this paper, we also use MobileNet model to classify music genres for mobile, and it has good accuracy compared with the best model.

The approach shown in this paper has the advantages of better data processing and feature extraction methods, a relatively new and advanced classification model, and the ability to automate the classification application with good classification results.

Future work can be focused on other deep learning model optimization improvements and other datasets for configuration experiments. The next step will be to determine the classification of the problems that occur in song singing.

Funding. This work was supported in part by the National Research and Development Program of China under 2020YFB1710401, and in part by the National Natural Science Foundation of China under Grant 61902367 and Grant 41976185.

References

1. Tao, H., et al.: An unsupervised fault diagnosis method for rolling bearing using STFT and generative neural networks. J. Franklin Inst. **357**(11) (2020)
2. Liu, C., et al.: Bottom-up broadcast neural network for music genre classification (2019)
3. Basili, R., Serafifini, A., Stellato, A.: Classifification of musical genre: a machine learning approach. In: ISMIR (2004)
4. Kostrzewa, D., Brzeski, R., Kubanski, M.: The classifification of music by the genre using the KNN classififier. In: Kozielski, S., Mrozek, D., Kasprowski, P., Malysiak-Mrozek, B., Kostrzewa, D. (eds.) BDAS 2018. CCIS, vol. 928, pp. 233– 242. Springer, Cham (2018). https://doi.org/10.1007/978-3-319-99987-618
5. Silla, C.N., Koerich, A.L., Kaestner, C.A.: A machine learning approach to automatic music genre classifification. J. Braz. Comput. Soc. **14**(3), 7–18 (2008)
6. Choi, K., Fazekas, G., Sandler, M., Cho, K.: Transfer learning for music classifification and regression tasks. arXiv preprint arXiv:1703.09179 (2017)
7. Kereliuk, C., Sturm, B.L., Larsen, J.: Deep learning and music adversaries. IEEE Trans. Multimedia **17**(11), 2059–2071 (2015)
8. Oramas, S., Nieto, O., Barbieri, F., Serra, X.: Multi-label music genre classifification from audio, text, and images using deep features. arXiv preprint arXiv:1707.04916 (2017)
9. Kim, T., Lee, J., Nam, J.: Sample-level CNN architectures for music auto-tagging using raw waveforms. In: 2018 IEEE International Conference on Acoustics, Speech and Signal Processing (ICASSP), pp. 366–370. IEEE (2018)
10. Lee, J., Nam, J.: Multi-level and multi-scale feature aggregation using pretrained convolutional neural networks for music auto-tagging. IEEE Signal Process. Lett. **24**(8), 1208–1212 (2017)
11. Lim, M., et al.: Convolutional neural network based audio event classifification. KSII Trans. Internet Inf. Syst. **12**(6), 2748–2760 (2018)
12. Choi, K., Fazekas, G., Sandler, M., Cho, K.: Convolutional recurrent neural networks for music classification. In: 2017 IEEE International Conference on Acoustics, Speech and Signal Processing (ICASSP), pp. 2392–2396. IEEE (2017)
13. Gunawan, A.A., et al.: Music recommender system based on genre using convolutional recurrent neural networks. Procedia Comput. Sci. **157**, 99–109 (2019)
14. Ahmad, F., et al.: Music genre classification using spectral analysis techniques with hybrid convolution-recurrent neural network. Int. J. Innov. Technol. Explor. Eng. (IJITEE) **9**(1) (2019)

15. Li, C., Feng, Y., Sun, T., Zhang, X.: Long term Indian Ocean Dipole (IOD) index prediction used deep learning by convLSTM. Remote Sens. **14**, 523 (2022)
16. Sun, T., Feng, Y., Li, C., Zhang, X.: High precision sea surface temperature prediction of long period and large area in the Indian ocean based on the temporal convolutional network and internet of things. Sensors **22**, 1636 (2022)
17. Kostrzewa, D., Kaminski, P., Brzeski, R.: Music genre classification: looking for the perfect network. In: Paszynski, M., Kranzlmüller, D., Krzhizhanovskaya, V.V., Dongarra, J.J., Sloot, P.M.A. (eds.) ICCS 2021. LNCS, vol. 12742, pp. 55–67. Springer, Cham (2021). https://doi.org/10.1007/978-3-030-77961-0_6
18. Sola, J., Sevilla, J.: Importance of input data normalization for the application of neural networks to complex industrial problems. IEEE Trans. Nucl. Sci. **44**(3), 1464–1468 (1997)
19. Mel Frequency Ceptral Coefficient (MFCC) tutorial. Available at: http://practicalcryptography.com/miscellaneous/machine-learning/guide-mel-frequency-cepstral-coefficients-mfccs/
20. Wang, Z., Muknahallipatna, S., Fan, M., Okray, A., Lan, C.: Music classifification using an improved CRNN with multi-directional spatial dependencies in both time and frequency dimensions. In: 2019 International Joint Conference on Neural Networks (IJCNN), pp. 1–8. IEEE (2019)
21. Yi, Y., Chen, K.Y., Gu, H.Y.: Mixture of CNN experts from multiple acoustic feature domain for music genre classifification. In: 2019 Asia-Pacifific Signal and Information Processing Association Annual Summit and Conference (APSIPA ASC), pp. 1250–1255. IEEE (2019)
22. Zhang, C., Zhang, Y., Chen, C.: SongNet: Real-Time Music Classifification. Stanford University Press, Palo Alto (2019)

Individual Identification Based on ECG Signal Driven by Multi-layer LSTM and EEMD Algorithm

Xueting Wang[✉] and Xiaohong Zhang

Hangzhou Dianzi University, Hangzhou 300318, China
Wangxue_ting@126.com, xhzhang@hdu.edu.cn

Abstract. As people attach great importance to the field of information security, identification technology based on biometrics has been widely developed and applied. However, biometric identification technology based on face and fingerprint has the disadvantage of weak anti-counterfeiting and easy to prevent. Electrocardiogram (ECG) signals have high anti-counterfeiting properties of living body recognition, which makes the identification technology based on ECG signals have great development potential in the field of information security. This paper proposes an ECG identification algorithm based on Ensemble Empirical Mode Decomposition (EEMD) and Long Short-Term Memory (LSTM). First, the one-dimensional non-stationary and nonlinear ECG signals are decomposed by EEMD, and the Intrinsic Mode Functions (IMFs) of each layer are extracted in the time-frequency domain. The vector is used as the input layer of the multi-layer LSTM to complete the feature classification and output the individual identification result. The recognition accuracy of the proposed model is 95.47% (ECG-ID datasets) and 96.74% (Physionet/Cinc Challenge 2011 datasets), indicating that the proposed model can achieve a high recognition accuracy and capacity for generalization.

Keywords: ECG biometrics · Human identification · Long short-term memory · Ensemble empirical mode decomposition

1 Introduction

The rapid development of Internet of things and artificial intelligence technology provides necessary technical support for the new identity recognition technology with high security and high privacy. However, while the technology is developing, it also provides the possibility for fake fingerprints, dummy faces and other forgery technologies, increases the risk of personal information theft, and causes great damage and attack to the information security system. Therefore, it is particularly important to seek an identity recognition method with high security and high privacy.

With the continuous excavation and exploration of domestic and foreign researchers in the field of biometric technology, a biometric identification technology based on ECG

© ICST Institute for Computer Sciences, Social Informatics and Telecommunications Engineering 2022
Published by Springer Nature Switzerland AG 2022. All Rights Reserved
Y. Chenggang et al. (Eds.): MobiMedia 2022, LNICST 451, pp. 224–237, 2022.
https://doi.org/10.1007/978-3-031-23902-1_17

has rapidly become a research hotspot of biometric technology with the characteristics of high anti-counterfeiting. It is considered to be the biometric technology with the most security potential [1].

However, such a system must still overcome the technical challenges reflected in the following aspects. The first is that it is difficult to extract the detailed features of complex ECG signals, and the second is that the processing speed of the model on the two-dimensional ECG feature map is slow. This paper proposes an identity recognition model based on EEMD-LSTM, uses EEMD to decompose the original ECG signal, and inputs the IMFs component at each time into the multi-layer timing network LSTM for feature learning, so as to complete individual identity recognition and authentication, the detailed structure of the model is shown in Fig. 1.

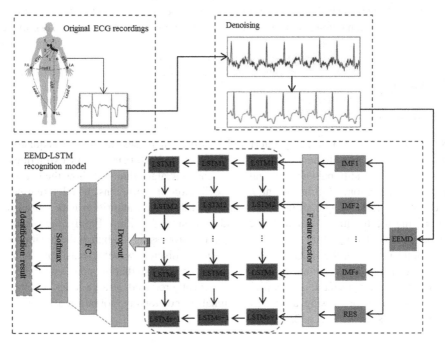

Fig. 1. Structure diagram of ECG recognition model based on EEMD-LSTM

Firstly, the collected individual ECG signal is denoised to obtain a clean ECG signal. Then, the denoised ECG signal is decomposed by n-layer EEMD to obtain the IMFs component of the signal, so as to ensure that each local detail feature of the ECG signal is considered. Secondly, the IMFs component of ECG signal is extracted in time-frequency domain, and the input layer of network model is constructed. Finally, multi-layer LSTM combined with dropout recognition model is designed to capture the change of feature dimension of ECG timing signal in time and space, complete the classification of feature vector and output individual identification results.

2 Related Works

Since L. Biel first proposed the use of ECG signal waveform characteristics as the basis for identification in 2001. ECG biometrics has been widely studied by researchers worldwide using various methods. Semwa [17], Labati [16], X Zhang [18], among others, manually extract the complex time-domain and morphological features of ECG waveform as feature vectors and input them into machine learning or deep learning models for classification training. However, as non-stationary, nonlinear and weak physiological signal, it is difficult to obtain all the detailed features of the ECG signal by manually extracting features, which will eventually affect the recognition accuracy. Zhang Y successively proposed ECG recognition models based on Convolutional Neural Networks (CNN) [19] and Transfer Learning (TL) [20], although the model of deep learning combined with transfer learning speeds up the training speed of the model, the model that uses two-dimensional images as the input layer of the network is slower to process image features.

3 Methods

3.1 Denoising

Since the ECG signal is easily interfered by different noises during the acquisition process, it is necessary to denoise the original ECG signal before the feature extraction of the signal. The traditional wavelet transform denoising algorithm will show the Pseudo-Gibbs phenomenon, resulting in the large oscillation of the reconstructed signal near the singular point. Cyclic shift wavelet threshold denoising algorithm is proposed by improving the traditional wavelet threshold denoising algorithm. Firstly, the original signal is subjected to 8 times of cyclic translation processing to change the position of the singular point in the ECG signal. Secondly, the discrete wavelet transform is used for wavelet decomposition and reconstruction processing, so that the noise components in the processed wavelet detail coefficients are greatly reduced. After 8 times of reverse cyclic translation processing, a clean ECG signal after denoising is obtained after reverse translation, as shown in Fig. 2.

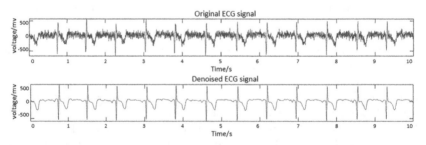

Fig. 2. Comparison of ECG signal before and after denoising

3.2 Ensemble Empirical Mode Decomposition

Norden E. Huang et al. [3] first proposed an analysis method for nonlinear and non-stationary signals empirical mode decomposition (EMD) algorithm, which has been widely used at present. However, EMD algorithm has the problem of mode aliasing when the same IMFs component may contain IMFs of different decomposition scales or the signal of the same scale is decomposed into different IMFs.

In order to avoid the mode aliasing problem of EMD algorithm, this paper adopts the EEMD algorithm proposed by Huang et al. The core idea of the algorithm is to decompose the original signal into several continuous IMFs with different scales by adding Gaussian white noise with normal frequency distribution during the decomposition of the signal to be processed, so as to weaken and even eliminate the phenomenon of mode aliasing. The EEMD algorithm process is similar to the EMD algorithm. The main difference is that Gaussian white noise is introduced into the decomposition process. The detailed steps [4] are as follows:

(1) Determine the decomposition execution times of EEMD algorithm m.
(2) The newly processed signal $f_i(t)$ is the sum of the original signal $f(t)$ and the Gaussian white noise signal $n_i(t)$ whose amplitude follows the standard normal distribution. $f_i(t)$ is defined as:

$$f_i(t) = f(t) + n_i(t) \tag{1}$$

where $i = 1, 2, \ldots, m$.

(3) After EEMD algorithm decomposition, the signal $f_i(t)$ can be decomposed into the superposition of n IMFs components and 1 residual residue.

$$f_i(t) = \sum_{k=1}^{n} C_{j,k}(t) + r_{j,k}(t), 1 \leq j \leq m \tag{2}$$

where j is the number of times the EMD algorithm is performed, and k is the number of layers of IMFs decomposed at the j-th time.

(4) When $j < m$, repeat step (2) until j reaches the number of times m.
(5) To find the mean of each layer of IMFs, the formula is as follows:

$$\overline{C_k}(t) = \frac{1}{m} \left(\sum_{j=1}^{n} C_{j,k} \right), j = 1, 2, \ldots, m, k = 1, 2, \ldots, n \tag{3}$$

(6) The introduced white noise can be offset by the characteristic that the Gaussian white noise amplitude obeys the normal distribution mean value of 0,the average value $\overline{C_k}(t)$ of multiple times is output as the IMFs component of the k-th layer.

Figure 3 shows the ECG signal after EEMD decomposition. It can be shown that EEMD algorithm can not only eliminate the phenomenon of mode aliasing, but also avoid the influence of singular value on the feature matrix, and can better deal with nonlinear and non-stationary ECG signals.

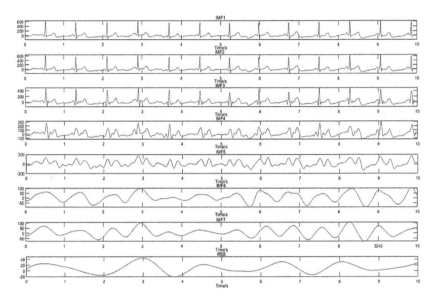

Fig. 3. ECG signal decomposed by EEMD algorithm

3.3 Long Short-Term Memory

Long short-term memory (LSTM) was first proposed by Hochreiter and schmidhuber [5]. It is a unique recurrent neural network (RNN) used for gate units and storage units to overcome the problem of vanishing or exploding gradients in traditional RNNs [6], and can effectively process nonlinear time series data on long time scales [7]. LSTM includes input layer, hidden layer and output layer, a single LSTM neuron [8] is shown in Fig. 4. Among them, f_t, i_t and O_t represent forgetting gate, input gate and output gate, respectively, and long short-term memory network learns long input sequence by using gating mechanism, so as to realize efficient processing of complex time series data.

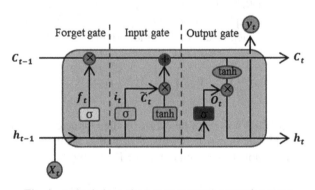

Fig. 4. A single long short-term memory network neuron

(1) Forgetting gate is used to screen memory and determining the amount of information.

$$f_t = \sigma\left(W_f \cdot \left[h_{t-1}, x_t\right] + b_f\right) \tag{4}$$

(2) Input gates are used to update the cell state and also store relevant information briefly.

$$i_t = \sigma\left(W_i \cdot \left[h_{t-1}, x_t\right] + b_i\right) \tag{5}$$

$$C_t = \tanh\left(W_c \cdot \left[h_{t-1}, x_t\right] + b_c\right) \tag{6}$$

(3) After obtaining the output of the forget gate and the input gate, the current cell state C_t can be known.

$$C_t = f_t C_{t-1} + i_t C_t \tag{7}$$

(4) The output gate is mainly used to control the final output of the cell state.

$$O_t = \sigma\left(W_o \cdot \left[h_{t-1}, x_t\right] + b_o\right) \tag{8}$$

$$h_t = O_t * \tanh(C_t) \tag{9}$$

where W is the weight coefficient and b is the bias term and x_t is the current input state, h_{t-1} is the output state at the previous moment, h_t is the unit output [9].

3.4 EEMD-LSTM ECG Authentication Model

This paper proposed an ECG identification algorithm based on EEMD-LSTM. EEMD has certain advantages for non-stationary and nonlinear signal decomposition, and LSTM model is more suitable for predicting long-term signal data. In order to achieve higher recognition accuracy, the EEMD-LSTM model mainly includes the following steps:

(1) **The input layer of EEMD-LSTM.** As shown in Fig. 5, the denoised ECG signal is decomposed into 8 layers by EEMD algorithm, including 7 IMFs components and one RES component. Then, the time domain and frequency domain features of the ECG signal components of each layer are extracted to construct a feature matrix, which is used as the input sample set of the LSTM layer.

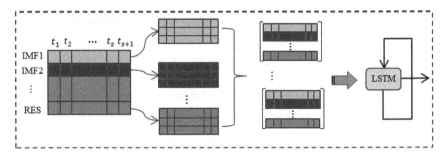

Fig. 5. Construct long and short-term neural network model input feature vector

(2) **The multi-layer LSTM model**. For complex time series ECG signals, it is difficult for a single-layer LSTM to achieve higher accuracy for identity recognition. In order to ensure that the deep detailed features of different time series signals are learned, this paper uses the output of the previous layer of LSTM network as the input of the latter layer of LSTM network, and builds a multi-layer LSTM network model, as shown in Fig. 6. The temporal signal features at each time are input into the multi-layer LSTM model for training.

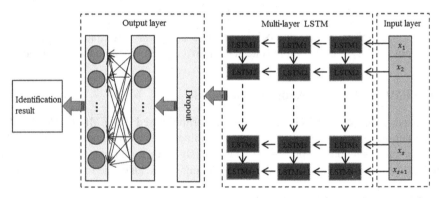

Fig. 6. Building multi-layer LSTM model

(3) **Model optimization**. The multi-layer LSTM is prone to over-fitting in the process of training model parameters, thus reducing the generalization ability of the model. To solve this problem, this paper adopts the method of adding dropout layer to multi-layer LSTM. In the training process, a neuron node is randomly stopped activation with certain probability, so as to reduce the coupling between neurons and the excessive dependence of the model on some features, so as to avoid over fitting and improve the generalization ability of the model. In addition, parameters such as the number of LSTM layers and model training batch size, the learning rate and the number of hidden layer units were determined by the grid optimization

method to determine the optimal values [10], which were set to 3, 50, 0.001 and 150, respectively.

4 Experimental Results and Discussion

4.1 Data Description

To evaluate the performance of the proposed EEMD-LSTM model, we carried out a large number of experiments using the ECG-ID dataset and Physionet/Cinc Challenge 2011 dataset from the Physionet database [11], the specific allocation of data sets is shown in Table 1.

The ECG-ID dataset is specially used to study ECG-based biometrics. It is obtained with ECG lead I from 90 volunteers (44 men and 46 women, of ages 13 to 75 years) in multi-sessions. This database is used to verify whether the ECG data of different collection cycles have an impact on the ECG recognition accuracy. The challenge data is standard multi-lead/single-lead ECG recordings, based on chest collection. Among them, Physionet/Cinc Challenge 2011 dataset is standard 12-lead ECG recordings (leads I, II, II, aVR, aVL, aVF, V1, V2, V3, V4, V5, and V6) with multiple sets of recordings. In this paper, the ECG data sets of lead I and lead II in Physionet/Cinc Challenge 2011 database are used to verify whether different lead acquisition methods have an impact on the ECG recognition accuracy.

Table 1. Characteristics of ECG database.

Protocol	Data source	Data size	Purpose	Characteristic
1	ECG-ID dataset	90 × 2	Training sample	Two groups are the same session
		90 × 1	Test sample	Another session
2	Physionet/Cinc Challenge 2011	90 × 2	Training sample	Lead I-collected
		90 × 1	Test sample	Different leads (leads I,II)

4.2 Model Evaluation Index

The identification process of the ECG signal determines whether it belongs to the same individual tested by the accuracy threshold set in advance. The performance of the proposed algorithm is evaluated using the most popular benchmark metrics, namely, accuracy (Acc), and equal error rate (EER):

(1) Recognition accuracy (Acc):

$$Acc_{\text{training}} = \frac{TP + TN}{TP + TN + FN + FP} \tag{10}$$

Here, TP and FN are the recognition results where a registered person is accepted correctly and rejected erroneously, respectively. TN and FP are the recognition results where a nonregistered person (illegal intruder) is rejected correctly and accepted erroneously, respectively.

$$Acc_{\text{test}} = \frac{N_{true}}{N_{total}} \tag{11}$$

where N_{true} means the number of true recognitions and N_{total} means the total samples number.

(2) The threshold is adjusted, and when the false rejection rate (FRR) is equal to the false acceptance rate (FAR), the FAR (or FRR) value is called the equal error rate (EER). Here:

$$FAR = \frac{Nunber\ of\ false\ acceptance}{Total\ number\ of\ interclass\ tests} \tag{12}$$

$$FRR = \frac{Nunber\ of\ false\ rejections}{Total\ number\ of\ intraclass\ tests} \tag{13}$$

4.3   Results of the ECG-Based Biometric Algorithm

Three recognition models are designed and tested and the detailed design of the models is shown in Table 2. Using the two protocols proposed in Table 1 to train the three network models respectively, and compare and analyze the advantages of the network model of EEMD-LSTM combined with Dropout in identity recognition, it reflects the importance of extracting local detail features after decomposing the signal.

Table 2. Overview of the three schemes.

Scheme	Structure	Note	Role
A	EEMD-LSTM	Multi-layer LSTM + Dropout	Performance of the multi-layer LSTM
B	EEMD-LSTM	Multi-layer LSTM	Influence of the dropout
C	Multi-layer LSTM	Without EEMD + Dropout	Influence of the EEMD

The Results of Equal Error Rate. Two ECG-ID datasets in different collection periods in protocol 1 are used as the input of the three model schemes for model training to verify the influence of ECG data of different collection periods on the performance of the recognition model. The samples of the training set are 90×2. The sample size of the test set is 90×1. The training results of the three models are shown in Fig. 7 (a).

Two ECG data sets with different lead acquisition methods in Protocol 2 were used as the input of the three model schemes for model training to verify the influence of ECG data under different lead acquisition methods on the recognition model performance. The samples in the training set are 90 × 2. The sample size of the test set is 90 × 1. The training results of the three models are shown in Fig. 7 (b).

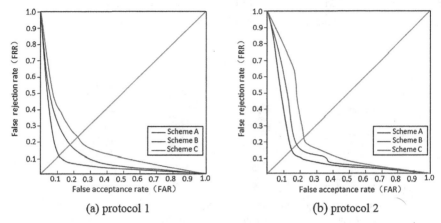

(a) protocol 1   (b) protocol 2

Fig. 7. EER results of protocol 1 and protocol 2 under the training of three network model schemes

It can be seen from Fig. 6 that the EER of scheme A under the two databases is smaller than the performance of EER in Scheme B, indicating that the Dropout layer in the multi-layer LSTM network model plays a key role in avoiding over-fitting. The comparison and analysis of scheme A and It can be seen from scheme C that by using the EEMD algorithm to decompose the ECG signal, some detailed features of the ECG signal can be extracted and the EER in the model training process can be reduced.

The Results of Recognition Accuracy. In view of the recognition accuracy of the network model for ECG signals, this paper uses the training sample sets and test sample sets of protocols 1 and 2 to recognize and train the three designed network models, and the results are shown in Tables 3 and 4, respectively. In addition, in order to more intuitively show the performance advantages and disadvantages of the three models, the experimental data is displayed on the bar chart, the results are shown in Fig. 8.

Table 3. Training set recognition results for different schemes.

Scheme	Structure	Protocol 1 (Training sample)		Protocol 2 (Training sample)	
		Acc (%)	EER (%)	Acc (%)	EER (%)
A	EEMD-LSTM + Dropout	96.58	10.24	94.85	11.12
B	EEMD-LSTM	88.21	16.36	90.78	14.69
C	Multi-layer LSTM	80.62	20.58	82.46	19.54

Table 4. Testing set recognition results for different schemes.

Scheme	Structure	Protocol 1 (Test sample) Acc (%)	Protocol 2 (Test sample) Acc (%)
A	EEMD-LSTM + Dropout	95.47	96.74
B	EEMD-LSTM	90.18	89.10
C	Multi-layer LSTM	79.37	82.59

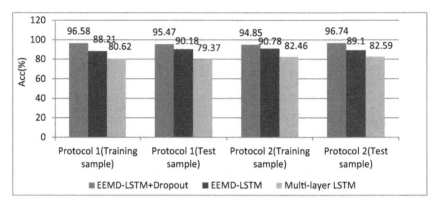

Fig. 8. Column chart of model training results

It can be seen from the recognition accuracy results under the three models that the network model combining EEMD-LSTM with Dropout can show high recognition accuracy for ECG signals with different acquisition periods and different acquisition methods. It shows that the EEMD-LSTM proposed in this paper can achieve highly accurate and robust identification results for non-stationary and nonlinear ECG signals.

Discuss with Other Methods. In order to better prove the pros and cons of the identification algorithm proposed in this paper, we compare and analyze the ECG-based identification algorithm proposed in the paper by other authors, as shown in Table 5.

Table 5. Comparative tabulation of experimental results for different identification algorithms.

Authors	Classifier	Database (Number)	Performance (Acc)
Zhang et al. (2018) [13]	CNN	MIT-Arrh (47)	91.10%
		MIT-NSR (18)	95.10%
Choi et al. (2019) [14]	Linear classifier	CU-ECG (100)	93.00%
Nuno et al. (2020) [15]	DenseNet	ECG-ID (90)	92.22%
Yang et al. (2021) [12]	GoogleNet	ECG-ID (90)	96.58%
Proposed	EEMD + LSTM	ECG-ID (90)	95.47%
		Physionet/Cinc Challenge 2011(90)	96.74%

Nuno uses the ECG signal feature map as the input of the deep learning network recognition model, and obtains a recognition accuracy of 92.22%. The possible reason for the lower than our method is that the training speed of the network model on the two-dimensional feature map is lower than the feature processing speed on the one-dimensional data. The author zhang uses the database MIT-Arrh and MIT-NSR to train the CNN network model, and achieved recognition accuracy of 95.10% and 91.10%, respectively. However, the recognition accuracy is slightly lower due to the small sample set for model training. The author Choi uses a machine learning classifier to identify ECG signals, and obtains a recognition accuracy of 93%, indicating that as long as the feature vector machine learning is processed well, a higher accuracy rate can also be achieved. Yang uses Googlenet with deep network structure as the input of one-dimensional ECG data, and obtains higher recognition accuracy. It is proved that properly increasing the number of network training layers can reflect better model performance.

5   Conclusion

In this paper, we propose an identity recognition model based on EEMD-LSTM for non-stationary and nonlinear time-series ECG signals. Firstly, EEMD algorithm can be well used to process the decomposition of non-stationary and nonlinear ECG signals, so as to extract the local detail features of ECG signals. Secondly, the LSTM method is very suitable for predicting one-dimensional long-time series signal. The recognition model of multi-layer LSTM neural network ensures higher recognition accuracy to a certain extent. In addition, the dropout network layer is introduced to avoid the over fitting phenomenon of multi-layer LSTM relying too much on a feature, so as to improve the generalization ability of the recognition model. During the experiment, the recognition model is trained for two kinds of ECG data under different acquisition cycles and different lead acquisition methods. The experiment shows that the identification model based on EEMD-LSTM proposed in this paper can show high recognition accuracy under two different ECG databases.

In addition, this paper also has some shortcomings. On the one hand, although the recognition model constructed has achieved high recognition accuracy in the process of training. However, the results of only two network data sets are difficult to show that the model has strong generalization ability, and there is still a certain gap compared with the model trained by measured ECG data sets. On the other hand, we should continue to study and optimize the deep learning algorithm, so as to obtain a higher recognition rate.

Acknowledgement. This work was supported by Zhejiang Province Public Welfare Technology Application Research Project (LGG20F010008).

References

1. Silva, H., et al.: ECG Biometrics: Principles and Applications. BIOSIGNALS 2013 (2013)
2. Biel, L., Pettersson, O., Philipson, L., Wide, P.: ECG analysis: a new approach in human identification. IEEE Trans. Instrum. Meas. **50**(3), 808–812 (2001)
3. Li, R., He, D.: Rotational machine health monitoring and fault detection using EMD-based acoustic emission feature quantification. IEEE Trans. Instrum. Meas. **61**(4), 990–1001 (2012)
4. Huang, N.E., et al.: A new view of nonlinear water waves: the Hilbert spectrum1. Annu. Rev. Fluid Mech. **31**, 417–457 (1999)
5. Hochreiter, S., Schmidhuber, J.: Long short-term memory. Neural Comput. **9**(8), 1735–1780 (1997)
6. Vu, M.T., Jardani, A., Massei, N., Fournier, M.: Reconstruction of missing groundwater level data by using Long Short-Term Memory (LSTM) deep neural network. J. Hydrol. (2020)
7. Li, et al.: GWO-LSTM deformation prediction model considering the deformation correlation of adjacent points. Railway Investigation and Surveying **47**(06), 26–32 (2021)
8. Jang, Y., et al.: Business failure prediction of construction contractors using a LSTM RNN with accounting, construction market, and macroeconomic variables. J. Manag. Eng. **36**(2) (2020)
9. Wei, X., et al.: Fault diagnosis of high-speed piston pump based on LSTM and CNN. J. Aeronaut. Astronaut. **42**(03), 435–445 (2021)
10. Deshwal, V., Sharma, M.: Breast cancer detection using SVM classifier with grid search technique. Int. J. Comput. Appl. **178**(31), 18–23 (2019)
11. Physionet. https://physionet.org/physiobank/. Last Accessed 1 Mar 2022
12. Yang, S., et al.: Arrhythmia detection based on wavelet decomposition and 1D googlenet. J. Electron. Inf. **43**(10), 3018–3027 (2021)
13. Zhang, Q., Zhou, D., Zeng, X.: HeartID: a multiresolution convolutional neural network for ECG-based biometric human identification in smart health applications. IEEE Access **5**, 11805–11816 (2017)
14. Choi, G.H., Bak, E.-S., Pan, S.B.: User identification system using 2D resized spectrogram features of ECG. IEEE Access **7**, 34862–34873 (2019)
15. Bento, N., Belo, D., Gamboa, H.: ECG biometrics using spectrograms and deep neural networks. Int. J. Mach. Learn. Comput. **10**(2) (2020)
16. Labati, R.D., et al.: Deep-ECG: Convolutional neural networks for ECG biometric recognition. Pattern Recognit. Lett. 78–85 (2018)
17. Semwal, V.B., et al.: An optimized feature selection technique based on incremental feature analysis for bio-metric gait data classification. Multimed. Tools Appl. (2017)
18. Zhang, X.: Research on ECG information acquisition and arrhythmia detection methods. Harbin Institute of Technology (2019). 10.27061

19. Zhao, Z., et al.: ECG authentication system design incorporating a convolutional neural network and generalized S-Transformation. Comput. Biol. Med. (2018)
20. Zhang, Y., et al.: Human identification driven by deep CNN and transfer learning based on multiview feature representations of ECG. Biomed. Signal Process. Control **68**, 102689 (2021)

Electromagnetic Signal Interference Based on Convolutional Autoencoder

Kaiyuan Zhao[1], Sa Xiao[2], Xiangyu Wu[1(✉)], Yang Wang[1], and Xian Cheng[1]

[1] College of Information and Communication Engineering, Harbin Engineering University, Harbin, China
[2] Beijing Institute of Astronautical Systems Engineering, Beijing, China

Abstract. At present, electromagnetic interference methods are mainly divided into traditional interference methods and intelligent interference methods. Traditional interference is currently dominated by barrage interference. Intelligent interference solves the shortcomings of barrage interference by sending out fixed-frequency and directional targeted interference waveform. However, most of the current intelligent interference methods require prior information and cannot deal with highly dynamic electromagnetic environments. Therefore, this study introduces an intelligent interference method without prior information. This study is based on a convolutional autoencoder model, which is used to extract high-order features of disturbed communication signal waveform without prior information. By covering some indistinct features and using a deconvolution network to generate similar signals to generate the best interference waveform, this method has an ideal bit error rate. The target signal is reconstructed by a convolutional autoencoder, and the optimal interference waveform is generated in the network by covering the high-order features of the input signal. Finally, the simulation is carried out using the method in this paper. In the BPSK communication system, a bit error rate of 48.7% can be achieved with a low signal-to-noise ratio. In practical engineering, the interference method in this paper can also realize covert jamming, which greatly improves the safety of jammer itself.

Keywords: Intelligent interference · Convolutional autoencoder · Signal to interference ratio

1 Introduction

Electromagnetic interference devices are widely used today. In terms of civilian use, electromagnetic interference equipment is used from signal shielding in the examination room to interference with unmanned aerial vehicle (UAV) communication. In the military field, electronic warfare and information warfare in modern warfare are becoming more and more important, and electromagnetic interference equipment is essential in electronic warfare. However, the traditional electromagnetic interference equipment has some shortcomings. The interference is less effective, and it cannot cope with the

Y. Chenggang et al. (Eds.): MobiMedia 2022, LNICST 451, pp. 238–243, 2022.
https://doi.org/10.1007/978-3-031-23902-1_18

highly dynamic electromagnetic environment [1]. So experts and scholars from many countries began to study new interference methods.

In 2006, American Abel S. Nunez et al. proposed a transform-domain communication interference waveform generation method that relies on prior knowledge. The method can interfere with the communication of the other party under the condition of correctly analyzing the other party's modulation method and some other information [2]. In the field of signal interference, the prior knowledge is mainly based on the modulation mode of the signal. Yun Lin et al. [3] identified the modulation mode of the physical layer signal based on the contour star image and deep learning. Ya Tu et al. [4] used Generative Adversarial Networks for modulation classification of digital signals. Changbo Hou et al. [5] used sliding window detection and complex convolutional networks in the frequency domain for modulation classification of aliased multi-signals. In 2017, Xingyu Xia et al. proposed an intelligent interference optimization waveform design method centered on Cell-Averaging (CA-CFAR). According to the CA-CFAR anti-interference mechanism, this method designs the interference waveform whose amplitude follows the Rayleigh distribution and is random in a finite interval. The interval is designed as a random interval based on the minimum interval [6]. In 2020, Pan Zhang et al. proposed an electronic interference method inspired by bionic systems, based on the "cognitive electronic interference" method for electronic interference, so that the interference method has the ability of autonomous perception and rapid decision-making [7]. In 2021, Zhe Su et al. proposed a new method based on the Stackelberg game, which can effectively interfere with specific signals while interfering with own signals as little as possible [8].

In this study, the interference signal generation method based on convolutional autoencoder (CAE) is used to realize the intelligent interference waveform generation without prior knowledge. In the system, the transmitter and receiver of the communication system and the RF front-end of the interference system are realized through USRP. The interference system consists of a USRP and a computer. The computer determines the optimal interference waveform and sends the interference signal by the software radio platform to achieve the interference effect, and the receiver evaluates the interference effect.

2 Method

2.1 System Model

In order to change the shortcoming of the intelligent interference method with prior knowledge mentioned above, the system model of this section is proposed. In this study, the features of the signal are extracted by the CAE, and the error function is designed through the classification effect and the minimum mean square error to improve the signal reconstruction performance. After the model is trained, the feature parameters in some fully connected layers are changed by occlusion and replacement to generate interference waveform. After the interference is implemented, the effect of the interference is evaluated by the receiver.

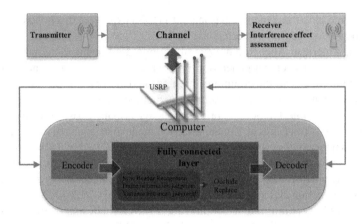

Fig. 1. System model structure diagram

2.2 Convolutional Auto-encoder

CAE [9–12] is based on autoencoder (AE) and introduces the idea of convolution into AE. In CAE, the encoder and decoder consist of convolutional layers and pooling layers. The convolutional layers in the encoder perform convolution operations, while the convolutional layers in the decoder perform deconvolution operations. Convolution is the process of multiplying and summing part of the data with the corresponding weights, while pooling is to extract invariant features. The structure of the CAE is shown in the following figure (Fig. 2):

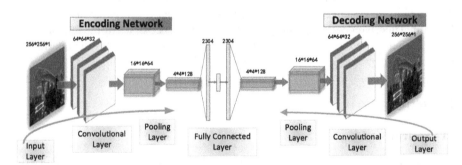

Fig. 2. CAE structure diagram

Assuming that there are k convolution kernels, each convolution kernel consists of parameters w^k and b^k, and h^k represents the convolution layer, then

$$h^k = \sigma(x * w^k + b^k) \tag{1}$$

where w^k represents is the weight, b^k represents the bias, x represents the input of the convolution kernel, and σ is the activation function.

Perform feature reconstruction on the obtained h^k, you can get:

$$y = \sigma\left(h^k * \hat{w}^k + c\right) \qquad (2)$$

where y is the output of the network, and the bias in the reconstruction process is c.

Comparing the input and output of the network with Euclidean, and optimizing through the BP algorithm, a complete CAE can be obtained:

$$E = \frac{1}{2n} \sum_{i=1}^{n} (x_i - y_i)^2 \qquad (3)$$

where n is the training times of CAE.

In the forward pass pooling layer, its output is:

$$a_{ij}^l = \max(a_{mn}^{l-1}), i \leq m, n \leq i+2 \qquad (4)$$

where m, n is the area covered by the pool core corresponding to a_{ij}^{l-1}.

Since the pooling layer of backpropagation has no parameters, the relevant gradients can be passed down:

$$\delta_{k,v}^{l-1} = \frac{\partial C}{\partial z_{k,v}^{l-1}} = \sum_{ij}^{i=3,j=3} \frac{\partial C}{\partial a_{ij}^l} \frac{\partial a_{ij}^l}{\partial a_{k,v}^{l-1}} \frac{\partial a_{k,v}^{l-1}}{\partial z_{k,v}^{l-1}} \qquad (5)$$

The loss function applied in the network is designed below, the input pure data is denoted as x_c^*, the parameters of the hidden part in the network are denoted as h_c, and the Taylor expansion of the Lagrangian remainder of the feature function of the autoencoder is as follows:

$$f\left(x_c^*\right) = f(x) + \left(x_c^* - x\right)^T \nabla f\left[x + \rho\left(x_c^* - x\right)\right] \qquad (6)$$

where $\nabla f\left[x + \rho\left(x_c^* - x\right)\right]$ is the first derivative of the coding part, and $\rho \in (0, 1)$, the loss function can be expressed as:

$$L\left(h_c, h_c^*\right) = L(h_c, f(g(h_c))) = \left\| h_c^* - h_c \right\| = \left\| f\left(x_c^*\right) - f(x) \right\|^2 \qquad (7)$$

3 Interference Effect Analysis

Apply the interference method above, and evaluate the interference effect by evaluating the bit error rate (BER) of the receiver after implementing the interference. The influence of the signal itself and different interference signals on the BER of the receiver is shown in the figure below, in which the interference waveform 1 and the interference waveform 2 are the interference waveform generated by the method used in this study (Fig. 3):

It can be seen from Fig. 4 that in the BPSK communication system, when the SIR is lower than -10 dB, the BER can reach up to 48.7%; in the QPSK communication system, when the SIR is lower than -10 dB, the BER can reach up to 33%; in the 8PSK

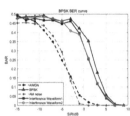
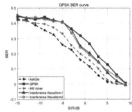
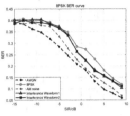

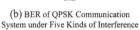

(a) BER of BPSK Communication System under Five Kinds of Interference	(b) BER of QPSK Communication System under Five Kinds of Interference	(c) BER of 8PSK Communication System under Five Kinds of Interference

Fig. 3. BER Curve Under Interference Waveform (SNR = 10 dB)

communication system, when the SIR is lower than −10 dB, the BER can reach up to 38.4%. It can be seen from the above results that the interference signal generated by this method can effectively interfere with the communication system. The method in this paper uses the I/Q two-way signal components to interfere with the signal, and distributes the power to the I/Q two-way, while the quadrature power of the QPSK signal is zero, so the method in this paper has a poor interference effect on the QPSK signal.

4 Conclusion

This study constructs a communication and interference system. The system can be used to develop and verify the generation of interference waveform based on CAE, as shown in Fig. 1. It can be concluded that the interference effect of the interference waveform intelligent generation method based on the CAE in this study is better than that of Gaussian noise interference, noise amplitude modulation and other interference signals.

The waveform generation method of the CAE in this study does not require prior information of the communication signal, and achieves the highest BER of 48.7% in the simulation. Through the continuous iteration of many experiments, the optimal convolution and deconvolution networks were obtained. The optimal parameter selection for implementing Gaussian perturbation in the fully connected layer of the CAE was found, and finally a better interference effect was achieved.

However, the interference method in this study still has some shortcomings, such as the poor interference effect on BPSK modulated signals in the actual situation, and the high dimension of the fully connected layer in the CAE, resulting in a high amount of computation. The above shortcomings will also be improved in future research.

References

1. Liu, Q.-F., Zheng, S.-Q., Zuo, Y., Zhang, H.-Q., Liu, J.-W.: Electromagnetic Environment Effects and Protection of Complex Electronic Information Systems. IEEE MTT-S International Conference on Numerical Electromagnetic and Multiphysics Modeling and Optimization (NEMO) **2020**, 1–4 (2020)

2. Nunez, A.S., Chakravarthy, V., Caldwell, J.T.: A transform domain communication and interference waveform. In: 2006 International Waveform Diversity and Design Conf6erence, pp. 1–5 (2006)
3. Lin, Y., Ya, T., Dou, Z., Chen, L., Mao, S.: Contour stella image and deep learning for signal recognition in the physical layer. IEEE Trans. Cogn. Commun. Netw. **7**(1), 34–46 (2020)
4. Ya, T., Lin, Y., Wang, J., Kim, J.-U.: Semi-supervised learning with generative adversarial networks on digital signal modulation classification. Comput. Mater. Continua. **55**(2), 243–254 (2018)
5. Hou, C., Liu, G., Tian, Q., Zhou, Z., Hua, L., Lin, Y.: Multisignal modulation classification using sliding window detection and complex convolutional network in frequency domain. IEEE Internet Things J. **9**(19), 19438–19449 (2022). https://doi.org/10.1109/JIOT.2022.316 7107
6. Xingyu, X., H. Daoliang, X., Li, Y., Xiaoyang, W.: Optimal waveform design for intelligent interference focused on CA-CFAR. In: 2017 International Conference on Computer Network, Electronic and Automation (ICCNEA), pp. 374–378 (2017)
7. Zhang, P., Huang, Y., Jin, Z.: A new electronic interference method inspried from bionics system. In: 2020 IEEE 5th International Conference on Signal and Image Processing (ICSIP), pp. 572–576 (2020)
8. Su, Z., et al.: Guarding legal communication with intelligent jammer: stackelberg game based power control analysis. China Commun. **18**(4), 126–136 (2021)
9. Ye, H., Liang, L., Li, G.Y.: Circular convolutional auto-encoder for channel coding. In: 2019 IEEE 20th International Workshop on Signal Processing Advances in Wireless Communications (SPAWC), pp. 1–5 (2019)
10. Lim, W., Lee, T.: Harmonic and percussive source separation using a convolutional auto encoder. In: 2017 25th European Signal Processing Conference (EUSIPCO), pp. 1804–1808 (2017)
11. Li, H., Meng, L., Zhang, J., Tan, Y., Ren, Y., Zhang, H.: Multiple description coding based on convolutional auto-encoder. IEEE Access **7**, 26013–26021 (2019)
12. Park, J., Lee, M., Chang, H.J., Lee, K., Choi, J.Y.: Symmetric graph bit error rate for unsupervised graph representation learning. IEEE/CVF Int. Conf. Comput. Vis. (ICCV) **2019**, 6518–6527 (2019)

Integrating Higher-Order Features for Structural Role Discovery

Qiang Tian[1], Wang Zhang[2], Pengfei Jiao[3], Kai Zhong[4], Nannan Wu[2,5], and Lin Pan[6(✉)]

[1] School of Computer and Information Engineering, Tianjin Normal University, Tianjin 300384, China
tianqiang@tjnu.edu.cn
[2] College of Intelligence and Computing, Tianjin University, Tianjin 300350, China
{wangzhang,nannan.wu}@tju.edu.cn
[3] School of Cyberspace, Hangzhou Dianzi University, Hangzhou 310018, China
pjiao@hdu.edu.cn
[4] The Joint College of SWJTU-Leeds, Southwest-Jiaotong University, Chengdu 610097, China
sc19k2z@leeds.ac.uk
[5] Shenzhen Research Institute, Tianjin University, Shenzhen 518063, China
[6] School of Marine Science and Technology, Tianjin University, Tianjin 300350, China
linpan@tju.edu.cn

Abstract. The role of node is able to denote its function and effect in the network, and can represent personal identity or status in real-world complex systems. It is defined on the local connective patterns and structural similarities. Compared to the community detection, the task of role discovery is independent to the node proximity which is generally related to the distance of density in the network. It is more likely to be determined by structural similarity, and the structural node representations have achieved great success in this field. Some existing methods focus on the local structural features to generate role-oriented node representations, but they consider too much on local structures and fail to learn multi-aspects representations of structural roles. More specifically, the local, global, and higher-order structures can denote different type of roles, and there are varying dependencies between them, leading to the difficulty to effectively integrate them. Thus, we propose a novel model HORD to integrate higher-order features into structural role discovery, aiming to learn multi-aspects structural node representations of roles. We leverage higher-order and local features and utilize the unified graph neural network (GNN) framework to organically combine them to generate structural node representations. We conduct extensive experiments on several real-world networks and the results demonstrate that our model is better than state-of-the art methods.

Keywords: Network embedding · Structural node representation · Role discovery

ⓒ ICST Institute for Computer Sciences, Social Informatics and Telecommunications Engineering 2022
Published by Springer Nature Switzerland AG 2022. All Rights Reserved
Y. Chenggang et al. (Eds.): MobiMedia 2022, LNICST 451, pp. 244–258, 2022.
https://doi.org/10.1007/978-3-031-23902-1_19

1   Introduction

The network or graph is the abstract model of real-world complex systems, such as the social network [33], traffic network, and protein network [39]. Analyzing the network structure can be beneficial to comprehending complex systems. In this case, one of the most effective method is the network embedding (also known as network representation learning), which aims to map the discrete and high-dimensional network structure into the continues and low-dimensional vector space while preserving some specific network information [36]. These representations can be applied to many downstream tasks such as node classification [30] and link prediction [34].

There are two research directions in the field of network representation learning: the positional node representations and structural node representations [29]. The positional node representation aims to encode node based on its relative position in the network, and preserves the node proximity in the embedding space. It can be applied to the task related to network distance or density, such as community detection [2]. Many methods are designed based on it, for example, the DeepWalk [25] and node2vec [5] leverage the random walk and generate node representations via Skip-Gram [20] model. Some methods based on GNNs also generate positional node representations, such as GraphSAGE [8] and ARGA [22]. These methods focus on the node proximity, but fail on the task of role discovery.

Opposite to community detection, the role of node is firstly defined as the equivalent class of isomorphic node [18]. It describes the local connective patterns of the node, and focuses on the structural similarity. For the task of role discovery, positional node representations cannot make it, while the structural node representations show the great potential. The existing methods usually leverage some structural features or similarities to generate node representations. RolX [10] utilizes the local features extracted by ReFeX [11] and decompose them to generate node representations, which recursively aggregate local and ego-net features to obtain deep information of network structure. The struc2gauss [23] leverages the global similarity RoleSim [13] while HONE [27] leverages some higher-order features.

However, these methods purely consider about single type of network structure, and considering the cost of computing complex features, most methods concentrate on the local structure. As shown in Fig. 1, the local features tend to represent the local structure of the center node, while the higher-order features describe the connective patterns with neighbors. As shown in the right part, we list out 9 graphlets (motifs) [12] with no more than 4 nodes. These two kinds of features are complementary for describing network structure, and there are varying dependencies among them. It is unclear to effectively make use of them.

To the best of our knowledge, there are a few methods that attempt to integrate multiple structural features. DMER [14] leverages the GCN [17] and VAE [15] on adjacency and local features respectively to integrate local topology structure and generate structural node representations. But it ignore that simply reconstructing the adjacency matrix is negative to role discovery to some degree.

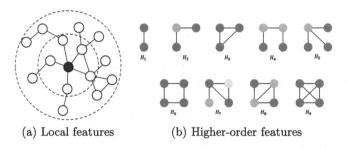

(a) Local features   (b) Higher-order features

Fig. 1. An illustration of local and higher-order features.

ARHOL [37] designs an adversarial learning framework to integrate some higher-order and local features, but it also suffers the problem of instability. We hope to integrate different type of features in an unified framework and generate multi-aspects structural node representations to discover roles.

Therefore, to address the above shortcomings, we aim to integrate higher-order features into structural role discovery and propose a novel deep-learning model HORD, which learns multi-aspects structural node representations of roles. We leverage the higher-order and local features and utilize the unified graph neural network (GNN) framework to organically combine them to generate structural node representations. Then we add the consistency constraint between them to reinforce the power of representing roles. The contributions of our model are summarized as follows:

- We propose a novel deep-learning model to effectively integrate higher-order features into role discovery, which can generate multi-aspects structural node representations.
- We utilize the unified GNN framework to generate node representations, and add the consistency constraint between features to reinforce the power of representing roles.
- We conduct extensive experiments on several real-world networks, and the results demonstrate that our model is better than state-of-the art methods.

2   Related Work

The positional and structural node representations are designed to preserve the node proximity and structural similarity in the embedding space respectively, and they are usually related to the task of community detection and role discovery. Over the past decades, most of the existing methods have been designed to generate positional node representations. DeepWalk [25] firstly introduces the random walk into network embedding, and leverages the Skip-Gram model which is widely used in NLP to generate node representation. Then node2vec [5] improves it and designs two hyper-parameters to control the probabilities of different walking mechanisms. LINE [30] optimizes a objective function and adopts a BFS-like strategy to preserve both pair-wise similarity and structural equivalence. These random-walk-based methods and some GNN-based methods such as VGAE [16] directly leverage the adjacency matrix and aim to preserve node proximity to generate positional node representations, but fail on the task of role discovery.

As for the role discovery, the existing methods apply various features to generate structural node representations. For example, ReFeX [11] proposes a novel method to extract local features, which recursively aggregate some local and ego-net features to obtain deep information of network structure. Then RolX [10], GLRD [4], DMER [14], REGAL [9], and RIDεRs [7] also leverage these features to discover roles. GAS [6] utilizes the GCN [17] to reconstruct some basic local features, and RESD [38] leverages variational auto-encoder (VAE) [15] to reconstruct ReFeX features constrained by node degree. These local features possess the strong power of representation the local connective structures, but ignore some more complex network information.

There are some methods based on global features to capture role information. REACT [24] leverages the RoleSim [13] to compute pair-wise structural similarities for each pair of nodes, and simultaneously discovers the community and role via matrix factorization. The struc2gauss [23] also leverages the similarity and designs the energy function based on the random walk on it to generate structural node representations. The struc2vec [26] firstly computes the structural similarities via Dynamic Time Warping (DTW) and constructs a multi-layer complete graph where the edge weights are based on them. Then it generates node representations with random walk. GraphWave [3] generates node representations via graph wavelet diffusion, and regards them as the probability distribution. This type of methods can capture more structural information, but may suffer the high computational complexity.

Recently, some methods attempt to introduce higher-order features into role discovery. Higher-order features are usually represented as graphlets or motifs, which describe the connective patterns of subgraphs with fixed number of nodes. The features can denote complex network structure, while computing them with large number of nodes causes high complexity. ARHOL leverages the auto-encoder to reconstruct some higher-order features, and use the GIN [35] to design an adversarial framework with the local features. HONE [27] constructs a wight graph, where the edge weights are represented as the number of times two nodes appear in the same motif, and then generate node representations via matrix factorization. Role2vec [1] designs a features-based random walk to overcome the traditional shortcomings. SEGK [21] uses another type of higher-order features. It computes structural similarities via WL [28] kernel and generate node representations with matrix factorization.

3   Method

3.1   Notions

We will first introduce the notions and definitions. Given a network or graph $G = \{V, E\}$ with adjacency matrix $\mathbf{A} \in \mathbb{R}^{n \times n}$, where $V = \{v_1, v_2, \cdots, v_n\}$ is the node set and $E \subseteq V \times V$ is the set of edges among nodes. The neighbors of the node v_i is denoted as $N(v_i) = \{v_j | (v_i, v_j) \in E\}$. The one-hop ego-net of node v_i is defined as $\mathcal{G}_i = \{V(g_i), E(g_i)\}$, where $V(g_i) = \{v_i\} \bigcup \{v_j \in V | (v_i, v_j) \in E\}$, and $E(g_i) = \{(u, v) \in E | u, v \in V(g_i)\}$. We use $\mathbf{X} \in \mathbb{R}^{n \times d_1}$ to denote the local features of nodes, while $\mathbf{M} \in \mathbb{R}^{n \times d_2}$ denotes the higher-order features, where $n = |V|$ is the number of nodes and d_1, d_2 are the dimension of features respectively. The goal of our model is to design a model to map the features into embedding space while preserving node structural similarity, and the dimension of the structural node representations is represented as d.

3.2   Model

Local Feature Extraction. It is known that two nodes u and v tend to share the same role if they have similar local structure. Though the adjacency matrix of graph contains the information of network topology, it's hard to compare the structural roles of two nodes, as the adjacency matrix is generally sparse and the nodes in the same role may be far away from each other. It is essential to extract effective local features from adjacency relationships. Here, we adopt ReFeX [11] for its high efficiency and effectiveness, which generates structural features by recursively aggregating simple local and ego-net features. This methods extracts one local feature and five ego-net-based features for each node. For the node v_i, the basic features based on $\mathcal{G}_i$ are defined as follows:

- Number of edges in $\mathcal{G}_i$: $f_1 = |E(g_i)|$.
- Sum of degree for nodes in $V(g_i)$: $f_2 = \sum_{u \in V(g_i)} d(u)$.
- The proportion of edges in $\mathcal{G}_i$ to all edges within and leaving $\mathcal{G}_i$: $f_3 = f_1/f_2$.
- The proportion of edges leaving $\mathcal{G}_i$ to all edges within and leaving $\mathcal{G}_i$: $f_4 = (f_2 - f_1)/f_2$.
- The degree of node v_i: $f_5 = |N(v_i)|$.
- The clustering coefficient for node v_i.

Then for each iteration, We compute the sum and mean value of neighbors' features and combine the new results with the last ones. With the increase of the number of iteration, the features can perceive deep information of network structure. The final local features are represented as $\mathbf{X}$.

Higher-Order Features Extraction. As shown in Fig. 1(b), we introduce the higher-order features that are known as graphlets or motifs. They describe the connective patterns of some subgraphs, and the color of node denotes the orbit. We observe that there are 15 orbits when the size of node is no more than 4.

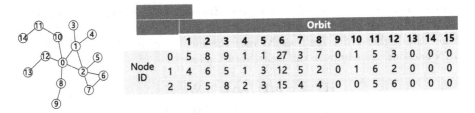

		Orbit														
		1	2	3	4	5	6	7	8	9	10	11	12	13	14	15
	0	5	8	9	1	1	27	3	7	0	1	5	3	0	0	0
Node ID	1	4	6	5	1	3	12	5	2	0	1	6	2	0	0	0
	2	5	5	8	2	3	15	4	4	0	0	5	6	0	0	0

Fig. 2. An illustration of the higher-order feature.

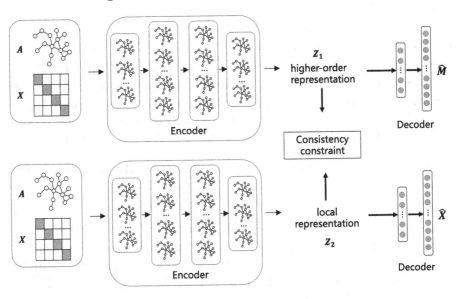

Fig. 3. An illustration of the proposed model HORD.

With the increase of the size, the features obtain more information of network structure, but need more computational complexity. We use the Graphlet Degree Vector (GDV) [12] to count these features, because it effectively counts orbits of nodes in linear time, which can be applied to large scale networks. We choose three nodes in the network and report the features of the first 15 dimensions in Fig. 2.

Considering the balance of complexity and effectiveness of features, we choose the size of node as 5, and we obtain the 73-dimensional higher-order features.

Graph Convolutional Network. As we have extracted the local and higher-order features, the next is to effectively integrate them to generate structural node representations. The most efficient method is to combines them, however, these features come from different parameter spaces, and the value of them may vary considerably. Thus, we design an novel framework based on the auto-encoder and graph convolutional network (GCN) [17] to reconstruct them and learn multi-aspects structural node representations. As shown in Fig. 3, we separately design two encoder-decoder framework with the same structure to reconstruct the higher-order features $\mathbf{M}$ and the local features $\mathbf{X}$. Specifically, for GCN encoder, we compute the representations as:

$$\begin{aligned}
\mathbf{H}_m^{(l+1)} &= \sigma(\tilde{\mathbf{D}}^{-\frac{1}{2}}\tilde{\mathbf{A}}\tilde{\mathbf{D}}^{-\frac{1}{2}}\mathbf{W}_m^{(l)}\mathbf{H}_m^{(l)}), \\
\mathbf{H}_x^{(l+1)} &= \sigma(\tilde{\mathbf{D}}^{-\frac{1}{2}}\tilde{\mathbf{A}}\tilde{\mathbf{D}}^{-\frac{1}{2}}\mathbf{W}_x^{(l)}\mathbf{H}_x^{(l)}).
\end{aligned} \tag{1}$$

The $\sigma(\cdot)$ is the non-linear activation function. The $\tilde{\mathbf{A}}$ denotes the adjacency matrix of the original network G added with self-loop edges, and $\tilde{\mathbf{A}} = \mathbf{A} + \mathbf{I}_n$, where $\mathbf{I}_n$ is the identity matrix. $\tilde{\mathbf{D}}$ is the diagonal matrix of node degree and $\tilde{\mathbf{D}}_{i,i} = \sum_j \tilde{\mathbf{A}}_{i,j}$. $\mathbf{W}_m^{(l)}$ and $\mathbf{W}_x^{(l)}$ denote the weight matrices in the GCN encoder with respect to the higher-order and local information. $\mathbf{H}_m^{(l)}$ and $\mathbf{H}_x^{(l)}$ are the hidden representation of the l-th layer respectively, and $l = 0, 1, 2, \cdots, L$. We use the identity matrix as the initial input of the GCN, then we have $\mathbf{H}_m^{(0)} = \mathbf{H}_x^{(0)} = \mathbf{I}_n$. With the increase of layer, the encoder can capture complex network structure, and we denote the higher-order representation and local representation as $\mathbf{Z}_1$ and $\mathbf{Z}_2$ respectively.

For the part of decoder, we use the multi-layer perceptrons to reconstruct the features:

$$\begin{aligned}
\hat{\mathbf{H}}_m^{(l+1)} &= \sigma(\hat{\mathbf{W}}_m^{(l)}\hat{\mathbf{H}}_m^{(l)} + \hat{\mathbf{b}}_m^{(l)}), \\
\hat{\mathbf{H}}_x^{(l+1)} &= \sigma(\hat{\mathbf{W}}_x^{(l)}\hat{\mathbf{H}}_x^{(l)} + \hat{\mathbf{b}}_x^{(l)}).
\end{aligned} \tag{2}$$

Similarly, the $\hat{\mathbf{W}}_m^{(l)}$ and $\hat{\mathbf{W}}_x^{(l)}$ denote the weight matrices in the decoder, while the $\hat{\mathbf{b}}_m^{(l)}$ and $\hat{\mathbf{b}}_x^{(l)}$ represent the bias. $\hat{\mathbf{H}}_m^{(l)}$ and $\hat{\mathbf{H}}_x^{(l)}$ denote the hidden representation in the decoder with $\hat{\mathbf{H}}_m^{(l)} = \mathbf{Z}_1, \hat{\mathbf{H}}_x^{(l)} = \mathbf{Z}_2$. We use $\hat{\mathbf{M}} = \hat{\mathbf{H}}_m^{(L)}$ and $\hat{\mathbf{X}} = \hat{\mathbf{H}}_x^{(L)}$ to denote the reconstructed features.

Joint Training. Through the process of reconstructing features, we can compute the loss function as:

$$\begin{aligned}
\mathcal{L}_M &= \|\hat{\mathbf{M}} - \mathbf{M}\|_2^2, \\
\mathcal{L}_X &= \|\hat{\mathbf{X}} - \mathbf{X}\|_2^2.
\end{aligned} \tag{3}$$

As we have obtain two types of structural node representations, we generate the final embedding $\mathbf{Z}$ as combing them. Note that if without additional constraints, the node representations are meaningless compared to combing features. Thus, to learn the multi-aspects node representation, we add a consistency constraint between the two parts as:

$$\mathcal{L}_{cons} = \|\mathbf{Z}_1 - \mathbf{Z}_2\|_2^2. \tag{4}$$

The consistency constraint makes our model learn multi-aspects representations of node roles in the same embedding space. To jointly train the whole model, we design the final loss as:

$$\mathcal{L} = \mathcal{L}_M + \mathcal{L}_X + \alpha\mathcal{L}_{cons}, \tag{5}$$

Table 1. The statistical information of the six networks.

Dataset	# nodes	# edges	# classes	Destiny (%)
Brazil	131	1,003	4	11.7792
Europe	399	5,995	4	7.5478
USA	1,190	13,599	4	1.9222
Actor	7,779	26,752	4	0.0886
Aminer-network	67,667	186,863	3	0.0082
Aminer-data	98,460	303,029	3	0.0063
Aminer-system	146,092	400,863	3	0.0038

where the α is the hyper-parameter to control the weight of consistency constraint.

4 Experiment

4.1 Dataset

We conduct extensive experiments on several real-world networks. The sizes of nodes in these networks range from 100 to 100,000, which can evaluate the ability be applied to large-scale networks. Some statistic information are shown in Table 1, and the detailed introductions are as follows:

- **Air-traffic networks** [26]: There are three air-traffic networks Brazilian, European, and American networks (shortly denoted as **Brazil, Europe**, and **USA**). Nodes represent the airports and edges represent flights between them. The class labels are between 0 and 3 reflecting the level of the airport activities.
- **Actor co-occurrence network** (shortly denoted as **Actor**) [19]: This is an actor only subgraph of a film-director-actor-writer network extracted from IMDb. The nodes denote actors and edges denote co-occurances on the same Wikipedia page. Nodes are sorted based on the number of words on their pages and split into four groups.
- **Aminer cooperation networks** [31,37]: This is a large network consisting of more than 1 million nodes and 4 million edges. Nodes represent papers and edges represent their cooperation relationships. We extract two subgraphs based on authors' keyterms (shortly denoted as **Aminer-network, Aminer-data**, and **Aminer-system**). Nodes are labeled based on their h-indexes.

4.2 Baseline

We compare our methods with following state-of-the-art embedding methods. The dimension of embeddings is set to 128 for all the baselines. As for other parameters, we tune them to the best according to their papers.

- **DeepWalk** [25]. This method applies random walk on node ids and learns node representations via the Skip-Gram model.
- **RolX** [10]. This method is based on non-negative matrix factorization (NMF) on the feature matrix which is extracted via ReFeX [11].
- **struc2vec** [26]. It learns role-based embeddings by encoding structural identity of nodes via some sequences of walks on a reconstructed multi-layer graph.
- **GraphWave** [3]. This method treats the features of spectral graph wavelets as probability distributions, and generates embeddings via empirical characteristic functions.
- **DRNE** [32]. This method proposes a layer normalized LSTM model to learn node embeddings recursively by assuming that the regular equivalent structure of a node has been encoded by the representations of its neighbors.
- **DMER** [14]. This methods jointly trains an auto-encoder and a GCN encoder to reconstruct ReFeX features and adjacency matrix, and makes the outputs of them to be similar.
- **RESD** [38]: This model applies variational auto-encoder on ReFeX features to reduce noise, and also uses MLP to reconstruct node degree as regularizer.

4.3 Experiment Setting

For our model HORD, we empirically use the ReLU as the activation function in both encoder and decoder. We set the number of hidden layers to 2. Then for each GCN encoder, the dimension of the representations is set to 64, so the dimension of the node embeddings is 128. In the process of training HORD, we set the max epochs to 500 with learning rate 0.001. We use the Adam optimizer to update parameters.

All the experiments are conducted on Linux server (Ubuntu 18.04.5 LTS) equipped with an Intel(R) Xeon(R) Silver 4210 CPU @ 2.20 GHz, 256 GB RAM and 2 NVIDIA 3090 GPUs. All models are implemented in PyTorch version 1.9.0, DGL version 0.7.1 with CUDA version 11.1, scikit-learn version 0.19.0 and Python 3.6.

4.4 Role Classification

We conduct the experiment of role classification to analyze our model on six real-world networks. The nodes are labeled based on their identities or functions that are related to their roles. For all the baselines and our model, we firstly generate node representations and then train a linear logistic regression classifier to classify nodes. We randomly choose 10% to 90% nodes as the training set and use the remain to test. We repeat the above process for 20 times and report their F1 scores. As shown in Fig. 4, we have the following observations.

Among all the baselines, the DeepWalk is the method for positional node representations, and we find that it obtains the poorest scores for all the datasets. Other methods perform better than it, and with the increase of the number of training samples, the accuracy gets higher. The results clearly show the difference

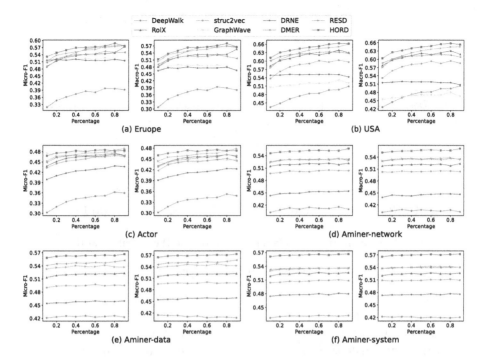

Fig. 4. The Micro-F1 and Macro-F1 scores of classification on the six real-world networks. The horizontal axis represents the different training ratios from 10% to 90%.

between the positional and structural node representations, and demonstrate that the positional node embeddings cannot qualify the task of role discovery.

As for the small networks (Europe, USA, and Actor), we observe that when we use 90% nodes to train the classifier, there is a downward trend in our proposed model HORD. The reason is that these datasets are not large enough, and too many training sample may cause over-fitting. For other percentage of training set, our model performs best in general.

We also conduct the classification experiment on some large network. We choose three academic cooperation network where the size of nodes is about 100,000 and analyze its efficiency on large datasets. Note that the GraphWave cannot get results because of the out-of-memory error. We observe that the scores become stable because small percentage of nodes are enough for the classifier to converge. Our model HORD display the obvious superiority and the scores are the highest. The experiment demonstrates that our model can effectively integrate higher-order and local features to generate multi-aspects structural node representations.

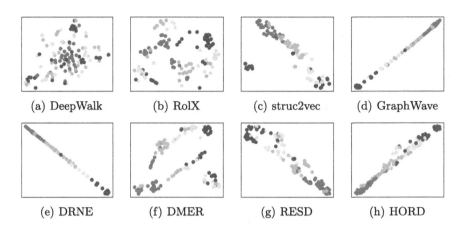

(a) DeepWalk   (b) RolX   (c) struc2vec   (d) GraphWave

(e) DRNE   (f) DMER   (g) RESD   (h) HORD

Fig. 5. Visualization of node representations on the Brazil network.

Table 2. The Micro-F1 scores of HORD and its variants on the six networks.

Model	Europe	USA	Actor	Aminer-network	Aminer-data	Aminer-system
Local	0.5601	0.6443	0.4755	0.5265	0.5408	0.5392
Higher	0.5469	0.6042	0.4779	0.5471	0.5511	0.5562
HORD	**0.5771**	**0.6604**	**0.4854**	**0.5573**	**0.5646**	**0.5647**

4.5   Visualization

In this subsection, we conduct the visualization experiment on the Brazil network to analyze the effectiveness. We firstly generate node embeddings and then map them into the 2-D space via t-SNE. In this experiment, nodes in the same role should be mapped into similar position in the embedding space, while nodes in different roles should be far away from each other. We report the results in Fig. 5. The circle denotes the node, and the color represents the role of node.

We observe that the distribution of nodes is nearly random in DeepWalk, while other methods display the tend of clustering. RolX simply decomposes the local features, and the nodes in the same role are still far away. DMER, struc2vec, and RESD can discover roles, while GraphWave and DRNE may suffer over-fitting, because they map all the nodes to a straight line. Our model HORD can effectively cluster nodes in the same role, and distinguish their differences.

4.6   Ablation Study

We conduct the ablation study to analyze the effectiveness of integrating the two types of features and the consistency constraint. We utilize the same classifier and randomly choose 70% samples to train it, and report the Micro-F1 scores in Table 2. Local denotes that our model only use the GCN to reconstruct the local features, while Higher denotes to reconstruct higher-order features. There

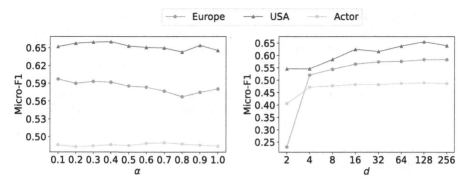

Fig. 6. The analysis of the weight of consistency constraint α and representation dimension d. We fix one parameter and adjust the other.

is no additional constraint on these two variants, and we compare the HORD with them. We mark the best scores in bold font, and we find that for all the six networks, the model HORD obtains the best performance. As for the local and higher-order features, there are different advantages on different datasets. The results prove the superiority of the proposed model.

4.7 Parameter Analysis

In this subsection, we analyze the influences of the two hyper-parameters in our model. As shown in the left figure of Fig. 6, the classification accuracy fluctuates with the change of α. The Europe and USA datasets have the similar network structures, and they both obtain the worst results when $\alpha = 0.8$. When the α is about 0.4, the model performs well. As for the Actor network, it performs best when $\alpha = 0.7$. The results demonstrate that there is the balance between the higher-order and local features, and our model can effectively integrate them.

As for the right figure, we evaluate the effect of dimension of node representations. We observe that when $d \leqslant 16$, the model cannot effectively capture enough structural information. While with the dimension becomes larger, the performance gets better. If the dimension continues to increase ($d \geqslant 256$), the scores will go down because of the over-fitting. It proves that our model HORD can generate expressive node representations with proper dimensions, which can be applied on many downstream tasks.

5   Conclusion

We introduce the challenges of the structural network representations, and find that the existing methods only concentrate on single type of structural features, and there are varying dependencies among them. To effectively integrate higher-order and local features to generate multi-aspects role-based network embeddings, we propose a novel framework HORD, which utilizes the unified graph convolutional network encoder to organically combine them to generate structural node representations. Then we add the consistency constraint between them to reinforce the power of representing roles. The experiments on real-world networks demonstrate the superiority and effectiveness of our model.

Acknowledgement. This work is supported by the Intelligent Manufacturing Special Foundation of Tianjin, China (20201198) and the Shenzhen Sustainable Development Project under Grant KCXFZ20201221173013036.

References

1. Ahmed, N., et al.: Role-based graph embeddings. IEEE Trans. Knowl. Data Eng. **34**(5), 2401–2415 (2020)
2. Cavallari, S., Zheng, V.W., Cai, H., Chang, K.C.C., Cambria, E.: Learning community embedding with community detection and node embedding on graphs. In: Proceedings of the 2017 ACM on Conference on Information and Knowledge Management, pp. 377–386 (2017)
3. Donnat, C., Zitnik, M., Hallac, D., Leskovec, J.: Learning structural node embeddings via diffusion wavelets. In: Proceedings of the 24th ACM SIGKDD International Conference on Knowledge Discovery and Data Mining, pp. 1320–1329 (2018)
4. Gilpin, S., Eliassi-Rad, T., Davidson, I.: Guided learning for role discovery (GLRD) framework, algorithms, and applications. In: Proceedings of the 19th ACM SIGKDD International Conference on Knowledge Discovery and Data Mining, pp. 113–121 (2013)
5. Grover, A., Leskovec, J.: node2vec: scalable feature learning for networks. In: Proceedings of the 22nd ACM SIGKDD International Conference on Knowledge Discovery and Data Mining, pp. 855–864 (2016)
6. Guo, X., Zhang, W., Wang, W., Yu, Y., Wang, Y., Jiao, P.: Role-oriented graph auto-encoder guided by structural information. In: International Conference on Database Systems for Advanced Applications, pp. 466–481 (2020)
7. Gupte, P.V., Ravindran, B., Parthasarathy, S.: Role discovery in graphs using global features: algorithms, applications and a novel evaluation strategy. In: 2017 IEEE 33rd International Conference on Data Engineering (ICDE), pp. 771–782 (2017)
8. Hamilton, W.L., Ying, R., Leskovec, J.: Inductive representation learning on large graphs. In: Advances in Neural Information Processing Systems, pp. 1025–1035 (2017)
9. Heimann, M., Shen, H., Safavi, T., Koutra, D.: REGAL: representation learning-based graph alignment. In: Proceedings of the 27th ACM International Conference on Information and Knowledge Management, pp. 117–126 (2018)
10. Henderson, K., et al.: RolX: structural role extraction & mining in large graphs. In: Proceedings of the 18th ACM SIGKDD International Conference on Knowledge Discovery and Data Mining, pp. 1231–1239 (2012)
11. Henderson, K., et al.: It's who you know: graph mining using recursive structural features. In: Proceedings of the 17th ACM SIGKDD International Conference on Knowledge Discovery and Data Mining, pp. 663–671 (2011)
12. Hočevar, T., Demšar, J.: A combinatorial approach to graphlet counting. Bioinformatics **30**(4), 559–565 (2014)

13. Jin, R., Lee, V.E., Hong, H.: Axiomatic ranking of network role similarity. In: Proceedings of the 17th ACM SIGKDD International Conference on Knowledge Discovery and Data Mining, pp. 922–930 (2011)
14. Ke, H., et al.: Deep mutual encode model for network embedding from structural identity. IEEE Access **7**, 177484–177496 (2019)
15. Kingma, D.P., Welling, M.: Auto-encoding variational bayes. In: International Conference on Learning Representations (2014)
16. Kipf, T.N., Welling, M.: Variational graph auto-encoders. NIPS Workshop on Bayesian Deep Learning (2016)
17. Kipf, T.N., Welling, M.: Semi-supervised classification with graph convolutional networks. In: International Conference on Learning Representations (2017)
18. Lorrain, F., White, H.C.: Structural equivalence of individuals in social networks. J. Math. Sociol. **1**(1), 49–80 (1971)
19. Ma, X., Qin, G., Qiu, Z., Zheng, M., Wang, Z.: RiWalk: fast structural node embedding via role identification. In: 2019 IEEE International Conference on Data Mining (ICDM), pp. 478–487 (2019)
20. Mikolov, T., Sutskever, I., Chen, K., Corrado, G., Dean, J.: Distributed representations of words and phrases and their compositionality. In: Advances in Neural Information Processing Systems, pp. 3111–3119 (2013)
21. Nikolentzos, G., Vazirgiannis, M.: Learning structural node representations using graph kernels. IEEE Trans. Knowl. Data Eng. **33**(5), 2045–2056 (2019)
22. Pan, S., Hu, R., Long, G., Jiang, J., Yao, L., Zhang, C.: Adversarially regularized graph autoencoder for graph embedding. In: Proceedings of the 27th International Joint Conference on Artificial Intelligence (IJCAI 2018), pp. 2609–2615 (2018)
23. Pei, Y., Du, X., Zhang, J., Fletcher, G., Pechenizkiy, M.: *struc2gauss*: structural role preserving network embedding via Gaussian embedding. Data Min. Knowl. Disc. **34**(4), 1072–1103 (2020). https://doi.org/10.1007/s10618-020-00684-x
24. Pei, Y., Fletcher, G., Pechenizkiy, M.: Joint role and community detection in networks via $L_{2,1}$ norm regularized nonnegative matrix tri-factorization. In: Proceedings of the 2019 IEEE/ACM International Conference on Advances in Social Networks Analysis and Mining, pp. 168–175 (2019)
25. Perozzi, B., Al-Rfou, R., Skiena, S.: DeepWalk: online learning of social representations. In: Proceedings of the 20th ACM SIGKDD International Conference on Knowledge Discovery and Data Mining, pp. 701–710 (2014)
26. Ribeiro, L.F., Saverese, P.H., Figueiredo, D.R.: struc2vec: learning node representations from structural identity. In: Proceedings of the 23rd ACM SIGKDD International Conference on Knowledge Discovery and Data Mining, pp. 385–394 (2017)
27. Rossi, R.A., Ahmed, N.K., Koh, E., Kim, S., Rao, A., Abbasi-Yadkori, Y.: A structural graph representation learning framework. In: Proceedings of the 13th International Conference on Web Search and Data Mining, pp. 483–491 (2020)
28. Shervashidze, N., Schweitzer, P., Van Leeuwen, E.J., Mehlhorn, K., Borgwardt, K.M.: Weisfeiler-lehman graph kernels. J. Mach. Learn. Res. **12**(9), 2539–2561 (2011)
29. Srinivasan, B., Ribeiro, B.: On the equivalence between positional node embeddings and structural graph representations. In: International Conference on Learning Representations (2020)
30. Tang, J., Qu, M., Wang, M., Zhang, M., Yan, J., Mei, Q.: Line: large-scale information network embedding. In: Proceedings of the 24th International Conference on World Wide Web, pp. 1067–1077 (2015)

31. Tang, J., Zhang, J., Yao, L., Li, J., Zhang, L., Su, Z.: Arnetminer: extraction and mining of academic social networks. In: Proceedings of the 14th ACM SIGKDD International Conference on Knowledge Discovery and Data Mining, pp. 990–998 (2008)
32. Tu, K., Cui, P., Wang, X., Yu, P.S., Zhu, W.: Deep recursive network embedding with regular equivalence. In: Proceedings of the 24th ACM SIGKDD International Conference on Knowledge Discovery and Data Mining, pp. 2357–2366 (2018)
33. Wasserman, S., Faust, K., et al.: Social Network Analysis: Methods and Applications, vol. 8. Cambridge University Press, Cambridge (1994)
34. Xie, Y., Gong, M., Wang, S., Liu, W., Yu, B.: Sim2vec: node similarity preserving network embedding. Inf. Sci. **495**, 37–51 (2019)
35. Xu, K., Jegelka, S., Hu, W., Leskovec, J.: How powerful are graph neural networks? In: International Conference on Learning Representations (2019)
36. Zhang, D., Yin, J., Zhu, X., Zhang, C.: Network representation learning: a survey. IEEE Trans. Big Data **6**(1), 3–28 (2018)
37. Zhang, W., et al.: Role-oriented network embedding based on adversarial learning between higher-order and local features. In: Proceedings of the 30th ACM International Conference on Information & Knowledge Management, pp. 3632–3636 (2021)
38. Zhang, W., Guo, X., Wang, W., Tian, Q., Pan, L., Jiao, P.: Role-based network embedding via structural features reconstruction with degree-regularized constraint. Knowl. Based Syst. **218**, 106872 (2021)
39. Zitnik, M., Leskovec, J.: Predicting multicellular function through multi-layer tissue networks. Bioinformatics **33**(14), i190–i198 (2017)

An Overview of Multimodal Fusion Learning

Fan Yang⬤, Bo Ning(✉)⬤, and Huaiqing Li⬤

Dalian Maritime University, Dalian 116000, Liaoning, China
ningbo@dlmu.edu.cn

Abstract. With the rapid development of modern science and technology, information sources have become more widely available and in more diverse forms, resulting in widespread interest in multimodal learning. With the various types of information captured by humans in understanding the world and perceiving objects, a single modality cannot provide all of the information about a specific object or phenomenon. Multimodal fusion learning opens up new avenues for tasks in deep learning, making them more scientific and human in their approach to solving many real-world problems. An important challenge confronting multimodal learning today is how to efficiently facilitate the fusion of multimodal features while retaining the integrity of modal information to reduce information loss. This paper summarizes the definition and development process of multimodality, analyzes and discusses briefly the main approaches to multimodal fusion, common models, and current specific applications, and finally discusses future development trends and research directions in the context of existing technologies.

Keywords: Multimodal learning · Multimodal fusion · Deep learning

1 Introduction

The goal of multimodal learning is to learn and understand a variety of different types of information. With the rapid development of deep learning in recent years, multimodal fusion has become a popular topic. Philosophers and artists used the term "multimodality" to define forms of expression and rhetorical methods that fused different contents as early as the fourth-century BC [1,2]. Since the twentieth century, the widespread use of the web and mobile devices has made multimodal data the primary form of data resource in recent times, and research into multimodal learning is critical for computers to understand heterogeneous data from multiple sources. Multimodal learning is currently used in a variety of applications, including face recognition [3], visual question answering [4], image captioning [5], sentiment analysis [6], and multimodal retrieval [7].

Y. Chenggang et al. (Eds.): MobiMedia 2022, LNICST 451, pp. 259–268, 2022.
https://doi.org/10.1007/978-3-031-23902-1_20

2   Definition and Development Process of Multimodal Learning

2.1   Definition of Multimodal Learning

The term "modality" encompasses a wide range of concepts. Humans gather information about a thing through sight, hearing, touch, and smell. A modality is a term used to describe any method of obtaining information. Likewise, sounds, images, and text obtained in various ways can be considered modalities. A typical form of multimodal information is depicted in Fig. 1.

While unimodal representation learning aims to convert information into numerical or feature vectors for further computer processing, multimodal learning improves the ability to understand and learn multimodal information by leveraging complementarity and filtering redundancy. Recent examples usually involve multimodal learning with images, text, and sounds.

The streets are sprinkled with fallen leaves in autumn and people take a leisurely stroll along the roads.

Fig. 1. Multimodal data for a "Autumn Streets" scene (image, sound and text)

2.2   Development of Multimodal Learning

Multimodal learning methods have made significant progress in several areas of intelligent information processing since the 1980s. McGurk et al. proposed the effect of vision on speech perception in 1976, which was used in Audio-Visual Speech Recognition (AVSR) technology [8] and served as a prototype for the multimodal concept. Many computer scientists, influenced by the McGurk effect, have worked on developing multimodal speech recognition systems based on vision and hearing, such as lip-sound speech recognition systems [9], which can effectively improve recognition accuracy when compared to audio alone. Atrey et al. classified existing multimodal fusion methods into fusion methods and fusion levels in 2010 [10]. Wang proposed the Deep Multimodal Hashing with Orthogonal Regularization Constraints (DMHOR) method [11] in 2015 as a method for reducing information redundancy in multimodal representations. Zhang et al. [12] and Wang et al. [13] have since made significant contributions to cross-modal information matching and retrieval; Liu et al. have analyzed and studied visual and haptic data and applied it to integrated robotic perception scenarios [14], and Fu et al. have made significant advances in the field of semantic annotation of images [15].

3   Multimodal Fusion Methods

Multimodal fusion is a key component of multimodal learning and is broadly classified into two types: model-independent fusion methods and model-based fusion methods. Model-independent methods do not directly rely on deep learning methods, which are simple but less practical in terms of information loss during fusion; Model-based methods, which are complex but more accurate, include the Multiple Kernel Learning (MKL) methods, Graphical Model (GM) methods, and the Neural Network (NN) methods.

3.1   Model-Independent Fusion Methods

Model-independent fusion methods are classed as early fusion, late fusion, and hybrid fusion depending on when the fusion happens. Early fusion incorporates features just after they're extracted, late fusion does so after each model's output, and hybrid fusion combine the advantages of the first two.

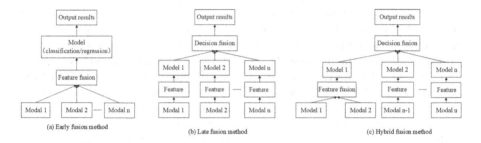

Fig. 2. Model-independent fusion methods

Early Fusion Methods. Early fusion is the technique of doing the fusion on both the feature and data levels immediately after feature extraction, most typically by using a simple join operation on the features. Early fusion methods can take advantage of the correlation and interactions between low-level elements of each modality when the modalities are highly linked. However, at the feature and data levels, this correlation is more difficult to extract, and Hinton et al. argue that the information contained in data from different modalities can only be correlated at a higher level [16]. According to Martinez et al., early fusion of multimodal data may not fully exploit the complementarity between the modalities and may even result in redundant vector inputs [17]. As a result, early fusion is not the best fusion procedure.

Furthermore, the issue of time synchronization between multimodal features must be considered during early fusion. Convolution and pool fusion, which can combine discrete event sequences with continuous signals, was proposed by ROBIN et al. to solve the time synchronization problem [18]. The structure of early fusion methods is depicted in Fig. 2(a), in which extracted features are fused directly first, then features from different modalities are integrated for model training, and finally the final output results.

Late Fusion Methods. Late fusion, also known as decision level fusion, entails first training a separate model for each modality and then fusing the outputs of several models. Late fusion methods, such as Bayesian rule fusion, maximum fusion, mean fusion, and other rule fusion methods, currently rely on rules to decide the combination of distinct model outputs [19].

When compared to previous fusion approaches, this sort of fusion can manage simple data asynchrony while providing greater flexibility in selecting the best-suited method for each modality to be analyzed, such as Hidden Markov Models (HMM) for audio and Support Vector Machines (SVM) for images. However, it ignores the low-level interaction of several modalities, making fusion harder. Figure 2(b) depicts the structure of the late fusion methods, which involves training each modal data individually in the first stage and fusing the output of several models in the second stage using a decision-making methodology.

Hybrid Fusion Methods. While hybrid fusion methods incorporate the benefits of early and late fusion, they also result in a more complicated model structure and higher training difficulty. Because the structure of deep learning models is flexible and diverse, hybrid fusion methods are ideal for this purpose, and so hybrid fusion methods have been widely applied in domains such as visual question answering and multimedia. Ni et al. [20] suggested a hybrid fusion strategy for multimedia analysis, for example, by presenting an image fusion method based on several BP (Back Propagation) networks. The combined elements of the video and sound signals are then sent into the audiovisual depth neural network model to generate model predictions, and the final results are generated by combining the predictions of each model [21]. The issue of the rationality of the hybrid fusion method's combination approach is a critical aspect in increasing the model's performance. Figure 2(c) shows the hybrid fusion method's structure, which is a blend of early and late fusion.

Each of the three methods has its own set of benefits and drawbacks. Early fusion can better capture the relationship between different features, but it is prone to overfitting; late fusion can solve the overfitting problem, but it does not allow the classifier to train all of the data at once; hybrid fusion methods can combine the benefits of the first two, but they must choose a suitable fusion method based on a combination of practical application problems.

3.2   Model-Based Fusion Methods

Model-based fusion methods are used to handle the problem of fusing disparate modalities by implementing technical and model viewpoints, and they have a broader variety of applications than model-independent methods. Multiple Kernel Learning (MKL) methods, Graphical Model (GM) methods, Neural Network (NN) methods, and so on are some of the most often used methodologies.

Multi-kernel Learning (MKL) Methods. Multi-kernel learning methods are a type of machine learning algorithm that extends the kernel Support Vector

Machine (SVM) method by replacing a single kernel with a collection of basic kernels, where different kernels correspond to different views of the data and are combined into a unified kernel after learning, as shown in Fig. 3. Multi-kernel learning methods are more flexible and capable of fusing heterogeneous data, and they're widely used in applications like multimodal sentiment recognition [22] and multimodal sentiment analysis, where different kernels are used for semantic, video, and text features to achieve better analysis results than single kernel modal fusion. McFee et al. employed MKL to rank the similarity of music artists based on auditory, semantic, and sociological triads to combine diverse data into a reasonable similarity space [23].

Flexible kernel selection, convex loss functions, and the ability to train models using common optimization packages and globally optimal solutions are advantages of the multi-kernel learning method, so a good MKL algorithm can improve accuracy while reducing complexity and training time. Its downside is that while testing, it is dependent on the training function and can consume a lot of memory.

The most basic way to construct a Multi-kernel model is to consider a convex combination of multiple elementary kernel functions:

$$K(x, z) = \sum_{i=1}^{M} \beta_i K_i(x, z) \tag{1}$$

$$\sum_{i=1}^{M} \beta_i = 1 \tag{2}$$

$$\beta_i \geq 0 \tag{3}$$

where K(x,z) is the basic kernel function, M is the total number of basic kernels, and β is the combination factor.

Graphical Model (GM) Methods. The Graphical Model (GM) Method is a popular fusion method that focuses on picture segmentation, stitching, and prediction to fuse shallow or deep layers to achieve the ultimate fusion result [24]. Graphical models are broadly classified as either joint probabilistic generative models or conditional probabilistic discriminative models. Initially, generative models were primarily used, particularly in statistical natural language processing. Examples include the Hidden Markov Model [25], Dynamic Bayesian Networks, and others. These models make extensive use of joint probabilities in their modeling. Subsequent discriminative models, such as Conditional Random Fields (CRF) techniques, are simpler and easier to learn than generative models and have been widely employed and demonstrated good results in multimedia classification tasks, multimodal session segmentation [26], and other applications.

Generative methods seek the best classification surface across distinct categories and adapt to differences in heterogeneous data, whereas discriminative

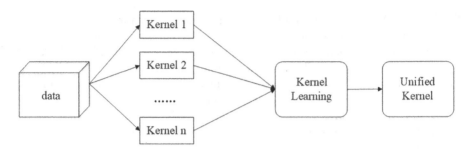

Fig. 3. Procedures multi-kernel learning

models seek to model posterior probabilities and describe data distribution statistically. Generic models require more data than discriminative models, but they are less accurate.

The advantages of Graphical Models include that they can easily uncover and exploit the geographical and temporal structure in the data, that they are suited for modeling time-series data, and that they enhance the model's interpretability by incorporating expert knowledge within the model. The downsides are that the models have limited generalization capabilities and that the feature relationships are complex.

Neural Network (NN) Methods. Neural networks have generated excellent results in unimodal feature extraction, particularly when processing data such as images, sound, and text. In multimodal tasks such as visual question answering [27], image captioning [28], and so on, neural networks are increasingly being used. Each modal data is initially transmitted through several different neural network layers, followed by several hidden layers to map the modalities to the joint space, resulting in the joint features, when utilizing neural networks to build multimodal feature representations.

Vo et al. proposed the Text Image Residual Gating (TIRG) method [29], where the gating module is used to preserve the spatial structure features of image modalities and the residual module obtains the modified features, which are added together to obtain the final combined features for image retrieval.

$$f_{gate}(\phi_x, \phi_t) = \sigma(W_{g2} * RELU(W_{g1} * [\phi_x, \phi_t]) \odot \phi_x) \qquad (4)$$

$$f_{res}(\phi_x, \phi_t) = W_{r2} * RELU(W_{r1} * ([\phi_x, \phi_t])) \qquad (5)$$

$$\phi_{xt}^{rg} = w_g f_{gate}(\phi_x, \phi_t) + w_r f_{res}(\phi_x, \phi_t) \qquad (6)$$

where f_{gate}, f_{res} are the gating and the residual features. W_g, W_r are learnable weights to balance them.

In 2019, Xu et al. proposed the Multi-Interactive MemoryNetwork, which uses the Aspect-guided attention mechanism to guide the model to generate

Attention vectors for text and images, while also using the Multi-interactive attention mechanism to capture interaction information between multimodalities and within a single modality [30]. This means that textual and visual information are fused via Attention over several hops. Zhang improved the algorithm for the multimodal machine translation task by deforming the Transformer to input the image representation at the Decoder side as well, implying that it should be coded as Q for the sentence and then K and V for the image features, i.e. finding semantically similar parts in the image for Attention fusion, and finally sending them together to the Decoder side for translation [31]. How to uncover the similarity and distinctiveness between multiple modalities is a critical topic in multimodal fusion. The information from several modalities is easily distinguishable and, at the same time, complementing. It is critical to understand how to locate these two representations, and Lu presented a new cross-modal shared feature transfer algorithm (cm-SSFT) to address this issue [32].

The neural network method has the advantage of being able to learn from large amounts of data and having high scalability. The downside is that it requires a significant amount of data to train, is difficult to achieve convergence, and gets less interpretable as the number of modalities grows.

4 Research Challenges in Multimodal Fusion Technology

By fully exploiting complementary information between modalities, the multimodal fusion technique provides for a more complete and accurate representation of features. When one of the modalities is lacking, the entire system can still function, such as when a person is unable to talk but can still gather and interpret emotions using visual data. Obtaining varying degrees of reinforcement for distinct features while ensuring the model's efficacy can aid in improving the performance of deep learning models. However, several issues, such as the heterogeneity gap and the semantic gap [33], remain unaddressed.

Different neural network structures characterize different data modalities, such as hierarchical networks for image features and sequential networks for text features. The various structures of neural networks result in various abstractions of data representation. As a result, they are not directly comparable, resulting in a heterogeneity gap.

Another issue in multimodal learning is maintaining semantic similarity, as it is difficult to record the intricate relationships between distinct modal inputs. Because neural networks' purpose is to normalize the properties of different modalities into a common space, the semantic similarity between modalities is critical. More effective semantic embedding approaches must be investigated to address these challenges and enable more effective communication and interoperability amongst modal information. There is also a need to develop a more universal evaluation standard to assess the value of feature fusion.

5 Summary and Outlooks

This study outlines multimodal data fusion approaches and the current state of research, as well as summarizes and analyzes the existing difficulties. Model-independent fusion methods and model-based fusion methods are the two forms of multimodal fusion methods. Model-independent methods are further classified as early, late, and hybrid fusion; model-based methods include multiple kernel learning, graphical models, and neural networks. Each of these strategies has benefits and drawbacks, and they all play a role in different domain applications. The current task is to bridge the heterogeneity and semantic gaps.

Multimodal learning is expected to be fully developed in the future because it is more closely aligned with human behavior in perceiving things than uni-modal information, and it is more in line with real-world applications. In-depth research on issues such as the semantic gap of modalities and feature fusion evaluation metrics will be conducted in the future to promote the application and development of multimodal fusion technology in the emerging field of machine learning.

References

1. Pedwell, R.K., Hardy, J.A., Rowland, S.L.: Effective visual design and communication practices for research posters: exemplars based on the theory and practice of multimedia learning and rhetoric. Biochem. Mol. Biol. Educ. **45**(3), 249–261 (2017)
2. Welch, K.E., Thompson, G.: Electric rhetoric: classical rhetoric, oralism, and a new literacy. Coll. Compos. Commun. **52**(1), 153 (2000)
3. Bilge, Y.C., Yucel, M.K., Cinbis, R.G., Ikizler-Cinbis, N., Duygulu, P.: Red carpet to fight club: partially-supervised domain transfer for face recognition in violent videos. In: Proceedings of the IEEE/CVF Winter Conference on Applications of Computer Vision, pp. 3358–3369 (2021). https://doi.org/10.1109/WACV48630.2021.00340
4. Chen, L., Yan, X.: Counterfactual samples synthesizing for robust visual question answering. IEEE (2020)
5. Alikhani, M., Sharma, P., Li, S.: Cross-modal coherence modeling for caption generation. The Association for Computational Linguistics (2020)
6. Mao, Y., Sun, Q., Liu, G.: DialogueTRM: exploring the intra- and inter-modal emotional behaviors in the conversation (2020)
7. Anwaar, M.U., Labintcev, E., Kleinsteuber, M.: Compositional learning of image-text query for image retrieval. WACV, pp. 1139–1148 (2021). https://doi.org/10.1109/WACV48630.2021.00118
8. Mcgurk, H., Macdonald, J.: Hearing lips and seeing voices. Nature **264**(5588), 746–748 (1976)
9. Petajan, E.D.: Automatic lip-reading to enhance speech recognition (1985)
10. Atrey, P.K., Hossain, M.A., El Saddik, A., et al.: Multimodal fusion for multimedia analysis: a survey. Multimed. Syst. **16**(6), 345–379 (2010). https://doi.org/10.1007/s00530-010-0182-0
11. Wang, D., Cui, P., Ou, M.: Deep multimodal hashing with orthogonal regularization. AAAI Press (2015)

12. Zhang, L., Zhao, Y., Zhu, Z.: Multi-view missing data completion. IEEE Trans. Knowl. Data Eng. **30**(7), 1296–1309 (2018)
13. Wang, L., Sun, W., Zhao, Z.: Modeling intra- and inter-pair correlation via heterogeneous high-order preserving for cross-modal retrieval. Signal Process. **131**, 249–260 (2017)
14. Liu, H., Li, F., Xu, X.: Multi-modal local receptive field extreme learning machine for object recognition. Neurocomputing **277**, 4–11 (2017)
15. Fu, K., Jin, J., Cui, R.: Aligning where to see and what to tell: image captioning with region-based attention and scene-specific contexts. IEEE Trans. Pattern Anal. Mach. Intell. **39**(12), 2321–2334 (2017)
16. Hinton, G.E., Salakhutdinov, R.R.: Reducing the dimensionality of data with neural networks. Science **313**(5786), 504–507 (2006)
17. Martínez, H.P., Yannakakis, G.N.: Deep multimodal fusion. In: The 16th International Conference (2014)
18. Murphy, R.R.: Computer vision and machine learning in science fiction. Sci. Robot. **4**(30), eaax7421 (2019)
19. Kahou, S.E., Pal, C., Bouthillier, X.: Combining modality specific deep neural networks for emotion recognition in video. In: ACM on International Conference on Multimodal Interaction, pp. 543–550 (2013). https://doi.org/10.1145/2522848.2531745
20. Ni, J., Ma, X., Xu, L.: An image recognition method based on multiple BP neural networks fusion. In: International Conference on Information Acquistition, pp. 323–326 (2004)
21. Gönen, M., Alpaydın, E.: Multiple kernel learning algorithms. J. Mach. Learn. Res. **12**, 2211–2268 (2011)
22. Jaques, N., Taylor, S.: Multi-task, multi-kernel learning for estimating individual wellbeing
23. Mcfee, B., Lanckriet, G.: Learning multi-modal similarity (2010)
24. He, J., Zhang, C.Q.: Survey of research on multimodal fusion technology for deep learning. Comput. Eng. **46**(5), 1–11 (2020)
25. Friedman, N.: Learning the structure of dynamic probabilistic networks. Comput. Sci. 139–147 (2010)
26. Reiter, S., Schuller, B., Rigoll, G.: Hidden conditional random fields for meeting segmentation. In: IEEE International Conference on Multimedia and Expo (ICME 2007), pp. 639–642 (2007)
27. Khademi, M.: Multimodal neural graph memory networks for visual question answering. In: Proceedings of the 58th Annual Meeting of the Association for Computational Linguistics, pp. 7177–7188 (2020)
28. Chen, S., Jin, Q., Wang, P., Wu, Q.: Say as you wish: fine-grained control of image caption generation with abstract scene graphs. In: IEEE, pp. 9962–9971 (2020)
29. Vo, N., Lu, J., Chen, S.: Composing text and image for image retrieval - an empirical odyssey. In: CVF Conference on Computer Vision and Pattern Recognition (CVPR), pp. 6432–6441 (2019). https://doi.org/10.1109/CVPR.2019.00660
30. Xu, N., Mao, W., Chen, G.: Multi-interactive memory network for aspect based multimodal sentiment analysis. In: 33rd AAAI Conference on Artificial Intelligence, pp. 371–378 (2019)
31. Zhang, Z., Chen, K., Wang, R.: Neural machine translation with universal visual representation. In: ICLR 2020: Eighth International Conference on Learning Representations (2020)

32. Lu, Y., Wu, Y., Liu, B.: Cross-modality person re-identification with shared-specific feature transfer. In: 2020 IEEE/CVF Conference on Computer Vision and Pattern Recognition (CVPR) (2020)
33. Wei, C.A.: New ideas and trends in deep multimodal content understanding: a review. Neurocomputing (2020)

Exploring Spatial Patterns of Emergency Call Behavior in a Metropolitan City of China

Ning Yuan[1]([✉]), Bo Yang[2], Kun Fu[2], Lei Du[1], Pengfei Jiao[3], Lin Pan[4], Qiang Tian[5], and Wenjun Wang[6]

[1] Tianjin Zhongtian Huitong Technology Co., Ltd., Tianjin 300121, China
yuanning@witapex.cn
[2] China Mobile Communications Group Jiangxi Co., Ltd., Nanchang 330038, China
[3] School of Cyberspace, Hangzhou Dianzi University, Hangzhou 310018, China
[4] School of Marine Science and Technology, Tianjin University, Tianjin 300072, China
[5] Computer and Information Engineering College, Tianjin Normal University, Tianjin 300382, China
[6] College of Intelligence and Computing, Tianjin University, Tianjin 300350, China

Abstract. Extensive analysis of human electronic footprints is of great importance for unveiling the patterns of collective reactions to extreme events. Several empirical results have been reported to reveal the influence of different scale events on human behavior using various social media datasets. But there is a lack of understanding of the patterns of emergency call behavior which is the direct evidence of unexpected events encountered by citizens. Here we explore the spatial patterns of emergency calls made by citizens in a metropolitan city in China. We find that there is strong randomness in the spatial conversion of emergency call behavior, the number of emergency calls made by an individual in a specific location of an incident follows a power-law distribution, and the spatial pattern of incident locations presents a bi-central aggregation feature. Then we propose an agent based model for the generation of incident location series. Our work has the potential value to help the government improve the efficiency of emergency management such as situation analysis, resource allocation and police deployment.

Keywords: Spatial pattern · Emergency call · Random walk model · Human behavior simulation

1 Introduction

With the wide application of mobile phones and other social media, human behavior can be aware through these electronic footprint data sets, which provide

Supported by the National Natural Science Foundation of China (61902278 and 62102262) and the National Key R&D Program of Jiangxi, China (20212ABC03W12).

multi-dimensional information for quantitative research on human dynamics [3, 6, 8, 30]. Moreover, on the basis of the study of normal human behavior, many researchers have carried out exploratory studies on the influence of unexpected events on spatiotemporal patterns of human behavior in recent years. Their work is of great importance to improving the efficiency of emergency management for governments [16].

Some anomalies that are triggered by different scale of emergencies, including sharp increased call volume [2, 11, 20], shortened call duration [20], anomalous information diffusion [11], unusual travel pattern [19–21], higher mobility predictability [19] and social activity [2, 20], have been uncovered using mobile phone records and applied in anomaly detection [1, 5, 7, 26]. Some other datasets such as Flicker [22], Twitter [18, 25, 27], Facebook [25], GPS [23, 24] and Air Transportation Network [29] are also used to study the influence of disasters on social communication or human mobility [10]. Meanwhile, emergency call records (ECR), which is considered as the direct evidence dataset of unexpected events encountered by citizens, has been studied for sociological perspective verification [9], hot spots analysis [14], event detection [13, 15] and call center workload prediction [4]. However, there is a lack of extensive understanding of the spatiotemporal patterns of emergency call behavior [12, 14, 28].

In this paper, we studied the spatial patterns of emergency calls made by citizens in a city in China. The character of strong randomness was found in the spatial conversion of emergency call behavior. The number of emergency calls made by an individual in a specific location of incident was detected to follow a power-law distribution, and the spatial pattern of incident locations presented a feature of bi-central aggregation. Then we proposed an agent based model for the generation of incident location series. Our work has potential value in applications in emergency management.

2   Materials and Methods

2.1   Dataset Description

To study the temporal dynamic of calling behavior in case of emergency, we applied for the right to use two datasets which have been encrypted to eliminate personal privacy:

(a) A dataset of ECR collected from a metropolitan city in China from Jan. 1, 2008 to Dec. 3, 2012. It contains a total of 22,358,046 incoming calls from 7,724,005 distinct phone numbers.
(b) A mobile phone signaling dataset from a Chinese operator covering ~2 billion calling records of ~6 million users in the city, same as dataset (a) from August 1, 2011 to October 31, 2011.

2.2 Methods

Data Preprocessing. We have collected the geographic coordinates of the incident locations from valid emergency call records in dataset (a). We focused our study on urban areas and finally obtained a dataset of 4,836,065 emergency call records with valid incident locations from 2,357,361 individuals.

The home and workplace of the individuals were extracted from dataset (b) using the similar method as described in [17]. Differently, we assigned the daytime and nighttime periods with 9 a.m. to 5 p.m. and 10 p.m. to 6 a.m. on weekdays, respectively to identify home and workplace.

Statistics for Incident Locations. The displacement Δr is defined as the distance between two consecutive incident locations of an individual. The trajectory of emergency call behavior is formed by an individual's consecutive incident locations, and its radius of gyration is defined as

$$r_g = \sqrt{\frac{1}{C}\sum_{i=1}^{C}(\vec{r_i} - \vec{r_{cm}})^2},\qquad(1)$$

where $\vec{r_i}$ represents the $i = 1, \ldots, C$ incident locations recorded for the individual and $\vec{r_{cm}} = \frac{1}{C}\sum_{i=1}^{C}\vec{r_i}$ is the center of mass of the trajectory.

The number of incident locations in one trajectory is denoted as L to measure the spatial activity of emergency calls for an individual. The number of emergency calls made at a single incident location is denoted as C_L to measure the emergency call activity at a fixed position for the individual.

Location Normalization. For investigating the aggregation characteristics of emergency call behavior, we took home and workplace as two reference points. A new coordinate system was constructed by mapping the geographic coordinates of each individual's home and workplace to $(-1, 0)$ and $(1, 0)$, respectively. Then an incident location could be mapped to a point in the new coordinate system according to its relative position to one's home and workplace points. Moreover, each incident location was classified as its nearer reference center defined as the origin point of a single step. And the displacement from home(workplace) to an incident location was denoted as D_h (D_w). The angle between the direction of home (workplace) to an incident location and the commuting direction counterclockwise is denoted as θ_h (θ_w). The number of home (workplace) that consecutive occurrenced in the series of reference centers for an individual is denoted as n_h (n_w).

Fit Test for Simulation Analysis. The original definition of Kullback-Leibler divergence is a non-symmetric measure of the difference between two probability distributions P and Q:

$$KL(P \parallel Q) = \sum_{i} P(i) \log \frac{P(i)}{Q(i)}.\qquad(2)$$

To evaluate the goodness-of-fit for statistical characteristics of simulation data, the symmetrical divergence was adopted here as:

$$D(P \parallel Q) = \frac{1}{2}(KL(P \parallel Q) + KL(Q \parallel P)). \tag{3}$$

Further, we specified the discrete random variable $x^{(m)}, m = 1, 2, \ldots, M$, whose distribution in real data is $P(x^{(m)})$, and $Q(x^{(m)}|\varphi^{(n)})$ is the distribution of simulation data generated under N groups of parameters $\varphi^{(n)}, n = 1, 2, \ldots, N$. Then the relative fitting deviation for distribution $P(x^{(m)})$ to $Q(x^{(m)})$ under the parameter set $\varphi^{(n)}$ is defined as:

$$R(X^{(m)}|\varphi^{(n)}) = \frac{D(P(X^{(m)}) \parallel Q(X^{(m)}|\varphi^{(n)}))}{\frac{1}{N}\sum\limits_{n=1}^{N} D(P(X^{(m)}) \parallel Q(X^{(m)}|\varphi^{(n)}))}. \tag{4}$$

For the probability distribution of all random variables $x^{(m)}$ used for evaluation, the average relative fitting deviation of the model under the parameter set $\varphi^{(n)}$ is:

$$\langle R \rangle(\varphi^{(n)}) = \frac{1}{M}\sum\limits_{m=1}^{M} R(X^{(m)}|\varphi^{(n)}), \tag{5}$$

which will be used as the basis for parameter optimization.

3   Empirical Results

3.1   Spatial Patterns of Emergency Call Behavior

To explore the spatial patterns of emergency call behavior, we studied the ECR data set in the urban area of a metropolitan city in China for five years. The distributions of displacement (Δr) and radius of gyration (r_g) of trajectories formed by incident locations were very consistent for different years. We tested the fitnesses of these two distributions with functions of power-law (POW), exponent (EXP), truncated power-law (TPL) and gauss (GAU), respectively. It was shown that the distributions $P(\Delta r)$ and $P(r_g)$ could be well fitted by the gauss function $P(x) = \frac{A}{\sqrt{2\pi}\sigma}\exp\left(-\frac{(x+\mu)^2)}{2\sigma^2}\right)$, where $A = 4.021, \mu = 8.873, \sigma = 8.989$ for $P(\Delta r)$ and $A = 0.385, \mu = 0.003, \sigma = 3.279$ for $P(r_g)$, respectively (See Fig. 1). It indicated that there was a strong randomness in the spatial pattern of emergency call behavior.

The number of incident locations for an individual (L) was considered to evaluate the activity of encountering emergency events. The distributions of L at the aggregated level for different years were observed as a consistent power-law decay $P(L) \sim L^{-\alpha}$, where $\alpha \approx 3.75$ as shown in Fig. 2 (a). Meanwhile, the number of emergency calls in a single incident location for an individual (C_L) also followed a power-law distribution $P(C_L) \sim C_L^{-\beta}$, where $\beta \approx 3.29$ as shown in

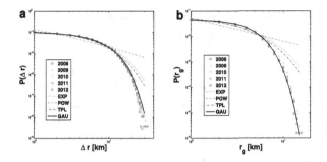

Fig. 1. Distributions of Δr and r_g in the log-log scale at aggregated level for different years. The tested fitting functions of exponent (EXP), power-law (POW), truncated power-law (TPL) and gauss (GAU) are shown as blue dot, green dashed, red dot-dashed and black solid curves, respectively. (Color figure online)

Fig. 2 (b). These phenomena indicate that the activity of emergency call behavior is very inhomogeneous for individuals. Then we studied the trends of average values of displacement (Δr), radius of gyration (r_g) and the number of emergency calls (C_i) for groups of individuals with the increase of L by 1 km interval. As shown in Fig. 2 (c), $\langle \Delta r \rangle$ and $\langle r_g \rangle$ increased rapidly and then tended to be saturated at about 4 km. It indicated that the number of events that an individual encountered averagely almost had no effect on the basic spatial patterns of emergency call behavior. And the saturation value should be associated to the scope of studied urban areas. As shown in Fig. 2 (d), $\langle C_i \rangle$ presented positive linear correlation with L as $\langle C_i \rangle = kL$, where $k = 1.25$.

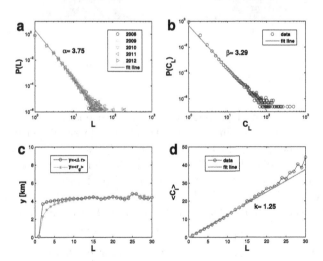

Fig. 2. (a) and (b) are the distribution of L and C_L in the log-log scale at the aggregated level. (c) and (d) shows the trends of $\langle \Delta r \rangle$, $\langle \Delta r \rangle$ and $\langle C_i \rangle$ for groups with different L.

3.2   Relative Position of Incident Location

Furthermore, we investigated the potential nonrandom characteristics in emergency call behavior. Considering the randomness of emergency events that individuals encountered, the generation of incident locations was not a strict continuous process, but occured randomly around the specific centers of their daily travel. In order to verify this hypothesis, we studied the characteristics of relative positions of incident locations, taking home and workplace for reference. Incident locations were transformed to a new coordinate system as described in Subsect. 2.2. The incident location points were separated into four groups by individuals with commuting distance (D_c) in different ranges of $0\,\mathrm{km} \leq D_c \leq 5\,\mathrm{km}$, $5\,\mathrm{km} < D_c \leq 10\,\mathrm{km}$, $10\,\mathrm{km} < D_c \leq 20\,\mathrm{km}$, $20\,\mathrm{km} < D_c \leq 30\,\mathrm{km}$, respectively. The normalized value of the number of incident location points in each grid of 0.1×0.1 in the new coordinate system was calculated and shown as heatmaps in Fig. 3. And we found that the spatial pattern of incident locations at the population level presented an obvious bi-central aggregation feature.

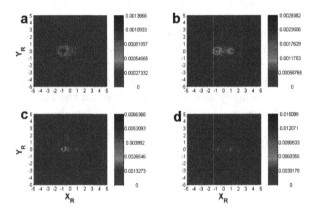

Fig. 3. Heatmap of the number of emergency calls in a relative coordinate system for four groups commuting distance.

To uncover the spatial patterns of the relative positions of emergency call behavior, we classified each incident location to its closer reference center (home or workplace). Then some statistics described in Subsect. 2.2 were calculated for further study. The distributions of D_h and D_w were shown in Fig. 4 (a) and (b), respectively. We tested the fitness of these two distributions with functions of power-law (POW), exponent (EXP), truncated power-law (TPL) and gauss (GAU). It was shown that $P(D_h)$ and $P(D_w)$ could be well fitted by the Gaussian function $P(x) = \frac{A}{\sqrt{2\pi}\sigma}\exp\left(-\frac{(x+\mu)^2)}{2\sigma^2}\right)$, where $A = 31.02, \mu = -18.98, \sigma = 10.04$ for $P(D_h)$ and $A = 15.42, \mu = -14.30, \sigma = 9.36$ for $P(D_w)$.

Figure 4 (c) showed the distributions of θ_h and θ_w, and the results were represented by blue circles and red triangles, respectively. The characteristics of $P(\theta_w)$ and $P(\theta_h)$ were consistent, which can be fitted by the Fourier series $f(x) = a_0 + a_1\cos(\omega x) + b_1\sin(\omega x) + a_2\cos(\omega x) + b_2\sin(\omega x)$, where $a_0 = 0.014, a_1 = -0.0044, b_1 = 0.0037, a_2 = 0.0046, b_2 = 0.00085, \omega = 0.017$. The results indicate that the incident locations are mainly concentrated in the vicinity of the commuting direction.

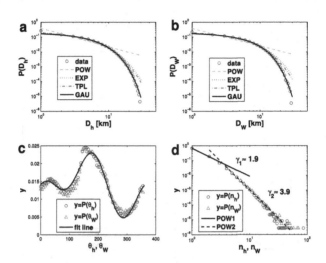

Fig. 4. (a) and (b) are the distribution of D_h and D_w, separately. A power-law distribution (the green dashed line), an exponential distribution (blue dot line), an exponentially truncated power-law distribution (red dashed line) and a Gaussian distribution (black line) of the two indicators are shown for fitting. (Color figure online)

In order to investigate whether the central reference point of the emergency call behavior is random, we analyzed the incident location series around home and workplace separately. Real data shows that the overall number of emergency calls around the two centers is almost equal. For an individual, the consecutive times of home (workplace) in the reference center sequence is identified by $n_h(n_w)$. If the conversion process of reference centers is random, the probability distribution $P(n_h)$ and $P(n_w)$ will appear exponential decay at the aggregated level. However, as shown in Fig. 4 (d), the patterns of $P(n_h)$ and $P(n_w)$ show two segments of the power-law decay, and the exponents are $\gamma_1 \approx 1.9$ and $\gamma_2 \approx 3.9$, where the inflection point is at 3. It indicates that the reference center of the incident locations where an individual makes emergency calls has a certain memory effect. That will provide a reference for our work on model construction.

4   Model

Based on the above results, the incident locations are mainly close to one's home or workplace. The distribution of the total number of these locations obeys a

power-law decay with memory effect. The displacement and the radius of gyration of trajectories obey a Gaussian distribution at aggregation level, respectively. Accordingly, a model of Double Center Memory effect Random Walk
(DCMRW) was proposed to generate the spatial series of emergency call behavior. Figure 5 (a) shows the simulation mechanism of the model which is assumed
as follows:

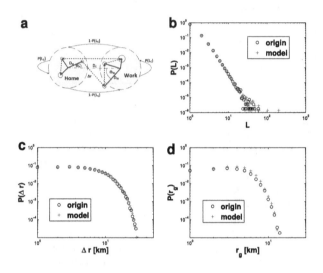

Fig. 5. (a) The DCMRW model. (b), (c) and (d) are the statistical characteristics of
real data (origin) and simulation results (model) for comparison.

(1) Each individual has a unique home and workplace, and D_c is identified as the
    commuting distance, which obeys an exponential distribution $D_c \sim \text{Exp}(\lambda)$;
(2) The locations where individual makes an emergency call are switched by the
    memory process, and the total number of these locations (L) is generated
    by the following memory function:

$$p(L) = \left(\frac{L}{L+1}\right)^{\nu}, \tag{6}$$

where ν is the parameter to control the memory strength;
(3) $\pi_h(\pi_w)$ is the probability of home (workplace) as the center for data gener-
    ation, and $0 \leq \pi_h \leq 1$ ($\pi_w = 1 - \pi_h$). The model with $\pi_h = 0$ or $\pi_h = 1$
    would become a single-center random walk model;
(4) The generation of consecutive incident locations for emergency call behavior
    around a center is effected by a memory process, and the number of these
    locations L_c is generated by the following function:

$$p(L_c) = \left(\frac{L_c}{L_c+1}\right)^{\nu_c}, \tag{7}$$

where ν_c is the parameter to control the memory strength;

(5) The distance of an incident location away from home is generated by Gaussian distribution $D_h \sim N(\mu_h, \sigma_h)$ $(D_h \geq 0)$. And the distance from workplace obeys the Gaussian distribution $D_w \sim N(\mu_w, \sigma_w)$ $(D_w \geq 0)$ in the same way;

(6) The angle θ_h and θ_w obey the following Fourier function:

$$f(x) = a_0 + a_1\cos(\omega x) + b_1\sin(\omega x) + a_2\cos(\omega x) + b_2\sin(\omega x). \qquad (8)$$

Through the simulation by model with parameters $\pi_H = 0.5, \lambda = 0.20, \nu = 2.28, \nu_c = 2.9, \mu_H = -19, \sigma_H = 10, \mu_w = -14.3, \sigma_w = 9.36, a_0 = 0.014, a_1 = -0.0044, b_1 = 0.0037, a_2 = 0.0046, b_2 = 0.00085, \omega = 0.017$, we collected about 1 million emergency call records from 0.5 million individuals. The spatial patterns of the real data can be well fitted by our simulation results as shown in Fig. 5 (b–d), which verified the effectiveness of the model.

Focusing on the parameters $\lambda, \nu, \nu_c, \mu_H, \sigma_H, \mu_w$ and σ_w, the fitting effect of simulation results generated by our model is measured by the method given in Subsect. 2.2. The referenced distributions include the probability distribution of the number of incident locations $P(L)$, the probability distribution of displacement $P(\Delta r)$ and the probability distribution of radius of gyration $P(r_g)$. As shown in Fig. 6–Fig. 9, the results (origin) of the real data, which is collected from $N = 100,000$ sampling individuals as a reference, are represented by black circles. The simulation results of model with different parameter values are represented by magenta triangle, yellow star, red cross, green square, blue diamond, etc. Detailed analyses of the parameters are as follows:

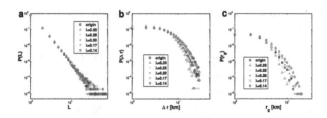

Fig. 6. The comparison of reproducing spatial patterns with different λ.

(1) λ: As shown in Fig. 6, λ has little effect on $P(L)$, but it has significant affect on the fitting goodness of the tail of $P(\Delta r)$ and $P(r_g)$. It indicates that with the increase of the average value of commute distance for agents, the generation probability of larger value of displacement and gyration radius will also increase. According to the results of KL-divergence given in Table 1, $\lambda = 0.20$ is the best choice for parameter to fit the real patterns, which means the average value of commute distance $\frac{1}{\lambda}$ in real data is about 5 km.

Table 1. The comparison of fitting results for reproducing spatial patterns by model with different λ.

λ	$D(P(L) \parallel Q(L\vert\varphi))$	$D(P(\Delta_r) \parallel Q(\Delta_r\vert\varphi))$	$D(P(r_g) \parallel Q(r_g\vert\varphi))$	$\langle R \rangle$
0.33	5.9×10^{-4}	0.0430	0.0101	1.3900
0.25	3.9×10^{-4}	0.0232	0.0055	0.8076
0.20	$\mathbf{3.4 \times 10^{-4}}$	**0.0032**	**0.0003**	**0.3078**
0.17	3.6×10^{-4}	0.0342	0.0046	0.8466
0.14	4.9×10^{-4}	0.0662	0.0122	1.6479

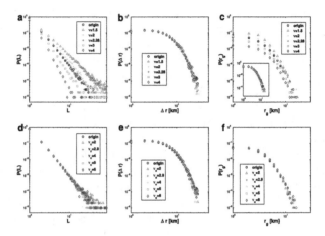

Fig. 7. The comparison of reproducing spatial patterns with different ν and ν_c.

Table 2. The comparison of fitting results for reproducing spatial patterns by the model with different ν.

ν	$D(P(L) \parallel Q(L\vert\varphi))$	$D(P(\Delta_r) \parallel Q(\Delta_r\vert\varphi))$	$D(P(r_g) \parallel Q(r_g\vert\varphi))$	$\langle R \rangle$
1.5	0.1220	0.0105	0.0922	1.4408
2	0.0129	0.0142	0.0136	0.4965
2.28	**0.0003**	**0.0032**	**0.0003**	**0.0812**
3	0.0408	0.0078	0.0291	0.5746
4	0.1808	0.0328	0.1145	2.4069

Table 3. The comparison of fitting results for reproducing spatial patterns by the model with different ν_c.

ν_c	$D(P(L) \parallel Q(L\vert\varphi))$	$D(P(\Delta_r) \parallel Q(\Delta_r\vert\varphi))$	$D(P(r_g) \parallel Q(r_g\vert\varphi))$	$\langle R \rangle$
2	4.0×10^{-4}	0.0052	0.0012	0.5895
2.9	$\mathbf{3.4 \times 10^{-4}}$	**0.0032**	**0.0003**	**0.3649**
4	4.4×10^{-4}	0.0232	0.0030	1.2415
5	4.8×10^{-4}	0.0286	0.0028	1.3419
6	5.4×10^{-4}	0.0284	0.0033	1.4622

(2) ν, ν_c: As shown in Fig. 7(a)-(c), ν has little effect on $P(\Delta r)$, but can affect the exponent of power-law function $P(L)$ and the proportion of the number of agents with small radius of gyration. It indicates that with the increase of ν, the memory effect on generation of incident locations will be stronger and the scope of emergency call activity for agents will also increase. As shown in Fig. 7(d)-(f), although ν_c potentially affects the memory strength of generation of incident locations around a single-center for an agent, it has no significant impact on patterns of $P(L)$, $P(\Delta r)$ and $P(r_g)$ at the aggregated level. According to the results of KL-divergence given in Table 2 and Table 3, the parameters $\nu \approx 2.28$ and $\nu_c \approx 2.9$ are the best choices for the model to fit the real patterns.

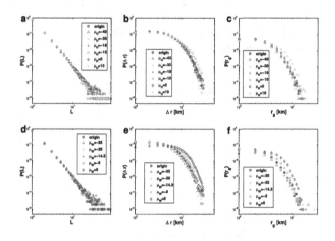

Fig. 8. The comparison of reproducing spatial patterns with different μ_H and μ_W.

Table 4. The comparison of fitting results for reproducing spatial patterns by the model with different μ_H.

μ_H	$D(P(L) \| Q(L|\varphi))$	$D(P(\Delta_r) \| Q(\Delta_r|\varphi))$	$D(P(r_g) \| Q(r_g|\varphi))$	$\langle R \rangle$
−40	5.1×10^{-4}	0.0044	0.0005	0.4605
−30	5.4×10^{-4}	0.0035	0.0004	0.4548
−19	$\mathbf{3.4 \times 10^{-4}}$	**0.0032**	**0.0003**	**0.3117**
−10	5.7×10^{-4}	0.0051	0.0012	0.5476
0	4.7×10^{-4}	0.0122	0.0071	0.9113
10	6.1×10^{-4}	0.0574	0.0352	3.3143

(3) μ_H, μ_W: As shown in Fig. 8, μ_H and μ_W have no effect on $P(L)$. If $\mu_H > 0$ and $\mu_W > 0$, the distribution $P(\Delta r)$ and $P(r_g)$ for simulation data will deviate from real patterns significantly. Meanwhile, if $\mu_H < 0$ and $\mu_W < 0$, the spatial patterns of real data can be fitted well, but small μ_H and μ_W

Table 5. The comparison of fitting results for reproducing spatial patterns by the model with different μ_W.

μ_W	$D(P(L) \parallel Q(L|\varphi))$	$D(P(\Delta_r) \parallel Q(\Delta_r|\varphi))$	$D(P(r_g) \parallel Q(r_g|\varphi))$	$\langle R \rangle$
-35	4.9×10^{-4}	0.0402	0.0061	0.6386
-25	5.2×10^{-4}	0.0167	0.0024	0.4912
-14.3	$\mathbf{3.4 \times 10^{-4}}$	**0.0032**	**0.0003**	**0.2646**
-5	4.7×10^{-4}	0.0404	0.0111	0.7159
5	4.9×10^{-4}	0.2842	0.0718	2.8898

will cause the simulation to generate a large number of negative samples which will be discarded. According to the results of KL-divergence given in Table 4 and Table 5, the parameter $\mu_H \approx -19$ and $\mu_W \approx -14.3$ are the best choices for model to fit the real patterns.

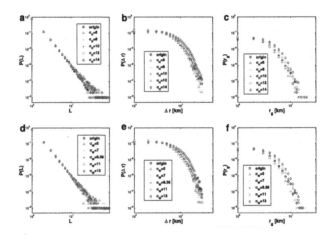

Fig. 9. The comparison of reproducing spatial patterns with different σ_H and σ_W.

(4) σ_H, σ_W: As shown in Fig. 9, σ_H and σ_W have no effect on $P(L)$. If the values of σ_H and σ_W are large, the distribution $P(\Delta r)$ and $P(r_g)$ for simulation data will deviate from real patterns significantly. Meanwhile, if σ_H and σ_W are small, spatial patterns of real data can be fitted well, but it will also cause the simulation to generate a large number of negative samples which will be discarded. According to the results of KL-divergence given in Table 6 and Table 7, the parameters $\sigma_H \approx 10$ and $\sigma_W \approx 9.36$ are the best choices for the model to fit the real patterns.

Table 6. The comparison of fitting results for reproducing spatial patterns by the model with different σ_H.

σ_H	$D(P(L) \parallel Q(L|\varphi))$	$D(P(\Delta_r) \parallel Q(\Delta_r|\varphi))$	$D(P(r_g) \parallel Q(r_g|\varphi))$	$\langle R \rangle$
6	4.9×10^{-4}	0.0151	0.0021	0.6237
8	3.6×10^{-4}	0.0041	0.0004	0.3416
10	$\mathbf{3.4 \times 10^{-4}}$	**0.0032**	**0.0003**	**0.3129**
12	4.5×10^{-4}	0.0477	0.0092	1.2171
14	4.6×10^{-4}	0.1121	0.0242	2.5047

Table 7. The comparison of fitting results for reproducing spatial patterns by the model with different σ_W.

σ_W	$D(P(L) \parallel Q(L|\varphi))$	$D(P(\Delta_r) \parallel Q(\Delta_r|\varphi))$	$D(P(r_g) \parallel Q(r_g|\varphi))$	$\langle R \rangle$
5	5.0×10^{-4}	0.0217	0.0037	0.6889
7	5.6×10^{-4}	0.0039	0.0013	0.4571
9.36	$\mathbf{3.4 \times 10^{-4}}$	**0.0032**	**0.0003**	**0.2633**
11	7.4×10^{-4}	0.0451	0.0085	1.2740
13	4.3×10^{-4}	0.1080	0.0234	2.3168

5   Conclusions

It is of great importance to capture and simulate human behavior to understand the internal mechanism of an emergency. Nowadays, electronic footprint data provides necessary materials for revealing the impact of emergencies on human behavior patterns. This paper explored the spatial patterns of emergency calls made by citizens in a metropolitan city in China using emergency call records and mobile phone signaling data. By measuring the spatial statistical characteristics of emergency calls, we find that there is a strong randomness in this behavior, but the number of emergency calls made by an individual in a specific location follows a power-law distribution, and the spatial pattern of incident locations presents a bi-central aggregation feature. These patterns provide the possibility to predict the trajectory of emergency call behavior. Then we propose an agent based model named DCMRW for the generation of incident location series. The effectiveness of the generation mechanism of our model has been verified by simulation experiments.

Our work could benefit to improve the efficiency of emergency management from the following aspects: situation analysis, resource allocation and police deployment.

References

1. Altshuler, Y., et al.: The social amplifier—reaction of human communities to emergencies. J. Stat. Phys. **152**(3), 399–418 (2013). https://doi.org/10.1007/s10955-013-0759-z

2. Bagrow, J.P., Wang, D., Barabási, A.L.: Collective response of human populations to large-scale emergencies. PLoS ONE **6**(3), e17680 (2011). https://doi.org/10.1371/journal.pone.0017680

3. Barabási, A.L.: The origin of bursts and heavy tails in human dynamics. Nature **435**(7039), 207–211 (2005). https://doi.org/10.1038/nature03459

4. Barrientos, F., Sainz, G.: Interpretable knowledge extraction from emergency call data based on fuzzy unsupervised decision tree. Knowl. Based Syst. **25**(1), 77–87 (2012). https://doi.org/10.1016/j.knosys.2011.01.014

5. Becker, R., et al.: Human mobility characterization from cellular network data. Commun. ACM **56**(1), 74 (2013). https://doi.org/10.1145/2398356.2398375

6. Brockmann, D., Hufnagel, L., Geisel, T.: The scaling laws of human travel. Nature **439**(7075), 462–465 (2006). https://doi.org/10.1038/nature04292

7. Candia, J., González, M.C., Wang, P., Schoenharl, T., Madey, G., Barabási, A.L.: Uncovering individual and collective human dynamics from mobile phone records. J. Phys. A: Math. Theor. **41**(22), 224015 (2008). https://doi.org/10.1088/1751-8113/41/22/224015

8. Chu, J., et al.: Passenger demand prediction with cellular footprints. IEEE Trans. Mob. Comput. **21**(1), 252–263 (2022). https://doi.org/10.1109/TMC.2020.3005240

9. Eriksson, M.: Conceptions of emergency calls: emergency communication in an age of mobile communication and prevalence of anxiety. J. Contingencies Crisis Manag. **18**(3), 165–174 (2010). https://doi.org/10.1111/j.1468-5973.2010.00613.x

10. Freudendal-Pedersen, M., Kesselring, S.: What is the urban without physical mobilities? COVID-19-induced immobility in the mobile risk society. Mobilities **16**(1), 81–95 (2021). https://doi.org/10.1080/17450101.2020.1846436

11. Gao, L., Song, C., Gao, Z., Barabási, A.L., Bagrow, J.P., Wang, D.: Quantifying information flow during emergencies. Sci. Rep. **4**, 3997 (2014). https://doi.org/10.1038/srep03997

12. Jasso, H., Fountain, T., Baru, C., Hodgkiss, W., Reich, D., Warner, K.: Spatiotemporal analysis of 9-1-1 call stream data. In: Proceedings of the 2006 International Conference on Digital Government Research, pp. 21–22. Digital Government Society of North America (2006). https://doi.org/10.1145/1146598.1146608

13. Jasso, H., Fountain, T., Baru, C., Hodgkiss, W., Reich, D., Warner, K.: Prediction of 9-1-1 call volumes for emergency event detection. In: Proceedings of the 8th Annual International Conference on Digital Government Research: Bridging Disciplines & Domains, pp. 148–154. Digital Government Society of North America (2007)

14. Jasso, H., Hodgkiss, W., Baru, C., Fountain, T., Reich, D., Warner, K.: Spatiotemporal characteristics of 9-1-1 emergency call hotspots. In: Proceedings of the National Science Foundation Symposium on Next Generation of Data Mining and Cyber-Enabled Discovery for Innovation (NGDM 2007), pp. 10–12. Citeseer (2007)

15. Jasso, H., Hodgkiss, W., Baru, C., Fountain, T., Reich, D., Warner, K.: Using 9-1-1 call data and the space-time permutation scan statistic for emergency event detection. Gov. Inf. Q. **26**(2), 265–274 (2009). https://doi.org/10.1016/j.giq.2008.12.005

16. Kenett, D.Y., Portugali, J.: Population movement under extreme events. Proc. Natl. Acad. Sci. **109**(29), 11472–11473 (2012). https://doi.org/10.1073/pnas.1209306109

17. Kung, K.S., Greco, K., Sobolevsky, S., Ratti, C.: Exploring universal patterns in human home-work commuting from mobile phone data. PLoS ONE **9**(6), e96180 (2014). https://doi.org/10.1371/journal.pone.0096180

18. Lin, Y.-R., Margolin, D.: The ripple of fear, sympathy and solidarity during the Boston bombings. EPJ Data Sci. **3**(1), 1–28 (2014). https://doi.org/10.1140/epjds/s13688-014-0031-z
19. Lu, X., Bengtsson, L., Holme, P.: Predictability of population displacement after the 2010 Haiti earthquake. Proc. Natl. Acad. Sci. **109**(29), 11576–11581 (2012). https://doi.org/10.1073/pnas.1203882109
20. Moumni, B., Frias-Martinez, V., Frias-Martinez, E.: Characterizing social response to urban earthquakes using cell-phone network data: the 2012 Oaxaca earthquake. In: Proceedings of the 2013 ACM Conference on Pervasive and Ubiquitous Computing Adjunct Publication, pp. 1199–1208. UbiComp 2013 Adjunct, ACM, New York (2013). https://doi.org/10.1145/2494091.2497350
21. Pastor-Escuredo, D., et al.: Flooding through the lens of mobile phone activity. In: Global Humanitarian Technology Conference (GHTC 2014), pp. 279–286. IEEE (2014). https://doi.org/10.1109/GHTC.2014.6970293
22. Preis, T., Moat, H.S., Bishop, S.R., Treleaven, P., Stanley, H.E.: Quantifying the digital traces of hurricane Sandy on Flickr. Sci. Rep. **3**(1), 1–3 (2013). https://doi.org/10.1038/srep03141
23. Song, X., Zhang, Q., Sekimoto, Y., Horanont, T., Ueyama, S., Shibasaki, R.: Modeling and probabilistic reasoning of population evacuation during large-scale disaster. In: Proceedings of the 19th ACM SIGKDD International Conference on Knowledge Discovery and Data Mining (KDD 2013), pp. 1231–1239. ACM, New York (2013). https://doi.org/10.1145/2487575.2488189
24. Song, X., Zhang, Q., Sekimoto, Y., Shibasaki, R.: Prediction of human emergency behavior and their mobility following large-scale disaster. In: Proceedings of the 20th ACM SIGKDD International Conference on Knowledge Discovery and Data Mining (KDD 2014), pp. 5–14. ACM, New York (2014). https://doi.org/10.1145/2623330.2623628
25. Szell, M., Grauwin, S., Ratti, C.: Contraction of online response to major events. PLoS ONE **9**(2), e89052 (2014). https://doi.org/10.1371/journal.pone.0089052
26. Traag, V.A., Browet, A., Calabrese, F., Morlot, F.: Social event detection in massive mobile phone data using probabilistic location inference. In: 2011 IEEE Third International Conference on Privacy, Security, Risk and Trust (PASSAT) and 2011 IEEE Third Inernational Conference on Social Computing (SocialCom), pp. 625–628 (2011). https://doi.org/10.1109/PASSAT/SocialCom.2011.133
27. Wang, Q., Taylor, J.E.: Quantifying human mobility perturbation and resilience in hurricane Sandy. PLoS ONE **9**(11), e112608 (2014). https://doi.org/10.1371/journal.pone.0112608
28. Wang, W., et al.: Temporal patterns of emergency calls of a metropolitan city in China. Phys. A Stat. Mech. Appl. **436**, 846–855 (2015). https://doi.org/10.1016/j.physa.2015.05.028
29. Woolley-Meza, O., Grady, D., Thiemann, C., Bagrow, J.P., Brockmann, D.: Eyjafjallajökull and 9/11: the impact of large-scale disasters on worldwide mobility. PLoS ONE **8**(8), e69829 (2013). https://doi.org/10.1371/journal.pone.0069829
30. Xu, F., Li, Y., Jin, D., Lu, J., Song, C.: Emergence of urban growth patterns from human mobility behavior. Nat. Comput. Sci. **1**(12), 791–800 (2021). https://doi.org/10.1038/s43588-021-00160-6

Event Annotation Enhanced Pre-trained Language Model in Event Extraction

Qisen Xi, Yizhi Ren, Guohua Wu, Qiuhua Wang, Lifeng Yuan[✉],
and Zhen Zhang[✉]

School of Cyberspace, Hangzhou Dianzi University, Hangzhou 310018, China
{xiqs, renyz, wugh, wangqiuhua, yuanlifeng, zhangzhen}@hdu.edu.cn

Abstract. Event extraction is a crucial task that aims to extract event information in texts. Existing methods usually use pre-trained language models to extract events and have achieved state-of-the-art performance. However, these models do not consider the complexity of the event structure and lack the use of event knowledge. To address these problems, we propose a new framework that integrates event annotation into the pre-trained model explicitly, termd as EABERT. Specifically, event annotations are incorporated into the model input to construct the form "[CLS]sentence[SEP]event annotation[SEP]", which allows the model to encode the semantic relationship between text and event knowledge. To incorporate appropriate event annotations into the model, we further use the bilateral-branch BERT network to train the event type classifier for better accuracy of event annotations. Experiments on the event extraction benchmark dataset (ACE 2005) show that our proposed framework has significantly improved compared to previous methods.

Keywords: Event extraction · Event annotation · Pre-trained language model

1 Introduction

Event extraction (EE) is a challenge extraction task in natural language processing (NLP). It targets to extract structured event information (triggers and arguments) from unstructured text. For example, given the sentence "The EU foreign ministers met hours after U.S. President George W. Bush gave Saddam 48 h to leave Iraq or face invasion.", it contains event detection task to identify event trigger (the word "met") and classify event type (Meet). As well as event argument extraction task to identify event arguments ("ministers" and "hours") and classify their argument roles (Entity and Time). By explicitly capturing the event structure in the text, some AI downstream applications such as financial analysis, public opinion analysis, sentiment analysis can develop.

Many efforts have been devoted to event extraction. Existing methods [1–3] mainly use deep neural networks to follow a supervised learning paradigm for

© ICST Institute for Computer Sciences, Social Informatics and Telecommunications Engineering 2022
Published by Springer Nature Switzerland AG 2022. All Rights Reserved
Y. Chenggang et al. (Eds.): MobiMedia 2022, LNICST 451, pp. 284–297, 2022.
https://doi.org/10.1007/978-3-031-23902-1_22

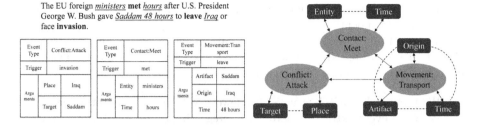

Fig. 1. Event extraction example and event structure

event extraction. Such methods can learn features from raw text and perform well in many publicly available benchmark datasets (ACE 2005, TAC KBP). Inspired by the successful application of pre-trained language models (PLMs) in NLP tasks, many approaches [4–6] have attempted to use PLMs for event extraction and achieved state-of-the-art performance. However, these PLMs-based method focused only on the fine-tuning phase, capturing only the internal pattern of the input text, and did not exploit the event type knowledge.

To alleviate the limitation, several studies have started to integrate event type labels into the PLMs and achieved positive effect. For example, CasEE [7] treats event type encoding as a priori encoding knowledge and uses a cascade decoding strategy for event extraction. GDAP [8] uses prefixed prompt learning to empower the automatic exploitation of event type label semantics on both input and output sides.

Although CasEE and GDAP integrate event type labels into pre-trained models, they do not consider the complex specificity of the event structure itself. The main challenge here is an event structure is far more complicated than a triad (head, relation, tail). As show in Fig. 1, event triggers, event arguments, and event types all have dependencies. Only by enabling the pre-trained model to understand this event structure knowledge better to perform modeling of event features can the event information be better extracted from texts.

To address these issues, we propose EABERT, a new framework with event annotation enhanced BERT for event extraction. Our framework contains two main modules: an event type classifier and an event extraction model. The event type classifier is a multi-label classification model. In particular, to solve the problem of low detection accuracy caused by imbalanced data distribution, we incorporate a bilateral-branch BERT network [9] structure consisting of a conventional branch trained with uniform sampling data and a re-balancing branch trained with reverse sampling according to the number of relevant instances. In event extraction, we use BERT as the basic model. It is worth noting that we add event annotations to BERT. Event annotations are predefined and can be considered as a complete event structure. We construct the token of "[CLS]sentence[SEP]event annotation[SEP]" and feed as the input of BERT. The semantic relationship between the input text and the event annotations is learned using the powerful self-attention mechanism in BERT to obtain the feature vector. Then, conditional random field (CRF) is used to extract event triggers and arguments.

We tested our model on benchmark dataset (ACE 2005). Our experiments show that our proposed framework achieves excellent performance. The main contributions of the paper can be summarized as follows:

(1) We propose EABERT, a novel framework with event annotation enhanced BERT in event extraction, explicitly integrating event annotation to encode the semantic relationship between text and event knowledge.
(2) We propose an end-to-end bilateral-branch BERT network and design a reverse sampling method according to the number of event samples for exhaustively boosting event type classification accuracy.
(3) We conducted experiments on the event extraction benchmark dataset ACE 2005. The experimental results show that our method achieves significant improvements compared with existing competitive methods.

2   Related Work

Event extraction is a crucial task in NLP. Traditional event extraction methods [10–12] rely on manually extracted features for event extraction, such as lexical and syntactic features. However, because such methods are based on existing NLP tools to do feature extraction, they will be limited by the tools' accuracy. This error propagation will be introduced into subsequent algorithms that cannot be modified. With the development of deep learning, various neural networks have been used for EE, e.g., Chen et al. [1] proposed a dynamic multi-pool convolutional neural networks. Nguyen et al. [2] proposed a joint extraction model JRNN based on RNN. These models can learn text features from the original text. Based on neural networks, researchers (Wadden et al. [3]; Liu et al. [13]; Zhang et al. [14]; Nguyen et al. [15]; Lai et al. [16]; Cui et al. [17]; Zhao et al. [18]) have also mined additional fine-grained information, including entity information, syntactic feature information, and chapter-level information, to enhance the feature representation in neural networks. For example, experiments have demonstrated that these methods achieve better results in public benchmark datasets.

Recently, because of the remarkable success of PLM in the field of NLP, many researchers have proposed PLM-based event extraction models. Yang et al. [4] directly applied BERT to build event extraction models. Wang et al. [5] combined with the dynamic multi-pool operation in DMCNN, BERT is used as the Encoding layer to extract text features for event extraction. Other researchers (Li et al. [6]; Liu et al. [19]; Du et al. [20]; Chen et al. [21]) proposed a BERT-QA-based question-and-answer event extraction method by drawing on the application of the QA approach in named entity recognition. Experimental results show that these event extraction methods based on pre-trained models have become a solution paradigm for event extraction tasks. However, previous work has focused only on the fine-tuning phase to obtain the Embedding form of tokens without exploiting the event type knowledge. Therefore, researchers have also explored pre-trained model approaches incorporating event type knowledge. For example, CasEE [7] mixes event type encoding into the embedding of BERT, and GDAP [8] adds prefixed event types based on cue learning. However, they still have shortcomings: the complexity of the event structure itself is not taken into account.

3   Method

In this section, we will introduce our EABERT framework in detail. Our framework aims to extract event information in texts. As illustrated in Fig. 2, we divide the event extraction task into two modules: an event type classifier and an event extraction model. In the event type classifier, we input the text to get the event types. In the event extraction module, we first obtain the corresponding event annotations. Then take the sentence and event annotations fed as the BERT input to identify event trigger and arguments and their span (start, end).

Formally: Given a text $\mathcal{D}, \boldsymbol{s} = (s_1, s_2, \ldots, s_n), \boldsymbol{s} \in \mathcal{D}$ is a set of sentences. The purpose of our model is to extract the event type $\mathcal{T}$ from $\boldsymbol{s}$, and then construct the input of $(s, event\ annotation)$ to extract the event trigger (Q, S_Q, E_Q) and the event argument (A, S_A, E_A).

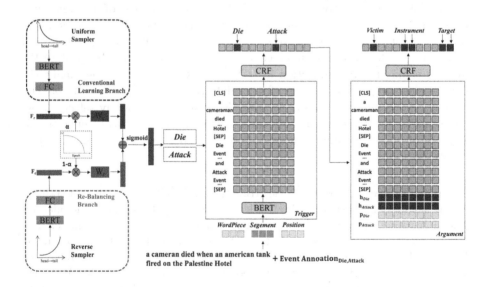

Fig. 2. Our EABERT framewokr for event extraction

3.1   Event Type Classifier

The event type classifier follows the idea of the bilateral-branch network [9]. Our model consists of two branches for representation learning and classifier learning, called the conventional branch and the re-balancing branch. Both branches use BERT as the backbone network and share all the weights. The input data of the conventional branch comes from a uniform sampler. The re-balancing branch designs a reverse sampling method to sample each class according to the sample size. After that, we use an adaptive learning strategy to balance the bilateral branch learning.

Data Samples. The input data for the conventional branch comes from a uniform sampler, where each sample in the training dataset is sampled only once with equal probability. This sampling method retains the original data distribution, so it facilitates representation learning. While, the re-balancing branch aims to alleviate the long-tailed label distribution. The input of this branch comes from a reverse sampler. For the reversed sampler, the sampling possibility of each class is proportional to the reciprocal of its sample size, i.e., the more instances in a class, the smaller sampling probability that class has. In particular, it can be noted that there are several categories in the event extraction dataset that have only very few instances, which can lead to extremely high sampling probabilities for these categories and thus reduce the classification ability of the model. To solve this problem, we use the average of the sample proportions of all the event categories available as the label proportion threshold to balance the sampling probability of most of the tail labels.

Formally, let N_i denote the number of revelant instances of an event type class i and N_{max} denote the maximum sample number of all event types. The reverse sampler operates in a five-step process: (1)Calculate the proportion of each class to the maximum number of class $w_i = N_{\max}/N_i$; (2)Calculate the average value of class proportion $\overline{w} = \sum_{i=1}^{C} w_i/C$, if $w_i > \overline{w}$, then make the current class proportion $w_i = \overline{w}$; (3)Calculate the sampling probability of class i based on the number of class $P_i = w_i/\sum_{j=1}^{C} w_j$; (4)Randomly select a class according to P_i; (5)Uniformly pick up a sample from class i with replacement. A batch of paired training data can be obtained by repeating this uniform and reverse sampling process.

Adaptive Learning. To avoid overfitting the tail labels and insufficient training on the head labels, we use an adaptive learning strategy to reconcile the bilateral branch learning. In concretely, by setting the adaptive learning parameter α to control the feature weights learned by the conventional and the re-balancing branches. In particular, α is automatically generated based on the training epoch T. The calculation of α can be expressed as follows: $\alpha = 1 - (T/T_{\max})^2$, where T_{max} is the total epoch of training, T is the current epoch. This approach allows to α exhibit a parabolic form of decay as the training period increases. This decay allows the model to focus on learning the conventional branches for most of the period until the final period when it shifts its training attention to the re-balancing branches.

In the training phase, let s denote a training sample and $t \in \{1, 2, 3, 4 \ldots, N\}$ is its corresponding class, where N is the number of classes. For the bilateral branches, we obtain a pair of samples (s_1^c, t_1^c) and (s_1^r, t_1^r) as input data using uniform sampling and reverse sampling for each branch, respectively. Then, the sampled data are fed into their corresponding branches to obtain the feature vectors f_c and f_r through a fully connected layer. Setting the adaptive learning parameter α to weight the control conventional branch features $f_c \in R^D$ and re-balancing branch features $f_r \in R^D$, i.e., αf_c and $(1 - \alpha)f_r$. Then, the two weighted feature vectors are sent into the classifiers $W_c \in R^{n \times D}$ and $W_r \in R^{n \times D}$ and the outputs are integrated by element addition. The final logits output is obtained by sigmoid activation function:

$$\hat{t}_i = \sigma \left(\alpha W_c f_c + (1 - \alpha) W_r f_r \right) \tag{1}$$

Finally, we apply a weighted binary cross-entropy loss, denoted by $E(.,.)$, for optimization of the pairwise inputs:

$$L = \alpha E \left(\hat{t}_i, t_i^c \right) + (1 - \alpha) E \left(\hat{t}_i, t_i^r \right) \tag{2}$$

During inference, we take the event proportion as α:

$$\alpha = \frac{\sum_{i=1}^C N_i}{N_{none}} \tag{3}$$

Test samples are fed into two branches with α and $1 - \alpha$. Then, we obtained the predicted event type labels.

3.2   Event Extraction Model

Our event extraction model is based on BERT and relies on event annotations. In the following, we will provide details on obtaining the event annotation and details on the event extraction model.

Event Annotation. In the ACE2005 event guideline[1], each event type is given a corresponding event annotation. Examples are shown in Table 1. Event annotations explain well the conditions under when an event occurs, the state and the associated event arguments, etc. Such event annotations can be well regarded as a complete event structure, i.e., an event contains event types, event trigger words and event arguments.

Event Trigger Extraction. Event trigger extraction aims to predict whether a token triggers an event or not and give the span S, i.e., the start index and the end index. The input of the model follows the standard BERT input forms, i.e., WordPiece embedding, positional embedding, and segment embedding. Specifically, to enable our model to learn the event semantic knowledge better, we focus on adding event annotations to the model.

---

[1] All label annotations are available at: https://www.ldc.upenn.edu/sites/www.ldc. upenn.edu/files/english-events-guidelines-v5.4.3.pdf.

Table 1. Event type and their corresponding event annotation.

Event type	Event annotation
LIFE:BE-BORN	A BE-BORN Event occurs whenever a PERSON Entity is given birth to
LIFE:MARRY	MARRY Events are official Events, where two people are married under the legal definition
MOVEMENT:TRANSPORT	A TRANSPORT Event occurs whenever an ARTIFACT (WEAPON or VEHICLE) or a PERSON is moved from one PLACE (GPE, FACILITY, LOCATION) to another

To achieve this goal, we utilize the SEP separator to construct the input of text and event annotations:

$$[\textbf{CLS}]\langle\textbf{sentence}\rangle[\textbf{SEP}]\langle\textbf{event annotation}\rangle[\textbf{SEP}]$$

where [CLS] is a special classification token for BERT, [SEP] is a special token to denote separation, and ⟨sentence⟩ is the tokenized input sentence. ⟨event annotation⟩ denotes the event annotation corresponding to the event type. It is worth noting that in practical cases, there are situations where there is a single sentence with multiple events. We use "AND" to splice the event annotations of multiple events. Since the input includes both the original sentence and the event annotation, the segment id of the original sentence is set to 0. The segment id of the event annotation is set to 1.

Then we get the contextualized representations of each token for trigger extraction with BERT. Formally, given a sentence $x = w_1, w_2, w_3, \ldots, w_{|x|}$ and corresponding event annotation $S_{annotation} = e_{s1}, e_{s2}, e_{s3}, \ldots, e_{sn}$.

We produce the input for trigger extractor as:

$$\text{Input} = [CLS]w_1, w_2, \ldots w_{|x|}[SEP]e_{s1}, e_{s2}, \ldots, e_{sn}[SEP] \tag{4}$$

Via BERT, we learn the hidden representations:

$$h_{[CLS]}, h_1^w, \ldots, h_{|x|}^w, h_{[SEP]}, h_1^e, \ldots, h_n^e = \text{BERT(Input)} \tag{5}$$

where $h_{[CLS]}$ and $h_{[SEP]}$ is the hidden state of [CLS] and [SEP]. h_i^w is the hidden state of the i-th input token and h_i^e is the hidden state of the corresponding event annotation.

In this paper, we use a linear CRF layer in the prediction phase for trigger labels. The hidden layer representation of the text after BERT encoding is fed to the CRF layer to learn the interdependencies between the output trigger labels and then find the best sequence of trigger labels.

Following Lafferty et al. [22], CRF defines a transition matrix $\mathbf{A}$ and use a score $A_{i,j}$ to model the transition from i^{th} label to the jth label. The scores $H_{i,t}$ of the martix is the score output by the BERT network, for the sentence $[x]_1^N$ and for the ith label, at the tth word. The score of a sequence of trigger label

$[t]_1^N$ for a particular sequence of words $[x]_1^N$ is the sum of the transfer fraction and network fraction efficiently calculated using dynamic programming:

$$S\left([x]_1^N, [t]_1^N\right) = \sum_{i=1}^{N} \left([A]_{[t]_{i-1},[t]_i}, + H_{[t]_i,i}\right) \tag{6}$$

The probability of predicting a sequence of triggers can be obtained by using the softmax function to do global normalization of all possible sequences:

$$P\left(T|X\right) = \frac{e^{S(X,T)}}{\sum_{\tilde{T} \in T_X} e^{S(X,\tilde{T})}} \tag{7}$$

where T_x denotes the sequence of all possible trigger prediction labels corresponding to X.

Event Argument Extraction. Given the identified trigger for a specific event type, event argument extraction aims to identify the arguments spans(start index and end index) and classify them into their corresponding roles.

The event argument extraction uses the exact hidden layer representation as to the trigger extraction, but it needs to know which token constitutes the event trigger. Therefore, when constructing the input to the argument extraction module, the corresponding token and position encoding of the trigger is embedded and concatenated with the original hidden layer. The format of the input is:

$$h_{[CLS]}, h_1^w, \ldots, h_{|x|}^w, h_{[SEP]}, h_1^e, \ldots, h_n^e, h_1^t, \ldots, h_n^t, h_1^p, \ldots, h_n^p \tag{8}$$

where h_i^t is the corresponding trigger embedding and h_i^p is the corresponding trigger position embedding.

We use the CRF layer proposed in trigger word extraction for the prediction of the argument sequences. The difference is that we use the feature vector mentioned in Eq. 8 as the input to the CRF.

Joint Training. The event extraction process consists of two parts: one is to extract the event trigger, and the other is to extract the event arguments. There is a high correlation between triggers and arguments in the event extraction domain. Inspired by the idea of multi-task learning, this paper uses joint learning for trigger extraction and argument extraction.

Specifically, the event trigger extraction training loss can be expressed as:

$$L_{Tri} = -\sum_{x \in X} \log\left(P\left(T_x|S_x\right)\right) \tag{9}$$

where $\mathcal{X}$ denotes the set of all sentences in the training data, S_x denotes the input sequence corresponding to sentence x, T_x and denotes the sequence of trigger prediction corresponding to sentence x.

Similarly, the event argument extraction training loss can be expressed as:

$$L_{Arg} = -\sum_{x \in X} \log\left(P\left(A_x | S_x\right)\right) \tag{10}$$

Then, we set the weight of the trigger extraction task loss to 1, and set λ to regulate the weight occupied by the argument extraction task loss, and the joint loss L of the two tasks can be expressed as: $L = L_{Tri} + \lambda L_{Arg}$, where $\lambda \in [0,1]$.

4   Expriment

4.1   Datasets and Evaluation Metric

We conducted experiments on dataset ACE 2005. ACE 2005 is the most widely used dataset in the field of event extraction. ACE 2005 consists of 8 main events and 33 sub-events. To comply with previous work, we use the same data split as the previous work [1,11,23]. This data split takes the test set with 40 newswire documents, while 30 other documents as the validation set and the remaining 529 documents to be the training set.

Following previous work [1,4,11], we use the following criteria to evaluate the correctness of each predicted event mention: (1) A trigger is correct if its event subtype and offsets match those of a reference trigger. (2) An argument is correctly identified if its event subtype and offsets match those of any of the reference argument mentions. (3) An argument is correctly classified if its event subtype, offsets and argument role match those of any of the reference argument mentions. Finally, we use Precision (P), Recall (R) and F1 scores (F1) as the evaluation metrics.

4.2   Implementation Details

Our implementation is in Pytorch. The BERT base model(uncased) from Hugging Face consists of 12 layers, 768 hidden units and 12 attention heads. In the event type classifier, the MLP consists of two layers with a hidden size of 768 and yields an output of 34 dimensions to predict the probability of the input sentence being assigned to the corresponding 34 classes. In event extraction, We set the sampling probability threshold w is 98.7 and α is 0.77. In event extraction, the trigger MLP consists of two layers with the hidden size being 768 and yields an output of 68 dimensions. The argument MLP yields an output of 58 dimensions. The batch size is 16. The learning rate is set as 2×10^{-5}. ADAM is the optimizer. All experiments are conducted on an NVIDIA RTX3090 GPU.

4.3   Overall Evaluation Results

We compare our method performance to a number of prior competitive models: **DMCNN** [1] adopts firstly dynamic multi-pooling CNN to extract sentence-level features automatically; **JRNN** [2] proposes a joint framework based on bidirectional RNN for event extraction; **DYGIE++** [3] is a BERT-based framework that models text spans and captures within-sentence and cross-sentence context; **BERT-QA** [6] is a BERT-based model converting event extraction into a QA task; **CasEE** [7] uses a cascade decoding strategy to model the relationship between event types and trigger words and argument elements for event extraction based on the BERT model; **GDAP** [8] takes event types as prefix prompt information to generate events based on T5 model.

Table 2. Overall performance on ACE 2005.

	Trigger identification			Trigger classification			Argument identification			Argument classification		
	P	R	F	P	R	F	P	R	F	P	R	F
DMCNN	80.4	67.7	73.5	75.6	63.6	69.1	68.8	51.9	59.1	62.2	46.9	53.5
JRNN	68.5	75.7	71.9	66.0	73.0	69.3	61.4	64.2	62.8	54.2	56.7	55.4
BERT-CRF	72.3	80.5	76.2	67.7	75.4	71.3	61.7	45.3	52.2	58.8	45.6	51.3
DYGIE++(ens)	–	–	76.5	–	–	73.6	–	–	55.4	–	–	52.5
BERT-QA	74.3	77.4	75.8	71.1	73.7	72.3	58.0	50.7	54.1	56.9	49.8	53.1
CasEE	78.0	79.8	78.8	74.7	76.8	75.7	62.5	48.7	54.7	59.2	48.4	53.2
GDAP	–	–	–	66.1	75.3	70.4	–	–	–	47.3	59.1	52.6
EABERT(ours)	77.5	82.2	**79.8**	75.4	**80.1**	**77.7**	67.1	51.2	58.1	**64.9**	50.3	**56.7**
EABERT-GOLD	**87.7**	**86.5**	**87.1**	**86.3**	**85.1**	**85.7**	**72.4**	54.7	62.3	**67.8**	51.5	**58.5**

The preformance of all methods on corpus is shown in Table 2. The table reveals that:

(1) In trigger identification and classification, the F1 scores are 79.8% and 77.7%. Our model has significant improvements over the basic neural-based methods (i.e., CNN and RNN). Compared to the same BERT-based classification model DYGIE++, it gains 4.1% on trigger classification F1 score. Compared to the BERT-based QA models BERT-QA, it gains 5.4% on trigger classification. Notably, our model improves 7.3% and 2% on trigger classification compared to the GDAP and CasEE models with the addition of event types. The results demonstrate the effectiveness of EABERT on event detection.

(2) While the improvement in argument extraction is not so obvious. This is probably due to the more rigorous evaluation metric we have taken and the difficulty of the argument extraction task. Compared with the BERT-based models DYGIE++ and BERT-QA, EABERT can achieve better results on the argument extraction task - the F1 score of argument identification is

3.4% higher than that of BERT-QA, and the F1 score of classification is 1.3% and 0.7%. Compared to the GDAP and CasEE, it gains 4.1% and 3.5% on arguments classification.

To further understand our proposed EABERT framework, we conducted experiments on the model EABERT-GOLD using gold annotations. Compared with EABERT, EABERT-GOLD achieved significant progress on the event extraction task, reaching SOTA results: 87.1%, 85.7%, 62.3%, 58.5%, respectively on F1 scores for trigger identification, trigger classification, argument identification and argument classification. It further illustrates that practical event annotation can substantially improve the performance of event extraction models.

4.4 Effectiveness of Event Annotations

To demonstrate the effectiveness of our incorporated event annotations, we constructed two EABERT variants: (1) GloVe event annotation embedding: we initialized the event annotation embedding with GloVe and then spliced it with the input text encoded using BERT. The F1 score dropped by 0.9%,2.3%,0.7%,1.6% on TI, TC, AI, AC, respectively. The results show that the improvement in our EABERT comes from understanding the event annotation. Using the self-attention mechanism, BERT can encode the semantic relationship between text and event annotations well. (2) Event Type Label Name: Replace the event annotations with the name of the event type label. The F1 score drops by 0.5%, 0.6%, 0.7%, 0.7%, respectively, indicating that the label name alone contains less semantic knowledge than the event annotation, which corresponds to a complete knowledge of the event structure.

Table 3. The performance of the EABERT variants. The values in table are F1 scores on test sets.

	TI	TC	AI	AC
EABERT	**79.8**	**77.7**	**58.1**	**56.7**
−GEAE	78.9(↓0.9)	75.4(↓2.3)	57.4(↓0.7)	55.1(↓1.6)
−ETLN	79.3(↓0.5)	77.1(↓0.6)	57.4(↓0.7)	56.0(↓0.7)

4.5   Effect of w and α

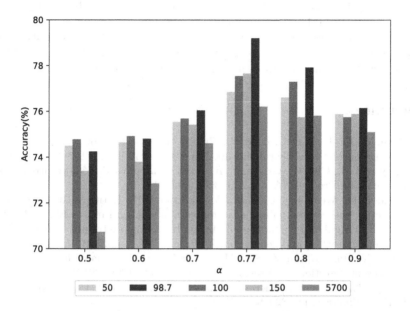

Fig. 3. Event type classifier performance on ACE2005 with different α and w

In this section, we conduct experiments on the ACE 2005 corpus to demonstrate the role of the label proportion threshold w in reverse sampler and the weight parameter α in the inference phase on the performance of the event classifier. To achieve this goal, we design relevant experimental parameters for comparison.

According to Sect. 3.1 and Eq. 3, we can calculate the label proportion threshold w to be 98.7 and the weight parameter α to be 0.77. We selected W from $\{50,98.7,100,150,5700^2\}$ and α from $\{0.5,0.6,0.7,0.77,0.8,0.9\}$. Figure 3 shows that the event classifier has the highest accuracy of 79.2% when W is selected as 98.7 and α is selected as 0.77, which is an improvement of 4.1% compared to the standard BERT multi-label classifier. This shows that our proposed data enhancement strategy of inverse sampling in bilateral-branch BERT network is very useful for the task of event classification.

5   Conclusion

In this paper, we propose a new framework that integrates event annotation into the BERT explicitly, termd as EABERT. We further use a bilateral-branch network to train the event type classifier to get the appropriate event annotations. Our method allows the model to encode the semantic relationship between text

---

[2] 5700 is the maximum proportion calculated according to Sect. 3.1.

and event knowledge. To demonstrate the effectiveness of the proposed framework, we systematically conducted a series of experiments on the widely used benchmark dataset ACE 2005. The experimental results show that our proposed method performs better than the previous methods.

In the future, we will: (1) explore how to effectively use the hierarchical information among event types to generate optimal event annotations;(2) explore how to make good use of this event knowledge more effectively.

References

1. Chen, Y., Xu, L., Liu, K., Zeng, D., Zhao, J.: Event extraction via dynamic multi-pooling convolutional neural networks. In: Proc. of ACL, pp. 167–176 (2015)
2. Nguyen, T.H., Cho, K., Grishman, R.: Joint event extraction via recurrent neural networks. In: Proc. of NAACL, pp. 300–309 (2016)
3. Wadden, D., Wennberg, U., Luan, Y., Hajishirzi, H.: Entity, relation, and event extraction with contextualized span representations. In: Proc. of EMNLP (2019)
4. Yang, S., Feng, D., Qiao, L., Kan, Z., Li, D.: Exploring pre-trained language models for event extraction and generation. In: Proc. of ACL, pp. 5284–5294 (2019)
5. Wang, X., Han, X., Liu, Z., Sun, M., Li, P.: Adversarial training for weakly supervised event detection. In: Proc. of NAACL, pp. 998–1008 (2019)
6. Li, F., et al.: Event extraction as multi-turn question answering. In: Proc. of EMNLP Findings, pp. 829–838 (2020)
7. Sheng, J., et al.: CasEE: a joint learning framework with cascade decoding for overlapping event extraction. In: Proc. of ACL Findings (2021)
8. Si, J., Peng, X., Li, C., Xu, H., Li, J.: Generating disentangled arguments with prompts: a simple event extraction framework that works. arXiv preprint arXiv:2110.04525 (2021)
9. Zhou, B., Cui, Q., Wei, X., Chen, Z.: BBN: bilateral-branch network with cumulative learning for long-tailed visual recognition. In: Proc. of CVPR, pp. 9719–9728 (2020)
10. Hong, Y., Zhang, J., Ma, B., Yao, J., Zhou, G., Zhu, Q.: Using cross-entity inference to improve event extraction. In: Proc. of ACL, pp. 1127–1136 (2011)
11. Li, Q., Ji, H., Huang, L.: Joint event extraction via structured prediction with global features. In: Proc. of ACL, pp. 73–82 (2013)
12. Li, Q., Ji, H., Hong, Y., Li, S.: Constructing information networks using one single model. In: Proc. of EMNLP, pp. 1846–1851 (2014)
13. Liu, S., Chen, Y., Liu, K., Zhao, J.: Exploiting argument information to improve event detection via supervised attention mechanisms. In: Proc. of ACL, pp. 1789–1798 (2017)
14. Zhang, Y., Xu, G., Wang, Y., Liang, X., Wang, L., Huang, T.: Empower event detection with bi-directional neural language model. Knowl. Based Syst. **167**, 87–97 (2019)
15. Nguyen, T.M., Nguyen, T.H.: One for all: Neural joint modeling of entities and events. In: Proc. of AAAI, pp. 6851–6858 (2019)
16. Lai, V.D., Nguyen, T.N., Nguyen, T.H.: Event detection: gate diversity and syntactic importance scores for graph convolution neural networks. In: Proc. of EMNLP (2020)

17. Cui, S., Yu, B., Liu, T., Zhang, Z., Wang, X., Shi, J.: Edge-enhanced graph convolution networks for event detection with syntactic relation. In: Proc. of EMNLP Findings (2020)
18. Zhao, Y., Jin, X., Wang, Y., Cheng, X.: Document embedding enhanced event detection with hierarchical and supervised attention. In: Proc. of ACL, pp. 414–419 (2018)
19. Liu, J., Chen, Y., Liu, K., Bi, W., Liu, X.: Event extraction as machine reading comprehension. In: Proc. of EMNLP, pp. 1641–1651 (2020)
20. Du, X., Cardie, C.: Event extraction by answering (almost) natural questions. In: Proc. of EMNLP (2020)
21. Chen, Y., Chen, T., Ebner, S., White, A.S., Van Durme, B.: Reading the manual: event extraction as definition comprehension. In: Proceedings of the Fourth Workshop on Structured Prediction for NLP (2020)
22. Lafferty, J.D., McCallum, A., Pereira, F.C.N.: Conditional random fields: probabilistic models for segmenting and labeling sequence data. In: Proc. of ICML (2001)
23. Liu, X., Luo, Z., Huang, H.: Jointly multiple events extraction via attention-based graph information aggregation. In: Proc. of EMNLP (2018)

Dynamic Style Transferring and Content Preserving for Domain Generalization

Chaoyi Wang[1], Liang Li[2(✉)], Yuhan Gao[3], Jiehua Zhang[1], Yefei Zhang[1], Yaoqi Sun[1], Weijun Qin[4], Jun Yin[5], and Zhongyuan Wang[4]

[1] Hangzhou Dianzi University, Hangzhou, Zhejiang, China
{chaoyiwang,jh.zhang,zhangyf,syq}@hdu.edu.cn
[2] Institute of Computing Technology, CAS, Beijing, China
liang.li@ict.ac.cn
[3] Lishui Institute of Hangzhou Dianzi University, Hangzhou, China
yuhangao@hdu.edu.cn
[4] Kuaishou Technology, Beijing, China
{qinweijun,wangzhongyuan}@kuaishou.com
[5] Zhejiang Dahua Technology CO., LTD., Hangzhou, Zhejiang, China
yin_jun@dahuatech.com

Abstract. Although convolutional neural networks (CNNs) have shown remarkable ability in different computer vision tasks, they do not cope well with domain shifts. Recent studies show that the domain shift mainly results from the style or texture variation of images rather than the content. Inspired by this, we propose dynamic style transferring to overcome the style bias of CNNs. Specifically, we design a knowledge-injected attention mechanism for learning adaptive fusion weights and embedding the style knowledge of dynamic chosen images in latent space. So the extent of transferred style is controlled, and we can retain content-related information. Furthermore, we introduce the content preserving module, which builds an adversarial structure with the encoder to make the extracted style information more precise. For balancing the adversarial relationship between encoder and auxiliary predictor, we also introduce a consistency loss to empower the style-biased predictor and indirectly boost the encoder's ability by extending the back-propagation process. We conduct extensive experiments on PACS and Office-Home datasets to evaluate the effectiveness of our method. Experiment results show remarkable performance over the state-of-the-art methods in the domain generalization.

Keywords: Transfer learning · Domain generalization · Style transfer · Content preserving

1 Introduction

In the past few years, Convolutional Neural Networks (CNNs) achieved satisfactory performance in many computer vision tasks with the help of large scale

© ICST Institute for Computer Sciences, Social Informatics and Telecommunications Engineering 2022
Published by Springer Nature Switzerland AG 2022. All Rights Reserved
Y. Chenggang et al. (Eds.): MobiMedia 2022, LNICST 451, pp. 298–315, 2022.
https://doi.org/10.1007/978-3-031-23902-1_23

well-labelled data. However, most CNN models are trained based on the i.i.d. assumption that training and testing data share the same data distribution. In the real world, the hypothesis is not always satisfied, and models often suffer from poor generalization ability in unseen domains. For boosting the performance of CNN models in unseen environments, annotating extensive amounts of data for each scenario to train networks is expensive and unpractical. To solve this problem, Unsupervised Domain Adaptation (UDA) [1–5] is an alternative method without the requirement of extra labelled data.

UDA methods intend to transfer the knowledge learned from the labelled source domain/task to the unlabeled target domain/task. Most UDA methods strive to align the domain distribution by learning domain invariant features of the source and target domains. In general, UDA methods can be divided into two categories, the discrepancy-based method and the adversarial-based method. The discrepancy-based methods alleviate the domain discrepancy by minimizing some predefined statistic metrics between the source and target domains in a high dimensional space. For aligning domain distributions, adversarial-based methods optimize the feature encoder in an adversarial training paradigm. Despite the success of UDA methods, unlabeled target domain data is still required for aligning domain distributions. Therefore the target domain is fixed during the training process, and models may suffer from poor generalization ability in environments out of training distribution.

As a transfer learning method with relaxed data constraints, Domain Generalization (DG) [6–8] intends to boost the generalization ability of models in arbitrary domains out of source distribution with only labelled source data. The existing DG approaches have tried to learn invariant features across multiple domains by minimizing feature divergences between the source domains [1,9–12], normalizing domain-specific gradients based on meta-learning [7,13–16], robust optimization [17–20], or augmenting source domain examples [6,21–25]. For example, Zhou et al. [25]randomly select two instances from different domains and adopt a probabilistic convex combination between instance-level feature statistics of bottom CNN layers. Despite the success of the above methods in mitigating the domain shift, they only reduce the domain gap in an ambiguous manner, which lacks specific optimizing orientation upon the cause of domain shifts. Recent studies [22,26] show that the domain shift mainly results from the style or texture variation of images rather than the content.

Motivated by this observation, Generative Adversarial Networks (GANs) are adopted by many researchers to reduce domain gaps by transferring image appearances. Nevertheless, the GAN-based approaches usually contain large scale parameters, which is time-consuming and hard training. Recently, normalization methods (e.g. BN [27], IN [28], CIN [29]) attracted increasing attention for style transferring as it's efficiency. One of the popular approaches is AdaIn [26], which is proposed to transfer image styles by normalizing feature statistics. Inspired by this work, many normalization-based domain generalization methods are proposed, including SagNet [22] and CrossNorm [30]. SagNet [22] provides a new idea for mitigating the difference between domain distributions, which dis-

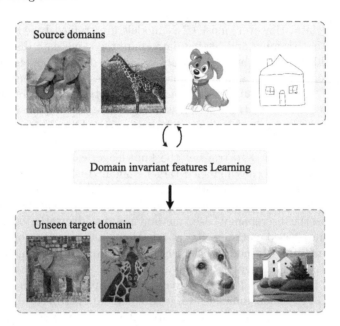

Fig. 1. Classification task about multi-source domain generalization. Given labelled data sampled from several source domains, training the model to learn domain invariant features. Then apply the model to an unseen target domain.

entangles style features from categories information and exchanges statistics of features randomly to prevent style biased predictions and focus more on the contents. Similarly, the CrossNorm also proposes to exchange channel-wise statics between features for enlarging the training distribution. Although both methods improved the model generalization ability under image style shifts, they cannot control the extent of the statistics exchange. Therefore, they tend to ignore some content-related information or pay too much attention to trivial information such as one-sided style features (Fig. 1).

To solve the above problem, we propose the dynamic style transferring and content preserving for domain generalization, which makes the extent of transferred style controllable and reduces the intrinsic style-bias of CNNs in an adversarial learning paradigm. Specifically, we first design a knowledge-injected attention mechanism to learn weight vectors for adaptively fusing style knowledge of mini-batch instances in feature space. This enables an adaptive style integration to capture content-related information hidden in the style knowledge. Second, we introduce the dynamic content preserving module by building an adversarial learning paradigm between the feature encoder and the auxiliary predictor to make the extracted feature irrelevant to the image appearance. Further, in order to enable the encoder to learn the content-biased representation in a long phase, we impose a content consistency loss to boost the optimizing of auxiliary classifier during the minimax game. Therefore, our approach can mitigate the inherent style bias of CNNs by capturing the content-biased representation.

Our main contributions can be summarized as follows:

- We propose a domain generalization method with dynamic style transferring and content preserving, which makes the extent of transferred style controllable and overcomes the intrinsic style bias of CNNs in an adversarial learning paradigm.
- We introduce consistency loss to balance the encoder and auxiliary predictor, which build an adversarial structure. Therefore the encoder can learn the content-biased representation in an extended phase by the back-propagation.
- We conduct extensive experiments on three widely used domain generalization benchmarks, including PACS and Office-Home. The results demonstrate that our method achieves comparable performance to state-of-the-art methods.

2   Related Work

Unsupervised Domain Adaptation (UDA) tackles the domain shift problem where labelled source data and unlabelled target data are available for training. Most UDA methods derive from the point of view of reducing the domain gap between different domains. Maximum Mean Discrepancy (MMD) [31] is an important statistic metric to mitigate the domain distribution shift in previous works. Ganin *et al.* [1] introduced Domain Adversarial Neural Network (DANN) to align the feature distributions. DDC [32] was proposed to alleviate the domain discrepancy by adding adaptation layers for matching high-order moments of feature distributions. Saito *et al.* proposed MCD [33] by devising a domain discriminator to learn domain-invariant features in an adversarial manner for bridging the domain gaps. Inspired by the image translation idea of CycleGAN [34], some methods [35–37] translate the target style into source images to close the domain gap at the image level.

Domain generalization aims to make the model more robust against unseen domains with only access to the source data. Similar to domain adaptation, some multi-source domain generalization works utilize domain alignment methods to minimize the domain discrepancy among source domains for learning domain invariant features. These methods [38,39] argue that feature distributions aligned among source domains should also be robust to unseen target domains. The popular feature aligning methods include minimizing Maximum Mean Discrepancy (MMD) [39,40], minimizing the KL divergence [41] and adversarial learning [9,42]. The works [43,44] design the model with certain parts for learning domain-specific and domain shared representations. For instance, Chattopadhyay *et al.* [43] proposed to learn a balance of domain-invariant and domain-specific features by domain-specific masks. Thus both in-domain and out-of-domain generalization performance are improved. Work [45] proposed to iteratively discard the dominant features activated on the training data, and encourage the network to activate remaining features that correlates with labels. The domain generalization method we proposed is more lightweight compared to previous methods and adaptive learning is performed to enable a controlled degree of style transformation.

Normalization plays a vital role in deep neural network training and image style transferring. Ioffe *et al.* [27] introduced a Batch Normalization (BN) layer to speed up the convergence of models and alleviate the "gradient diffusion" problem in deep networks by normalizing the feature statistics. Batch Normalization is a benchmark technology that has inspired many following normalization methods [26,28,29,46,47]. Ulyanov *et al.* [28] found that significant improvement could be achieved simply by replacing batch normalization with instance normalization. Dumoulin *et al.* [29] proposed a Conditional Instance Normalization (CIN) to learn different affine parameters for different styles. Nevertheless, CIN cannot be adapted to arbitrary new styles without re-training the model. Adaptive Instance Normalization (AdaIN) [26] enables arbitrary style transfer in real-time by aligning the mean and variance of the content features with those of the style features. Compared to BN, IN and CIN, AdaIN adaptively computes affine parameters from style inputs to achieve arbitrary style transfer.

3   Methodology

In this section, we elaborate our dynamic style transferring and content preserving for multiple/single source domain generalization. We first review the background knowledge about instance normalization and style transferring in Sect. 3.1. Secondly, we overview the basic paradigm of domain generalization and the proposed method in Sect. 3.2. Thirdly, we detail the dynamic style transferring and content preserving modules in Sect. 3.3 and Sect. 3.4, respectively.

3.1   Preliminary

As revealed by recent studies [48–50], CNNs are sensitive to the style of images extracted from domains with different data distributions. For inducing the intrinsic style bias of CNNs, both GAN-based and instance normalization-based methods [26,28,29] are proposed. Compared with GAN-based methods, instance normalization-based methods are more efficient and easy inserted into other methods. They [26,51] utilize the channel-wise mean and standard deviation as style representation and transfer image styles by normalizing feature statistics.

Let $x \in \mathbb{R}^{B \times C \times H \times W}$ denotes a batch of feature maps, where B, C, H and W indicate the dimension of batch, channel, height and width, respectively. Instance normalization transforms the normalized feature map, which is formulated as,

$$\text{IN}(x) = \gamma \frac{x - \mu(x)}{\sigma(x)} + \beta, \tag{1}$$

where $\gamma, \beta \in \mathbb{R}^C$ are learnable parameters of the affine transformation. And $\mu(x), \sigma(x) \in \mathbb{R}^{B \times C}$ indicate the mean and standard deviation of each feature map at the spatial dimension within the channel according to Eq. 2 and 3, respectively.

$$\mu(x)_{b,c} = \frac{1}{HW} \sum_{h=1}^{H} \sum_{w=1}^{W} x_{b,c,h,w} \tag{2}$$

$$\sigma(x)_{b,c} = \sqrt{\frac{1}{HW} \sum_{h=1}^{H} \sum_{w=1}^{W} (x_{b,c,h,w} - \mu(x)_{b,c})^2} \qquad (3)$$

Inspired by this, some researchers [26,28,29] utilize the mean and the variance of the features for style transferring. Huang et $al.$ [26] propose Adaptive Instance Normalization (AdaIN) for arbitrary style transfer by recombining the mean and variance of the content features with those of the style features.

$$\text{AdaIN}(x) = \sigma(y)\frac{x - \mu(x)}{\sigma(x)} + \mu(y), \qquad (4)$$

where x, y denote the content feature and the target style feature, respectively.

3.2 Overview of Proposed Method

In terms of data availability for training, we assume that we have only access to the source instances $x_s \in X_s$ and the corresponding labels $y_s \in Y_s$ from the source distribution $p_s(x, y)$. Under the scenario of domain generalization, the target image and label are not available for training. Our main goal is to train a neural network on the source domain and generalize well to unseen target domains by inducing the style bias of network.

As illustrated in Fig. 2, our framework consists of three sub-modules, i.e. the shared feature encoder, dynamic style transferring with a style-agnostic classifier and content preserving module with an auxiliary predictor. The shared encoder E extracts features of instances for predicting the categories of inputs. As the target data is unavailable in the training phase, we adopt the dynamic style transferring module to enrich the style information by knowledge-injected attention mechanism for learning content invariant representations. The style-agnostic classifier G_s is supervised by a task loss L_s for accurately predicting image classes. Meanwhile, the dynamic content preserving module builds an adversarial structure between the encoder and auxiliary predictor G_a. The minimax game between them encourages the encoder to generate less style-biased representations. Furthermore, we design a content consistency loss for balancing the adversarial relationship between encoder E and auxiliary predictor G_a. And it also makes the content features extracted by the encoder more style irrelevant. It is worth noting that we only employ the encoder E and auxiliary predictor G_a during the evaluation stage.

3.3 Dynamic Style Transferring

In domain generalization, the alignment of domain distributions plays a significant role. Recent studies [48–50] show that domain distribution shifts mainly result from the style or texture variation of images. Inspired by these studies, SagNet [22] proposed style randomization to reduce this gap so that the encoder can focus on capturing content-related features. However, the extent of

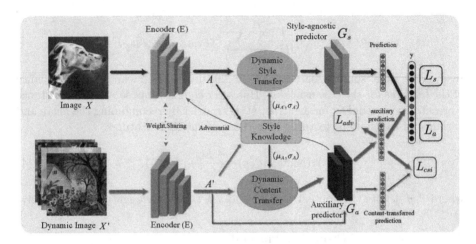

Fig. 2. An illustration of our method, which consists of three sub-modules, including the shared feature encoder, dynamic style transferring with style-agnostic classifier, and dynamic content preserving module with auxiliary predictor. The dynamic style transferring module leads the style-agnostic classifier to focus on content information in the feature map. The dynamic content preserving module guides the auxiliary classifier to focus on the style information, while adversarial learning makes the feature extractor generate less style-related representation.

statistics exchanges is uncontrollable. And they tend to ignore some content-related knowledge hidden in style features. To solve this problem, we propose the dynamic style transferring (DST) module, which can control the extent of transferred knowledge by introducing a knowledge-injected attention mechanism. This mechanism helps achieve the goal of adaptively fusing style knowledge of mini-batch instances in latent space by learning weight vectors. This enables an adaptive style integration to capture content-related information hidden in the style knowledge.

Our knowledge-injected attention mechanism is inspired by the channel-attention mechanism [52], and we implement the attention function $a(\cdot, \cdot)$ by a single linear layer to process both the mean and standard deviation of feature maps. Given a training image x and a dynamic selected image x', we extract their intermediate feature maps by $E(x) = \mathbf{A}, E(x') = \mathbf{A}' \in \mathbb{R}^{D \times H \times W}$ from the encoder E, where H and W indicate spatial dimensions, and D is the number of channels. Then we calculate the statistic $\mu_A, \sigma_A \in \mathbb{R}^D$ as the style representation by Eq. 5 and 6:

$$\mu(A)_{b,c} = \frac{1}{HW} \sum_{h=1}^{H} \sum_{w=1}^{W} A_{h,w}; \qquad (5)$$

$$\sigma(\mathbf{A}) = \sqrt{\frac{1}{HW} \sum_{h=1}^{H} \sum_{w=1}^{W} (\mathbf{A}_{hw} - \mu(\mathbf{A}))^2}. \qquad (6)$$

The dynamic style transferring constructs the transferred style knowledge $\mu, \sigma \in \mathbb{R}^D$ through the knowledge-injected attention mechanism based on A and A':

$$\mu = a\left(\mu_A, \mu_{A'}\right); \tag{7}$$

$$\sigma = a\left(\sigma_A, \sigma_{A'}\right), \tag{8}$$

where $a(\cdot, \cdot)$ denote our attention function, and $\mu_{A'}, \sigma_{A'}$ indicate the channel-wise statics of A'.

Then we implement style transfer by conducting affine transformation on normalized A:

$$\mathrm{DST}(A, A') = \sigma \cdot \frac{A - \mu_A}{\sigma_A} + \mu. \tag{9}$$

The transferred feature map is fed to G_s for a content-biased prediction, and we obtain the cross-entropy loss L_s to jointly optimize $\mathbf{E}$ and $\mathbf{G_s}$:

$$\underset{\mathbf{E,G_s}}{arg\ \min} L_s = -\mathbb{E}_{(\mathbf{x,y})\in S} \sum_{k=1}^{K} \mathbf{y}_k \log \mathbf{G_s}\left(\mathrm{DST}\left(A, A'\right)\right)_k, \tag{10}$$

where K is the number of classification categories, $\mathbf{y} \in \{0,1\}^K$ is the one-hot label for input x and $S = \{X_s, Y_s\}$ is the training set.

The introduction of the knowledge-injected attention mechanism recalibrates the statistics to control fusion extents and increases the diversity of style combinations by adjusting the injecting weights. Therefore the style-agnostic classifier G_s can be robust against the style change and predicts categories based on the content information.

3.4 Dynamic Content Preserving

In addition to learn a style-agnostic predictor, we design the dynamic content preserving module to further mitigate the style bias of network by learning style-related feature representations. Concretely, we first construct an adversarial structure between feature encoder E and auxiliary predictor G_a to constrain the encoder to learn content-agnostic features. In other words, the style knowledge would be captured by the feature encoder to contain as little content information as possible. To achieve this goal, G_a is encouraged to make auxiliary decisions according to the content preserved features $DCP(A, A')$ by L_a. Besides, the predictor tries to predict x accurately, which adversarially makes the encoder capture the discriminative representations. Lastly, we impose a content consistency loss L_{csi} to balance the adversarial structure in the minimax game and preserve the ability of the encoder to encode content-related feature.

In contrast to the dynamic style transferring module, this module retains the style knowledge of feature map A and replaces its content with a dynamically selected representation A' as,

$$\mathrm{DCP}(A, A') = \sigma_A \cdot \frac{A' - \mu_{A'}}{\sigma_{A'}} + \mu_A. \tag{11}$$

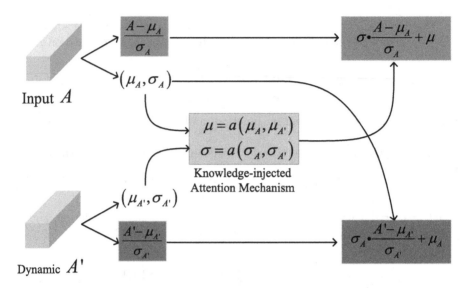

Fig. 3. Illustration of the knowledge-injected attention mechanism. It learns adaptive fusion weights and embedding the style knowledge of dynamic chosen images in latent space.

Figure 3 illustrates the process of the dynamic content preserving. Once the content transformation is finished, the transferred feature maps are fed into the auxiliary classifier G_a to compute the auxiliary predictions. We employ a cross-entropy loss L_a to optimize $\mathbf{G_a}$:

$$\underset{\mathbf{G_a}}{arg\min} L_a = -\mathbb{E}_{(\mathbf{x},\mathbf{y}) \in S} \sum_{k=1}^{K} \mathbf{y}_k \log \mathbf{G_a}\left(\mathrm{DCP}\left(A, A'\right)\right)_k, \tag{12}$$

where $\mathbf{y}_k$ is the label of the instance x, and the optimization goal of the loss function L_a is to promote $\mathbf{G_a}$ make correctly predictions based on the content transferred feature of x $(DST(A, A'))$. On the other hand, we train encoder E to fool G_a by minimizing an adversarial loss L_{adv} as follows.

$$\underset{\mathbf{E}}{arg\min} L_{\mathrm{adv}} = -\lambda_{\mathrm{adv}} \mathbb{E}_{(\mathbf{x},\cdot) \in S} \sum_{k=1}^{K} \frac{1}{K} \log \mathbf{G_a}\left(\mathrm{DCP}\left(A, A'\right)\right)_k \tag{13}$$

where λ_{adv} is a hype-parameter for adjusting the adversarial extent.

Although the two networks and objective functions construct an adversarial structure, the capability between them may not be balanced as the discriminator is weak, which results in the learning of the encoder being terminated in early phase. Essentially, the improvements of generators or encoders come from the gradient back-propagation of the discriminator's loss. When the predictor is fooled easily by generators, the marginal cost in the later training phase is insufficient to drive the generator to jump out the local optimum point in

---

Algorithm 1. Training algorithm of our method.

Input: training data $S = (x_i, y_i)_{i=1}^{M}$; batch size$N$;

Initialize: feature extractor $\mathbf{E}$; style-agnostic classifier $\mathbf{G}_s$; auxiliary classifier $\mathbf{G}_a$

While not converged $\mathbf{X}, \mathbf{Y} = Minibatch(S, N)$

$\mathbf{A} = \mathbf{E}(\mathbf{X})$

$\mathbf{A'} = SHUFFLE(\mathbf{A})$

$\mathbf{A}^s = DST(\mathbf{A}, \mathbf{A'})$

$\underset{\mathbf{E},\mathbf{G}_s}{arg\,\min}\, L_s = -\frac{1}{N} \sum_{j=1}^{N} \sum_{k=1}^{K} \mathbf{Y}_{j,k} \log \mathbf{G}_s(A_j^s)_k$

$\mathbf{A}^c = DCP(\mathbf{A}, \mathbf{A'})$

$\underset{\mathbf{G}_a}{arg\,\min}\, L_a = -\frac{1}{N} \sum_{j=1}^{N} \sum_{k=1}^{K} \mathbf{Y}_{j,k} \log \mathbf{G}_a(A_j^c)_k$

$\underset{\mathbf{E}}{arg\,\min}\, L_{\mathrm{adv}} = -\lambda_{\mathrm{adv}} \frac{1}{N} \sum_{j=1}^{N} \sum_{k=1}^{K} \frac{1}{K} \log \mathbf{G}_a \left(\mathbf{A}_j^c\right)_k$

$\underset{\mathbf{E},\mathbf{G}_a}{arg\,\min}\, L_{\mathrm{csi}} = -\lambda_{\mathrm{csi}} \frac{1}{N} \sum_{j=1}^{N} \sum_{k=1}^{K} \|\mathbf{G}_a(A_j^c) - A_j^c\|_k^2$

end

Output: $\mathbf{E} \circ \mathbf{G}_s$

---

optimization space. Motivated by this, we impose the consistency loss L_{csi} to empower the auxiliary classifier, which minimizes the mean square error between auxiliary predictions and content preserving predictions. Therefore, it not only promotes the adversarial relationship between encoder and auxiliary predictor, but also makes the encoder learn content-biased representations in an extended phase and protects the encoder's ability to capture content-related features. The above consistency loss is computed as,

$$\underset{\mathbf{E},\mathbf{G}_a}{arg\,\min}\, L_{\mathrm{csi}} = \lambda_{\mathrm{csi}} \mathbb{E}_{\mathbf{x} \in S} \sum_{k=1}^{K} \left\{\mathbf{G}_a \left(\mathrm{DCP}\left(A, A'\right)\right)_k - \mathbf{G}_a \left(A'\right)_k\right\}^2 \quad (14)$$

where λ_{csi} is the weight coefficient which controls balance of the adversarial game. We analyze the influence of different λ_{csi} value in ablation study (Sect. 4.3).

4 Experiments

In this section, we conduct extensive experiments to validate the effectiveness of our methods on three widely-used benchmarks, including PACS [44] and Office-Home [53]. We first introduce the datasets and implementation details. Then we analyse the experimental results on datasets and discuss the ablation study. Finally, we analyse the visualization result domain alignment of the proposed method.

4.1   Datasets and Implementation Details

In this section, we first introduce three widely used benchmarks, including PACS [44] and Office-Home [53]. Then we describe the implementation details of our method.

PACS is a domain generalization dataset that consists of 9991 images across four domains, namely Photo, Art Painting, Cartoon and Sketch. Each domain contains seven categories. Following the official split [44], we split the data of PACS into 70% training and 30% validation.

Office-Home is a benchmark dataset for domain adaptation that contains four domains, including Art, Clipart, Product and Real-World. Each domain consists of 65 categories with an average of about 70 instances per class. We split the 15588 instances of Office-Home into 90% training and 10% validation following [8].

Implementation Details. The proposed method is implemented on PyTorch and trained on a single NVIDIA RTX 2080TI GPU. During the training, we adopt the Stochastic Gradient Descent (SGD) optimizer with a weight decay of 0.0001, momentum of 0.9 and an initial learning rate of 0.0004 for all datasets. We adopt the cosine scheduling for the learning rate adjusting, and the adjusting iterations is 2k. The adversarial weight are fixed to 0.1. Limited by the GPU memory, we set the training batchsize to 96 on PACS and 32 on others.

4.2   Results on PACS

In this section, we conduct the experiments of single-source domain generalization and multi-source domain generalization on PACS. We employ the ResNet-18 [54] as our feature extractor for all experiments on the PACS dataset.

For demonstrating the effectiveness of our method under single-source domain generalization setting, we conduct experiments on the PACS dataset where only a single source domain data is accessible. We train our network on each domain of PACS and validate the model on the remaining domains. As can be seen in Table 1, our model outperforms the state-of-the-art method by a large margin in most domains. Specifically, we outperform JiGen [6] by 11.7% and higher than Sagnet [22] by 4.4%, in average. The reason may be that the proposed dynamic style transferring significantly benefits the robustness of CNNs against the appearance variation. And the content preserving module further improves the performance by balancing the adversarial learning between the encoder and auxiliary classifier.

Furthermore, for demonstrating the effectiveness of our method under multi-source domain generalization task, we compare it with recent works, including Epi-FCR [15], D-SAM [8], JiGen [6], MASF [7], MMLD [10], RSC [45], StableNet [56] and SagNet [22]. The results of RSC and StableNet are from the original paper, and the results of other methods in Tabel 2 are copied from [22]. The experimental comparison results are shown in Table 2. We observe that the proposed method achieves competitive performance against all the methods with 0.45–7.64% improvements in average accuracy, proving our method is robust to

Table 1. Performance comparison at the single-source domain generalization on PACS (A: Art Painting, C: Cartoon, S: Sketch, P: Photo).

Method	A→C	A→S	A→P	C→A	C→S	C→P	S→A	S→C	S→P	P→A	P→C	P→S	Avg.
ResNet-18 [54]	62.3	49.0	95.2	65.7	60.7	83.6	28.0	54.5	35.6	64.1	23.6	29.1	54.3
JiGen [6]	57.0	50.0	96.1	65.3	65.9	85.5	26.6	41.1	42.8	62.4	27.2	35.5	54.6
ADA [55]	64.3	58.5	94.5	66.7	65.6	83.6	37.0	58.6	41.6	65.3	32.7	35.9	58.7
SagNet [22]	67.1	56.8	95.7	**72.1**	69.2	85.7	41.1	62.9	46.2	**69.8**	35.1	40.7	61.9
Ours	**67.2**	**62.4**	**96.3**	67.8	**69.7**	**87.7**	**59.0**	**65.1**	**54.3**	67.2	**41.3**	**56.3**	**66.3**

Table 2. Performance comparison at multi-source domain generalization on PACS.

Method	Venue	Art painting	Cartoon	Sketch	Photo	Avg.
Epi-FCR [15]	AAAI 2018	82.10	77.00	73.00	93.9	81.50
D-SAM [8]	ICPR 2018	77.33	72.43	77.83	95.30	80.72
JiGen [6]	CVPR 2019	79.42	75.25	71.35	96.03	80.51
MASF [7]	NIPS 2019	80.29	77.17	71.69	94.99	81.04
RSC [45]	ECCV 2020	75.72	68.50	66.10	93.93	76.06
MMLD [10]	AAAI 2020	81.28	77.16	72.29	96.09	81.83
SagNet [22]	CVPR 2021	**83.58**	**77.66**	76.30	95.47	83.25
StableNet [56]	CVPR 2021	80.16	74.15	70.10	94.24	79.66
Ours	–	82.32	76.62	**80.00**	**95.87**	**83.70**

the style variations. Particularly, our approach brings significant improvement on the Sketch domain, with a maximum improvement of 13.9% and a minimum improvement of 2.17%. The improvement demonstrates that the dynamic style transferring and content preserving are effective in reducing the intrinsic style bias of the feature extractor. Therefore the generalization ability of our model against style variations is improved. Besides, we also find SagNet [22] exceed our model in Art Painting and Cartoon domains. We attribute this inferior performance to two aspects. On the one hand, our method may not be as stable as other methods due to the hype parameters are not fine-tuned. On the other hand, we may suffer from a relatively high source risk in mussy backgrounds such as Art painting, as our method performs well in Sketch and Photo domains which have salient objects and brief background.

We also notice that the performance of our model decreases sharply under the single-source DG setting, compared to the results of multi-source DG in Table 2. On the one hand, this demonstrates the number of training instances plays a vital role in DG, and the single-source DG is a challenging task. On the other hand, this validates that the rich variations of domain style benefit our method to capture and induce the style bias as the multi-source experiments are conducted on mixed data.

4.3 Ablation Study

In this section, we verify the effectiveness of the proposed dynamic style transferring (DST) and content preserving (DCP) under a single source domain gener-

Table 3. Ablation study of our method on PACS for single-source domain generalization (A: Art Painting, C: Cartoon, S: Sketch, P: Photo). λ_{csi} is the coefficient of content consistency loss.

Method	A→C	A→S	A→P	C→A	C→S	C→P	S→A	S→C	S→P	P→A	P→C	P→S	Avg.
Baseline	67.1	56.8	95.7	**72.1**	69.2	85.7	41.1	62.9	46.2	**69.8**	35.1	40.7	61.9
DST w/o DCP	63.7	**65.1**	**96.8**	70.1	**72.2**	**89.9**	43.7	62.1	53.1	68.8	32.9	50.0	64.0
DST w/DCP ($\lambda_{csi}=1$)	66.2	61.2	96.3	66.0	70.3	86.8	41.2	64.3	47.7	67.2	**41.6**	48.8	63.1
DST w/DCP ($\lambda_{csi}=0.01$)	66.8	60.1	95.9	70.2	69.4	89.0	50.7	62.1	**54.5**	66.5	40.8	52.2	64.8
DST w/DCP ($\lambda_{csi}=0.1$)	**67.2**	62.4	96.3	67.8	69.7	87.7	**58.9**	**65.1**	54.3	67.2	41.3	**56.3**	**66.3**

alization setting on PACS, and we also show the influence of content consistency loss in Eq. 14.

We adopt SagNet [22] as our baseline. First, we validate the effect of the proposed DST based on the baseline (denoted as 'DST w/o DCP' in Table 3), where the content consistency loss is not involved into the optimizing process. Then we balance the adversarial learning between feature encoder and auxiliary predictor by introducing the content consistency criterion. We explore the consistency loss by varying the coefficient λ_{csi} in Eq. 14 while the DST module is fixed.

As illustrated in Table 3, all variants of our method significantly surpass the baseline [22] in average accuracy. The comparison between baseline and 'DST w/o DCP' demonstrates that the adaptive style fusion weights can guide the model to concentrate on useful information by dynamically adjusting the extent of style knowledge transferring. As can be seen in the second and third rows of Table 3, the performance of 'DST w/ DCP($\lambda_{csi} = 1$)' is worse than original 'DST w/o DCP'. Such this accuracy degeneration may results from the imbalance between feature extractor and auxiliary predictor. The large coefficient of content consistency loss leads to the encoder failing in the minimax game, and the style bias of CNNs impacts the extraction of domain invariant features.

The last three rows of Table 3 show the influence of hype parameters λ_{csi}. We observe that the best performance occurs in 'DST w/ DCP ($\lambda_{csi} = 0.1$)'. And the performance of 'DST w/ DCP ($\lambda_{csi} = 0.01$)' surpasses 'DST w/ DCP ($\lambda_{csi} = 1$)' with 1.7% in average accuracy. Particularly, 'DST w/ DCP ($\lambda_{csi} = 0.01$)' exceed 'DST w/ DCP ($\lambda_{csi} = 1$)' in task $S \to A$ by 9.5%. We attribute such phenomenon to the balance of adversarial training process between encoder and auxiliary predictor. The large coefficient of content consistency leads to the encoder failing to reduce the style bias. On the contrary, a small coefficient makes the encoder surpass the predictor in early-stage and unable to learn further via the adversarial process. Therefore a proper coefficient is necessary for the content preserving loss which intends to balance the minimax two-player game. And the encoder can preserves the content feature benefiting from the DCP. Finally, we set DCP($\lambda_{csi} = 0.1$) in the following experiments.

Table 4. Performance comparison at single-source domain generalization on Office-Home (A: Art , C: Clipart, P: Product, R: Real_World).

Method	A→C	A→P	A→R	C→A	C→P	C→R	P→A	P→C	P→R	R→A	R→C	R→P	Avg
ResNet-50 [54]	34.9	50.0	58.0	37.4	41.9	46.2	38.5	31.2	60.4	53.9	41.2	59.9	46.1
ERM [61]	40.0	47.7	57.9	39.0	51.8	52.3	37.4	30.3	56.4	53.3	41.5	69.7	48.1
ARM [57]	41.0	48.7	63.1	36.4	45.6	47.7	44.6	32.8	56.9	51.8	42.6	69.2	48.4
Fish [20]	40.5	54.4	63.1	41.5	52.8	58.5	41.0	36.4	66.7	53.8	41.5	73.8	52.0
SD [58]	45.6	57.4	66.2	43.6	53.3	52.8	40.0	34.4	65.1	56.9	47.7	72.8	53.0
DAN [2]	43.6	57.0	67.9	45.8	56.5	60.4	44.0	43.6	67.7	63.1	51.5	74.3	56.3
DANN [1]	45.6	59.3	70.1	47.0	58.5	60.9	46.1	43.7	68.5	**63.2**	51.8	76.8	57.6
SagNet [22]	48.7	61.0	70.3	48.7	55.4	62.1	50.8	45.6	69.2	62.6	**54.9**	**76.9**	58.8
Ours	**49.7**	**62.6**	**73.8**	**50.8**	**59.0**	**64.1**	**52.3**	**46.7**	**73.3**	63.1	48.2	**76.9**	**60.0**

4.4   Results on Office-Home

In this section, we further compare our method with recent state-of-the-art works [1,2,20,22,54,57,58] under single-source domain generalization setting on the Office-Home dataset. The results of ResNet-50 [54], DAN [2] and DANN [1] are copied from [59], and the results of other methods in Tabel 4 are reproduced from the code in DomainBed library [60].

The comparison results are shown in Table 4. We can observe that the proposed method exceeds all of the comparison approaches in most tasks and averages accuracy by a large margin. In particular, our approach achieves 4.1% gain on $P \rightarrow R$ task and 1.2% gain on average, compared to the state-of-the-art Sag-Net [22] on accuracy. We note that SagNet exchanges the style statistics in a random interpolation manner. Therefore, they tend to ignore some content-related information or pay too much attention to trivial information such as one-sided style features which are unrelated to the prediction. Besides, the adversarial training in SagNet is also unbalanced, which results in the back-propagation disabled in the later phase.

5   Conclusion

This paper proposes the dynamic style transferring and content preserving to alleviate the style bias of CNNs. Concretely, we design a knowledge-injected attention mechanism to control the extent of embedding the style knowledge of dynamic chosen images in latent space. So the content-related information hidden in style knowledge can be retained. Furthermore, we introduce the content preserving module, which builds an adversarial structure with the encoder to make the captured style information more precise. Experiment results show our method achieve remarkable performance over the SOTA methods in the single/multiple source domain generalization.

Limitation. Because of the adversarial relationship between the encoder and the auxiliary classifier, our model suffers from the performance degradation in some sub-tasks. As our approach does not leverage domain labels, it may be significant to further improve the performance under multi-source domain setting by adding a domain discriminator to capture the domain information.

References

1. Ganin, Y., et al.: Domain-adversarial training of neural networks. J. Mach. Learn. Res. **17**(1), 2096–2130 (2016)
2. Long, M., Cao, Y., Wang, J., Jordan, M.: Learning transferable features with deep adaptation networks. In: International Conference on Machine Learning, pp. 97–105. PMLR (2015)
3. Long, M., Cao, Z., Wang, J., Jordan, M.I.: Conditional adversarial domain adaptation. Adv. Neural Inf. Process. Syst. **31** (2018)
4. Peng, X., Bai, Q., Xia, X., Huang, Z., Saenko, K., Wang, B.: Moment matching for multi-source domain adaptation. In: Proceedings of the IEEE/CVF International Conference on Computer Vision, pp. 1406–1415 (2019)
5. Tzeng, E., Hoffman, J., Saenko, K., Darrell, T.: Adversarial discriminative domain adaptation. In: Proceedings of the IEEE Conference on Computer Vision and Pattern Recognition, pp. 7167–7176 (2017)
6. Carlucci, F.M., D'Innocente, A., Bucci, S., Caputo, B., Tommasi, T.: Domain generalization by solving jigsaw puzzles. In: Proceedings of the IEEE/CVF Conference on Computer Vision and Pattern Recognition, pp. 2229–2238 (2019)
7. Dou, Q., Coelho de Castro, D., Kamnitsas, K., Glocker, B.: Domain generalization via model-agnostic learning of semantic features. Adv. Neural Inf. Process. Syst. **32** (2019)
8. D'Innocente, A., Caputo, B.: Domain generalization with domain-specific aggregation modules. In: Brox, T., Bruhn, A., Fritz, M. (eds.) GCPR 2018. LNCS, vol. 11269, pp. 187–198. Springer, Cham (2019). https://doi.org/10.1007/978-3-030-12939-2_14
9. Li, H., Pan, S.J., Wang, S., Kot, A.C.: Domain generalization with adversarial feature learning. In: Proceedings of the IEEE Conference on Computer Vision and Pattern Recognition, pp. 5400–5409 (2018)
10. Matsuura, T., Harada, T.: Domain generalization using a mixture of multiple latent domains. In: Proceedings of the AAAI Conference on Artificial Intelligence, vol. 34, pp. 11749–11756 (2020)
11. Sun, B., Saenko, K.: Deep CORAL: Correlation alignment for deep domain adaptation. In: Hua, G., Jégou, H. (eds.) ECCV 2016. LNCS, vol. 9915, pp. 443–450. Springer, Cham (2016). https://doi.org/10.1007/978-3-319-49409-8_35
12. Zhao, S., Gong, M., Liu, T., Fu, H., Tao, D.: Domain generalization via entropy regularization. Adv. Neural. Inf. Process. Syst. **33**, 16096–16107 (2020)
13. Balaji, Y., Sankaranarayanan, S., Chellappa, R.: MetaReg: towards domain generalization using meta-regularization. Adv. Neural. Inf. Process. Syst. **31** (2018)
14. Li, D., Yang, Y., Song, Y.Z., Hospedales, T.M.: Learning to generalize: meta-learning for domain generalization. In: Thirty-Second AAAI Conference on Artificial Intelligence (2018)
15. Li, D., Zhang, J., Yang, Y., Liu, C., Song, Y.Z., Hospedales, T.M.: Episodic training for domain generalization. In: Proceedings of the IEEE/CVF International Conference on Computer Vision, pp. 1446–1455 (2019)
16. Zhang, M.M., Marklund, H., Dhawan, N., Gupta, A., Levine, S., Finn, C.: Adaptive risk minimization: a meta-learning approach for tackling group shift (2020)

17. Arjovsky, M., Bottou, L., Gulrajani, I., Lopez-Paz, D.: Invariant risk minimization. arXiv preprint arXiv:1907.02893 (2019)
18. Krueger, D., et al.: Out-of-distribution generalization via risk extrapolation (rex). In: International Conference on Machine Learning, pp. 5815–5826. PMLR (2021)
19. Sagawa, S., Koh, P.W., Hashimoto, T.B., Liang, P.: Distributionally robust neural networks. In: International Conference on Learning Representations (2019)
20. Shi, Y., et al.: Gradient matching for domain generalization. arXiv preprint arXiv:2104.09937 (2021)
21. Bai, H., et al.: DecAug: out-of-distribution generalization via decomposed feature representation and semantic augmentation. arXiv preprint arXiv:2012.09382 (2020)
22. Nam, H., Lee, H., Park, J., Yoon, W., Yoo, D.: Reducing domain gap by reducing style bias. In: Proceedings of the IEEE/CVF Conference on Computer Vision and Pattern Recognition, pp. 8690–8699 (2021)
23. Shankar, S., Piratla, V., Chakrabarti, S., Chaudhuri, S., Jyothi, P., Sarawagi, S.: Generalizing across domains via cross-gradient training. arXiv preprint arXiv:1804.10745 (2018)
24. Zhou, K., Yang, Y., Hospedales, T., Xiang, T.: Learning to generate novel domains for domain generalization. In: Vedaldi, A., Bischof, H., Brox, T., Frahm, J.-M. (eds.) ECCV 2020. LNCS, vol. 12361, pp. 561–578. Springer, Cham (2020). https://doi.org/10.1007/978-3-030-58517-4_33
25. Zhou, K., Yang, Y., Qiao, Y., Xiang, T.: Domain generalization with mixstyle. arXiv preprint arXiv:2104.02008 (2021)
26. Huang, X., Belongie, S.: Arbitrary style transfer in real-time with adaptive instance normalization. In: Proceedings of the IEEE International Conference on Computer Vision, pp. 1501–1510 (2017)
27. Ioffe, S., Szegedy, C.: Batch normalization: Accelerating deep network training by reducing internal covariate shift. In: International Conference on Machine Learning, pp. 448–456. PMLR (2015)
28. Ulyanov, D., Vedaldi, A., Lempitsky, V.: Improved texture networks: maximizing quality and diversity in feed-forward stylization and texture synthesis. In: Proceedings of the IEEE Conference on Computer Vision and Pattern Recognition, pp. 6924–6932 (2017)
29. Dumoulin, V., Shlens, J., Kudlur, M.: A learned representation for artistic style. arXiv preprint arXiv:1610.07629 (2016)
30. Tang, Z., Gao, Y., Zhu, Y., Zhang, Z., Li, M., Metaxas, D.N.: Crossnorm and self-norm for generalization under distribution shifts. In: Proceedings of the IEEE/CVF International Conference on Computer Vision, pp. 52–61 (2021)
31. Long, M., Cao, Y., Cao, Z., Wang, J., Jordan, M.I.: Transferable representation learning with deep adaptation networks. IEEE Trans. Pattern Anal. Mach. Intell. 41(12), 3071–3085 (2018)
32. Tzeng, E., Hoffman, J., Zhang, N., Saenko, K., Darrell, T.: Deep domain confusion: maximizing for domain invariance. arXiv preprint arXiv:1412.3474 (2014)
33. Saito, K., Watanabe, K., Ushiku, Y., Harada, T.: Maximum classifier discrepancy for unsupervised domain adaptation. In: Proceedings of the IEEE Conference on Computer Vision and Pattern Recognition, pp. 3723–3732 (2018)
34. Zhu, J.Y., Park, T., Isola, P., Efros, A.A.: Unpaired image-to-image translation using cycle-consistent adversarial networks. In: Proceedings of the IEEE International Conference on Computer Vision, pp. 2223–2232 (2017)
35. Hoffman, J., et al.: CyCADA: cycle-consistent adversarial domain adaptation. In: International Conference on Machine Learning, pp. 1989–1998. PMLR (2018)

36. Li, Y., Yuan, L., Vasconcelos, N.: Bidirectional learning for domain adaptation of semantic segmentation. In: Proceedings of the IEEE/CVF Conference on Computer Vision and Pattern Recognition, pp. 6936–6945 (2019)
37. Long, J., Shelhamer, E., Darrell, T.: Fully convolutional networks for semantic segmentation. In: Proceedings of the IEEE Conference on Computer Vision and Pattern Recognition, pp. 3431–3440 (2015)
38. Motiian, S., Piccirilli, M., Adjeroh, D.A., Doretto, G.: Unified deep supervised domain adaptation and generalization. In: Proceedings of the IEEE International Conference on Computer Vision, pp. 5715–5725 (2017)
39. Muandet, K., Balduzzi, D., Schölkopf, B.: Domain generalization via invariant feature representation. In: International Conference on Machine Learning, pp. 10–18. PMLR (2013)
40. Ghifary, M., Balduzzi, D., Kleijn, W.B., Zhang, M.: Scatter component analysis: a unified framework for domain adaptation and domain generalization. IEEE Trans. Pattern Anal. Mach. Intell. **39**(7), 1414–1430 (2016)
41. Li, H., Wang, Y., Wan, R., Wang, S., Li, T.Q., Kot, A.: Domain generalization for medical imaging classification with linear-dependency regularization. Adv. Neural. Inf. Process. Syst. **33**, 3118–3129 (2020)
42. Li, Y., Tian, X., Gong, M., Liu, Y., Liu, T., Zhang, K., Tao, D.: Deep domain generalization via conditional invariant adversarial networks. In: Proceedings of the European Conference on Computer Vision (ECCV), pp. 624–639 (2018)
43. Chattopadhyay, P., Balaji, Y., Hoffman, J.: Learning to balance specificity and invariance for in and out of domain generalization. In: Vedaldi, A., Bischof, H., Brox, T., Frahm, J.-M. (eds.) ECCV 2020. LNCS, vol. 12354, pp. 301–318. Springer, Cham (2020). https://doi.org/10.1007/978-3-030-58545-7_18
44. Li, D., Yang, Y., Song, Y.Z., Hospedales, T.M.: Deeper, broader and artier domain generalization. In: Proceedings of the IEEE International Conference on Computer Vision, pp. 5542–5550 (2017)
45. Huang, Z., Wang, H., Xing, E.P., Huang, D.: Self-challenging improves cross-domain generalization. In: Vedaldi, A., Bischof, H., Brox, T., Frahm, J.-M. (eds.) ECCV 2020. LNCS, vol. 12347, pp. 124–140. Springer, Cham (2020). https://doi.org/10.1007/978-3-030-58536-5_8
46. Ba, J.L., Kiros, J.R., Hinton, G.E.: Layer normalization. arXiv preprint arXiv:1607.06450 (2016)
47. Wu, Y., He, K.: Group normalization. In: Proceedings of the European conference on computer vision (ECCV), pp. 3–19 (2018)
48. Baker, N., Lu, H., Erlikhman, G., Kellman, P.J.: Deep convolutional networks do not classify based on global object shape. PLoS Comput. Biol. **14**(12), e1006613 (2018)
49. Geirhos, R., Rubisch, P., Michaelis, C., Bethge, M., Wichmann, F.A., Brendel, W.: ImageNet-trained CNNs are biased towards texture; increasing shape bias improves accuracy and robustness. arXiv preprint arXiv:1811.12231 (2018)
50. Hermann, K., Chen, T., Kornblith, S.: The origins and prevalence of texture bias in convolutional neural networks. Adv. Neural. Inf. Process. Syst. **33**, 19000–19015 (2020)
51. Karras, T., Laine, S., Aila, T.: A style-based generator architecture for generative adversarial networks. In: Proceedings of the IEEE/CVF Conference on Computer Vision and Pattern Recognition, pp. 4401–4410 (2019)
52. Hu, J., Shen, L., Sun, G.: Squeeze-and-excitation networks. In: Proceedings of the IEEE Conference on Computer Vision and Pattern Recognition, pp. 7132–7141 (2018)

53. Venkateswara, H., Eusebio, J., Chakraborty, S., Panchanathan, S.: Deep hashing network for unsupervised domain adaptation. In: Proceedings of the IEEE Conference on Computer Vision and Pattern Recognition, pp. 5018–5027 (2017)

54. He, K., Zhang, X., Ren, S., Sun, J.: Deep residual learning for image recognition. In: Proceedings of the IEEE Conference on Computer Vision and Pattern Recognition, pp. 770–778 (2016)

55. Volpi, R., Namkoong, H., Sener, O., Duchi, J.C., Murino, V., Savarese, S.: Generalizing to unseen domains via adversarial data augmentation. Adv. Neural Inf. Process. Syst. **31** (2018)

56. Zhang, X., Cui, P., Xu, R., Zhou, L., He, Y., Shen, Z.: Deep stable learning for out-of-distribution generalization. In: Proceedings of the IEEE/CVF Conference on Computer Vision and Pattern Recognition, pp. 5372–5382 (2021)

57. Zhang, M., Marklund, H., Dhawan, N., Gupta, A., Levine, S., Finn, C.: Adaptive risk minimization: learning to adapt to domain shift. Adv. Neural Inf. Process. Syst. **34** (2021)

58. Pezeshki, M., Kaba, O., Bengio, Y., Courville, A.C., Precup, D., Lajoie, G.: Gradient starvation: a learning proclivity in neural networks. Adv. Neural Inf. Process. Syst. **34** (2021)

59. Bucci, S., D'Innocente, A., Liao, Y., Carlucci, F.M., Caputo, B., Tommasi, T.: Self-supervised learning across domains. IEEE Trans. Pattern Anal. Mach. Intell. **44**, 5516–5528 (2021)

60. Gulrajani, I., Lopez-Paz, D.: In search of lost domain generalization. arXiv preprint arXiv:2007.01434 (2020)

61. Volk, G., Müller, S., Von Bernuth, A., Hospach, D., Bringmann, O.: Towards robust cnn-based object detection through augmentation with synthetic rain variations. In: 2019 IEEE Intelligent Transportation Systems Conference (ITSC), pp. 285–292. IEEE (2019)

Graph Representation Learning for Assisting Administrative Penalty Decisions

Xue Chen[1], Chaochao Liu[2], Shan Gao[3], Pengfei Jiao[4], Lei Du[5], and Ning Yuan[5(✉)]

[1] School of Law, Tianjin University, Tianjin 300372, China
[2] Chinese Academy of Cyberspace Studies, Beijing 100048, China
[3] School of Information Engineering, Tianjin University of Commerce, Tianjin 300134, China
[4] School of Cyberspace, Hangzhou Dianzi University, Hangzhou 310018, China
[5] Tianjin Zhongtian Huitong Technology Co., Ltd, Tianjin 300121, China
yuanning@witapex.cn

Abstract. The application of artificial intelligence opens up a new path for administrative punishment and law enforcement, which is of great significance to the modernization of the country's governance capacity. Graph representation learning has been widely used in many judicial scenarios. Most existing administrative legal documents for cause determination and penalty decision are made by means of natural language processing. Due to the many representation methods of information elements in the administrative law enforcement documents, the identification of the cause of action and the decision of punishment are difficult to make, which makes the low accuracy and lack of interpretable. In order to solve these problems, this paper constructs a knowledge graph-based information embedding method to effectively embed knowledge graphs into the network, and builds two graph convolutional neural network frameworks based on node classification and graph classification to realise intelligent assisted case determination and penalty decision based on graph representation. The experimental results show that the graph neural network-based framework is a better choice and the results of multi-task classification are significantly better than using only a single task.

Keywords: Administrative penalties · Graph neural networks · Network embedding · Complex networks

1 Introduction

In July 2017, China's President Xi Jinping gave important instructions on the reform of the judicial system, stressing that "we should follow the laws of justice and combine the deepening of the reform of the judicial system with the application of modern technology". This requires us to deepen the application of modern technology in the judicial field, increase the construction and application of information technology, promote the

Supported by the National Key R&D Program of Jiangxi, China (20212ABC03W12) and National Key R&D Program of China (2020YFC0833303).

Y. Chenggang et al. (Eds.): MobiMedia 2022, LNICST 451, pp. 316–325, 2022.
https://doi.org/10.1007/978-3-031-23902-1_24

upgrading of information technology and intelligence in judicial work, use technology to enhance judicial efficiency, and promote the overall quality and efficiency of trial and execution work.

Deep learning, one of the hottest research directions in the field of machine learning and indeed in computing and the Internet today, has in many ways surpassed previous machine learning algorithms in terms of predictive accuracy since its introduction, showing amazing advantages in image processing, natural language, audio recognition and more. In particular, in recent years, the emergence of convolutional neural networks (CNN) [1], recurrent neural networks (RNN) [2] and adversarial neural networks (GAN) [3] have made deep learning algorithms soar and have received a lot of attention from academia and industry. The emergence of CNN, RNN and GAN in recent years has led to a surge in deep learning algorithms, which have received widespread attention from both academia and industry. The application of deep learning opens up new paths for administrative punishment and law enforcement, and is of great significance to the modernization of the country's governance capacity [4, 5].

In this paper, we construct a knowledge graph-based information embedding method to effectively embed knowledge graphs into the network, and build two graph convolutional neural network frameworks based on node classification and graph classification to realize intelligent assisted case determination and penalty decision based on graph representation. In summary, the contributions of this paper are as follows:

i. We are the first to use graph learning techniques to solve cause inference and sentence penalties.
ii. We propose two frameworks for intelligent assisted penalty decisions based on node classification and graph classification, which can transform administrative legal documents into attribute graphs for adjudication decisions.
iii. Experimental results demonstrate the effectiveness of our proposed framework.

2 Related Work

Current deep learning techniques are becoming increasingly sophisticated, and their end-to-end learning has achieved significant success in text processing tasks by avoiding the error propagation problems associated with heavy feature engineering and natural language processing tools, achieving performance well beyond that of traditional methods [6, 7]. In terms of text feature representation, Mikolov et al. proposed word2vec, a method for training word vectors through neural networks [8]; Later, Joulin et al. proposed fastText [9], an efficient method for text classification and representation learning based on word vectors, using an n-gram model to more effectively represent the relationship between words before and after; The proposed pre-training model of BERT [10] pushed the text feature representation to the top. In text classification matching, Kim proposed the TextCNN approach [11] to apply convolutional neural networks to text classification tasks, which capture key n-gram-like information in sentences through one-dimensional convolutional kernels; Liu et al. proposed a network design that uses RNNs for classification problems [12], taking into account the temporal characteristics of text; A number of network variants, such as LSTM, RCNN, and network models that introduce the attention [13] mechanism, have since emerged.

In recent years, with the continuous disclosure of judicial data represented by judicial documents and the breakthrough of natural language processing technology, how to apply artificial intelligence technology in the judicial field to improve the efficiency of judicial personnel in the case processing process has gradually become a hot topic of legal technology research, and some scholars have been studying the legal text processing technology related to deep learning. Luo et al. [14] proposed a neural network approach based on an attention mechanism to integrate the law information into the charge prediction task to rationalize the charge prediction more and help improve the efficiency of the legal assistant system. Hu et al. [15] proposed an attribute-attentive offense prediction model to classify offenses according to legal attributes and manually tag relevant offense attribute information to significantly improve the prediction accuracy of low-frequency and confusing offenses. Zhong et al. [16] used directed acyclic topological graphs to model logical dependencies among multiple tasks, fusing statutes, charges and sentences into a unified judicial sentencing framework, achieving consistent and significant improvements in the effects of all tasks across multiple datasets. To our knowledge, we have not seen a relevant area where graph neural networks have been used to intelligently assist in penalty decisions.

3 The Proposed Framework

This paper proposes two frameworks for assisting penalty decisions from node classification and graph classification perspectives.

3.1 The Framework for Intelligent Assisted Penalty Decisions Based on Node Classification

This framework constructs the entire administrative penalty instrument data as an administrative penalty network, where each administrative penalty instance is a node and the connected edges between nodes are determined by the relevance of the type of offence and the fact of the offence between penalty instances. Specifically, for single task classification, the penalty category of each administrative penalty instance is used as the label of the node to train the node classification model; for multi-task classification, the penalty category and penalty basis of each administrative penalty instance are used as different labels of the node to train the multi-task model; for multi-label fusion, the penalty category and fine amount of each administrative penalty instance are fused into one label.

3.1.1 Label Generation

The label generation rules are as follows:

(1) The generation of penalty category label: In the "penalty category" field, each category is divided by a semicolon. Firstly, all the penalty categories are counted and labelled numerically. Secondly, one hot vector is generated for each administrative instrument, setting the position of the penalty category to which the administrative instrument is set to 1.

(2) Fine amount label generation: As each administrative instrument penalty instance involves a different fine amount, the fine amount interval is set for labeling. The interval division rules are shown in Table 1 and Table 2.

Table 1. Label division rules of fine amount (unbalanced label)

Amount of penalty ($ million)	Label
0	0
0–1	1
1–10	2
10–50	3
50–100	4

Table 2. Label division rules of fine amount (balanced label)

Amount of penalty ($ million)	Label
0	0 (20000 records)
0–0.1	1 (20972 records)
0.1–0.5	2 (14596 records)
0.5–10	3 (12020 records)
>10	4 (10000 records)

(3) Penalty basis label generation: In the "penalty basis" field, there are specific legal provisions. Firstly, the legal basis of all instruments are counted and labeled numerically. Secondly, one-hot vectors are generated for the legal basis of each administrative instrument, and the corresponding position of it involved in the administrative instrument is set to 1.

3.1.2 The Generation of Sentence Vectors

Two different approaches are used for vector generation at this stage. The first method is generated by word2vec; the second is generated by Bert. Firstly, using python's jieba splitting, the type of offence and the fact of offence for each instance of the administrative instrument are split; secondly, the splitting results are eliminated by stop words; finally, the results are input into the two models respectively to obtain the sentence vectors of the corresponding models.

3.1.3   Graph Structuring Stage

The cosine similarity between any two sentence vectors is first calculated from the obtained sentence vectors, and a graph adjacency matrix with weights is constructed from the similarity matrix. Where each case is treated as a node in the graph. The cosine similarity can be formulated as follows:

$$\cos(\theta) = \frac{\sum_{i=1}^{n}(x_i \times y_i)}{\sqrt{\sum_{i=1}^{n}(x_i)^2} \times \sqrt{\sum_{i=1}^{n}(y_i)^2}} \qquad (1)$$

Next, the interval corresponding to the weights is set and the resulting cosine similarity matrix is converted into an adjacency matrix with a weighted graph. The weight correspondences are shown in Table 3.

Table 3. Weight corresponding conversion table

Cosine similarity interval	Weight
0–0.5	0
0.5–0.6	1
0.6–0.7	2
0.7–0.8	3
0.8–0.9	4
0.9–1	5
1	0

3.1.4   The Stage of Graph Neural Network

We built a two-layer GCN [19] model to learn the administrative penalty document node vectors, which are then classified by a one-layer MLP. For multi-label classification, the penalty category and penalty are classified by two different MLP according to two different labels.

A two-layer *graph neural network is as follows:*

$$Z = f(X, A) = softmax(\hat{A}ReLU(\hat{A}XW^{(0)})W^{(1)}) \qquad (2)$$

where $\hat{A} = \tilde{D}^{-\frac{1}{2}}\tilde{A}\tilde{D}^{-\frac{1}{2}}$, X is the attribute matrix.

3.2   The Framework for Intelligent Assisted Penalty Decisions Based on Graph Classification

Each administrative penalty instance is constructed as a network, and the nodes of the network are phrases in the text of the type of offence and the fact of the offence in that penalty instance. The connected edges between the nodes are determined by the correlation between the phrases, and the word vectors of the phrases are used as attributes of the corresponding nodes. The penalty category of each administrative penalty instance is used as the label of the corresponding network to train the graph classification model. The final result is a graph mining-based intelligent aid for cause determination and penalty decision.

Specifically, the label generation rules and word and sentence vector generation phases are the same framework as the intelligent assisted penalty decision based on node classification, differing mainly in the graph generation and word vectorisation, and graph neural network phases.

3.2.1 Graph Generation and Word Vectorisation

Each case is constructed as a word network, with each word being a node, by calculating the PMI values between words in each case (text). The word2vec model is used to find the representation vector of each word in the word network, which is used as the attribute vector of that word. The PMI is given by the following formula.

$$PMI = log \frac{p(i,j)}{p(i)p(j)} \tag{3}$$

where $p(i,j) = \frac{\#W(i,j)}{\#W}, p(i) = \frac{\#W(i)}{\#W}$. $\#W(i)$ refers to the number of sliding windows which contain the word i, $\#W(i,j)$ is the number of sliding windows containing both the word i and the word j, $\#W$ refers to the total number of sliders in the corpus.

3.2.2 The Stage of Graph Neural Network

For graph classification, we learn graph vectors through a two-layer GCN [19] model and a readout layer [18], and then classify them through a layer of MLP.

4 Results

In this section, we use administrative penalty instrument data to verify the effectiveness of our proposed framework. The experimental results show that the graph neural network-based framework is a better choice.

4.1 Evaluation Metric

We use Accuracy [20] and Hamming [21] to evaluate our framework performance. Two metrics are defined as follows:

(1) The accuracy is defined as the proportion of the total sample that is correctly predicted, namely

$$Accuracy = \frac{(TP + TN)}{(TP + TN + FP + FN)} \tag{4}$$

(2) Hamming is used to measure the number of times a label is misclassified, i.e. a label belonging to a sample is not predicted and a label that does not belong to that sample is predicted to belong to that sample.

$$\text{Hamming}_{\text{loss}} = \frac{1}{n} \sum_{i=1}^{n} \frac{1}{m} \left| h(x_i) \Delta y_i \right| \tag{5}$$

the single-task node classification task uses two different metrics: $\text{Hamming}_{\text{loss}}$ and Accuracy. We use 10% of task metrics for $\text{Hamming}_{\text{loss}}$ and the other task metrics are for Accuracy. We use 10% of datasets for the validation and 20% for the test set. Obviously, the higher accuracy means the better performance, while the smaller the loss, the better for Hamming loss.

4.2 Parameters Setting

For the sentence vector generation phase, we follow the base settings of both papers, where word2vec [17] has a sentence vector dimension of 300 and Bert [10] has the dimension of 768. For the node classification and graph classification tasks, we set the number of iterations of the GCN [19] model to 200 and 100, respectively, and the output node vector and graph vector dimension set to 128.

4.3 Datasets

The administrative penalty instrument dataset is used in this dataset. 82,363 records are recorded in this dataset, and 71,457 data were obtained after data cleaning for single-task node classification, label fusion node classification and graph classification, and 65,374 data were used for multi-task node classification. The number of processed dataset is 71,457.

4.4 Experiment Analysis

In this section, we explore the performance of the model in three directions: single-label, multi-label and multi-label fusion.

Figure 1 gives the results of sentencing penalties for single-label administrative instruments based on node classification and graph classification. (a) and (b) correspond to the results of the node classification. The horizontal axis represents the proportion of the training set and the vertical axis corresponds to the evaluation index. As can be seen from Fig. 1, the performance of the model tends to increase as the training ratio increases. Good results were achieved for both the node classification and graph classification tasks, indicating that the graph neural network based approach is a better choice.

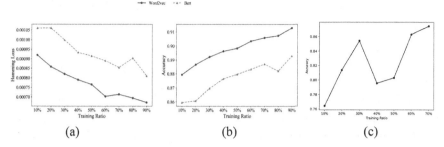

Fig. 1. Results of sentencing penalties for single-label administrative instruments

Figure 2 gives the results of multi-labelled administrative instruments based on node classification for sentencing penalties. It is obvious to see from the figure that the results for multi-task classification are significantly better than using only a single label.

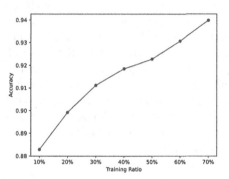

Fig. 2. Results of sentencing penalties in multi-label administrative instruments

Figure 3 shows the results of sentencing penalties in multi-label fusion administrative instruments. The three graphs correspond from left to right to label fusion node classification (unbalanced), label fusion node classification (balanced), and label fusion graph classification. When fusing the penalty category and the fine amount of the sample into one label, similar results to the single task are achieved, but when equalizing the division of the fine amount labels, the results are unsatisfactory. The equalization of the penalty amount labels caused an imbalance in the fused label categories and so led to poorer final results.

Overall, our model achieved good results for both the node classification and graph classification tasks, illustrating that a graph neural network-based approach is a better choice.

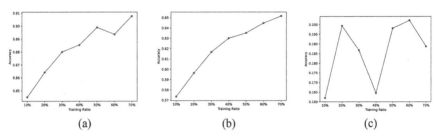

(a)   (b)   (c)

Fig. 3. Results of sentencing penalties in multi-label fusion administrative instruments

5 Conclusion

In this paper, we propose two intelligent assisted punishment frameworks, which are graph neural network frameworks based on node classification and graph classification respectively. To the best of our knowledge, this is the first time that graph learning techniques have been used to solve such problems. Overall, good results are achieved for both the node classification and graph classification tasks, indicating that the graph neural network approach is a better choice. The results for multi-task classification are significantly better than using only a single label. Similar results to the single task are achieved when fusing the penalty category and the fine amount of the sample into one label, but poorer results are achieved when the fine amount of labels are equalized. The equalization of the penalty amount labels caused an imbalance in the fused label categories and so led to poorer final results. A possible improvement solution would be to process the fused labels by removing some of the samples from a few categories or by combining them into one category.

References

1. Alzubaidi, L., Zhang, J., Humaidi, A.J., et al.: Review of deep learning: concepts, CNN architectures, challenges, applications, future directions. J. Big Data **8**(1), 1–74 (2021)
2. Nasir, J.A., Khan, O.S., Varlamis, I.: Fake news detection: a hybrid CNN-RNN based deep learning approach. Int. J. Inf. Manag. Data Insights **1**(1), 100007 (2021)
3. Zhou, F., Yang, S., Fujita, H., et al.: Deep learning fault diagnosis method based on global optimization GAN for unbalanced data. Knowl. Based Syst. **187**, 104837 (2020)
4. Raaijmakers, S.: Artificial intelligence for law enforcement: challenges and opportunities. IEEE Secur. Priv. **17**(5), 74–77 (2019)
5. Berk, R.A.: Predictive policing, and risk assessment for law enforcement. Annu. Rev. Criminol **4**, 209–236 (2021)
6. LeCun, Y., Bengio, Y., Hinton, G.: Deep learning. Nature **521**(7553), 436–444 (2015)
7. Young, T., Hazarika, D., Poria, S., et al.: Recent trends in deep learning based natural language processing. IEEE Comput. Intell. Mag. **13**(3), 55–75 (2018)
8. Mikolov, T., Sutskever, I., Chen, K., et al.: Distributed representations of words and phrases and their compositionality. In: Proceedings of the 26th International Conference on Neural Information Processing Systems, pp. 3111–3119 Lake Tahoe, NV, USA (2013)
9. Joulin, A., Grave, E., Bojanowski, P., et al.: Bag of tricks for efficient text classification. In: Proceedings of the 15th Conference of the European Chapter of The Association for Computational Linguistics, pp. 427–431, Valencia, Spain (2017)

10. Devlin, J., Chang, M.W., Lee, K., et al.: BERT: pre-training of deep bidirectional transformers for language understanding. In: Proceedings of 2019 Conference of the North American Chapter of the Association for Computational Linguistics, 4171–4186, Minneapolis, MN, USA (2019)

11. Kim, Y.: Convolutional neural networks for sentence classification. In: Proceedings of 2014 Conference on Empirical Methods in Natural Language Processing, pp. 1746–1751, Doha, Qatar (2014)

12. Liu, P.F., Qiu, X.P., Huang, X.J., et al.: Recurrent neural network for text classification with multi-task learning. In: Proceedings of the 25th International Joint Conference on Artificial Intelligence, 2873–2879, New York, NY, USA (2016)

13. Vaswani, A., Shazeer, N., Parmar, N., et al.: Attention is all you need. In: Proceedings of the 31st International Conference on Neural Information Processing Systems, pp. 5998–6008, Red Hook, NY, USA (2017)

14. Luo, B.F., Feng, Y.S., Xu, J.B., et al.: Learning to predict charges for criminal cases with legal basis. In: Proceedings of 2017 Conference on Empirical Methods in Natural Language Processing, pp. 2727–2736, Copenhagen, Denmark (2017)

15. Hu, Z.K., Li, X., Tu, C.C., et al.: Few-shot charge prediction with discriminative legal attributes. In: Proceedings of the 27th International Conference on Computational Linguistics, pp. 487–498, Santa Fe, NM, USA (2018)

16. Zhong, H.X., Guo, Z.P., Tu, C.C., et al.: Legal judgment prediction via topological learning. In: Proceedings of 2018 Conference on Empirical Methods in Natural Language Processing, pp. 3540–3549, Brussels, Belgium (2018)

17. Goldberg, Y., Levy, O.: word2vec explained: deriving Mikolov et al.'s negative-sampling word-embedding method. arXiv preprint. arXiv:1402.3722 (2014)

18. Yao, L., Mao, C., Luo, Y.: Graph convolutional networks for text classification. In: Proceedings of the AAAI conference on artificial intelligence, vol. 33, no. 1, pp. 7370–7377 (2019)

19. Kipf, T.N., Welling, M.: Semi-supervised classification with graph convolutional networks. arXiv preprint. arXiv:1609.02907 (2016)

20. Kaya, İ, Kahraman, C.: Development of fuzzy process accuracy index for decision making problems. Inf. Sci. **180**(6), 861–872 (2010)

21. Butucea, C., Ndaoud, M., Stepanova, N.A., et al.: Variable selection with Hamming loss. Ann. Stat. **46**(5), 1837–1875 (2018)

Object Recognition and Detection

A Robust Signal Modulation Recognition Method Against Black-Box Detection Attack

Zhihui An, Peihan Qi$^{(\boxtimes)}$, Xiaoyu Zhou, and Yongchao Meng

State Key Laboratory of Integrated Service Networks, Xidian University,
Xi'an 710071, China
phqi@xidian.edu.cn

Abstract. Deep learning (DL) models have been widely used in the recognition of modulation types with outstanding recognition effects. With the improvement of modulation recognition, the perturbation from the attacker has also changed from adding physical interference to the original signal to an adversarial attack based on the neural network. The adversarial attack adding subtle perturbation which is imperceptible to the human eye, makes the neural network produce false recognition results with high confidence. This kind of perturbation is hard to be reflected in spectrogram or constellation diagram, so it is seriously destructive to the modulation recognition algorithm based on neural networks. In response to adversarial attacks, we propose a modulation recognition method against black-box detection attacks. In this paper knowledge distillation is used to defend against the attack that comes from the attacker's black-box detection. The experimental results demonstrated that the defense method constructed in this paper can improve the ability to defend adversarial samples and keep the recognition accuracy of the recognition network. This article aims at improving the robustness of the network and constructing a robust modulation recognition network.

Keywords: Modulation recognition · Adversarial attack · Knowledge distillation · Robust network

1 Introduction

With the continuous development of modern communication systems, the signal environment is becoming more and more complex. In such a complex scenario, human comprehension ability can neither complete the perception of large amounts of data, nor can its comprehension speed match the update speed of information, which can easily cause a series of key goals and situation perception errors or untimely perception problem.

This work was supported in part by the National Natural Science Foundation of China under Grant No. 62171334.

Y. Chenggang et al. (Eds.): MobiMedia 2022, LNICST 451, pp. 329–339, 2022.
https://doi.org/10.1007/978-3-031-23902-1_25

With the rapid development of artificial intelligence in recent years, deep learning as one of its core technologies has been widely used in many fields and has already demonstrated breakthrough progress in signal recognition technology [1]. O'Shea et al. [1] proposed to use the convolutional neural network (CNN) structure for automatic modulation classification of 11 modulation signals and to automatically learn and classify the originally collected signals. Peng et al. [2] proposed a constellation diagram (CD) to transform a time-series IQ signal into an image for adopting AlexNet and GoogLeNet which have a better performance on image classification. N. E. West and T. O'Shea [3] studied the effects of convolution kernel size, network depth, and the number of neurons in each layer of convolution neural network on modulation classification performance, and compared convolution neural network, residual network and convolution-based long short-term memory network (LSTM) for modulation classification. Zhang et al. [4] proposed a CNN-LSTM structure based on a dual-stream structure that can explore the feature interaction and spatial-temporal properties of radio signals.

However, due to the interpretability of neural networks and a large number of non-linear high-dimensional operations, neural networks often make false judgments with high confidence when faced with some subtle perturbation that is hardly detectable by the human eye. In response to this phenomenon, Christian Szegedy et al. [6] proposed the concept of adversarial samples. They used the L-BFGS method to generate adversarial examples to solve general target problems. Goodfellow et al. [7] proposed the Fast Gradient Sign Method (FGSM) which is used to fool CNN-based classification networks. FGSM generates adversarial examples by computing the gradient of the neural network loss function knowledge distillation. Kurakin et al. [8] applied adversarial examples to the physical world. They extended the FGSM by running finer optimizations (smaller changes) for multiple iterations. Papernot et al. [9] proposed Jacobian-based saliency map attack (JSMA). This approach produces adversarial perturbations by forwarding derivatives. Dezfooli et al. [13] proposed the DeepFool algorithm to find the closest distance from the original input to the adversarial sample decision boundary.

Research on defending adversarial samples has achieved results in some fields, such as image classification, speech recognition, target detection, etc. Using adversarial examples for training is one of the strategies to improve the robustness of neural networks. Goodfellow et al. use adversarial examples during training [7]. They will generate adversarial examples at every step of the training and send them into the training set. From the results, adversarial training can improve the robustness of the network, but an expanded training set cannot defend against black-box attacks. Metzen et al. [14] created a detector for adversarial examples as an auxiliary network to the original neural network.

In order to reduce the influence of adversarial samples on the signal modulation recognition network and improve the robustness of the network, this paper proposes a method based on knowledge distillation to update the parameters of the signal modulation recognition network through the teacher model and the student model to achieve the effect of against black-box detection attack. The research data in this paper is drawn from the public data set RML2016.10a. The student network uses the VTCNN2, and the teacher network uses a 16-layer ResNet network. The results showed that the teacher network has a high recognition accuracy for the adversarial samples. After knowledge distillation and parameter transfer, the recognition accuracy of the signal modulation recognition network in adversarial samples has increased from 0.37 to 0.69 (SNR = 10 dB). It can be seen that the method proposed in this paper has excellent defensive capabilities in defending black-box detection attacks. In addition, the methods mentioned in this paper also have a generalization ability and show good defensive capabilities against adversarial samples generated in different ways.

2   Methodology

2.1   Black-Box Detection Attack

Adversarial attacks can be divided into black-box attacks and white-box attacks. The difference between the two is the degree of knowledge acquisition of the target model. In practical applications, attackers can't directly obtain all the knowledge of the target model but obtain the relevant parameters of the target model by accessing the target model a limited number of times. In this paper, we set up a black-box detection attack, assuming that the attacker has detected the recognition network structure of the target model through previous access, and trained the attack samples on the same recognition network structure. In other words, the attacker knows the network structure of the modulation recognition network and trains the modulation recognition network. The adversarial sample is generated according to the trained modulation recognition network to attack the target model.

In the experiment, the same network structure and training set as the modulation recognition network is used to train the attacker's network, and the FGSM method is used to generate adversarial samples on the attacker's network to simulate the black-box detection attack.

2.2   Defensive Distillation

Knowledge distillation methods are widely used in network pruning and network structure compression. Taking advantage of its property of transferring knowledge from complex networks to simple networks, knowledge distillation is applied to defend against black-box detection attacks. The black-box detection attack considers that the attacker knows the structure of the modulation recognition network, and the attacker achieves the purpose of simulating the network performance by training the attack network with the same structure. On the premise of keeping the structure of the modulation recognition network unchanged, defensive distillation transfers the knowledge of the complex network to the modulation recognition network through distillation, so that it can achieve the performance of the complex network under the condition of having a simple structure. Thereby preventing black-box detection attacks from attackers.

The teacher network and the student network are also constructed in the defense distillation. The structure of the teacher network is complex and the performance is better, but due to the long training time and the huge structure, it is not easy to deploy. The student network has a simpler structure and is convenient for training. In this paper, the student network adopts the same network structure as the modulation recognition network.

$$q_i = \left[\frac{\exp(Z_i/T)}{\sum_{j=0}^{N-1} \exp(Z_j/T)} \right]_{i \in 0,\cdots,N-1} \tag{1}$$

In the formula, q_i is the current category classification probability, N represents N categories, and Z_i is the logits output of the current category into the activation function. The process of defensive distillation can be described as using the training set and the hard labels to train the teacher network, and after the training is completed, the teacher network is used to label the corresponding soft labels for the training data. The specific method for generating soft labels is to introduce a temperature function T into the softmax layer of the teacher network. When T = 1, it is the original softmax function. The larger T is, the softer the distribution between various classes output by the function is. Compared with hard labels, soft labels can not only classify the data correctly but also reflect the similarity between categories.

2.3   Framework of Teacher Network and Student Network

The structure of the student network and teacher network constructed in the process of knowledge distillation in this paper is shown in Fig. 1 and Fig. 2. We designed a teacher network for modulation recognition, and the student network is VTCNN2.

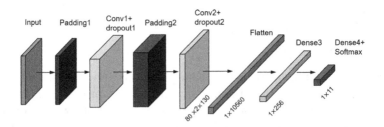

Fig. 1. The structure of the student network (VTCNN2)

The structure of teacher network is designed as follows:

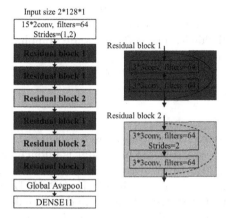

Fig. 2. The structure of the teacher network

The first convolutional layer performs simple preliminary feature extraction on the signal data input to the network and feeds the feature map into the ResNet blocks.

We add ResNet blocks to further extract the features of the signal. ResNet introduces jump connections between different convolutional layers, which can better learn data features than simple convolutional layers.

The function of the fully connected (FC) layer is to output the final recognition result according to the feature map extracted by the ResNet blocks. Here we rewrite the activation function softmax, and introduce the temperature parameter T into it, so as to achieve the effect of generating soft labels by the teacher network.

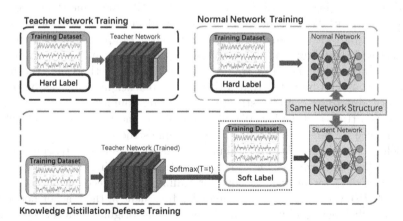

Fig. 3. Knowledge distillation defense training process and normal network training process

The knowledge distillation defense training process and the normal network training process are shown in Fig. 3. The knowledge distillation defense training uses datasets and hard labels to train a teacher network with a complex structure. After the teacher network training is completed, the teacher network is used to generate soft labels. The soft labels are combined with the dataset to retrain the student network. The normal training process is to directly use the data set and hard labels to train the recognition network.

2.4 Datasets

We chose the open-source simulation dataset RADIOML 2016.10A designed by DeepSiG. This dataset was selected because it is publicly available and is based on CNN. RADIOML 2016.10A consists of modulation signals at different SNRs, including eight kinds of digital signals: 8PSK, QPSK, BPSK, GFSK, CPFSK, PAM4, QAM16, and QAM64, and three kinds of analog signals: wide band frequency modulation (WBFM), amplitude modulation-double side band (AM-DSB), and amplitude modulation-single side band (AM-SSB). The dataset generates a total of 220 000 data samples with 20 kinds of SNRs, from 18 to–20 dB in steps of 2 dB, which means 2000 samples for each signal category. We used 80% of the samples as the training set and the rest samples as the test set. Each signal vector consists of an in-phase component and an orthogonal component, and each component has a length of 128.

3   Experiments

To analyze the performance of the proposed defense method, we conduct a series of comparative experiments. In this section, the complex network in the distillation step is called the teacher network, and the simple network model is called the student network. In the comparative experiments, the recognition network without defense training is called a normal network (with the same structure as the student network). We call the samples without adversarial attacks clean samples and the samples with adversarial attacks adversarial samples (FGSM-Adversarial Samples and BIM-Adversarial Samples). The main performance improvement is between the student network trained by the defense method and the normal network. It should be noted that although the teacher network has better performance, due to its complex structure and a large number of parameters, it is not easy to train and deploy. We only care about the improvement of network performance by defense methods under a simple structure.

Before conducting defense training, we need to select a teacher network with excellent performance for knowledge distillation. Using the teacher network model and data set proposed above for training, good recognition accuracy is obtained. Use the temperature parameter adjustment in the teacher network to generate soft labels, and use the soft labels and the original data set to train the student network. Figure 4 shows the recognition effect of the teacher network on

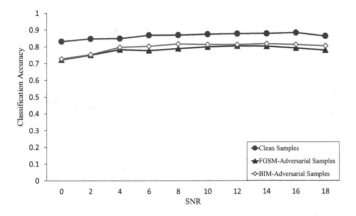

Fig. 4. Recognition accuracy of teacher network on clean samples and adversarial samples

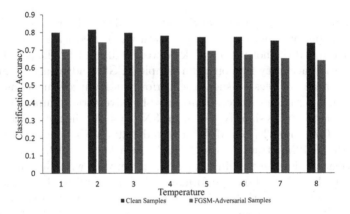

Fig. 5. The recognition accuracy of the student network on clean samples and adversarial samples (SNR = 10 dB) at different temperatures

clean samples and adversarial samples. It can be seen that the teacher network has a good recognition effect on both clean data and adversarial samples.

Next, we determine how changes in the temperature parameter affect the knowledge distillation defense effect. We use 10 dB data to conduct experiments, adjust the parameter T in the teacher network, generate different soft labels to train the student network, and compare the recognition performance of the student network under the soft label training generated by different temperature parameters. It can be seen from Fig. 5 that when the temperature T = 2, the performance of the student network is slightly improved, and as the temperature increases, the performance begins to decline.

So we decided to perform knowledge distillation defense when the temperature parameter T = 2. We used FGSM and BIM to generate adversarial samples,

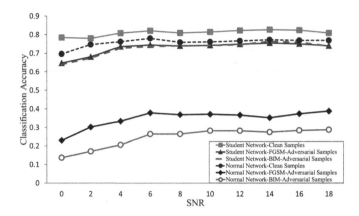

Fig. 6. The performance of student network and normal network on clean samples and adversarial samples

and the perturbation parameter of the adversarial samples was set to 0.001. We compare the performance of the student network trained with knowledge distillation defense and the normal network between 0 dB and 18 dB, mainly through the recognition accuracy rate on clean samples, FGSM adversarial samples, and BIM adversarial samples to show the performance improvement, as shown in Fig. 6, when the student network is attacked by adversarial samples, the recognition performance drops sharply. When the SNR = 4 dB, the recognition accuracy drops from 0.76 to 0.33 (FGSM-Attack) and 0.20 (BIM-Attack). It drops from 0.77 to 0.40 (FGSM-Attack) and 0.29 (BIM-Attack) at 18 dB. After the knowledge distillation defense training, the student network with the same structure as the normal network shows performance improvement on the same test samples. The student network has demonstrated good defense capabilities. When the SNR = 4 dB, the recognition accuracy is improved to 0.73 (FGSM-Attack) and 0.72 (BIM-Attack), and when the SNR = 18 dB, the recognition accuracy is 0.74 (FGSM-Attack) and 0.74 (BIM-Attack). Not only in the defense of adversarial samples, but also on clean samples, the recognition accuracy of the student network is also improved.

In order to further understand the positive impact of the knowledge distillation defense method on the recognition results, we plot the confusion matrix of 11 recognition results of the student network and the normal network when SNR = 4 dB. As shown in Fig. 7. From Fig. 7a, it can be seen that when not attacked by adversarial examples, the normal network produces serious confusion between analog signals 8PSK and QPSK, AM-DSB and WBFM, and between digital signals QAM16 and QAM64. After the normal network is attacked by adversarial samples, as shown in Figs. 7b and 7c, the confusion matrix is very chaotic, and the classification accuracy of the normal network is seriously affected. And the damage caused by BIM is even more serious. Figure 7d shows the case where the student network is not attacked by adversarial examples, and Fig. 7e and 7f are the confusion matrices of the student network under the attack of adversarial

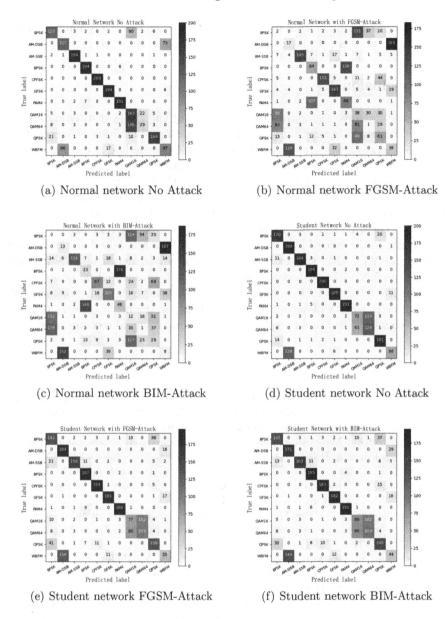

(a) Normal network No Attack

(b) Normal network FGSM-Attack

(c) Normal network BIM-Attack

(d) Student network No Attack

(e) Student network FGSM-Attack

(f) Student network BIM-Attack

Fig. 7. Confusion matrix of student network and normal network

examples. It can be seen that when there is no attack, the student network guarantees the classification accuracy with a slight improvement. Except for QAM16 and QAM64, the student network shows a dramatic improvement in classification accuracy when attacked by adversarial examples. Figure 7 confirms that the knowledge distillation defense method can exhibit a relatively prominent defense capability in the field of electromagnetic signal modulation recognition.

4 Conclusion

In this work, we investigate the defense method of knowledge distillation against adversarial attacks in the field of electromagnetic signal modulation recognition. The effectiveness of the knowledge distillation defense method is verified through experiments, and the optimal temperature is obtained by adjusting the temperature parameters, it is not found that the higher the temperature, the softer the label, the better the student's network learning effect. Using the knowledge distillation method can resist the black-box detection attack of the attacker on the premise of ensuring that our recognition network structure remains unchanged. Specifically, in the face of FGSM-Attack and BIM-Attack, based on the network structure of VTCNN2, the distribution of accuracy increases by 40% (FGSM-Attack) and 52% (BIM-Attack) when SNR = 4 dB. It also slightly improves the performance of the network on clean samples. We believe that our work will help improve the reliability of deep learning algorithms in the field of electromagnetic signal recognition and build a robust electromagnetic signal recognition system.

References

1. O'Shea, T.J., Corgan, J., Clancy, T.C.: Convolutional radio modulation recognition networks. In: Jayne, C., Iliadis, L. (eds.) EANN 2016. CCIS, vol. 629, pp. 213–226. Springer, Cham (2016). https://doi.org/10.1007/978-3-319-44188-7_16
2. Peng, S., et al.: Modulation classification based on signal constellation diagrams and deep learning. IEEE Trans. Neural Netw. Learn. Syst. 30(3), 718–727 (2019)
3. West, N.E., O'Shea, T.: Deep architectures for modulation recognition. In: Proceedings of the IEEE International Symposium on Dynamic Spectrum Access Networks (DySPAN), Piscataway, NJ, USA, pp. 1–6 (2017)
4. Zhang, Z., Luo, H., Wang, C., Gan, C., Xiang, Y.: Automatic modulation classification using CNN-LSTM based dual-stream structure. IEEE Trans. Veh. Technol. 69(11), 13 521–13 531 (2020)
5. Rajendran, S., Meert, W., Giustiniano, D., Lenders, V., Pollin, S.: Deep learning models for wireless signal classification with distributed low-cost spectrum sensors. IEEE Trans. Cogn. Commun. Netw. 4(3), 433–445 (2018)
6. Szegedy, C., et al.: Intriguing properties of neural networks (2013). https://arxiv.org/abs/1312.6199
7. Goodfellow, I., Shlens, J., Szegedyn, C.: Explaining and harnessing adversarial examples. In: Proceedinngs of the International Conference on Learning Representations, pp. 189–199 (2015)
8. Kurakin, A., Goodfellow, I., Bengio, S.: Adversarial examples in the physical world (2016). https://arxiv.org/abs/1607.02533
9. Papernot, N., McDaniel, P., Jha, S., Fredrikson, M., Celik, Z.B., Swami, A.: The limitations of deep learning in adversarial settings. Proceedings of the IEEE European Symposium on Security and Privacy, vol. 1, no. 1, pp. 372–387 (2016)

10. Zhou, R., Liu, F., Gravelle, C.W.: Deep learning for modulation recognition: a survey with a demonstration. Behav. Ecol. Sociobiol. **8**, 67366–67376 (2020)
11. Chen, P., Zhang, H., Sharma, Y., Yi, J., Hsieh, C.-J.: ZOO: zeroth order optimization based black-box attacks to deep neural networks without training substitute models (2017). https://arxiv.org/abs/1708.03999
12. Su, J., Vargas, D.V., Kouichi, S.: One pixel attack for fooling deep neural networks (2017). https://arxiv.org/abs/1710.08864
13. Dezfooli, S.M., Fawzi, A., Frossard, P.: DeepFool: a simple and accurate method to fool deep neural networks. In: Proceedings of the IEEE Conference on Computer Vision and Pattern Recognition, vol. 1, no. 1, pp. 2574–2582 (2016)
14. Metzen, J.H., Genewein, T., Fischer, V., Bischoff, B.: On detecting adversarial perturbations. In: Proceedings of the ICLR (2017). https://openreview.net/pdf?id=SJzCSf9xg
15. Zagoruyko, S., Komodakis, N.: Paying more attention to attention: improving the performance of convolutional neural networks via attention transfer. In: Proceedings of the International Conference on Learning Representation, pp. 1–13 (2017)
16. Yim, J., Joo, D., Bae, J., Kim, J.: A gift from knowledge distillation: fast optimization, network minimization and transfer learning. In: Proceedings of the IEEE Conference on Computer Vision and Pattern Recognition, pp. 7130–7138 (2017)

Electric Energy Meter Information Recognition System Based on Deep Learning

Shuai Gao⬮, Bo Ning$^{(\boxtimes)}$⬮, and Nan Jiang⬮

Dalian Maritime University, Dalian 116000, LN, China
ningbo@dlmu.edu.cn

Abstract. A new type of electric energy meter information recognition system based on deep learning is proposed. The system is mainly divided into OCR character recognition system and electric meter information verification system. OCR character recognition system mainly includes two parts: character detection and character recognition. The text detection uses the CTPN model, and the text recognition uses the CRNN network in deep learning for recognition, and then uses the CTC loss function for sequence processing to improve the accuracy of text recognition. Through the RCTW-17 data set training, an OCR text recognition system with high accuracy, strong stability and fast speed is obtained. The identified results are automatically checked with the information in the background database, and finally an electric energy meter information identification system is obtained. The verification of the RCTW-17 data set and the actual photo identification of the electric energy meter prove the effectiveness of this method.

Keywords: OCR technology · CTPN network · CRNN network · Electric energy meter information recognition

1 Introduction

The identification of electric energy meter information has always been a very important issue. With the rapid development of my country's economy, more and more places need to use electric energy, which is particularly important for the management of electric energy meters. The electric energy meter plays a very important role as an instrument for measuring electric energy. The method of manually copying the electric energy meter is inefficient and prone to errors. Therefore, it is extremely important to automatically identify the electric energy meter data. This method can not only save labor costs, but also it can also improve the accuracy and save time. The methods of identifying the data of electric energy meters can be roughly divided into two categories. One is the method of positioning and identifying according to the characteristics of artificial design [1–4]. Shape features for digital recognition. Yang Juan [5] completed the identification of electric energy meter numbers through image preprocessing, target positioning, and identification, but the positioning accuracy in complex scenes is low and the robustness is insufficient. Wang Chen et al. [6] used the TM-MSER algorithm to complete the

Y. Chenggang et al. (Eds.): MobiMedia 2022, LNICST 451, pp. 340–349, 2022.
https://doi.org/10.1007/978-3-031-23902-1_26

positioning and segmentation of digital instruments. Another method is to use a deep learning framework, using models such as convolutional neural networks, to extract features from images, and then perform detection and recognition to finally obtain data. Wu Binbin [7] et al. combined template matching and deep neural network technology, made full use of template calibration information, turned the indication detection under complex conditions into simple and effective isometric segmentation, and then identified, with better robustness. Li Ming et al. [8] used connected domain segmentation and localization and BP neural network for digit recognition. Chen Ying [9] and others proposed the Enhanced Faster R-RCNN network by using the features in the Faster-RCNN network, which improved the accuracy in identifying the information of the electric energy meter. Gong An [10] et al. proposed a recognition method of electric energy representation based on YOLOv3 network, which showed that this method has higher localization accuracy and recognition accuracy. It can be seen from the above literature that most of the digital recognition algorithms for electric energy meters are based on traditional image processing methods. However, the recognition accuracy of electric energy meters in complex scenarios is low, and there is a problem of insufficient robustness. This paper is based on deep learning. The method proposes a combination of CTPN [11] text detection model and CRNN [12] text recognition model to realize the digital recognition algorithm of electric energy meter, which improves the robustness and accuracy of the algorithm. After identification, the identified data will be transferred to the background database for comparison. If there is an electric meter of this type, the data will be updated. If not, a new data will be inserted to obtain a complete electric energy information table. It is hoped that in the future, the content of the electric energy meter can be identified by uploading photos to the system through mobile phones, which will benefit the society. The flow chart of the whole system is shown in Fig. 1:

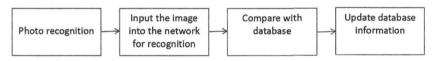

Fig. 1. System flow chart

2 OCR Text Detection Method

This paper mainly introduces the basic process of CTPN network detection and the basic structure of the network.

2.1 The Basic Process of CTPN Network Detection

The proposal of CTPN is based on the fact that text is usually written horizontally from left to right, and the width between words is roughly the same. Fixed width, to detect text height. It's essentially an RPN method that stitches together the detected boxes. Due to the above three characteristics, this model is particularly suitable for information identification of electric energy meters.

The specific process is as follows: First, the feature extraction is carried out through the backbone network VGG16, and the Conv5 layer outputs the feature map of N × C × H × W. Since the convolutional network of VGG16 has a cumulative stride of 16 after 4 pooling layers. That is, one pixel in the feature map output by the Conv5 layer corresponds to 16 pixels of the original image. Then do a 3 × 3 sliding window on Conv5, that is, each point is combined with the surrounding 3 × 3 area features to obtain a feature vector of length 3 × 3 × C. The final output is a feature map of N × 9C × H × W, which is still the spatial feature learned by CNN. Then continue to reshape the feature map output in the previous step:

$$\text{Reshape:} \quad N \times 9C \times H \times W(NH) \times W \times 9C \tag{1}$$

Then feed the Bi-LSTM with a data stream of Batch = NH and maximum time length Tmax = W, and learn the sequence features of each row. The Bi-LSTM output is (NH) × W × 256, which is then reshaped to restore the shape:

$$\text{Reshape:} \quad (NH) \times W \times 256 \, N \times 256 \times H \times W \tag{2}$$

This feature includes both spatial features and sequence features learned by Bi-LSTM. Then through the fully connected layer, it becomes a feature of N × 512 × H × W. Finally, through an RPN network similar to Faster RCNN, the text detection frame is obtained.

Since CTPN is aimed at the detection of horizontally arranged text, it adopts a set of (10) fixed reference frames of equal width to locate the text position. The fixed reference frame width and height are:

$$\text{Widths} = [16] \tag{3}$$

$$\text{Heights} = [11, 16, 23, 33, 48, 68, 97, 139, 198, 283] \tag{4}$$

Since CTPN uses the VGG16 model to extract features, the width and height of the Conv5 feature map are 1/16 of the width and height of the input original image. At the same time, the fully connected layer is equal to the width and height of Conv5. CTPN is equipped with 10 above-mentioned fixed reference frames for each point of the feature map of the fully connected layer. After obtaining the fixed reference frame, similar to Faster R-CNN, CTPN will do the following processing: use Softmax to determine whether the fixed reference frame contains text, That is, a positive fixed reference frame with a large Softmax score is selected; then the center y-coordinate and height of the fixed reference frame containing the text are corrected using bounding box regression.

$$Vc = \left(C_y - C_y^a\right)/h^a \tag{5}$$

$$V_h = \log\left(\frac{h}{h^a}\right) \tag{6}$$

$$V_c^* = \left(C_y^* - C_y^a\right)/h^a \tag{7}$$

$$V_h^* = \log\left(\frac{h^*}{h^a}\right) \tag{8}$$

Equation (5) and (6) are the coordinates of the regression prediction; C_y^a, h^a is the center y coordinate and height of the fixed reference frame, and V_c^*, V_h^* is the Ground Truth. After the fixed reference frame is processed by the above Softmax and bounding box regression, a set of vertical strip text detection boxes will be obtained. Subsequent text detection boxes only need to be connected together with the text line construction algorithm to obtain the text position.

The Loss function is:

$$\text{Loss}(S_i, V_j, O_k) = \frac{1}{N_s}\sum_i L_s^{cls}(S_i, S_I^*) + \frac{\lambda_1}{N_v}\sum_j L_v^{reg}(v_j, v_j^*) + \frac{\lambda_2}{N_o}\sum_k L_o^{reg}(O_k, O_k^*) \tag{9}$$

The main three errors of the above loss function come from the classification error of the fixed reference frame and the background, the vertical coordinate offset regression error, and the correction error of the fixed reference frame x at the boundary.

Network basic structure (Fig. 2):

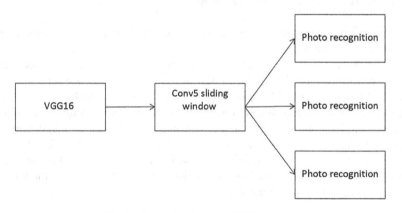

Fig. 2. Basic structure of CTPN network

Applied to the electric energy meter system proposed in this paper, the CTPN algorithm is used for segmentation detection, and the result is shown in Fig. 3:

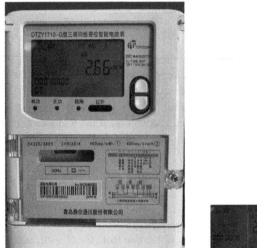 

Fig. 3. Text segmentation

3   OCR Text Recognition Method

This paper mainly introduces the basic process of CRNN network recognition and the basic structure of the network.

The CRNN model has many advantages. It can learn directly from sequence labels. Instead of labeling each character, you only need to label a sequence for a picture. For example, if the picture is "22.6 Kwh", the label is "22.6 Kwh" without having to label each character individually. Image features extracted by CNN. Using the input feature sequence of RNN training, the output is a sequence label. There is no length limit on the images to be trained, but normalize the height of the images. There are few parameters. Although CNN and RNN are combined, a loss function (CTC LOSS) is used for joint training in the end to achieve end-to-end training, which can directly get the final result we want and the recognition time is short.

3.1   The CRNN Network is Mainly Divided into Three Modules

1. Convolution module: The backbone network is an improved version based on the VGG model.
2. Recurrent network module: It consists of two steps of feature sequence extraction and two BLSTM training. B is bidirectional and can extract model information in two directions, not just one. The BLSTM of CRNN has two layers, and two layers can obtain higher-level sequence features.
3. Transcription module, the transcription module is mainly a CTC layer, and its main function is to train the loss function of the network.

3.2   The Specific Implementation Steps of CRNN

Feature sequence extraction is performed in the first step of the recurrent network module in the above figure. This is done by scaling the images to the same height. Then each feature vector of the feature sequence is generated from left to right in columns on the feature map. This means that the ith feature vector is the ith concatenation of all feature maps, and the width of each column is fixed to a single pixel in our setup. This approach can make the feature sequence in order, and can better perform the following cyclic network operations.

Transcription is the process of integrating all possible outcomes of the feature sequence predicted by the LSTM network into the final outcome. A CTC model is connected at the end of the bidirectional LSTM network to achieve end-to-end identification. The CTC model is connected to time classification. CTC can perform end-to-end training without requiring training data alignment and one-by-one labeling, and directly output sequence results of indeterminate lengths. CTC is generally connected in the last layer of the RNN network for sequence learning and training. For a sequence of length T, each sample point t (t is much larger than T) will output a softmax vector in the last layer of the RNN network, representing the predicted probability of the sample point, and these probabilities of all sample points are transmitted to After the CTC model, the most likely label is output, and after removing spaces and deduplication, the final sequence label can be obtained, that is, our final recognition result.

The structure of the CRNN model is shown in Fig. 4:

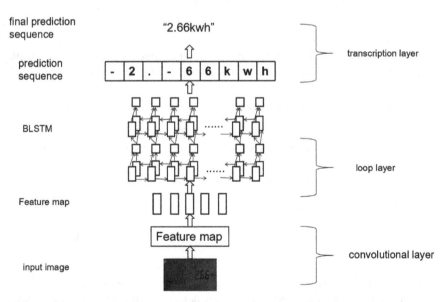

Fig. 4. CRNN model structure diagram

4 Experiment

4.1 Evaluation Indicators

The evaluation metrics for target detection are mAP (mean average precision) and accuracy. Before calculating mAP, it is necessary to understand the concepts of TP, TN, FP and FN. TP (true positives) refers to the predicted positive samples and matches the real results, TN (true negatives) refers to the predicted negative samples and matches the real results, FP (false positives) refers to predicting positive samples but does not match the real results, FN (false negatives) refers to predicting negative samples but does not match the real results. To judge whether it is consistent with the real results, it is necessary to obtain the intersection ratio (IoU) between the ground truthbox and the prediction box. When the IoU is greater than the set threshold (threshold_iou is generally set to 0.5), it means that the prediction box is the ground truth box, otherwise it means that the prediction box is the same as the predicted box. The actual results do not match.

The calculation of each category in object detection is shown in Eq. 10

$$precision_{class} = \frac{TP}{TP + FP} \tag{10}$$

The calculation formula of mAP is shown in 11, n represents the number of categories in target detection, and i represents the current category.

$$mAP = \frac{1}{n} * \sum_{t=0}^{n} precision_i \tag{11}$$

The calculation formula of accuracy is shown in Eq. 12

$$accuracy = \frac{TP + TN}{TP + TN + FP + FN} \tag{12}$$

The evaluation standard of classification is the accuracy rate, and the calculation method is the ratio of the number of correctly classified samples to the total number of samples.

4.2 Electric Energy Meter Detection

Table 1. Electric energy meter test results

Data set	Number of samples	CTPN	
		mAP	Accuracy
Test set	244	96.64%	97.12%
Training set	12034	93.34%	91.33%

Table 1 shows the experimental results of the electric energy meter detection. It can be seen from Table 1 that the mAP and accuracy detected by the electric energy meter are more than 91%, indicating that most of the images have detected the LCD screen area. The data set used in the detection process is 244 photos focusing on single-phase electric energy meters and three-phase electric energy meters taken from different angles. After experimental tests, as shown in Figs. 5 and 6, good results can be achieved.

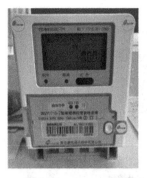

Fig. 5. Electric energy meter pictures taken from different angles

Fig. 6. Processed grayscale image and detection frame

4.3 Electric Energy Meter Identification

Table 2. Electric energy meter identification results

Data set	Number of samples	CTPN	
		mAP	Accuracy
Test set	244	92.42%	93.52%
Training set	12034	94.89%	92.73%

Table 2 shows the experimental results of digital recognition. It can be seen from Table 2 that the accuracy of digital recognition in the test set and training set is above 92%, and the number of samples is relatively large, which can represent the recognition results of electric energy meters taken from different angles, but A very small part of the recognition results have problems. The main reasons for the low accuracy in the test set are some blurred images, reflections and other problems. The recognition result is shown in Fig. 7.

Fig. 7. Picture of a successfully detected electric energy meter

4.4 Model Comparison

Table 3. Model Comparison Results

Model	mPA	Accuracy
EAST + CRNN	89.24%	88.45%
EAST + ATTENTION	84.95%	86.98%
SEGLINK + CRNN	90.94%	92.33%
SEGLINK + ATTENTION	85.26%	91.25%
FTSN + CRNN	93.36%	90.15%
FTSN + ATTENTION	83.94%	85.88%
CTPN + CRNN	**94.52%**	**94.26%**
CTPN + ATTENTION	92.72%	93.18%

Table 3 presents the comparison of eight models. Through the comparison experiment, it can be seen that the CTPN + CRNN model has the best effect. The model in this paper can effectively identify the data in the electric energy meter, so as to achieve the function of collecting electricity consumption information.

5   Conclusion

In order to improve the accuracy of automatic identification of electric energy meters, a text detection and recognition model based on CTPN + CRNN network is constructed in this paper. Faster and more robust, it can detect and identify pictures of electric energy meters with high complexity taken from different angles, which has certain feasibility.

References

1. Zhang, Z.: Research on the reading system of electric energy meter based on digital image recognition. Master's thesis. Beijing Jiaotong University, Beijing (2010)
2. Bei, C.: Research on image recognition technology of single-phase electricity meter. Master's Thesis. Nanjing University of Science and Technology, Nanjing (2014)
3. Zhang, X.: Research and implementation of digital image recognition technology of electric energy meter. Master's Thesis. Shanghai Jiaotong University, Shanghai (2007)
4. Ling, L.: Recognition technology of electric energy representation number based on image processing. In: Proceedings of the 2012 Academic Exchange Conference of the Electric Power System Automation Professional Committee of the Chinese Society of Electrical Engineering, pp. 1–5. Xiamen, China (2012)
5. Yang, J.: Research and Implementation of Electric Energy Meter Image Recognition Technology based on Digital Image Processing. Nanjing University of Science and Technology, Nanjing (2012)
6. Wang, C., et al.: Research on image-based digital instrument character wheel positioning and segmentation algorithm. Electron. Measur. Technol. **09**, 139–142 (2017)
7. Wu, B., Zhu, Y., Ge, Y., Lv, Y.: Information recognition of electric energy meter combined with template matching and deep neural network. Electr. Measur. Instrum. 1–9 (2021)
8. Li, M., et al.: Digital recognition method of electric energy meter based on image processing. Electron. Qual. **3**, 41–45 (2018)
9. Chen, Y., Jiang, W., Yang, F., Zhu, X.: Research on digital recognition algorithm of smart electric energy meter. Inform. Commun. (01), 17–21 (2020)
10. Gong, A., Zhang, Y., Tang, Y.: Recognition method of electric energy representation number based on YOLOv3 network. Comput. Syst. Appl. **29**(01), 196–202 (2020). https://doi.org/10.15888/j.cnki.csa.007215
11. Tian, Z., Huang, W., He, T., He, P., Qiao, Y.: Detecting text in natural image with connectionist text proposal network. In: Leibe, B., Matas, J., Sebe, N., Welling, M. (eds.) Computer Vision – ECCV 2016: 14th European Conference, Amsterdam, The Netherlands, October 11–14, 2016, Proceedings, Part VIII, pp. 56–72. Springer International Publishing, Cham (2016). https://doi.org/10.1007/978-3-319-46484-8_4
12. Baoguang, S., Xiang, B., Cong, Y.: An end-to-end trainable neural network for image-based sequence recognition and its application to scene text recognition. IEEE Trans. Pattern Anal. Mach. Intell. **39**(11), 2298–2304 (2017). https://doi.org/10.1109/TPAMI.2016.2646371

Towards Defending Adversarial Attacks with Temperature Regularization in Automatic Modulation Recognition

Tao Jiang[1,3], Huabao Xu[2], Linlin Liang[2], and Peihan Qi[1(✉)]

[1] State Key Laboratory of ISN, Xidian University, Xi'an 710071, China
phqi@xidian.edu.cn
[2] School of Cyber Engineering, Xidian University, Xi'an 710126, China
huabaoxu@stu.xidian.edu.cn, llliang@xidian.edu.cn
[3] Guangxi Key Laboratory of Cryptography and Information Security, Guilin, China

Abstract. Deep learning has been shown to perform extremely well at various machine learning tasks. However, these same architectures are highly vulnerable to adversarial examples: malicious inputs carefully crafted by adversaries which can force a neural network to produce erroneous predictions with high confidence. This undermines the security of deep learning algorithms when apply to those security-sensitive applications. Existing works have shown that the Signal Modulation Recognition (SMR) solutions based on deep learning are also susceptible to adversarial attacks. In this paper, we propose a new approach called temperature regularization to defense a deep learning scheme against white-box attacks in signal modulation recognition. Specifically, we introduce different temperatures to the softmax layer during the training of the neural network. Experimental results show that training a neural network with an appropriate high temperature can significantly enhance its robustness to three white-box attacks.

Keywords: Deep learning · Automatic modulation recognition · Adversarial defense · Temperature regularization

1 Introduction

With the rapid growth of the end-devices and wide deployment of wireless communication technology, the scarcity of spectrum resources becomes more and more severe and consequently reduces the network availability. However, a large portion of the assigned spectrum is used sporadically and geographically. The survey [10] shows that the utilization of licensed bands from 0 to 6 GHz is less than 6%. Moreover, according to the Federal Communications Commission (FCC) [8], temporal and geographical variations in the utilization of the assigned spectrum range from 15% to 85%, or even lower, thus wasting a lot of spectrum resources. Because of this, the FCC proposed a new concept, namely Cognitive Radio (CR), to use the spectrum opportunistically and overcome the

Y. Chenggang et al. (Eds.): MobiMedia 2022, LNICST 451, pp. 350–361, 2022.
https://doi.org/10.1007/978-3-031-23902-1_27

problem of low spectrum utilization [8]. CR is an intelligent wireless communication system, which builds upon software-defined radio technology and is aware of its operating environment. It helps to learn and readjust the transmission parameters dynamically based on the statistical variations in the environment. CR has been proved to be effective in using the spectrum holes without causing harmful interference to the primary users while maintaining a good quality of service.

Modulation recognition plays a key role in most intelligent communication systems and is considered as a major task of CR in both civilian and military systems. Generally, the existing wireless signal modulation recognition algorithms are mainly implemented in two approaches, i.e., the maximum likelihood method based on hypothesis testing and the pattern recognition method based on feature extraction. Since the later approach has much lower computational complexity and is applicable to real-time applications, it is considered as a promising alternative of the previous one [13]. Deep learning is one of the typical pattern recognition methods with impressive performance. However, Szegedy et al. [26] has found that Deep Neural Networks (DNNs) are highly vulnerable to adversarial examples. By applying well-crafted but subtle perturbations to natural examples, it is easy to fool a pre-trained model to produce erroneous predictions with high confidence. Thus, if a DNN is deployed in adversarial environment to perform automatic modulation recognition task, the normal modulation recognition may not be implemented.

In this paper, inspired by the defensive distillation [23], we propose a new method, called temperature regularization, to defend the DNN against adversarial attacks. Our empirical findings show that training a DNN with an appropriate high temperature can substantially improve its robustness to three white-box attacks, i.e., FGSM [9], MIM [7] and PGD [17].

Contributions. In this paper, we make the following contributions:

- We provide an intuition of why training the DNN with an appropriate high temperature *without distillation* may enhance its robustness to adversarial attacks.
- We analyze how temperature influences the DNN's sensitivity to subtle variations around the inputs from the prospect of the Jacobian matrix.
- We empirically prove the feasibility of the proposed method on modulation signal dataset and identify an "optimal" temperature for defending the VT-CNN2 model in modulation recognition.

2 Preliminaries

Szegedy et al. [26] first noticed the existence of adversarial examples in the field of computer vision and they proposed the L-BFGS algorithm for crafting adversarial examples. After that, various attack algorithms have been proposed for generating adversarial examples, such as FGSM [9], MIM [7], PGD [17], DeepFool [19], CW [4] and so on. Surprisingly, Moosavi-Dezfooli et al. [18] showed the existence of a universal and quasi-imperceptible perturbation that causes most natural images to be misclassified with high probability. And they proposed an iterative algorithm for generating such universal perturbations. [12,24] even demonstrated that it is feasible to learn the universal perturbations with a generative model. More troubling, adversarial examples misclassified by one model are often misclassified by another model, even if the two models have different network architectures or were trained on disjoint training sets, so long as both models were trained to perform the same task [28–30].

More recently, Lin et al. [16] showed that the classification accuracy of the modulation recognition model, VT-CNN2 [21], could be decreased by about 50% on average when adding a perturbation level of 0.001 to the natural modulation signals. Thus, when applying deep learning models to modulation recognition in adversarial settings, one must take into account certain vulnerabilities.

In the literature, various defense methods have been proposed to reduce the effects of adversarial examples. Typically, these defense methods can be divided into three categories. The first class is to detect the presence of adversarial perturbations in the input during inference. This is usually done by finding statistical outliers or training separate sub-networks that can distinguish between adversarial and benign inputs [6,14,15]. The second class denotes the various pre-processing methods which aim at removing or destroying structured perturbations on adversarial inputs before passing them to the classifier, including [1,11,25] and so on. This class of defenses can be easily used in conjunction with other defense mechanisms and is more practical due to its model- and attack-agnostic property. The third class is to enhance the robustness of neural networks itself, including Adversarial Training [3,27], Label Smoothing [5] and Defensive Distillation [23].

3   Methodology

3.1   Temperature Regularization

Defensive distillation was proposed in [23] to reduce the effectiveness of adversarial examples on DNNs. Their intuition is that knowledge extracted from teacher neural networks, in the form of probability vectors, and transferred in student neural networks can be beneficial to improving generalization capabilities of DNNs to unseen inputs and therefore enhances their robustness to adversarial examples. The authors also pointed out that an ideal training procedure would result in distilled network F^d converging to the original network F although this is not the case empirically.

We believe that *the distilled network F^d can learn what the original network F can, and vice versa, because their network architectures are the same.* Thus, different from the defensive distillation [23] we discard the distilled network training procedure and train the original network with high temperature. The specific analysis is as follow.

(1) Since softmax operation is to normalizes the logits into a probability vector $F(x)$, each component in $F(x)$ indicates the probability that current input x belongs to the corresponding class. For N classes classification problem (i.e. the output dimension of F is N), the output vector $F(x)$ of the last softmax layer can be expressed as

$$F(x) = \left[\frac{e^{z_i(x)/T}}{\sum_{n=0}^{N-1} e^{z_n(x)/T}} \right]_{i \in \{0...N-1\}} \quad (1)$$

where $z_i(x), i \in 0 \ldots N-1$ are the logits produced by the last hidden layer of a DNN, and parameter T is called temperature. As $T \to \infty$ the $e^{z_i(x)/T}$ converge to 1. Thus, all components in $F(x)$ are close to $1/N$. From the above analysis, we can see that there exists T_0, when $T \geq T_0$ the model's prediction probability assigning to all classes not greater than $p \in (1/N, 1)$ for all inputs. Thus, training a DNN with a high temperature will force it not to make overly confident predictions in any one class examples and reduce its sensitivity to small variations of its inputs [23]. In addition, from the perspective of the loss function, the higher the temperature is, the more ambiguous its probability distribution will be (i.e. all probabilities of the $F(x)$ are close to $1/N$). Therefore, the more stable the loss function will be (i.e. the cross-entropy for any input is close to $\log N$). This consequently can make the learned model smoother. Note that this change of temperature does not impact the relative ordering of classes.

(2) The neural network's sensitivity to input variations can be quantified by its Jacobian matrix. Let M denote the input dimension, we now consider one element $(i, j) \in [0..N-1] \times [0..M-1]$ of the $N \times M$ Jacobian matrix for a neural network F at temperature T:

$$\left. \frac{\partial F_i(x)}{\partial x_j} \right|_T = \frac{\partial}{\partial x_j} \left(\frac{e^{z_i(x)/T}}{\sum_{n=0}^{N-1} e^{z_n(x)/T}} \right) \quad (2)$$

Let $h(x) = \sum_{n=0}^{N-1} e^{z_n(x)/T}$, we then have:

$$
\begin{aligned}
\left. \frac{\partial F_i(x)}{\partial x_j} \right|_T &= \frac{\partial}{\partial x_j} \left(\frac{e^{z_i(x)/T}}{h(x)} \right) \\
&= \frac{1}{h^2(x)} \left(\frac{\partial e^{z_i(x)/T}}{\partial x_j} h(x) - e^{z_i(x)/T} \frac{\partial h(x)}{\partial x_j} \right) \\
&= \frac{1}{h^2(x)} \frac{e^{z_i(x)/T}}{T} \left(\sum_{n=0}^{N-1} e^{z_n(x)/T} \frac{\partial z_i(x)}{\partial x_j} - \sum_{n=0}^{N-1} e^{z_n(x)/T} \frac{\partial z_n(x)}{\partial x_j} \right) \\
&= \frac{1}{T} \frac{e^{z_i(x)/T}}{h^2(x)} \left[\sum_{n=0}^{N-1} e^{z_n(x)/T} \left(\frac{\partial z_i(x)}{\partial x_j} - \frac{\partial z_n(x)}{\partial x_j} \right) \right]
\end{aligned}
$$

$$(3)$$

Equation 3 shows that increasing the temperature T will reduce the absolute value of all elements of model F's Jacobian matrix when values of the logits

$z_0(x), ..., z_{N-1}(x)$ are fixed. Thus, using a high temperature during training will systematically reduce the model sensitivity to small perturbations of its inputs at test time.

From the above analysis, we can derive that choosing an appropriate high temperature T for training will improve the robustness of a DNN to adversarial attacks and maintain its performance on benign examples at the same time (Fig. 1).

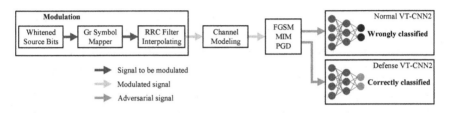

Fig. 1. An overview of defending the VT-CNN2 model against white-box attacks in modulation recognition. The only difference between the Normal VT-CNN2 and Defense VT-CNN2 is the softmax layer, where Defense VT-CNN2 has a much higher temperature than the Normal VT-CNN2.

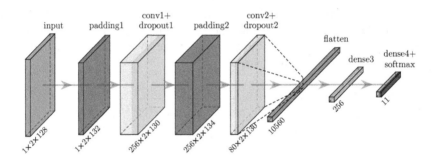

Fig. 2. Structure of VT-CNN2

3.2 Datasets and Target Model

To have a thorough study of our defense technique in the field of wireless communications, we choose the open-source dataset RADIOML 2016.10A generated with GNU Radio [2]. This dataset consists of 11 modulation signals at varying signal-to-noise ratios, including eight kinds of digital signals: 8PSK, BPSK, CPFSK, GFSK, PAM4, QAM16, QAM64, and QPSK, and three kinds of analog signals: AM-DSB, AM-SSB and WBFM. It has 220,000 data samples totally with 20 kinds of SNRs range from -20 dB to 18 dB in steps of 2 dB. Each SNR category has 11,000 data samples. We use 8 800 samples for training and the remaining 2,200 samples for testing at each SNR. For target model, we use the VT-CNN2 [20,21] which is optimized for the dataset RADIOML 2016.10A [2] to perform the modulation classification task. The network depth of VT-CNN2 is roughly equivalent to neural networks which work well on similar simple datasets in the field of computer vision. The specific architecture of VT-CNN2 is shown in Fig. 2.

3.3 Implementation

All the experiments in this work were performed on an NVIDIA GeForce RTX 2080 Ti and the code for the experiments was written in Python 3 using Tensorflow 2.4.1. An Adam solver and a categorical-crossentropy loss function were used to train the target model VT-CNN2 with a batch size of 1024. The three white-box attacks, FGSM, MIM, and PGD were implemented by an open-source software library, i.e., Cleverhans [22]. After the training converges, we obtain $\approx 72\%$ and $\approx 38\%$ test accuracy on benign examples under SNR = 10 dB and SNR = -10 dB respectively when there is no attack and no defense.

4 Experiments

4.1 Temperature Parameter Space Exploration

Firstly, we measure how temperature improves the resilience of the VT-CNN2 to adversarial attacks. Since the softmax mainly normalizes the logits into a probability vector $F(x)$ and does not change the relative ordering of classes, the parameter temperature T only matters during training. In order to produce more discrete distributions of probabilities, the softmax temperature is set back to 1 at test time.

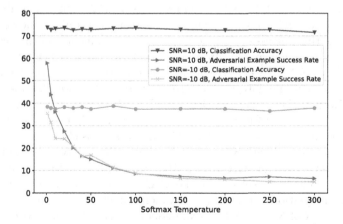

Fig. 3. An exploration of the temperature parameter space. We plot the VT-CNN2's classification accuracy on test set and the success rate of adversarial examples generated with PGD attack. Note that perturbations norm $\varepsilon = 0.0015$.

To identify the "optimal" softmax temperature, we train the VT-CNN2 under SNR = 10 dB and SNR = −10 dB with different temperatures {T: 1, 5, 10, 20, 30, 50, 75, 100, 150, 200, 300}. Then we use the attack algorithm PGD to generate adversarial examples. The classification accuracy of benign examples and the success rate of adversarial examples with respect to temperature is shown in Fig. 3. We observe that with the increase of temperature, the adversarial example success rate decreases rapidly and then largely remains constant. Specifically, when the temperature increases from 1 to 100, the adversarial example success rate decreased from 57.91% and 35.45% to 8.59% and 8.77% under SNR = 10 dB and SNR = −10 dB respectively. Based on the above observations, we choose temperature $T = 100$ to train the VT-CNN2 to effectively defense against adversarial attacks.

4.2 Defending Against Adversarial Attacks

To analyze the performance of our defense method, we conduct a series of comparative experiments. In the following sections, we refer to the model without defense as the Normal VT-CNN2 while the model with defense (trained with an appropriate high temperature) as the Defense VT-CNN2. Note that we do not care about the relationship between these different attack methods, but just how our Defense VT-CNN2 behaves under attacks.

Under Different Perturbations Magnitude. Figure 4 shows the classification accuracy of Normal VT-CNN2 and Defense VT-CNN2 under three attack algorithms (i.e., FGSM, MIM, and PGD) with different perturbations magnitude ε at SNR = 10 dB and SNR = −10 dB. We can observe that the proposed defense method can improve the classification accuracy of VT-CNN2 on adversarial examples largely, especially those generated with iterative-step attack algorithms (i.e. MIM and PGD). Concretely, at SNR = 10 dB, the classification accuracy of Defense VT-CNN2 on iterative adversarial examples is about three times of that Normal VT-CNN2 when the perturbations magnitude $\varepsilon > 0.001$. Furthermore, this defense technique has almost no influence on the accuracy of VT-CNN2 on benign examples. In some cases, for example, when SNR = 10 dB, the Defense VT-CNN2 even have higher accuracy than the Normal VT-CNN2.

To get more insight into the defense method further, we plot the confusion matrix of Normal VT-CNN2 and Defense VT-CNN2 for all 11 categories at SNR = 10 dB, as is shown in Fig. 5. It can be seen from Fig. 5a that when there is no attack and no defense, the Normal VT-CNN2 has serious classification confusion between analog signals 8PSK and QPSK, AM-DSB and WBFM, and between digital signals QAM16 and QAM64. In [16], they claimed that analog modulation confusion is difficult to solve, but the QAMs confusion can be improved by better synchronization and reducing channel impairments. Figure 5b shows the confusion matrix of Normal VT-CNN2 under adversarial attack. As can be seen, the MIM attack has a strong negative effect on the classification accuracy and the confusion matrix is extremely chaotic. Particularly, BPSK and PAM4 are

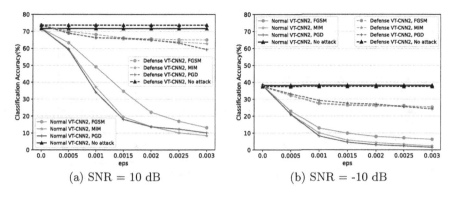

Fig. 4. Classification accuracy of VT-CNN2 with different perturbations magnitude ε.

misclassified to each other with a higher probability. And CPFSK and GFSK both are more likely misclassified as 8PSK. At the same time, the AM-DSB has a great possibility misclassified as WBFM. That is, compared to other modulation signals, FSKs, PSKs and AM-DSB signals are more vulnerable to adversarial attacks.

Figure 5c shows the confusion matrix of Defense VT-CNN2 before attack. Compare Fig. 5c with Fig. 5a, we notice that the defense method has some impact on the accuracy of 8PSK and WBFM benign examples. But overall, this impact is negligible. Figure 5d shows the confusion matrix of Defense VT-CNN2 under attack. Compare Fig. 5d with Fig. 5b, it can be clearly seen that the defense method can mitigate the adversarial effect significantly with the exception of QAM16. We do not exactly know why the accuracy of Defense VT-CNN2 on QAM16 is lower than that of Normal VT-CNN2 under attack, but this may be caused by the low accuracy of Normal VT-CNN2 on the QAM16 benign examples. Because when the classification accuracy is low, attack or defense does not make much sense.

Under Different SNRs. Figure 6 shows the classification accuracy of Normal VT-CNN2 and Defense VT-CNN2 under three white-box attacks at different SNRs, where $\varepsilon = 0.001$ for subplot Fig. 6a and $\varepsilon = 0.0015$ for subplot Fig. 6b. As shown in Fig. 6a and 6b, when there is no attack, the classification accuracy of Normal VT-CNN2 exhibits an increasing trend first and then almost remains constant ($\approx 72\%$) with the increase of SNR. Specifically, the classification accuracy of Normal VT-CNN2 increases rapidly from 38% to 72% as the SNR increases from -10 dB to 0 dB. But under adversarial attacks, the classification accuracy of Normal VT-CNN2 drops by almost one half at all SNRs. Obviously, the strength of iterative-step attacks is stronger than that of one-step attack. We find that our defense method is very effective against these adversarial attacks, especially against the iterative-step attacks. In detail, the classification accuracy of Defense VT-CNN2 under the three white-box attacks decreases by

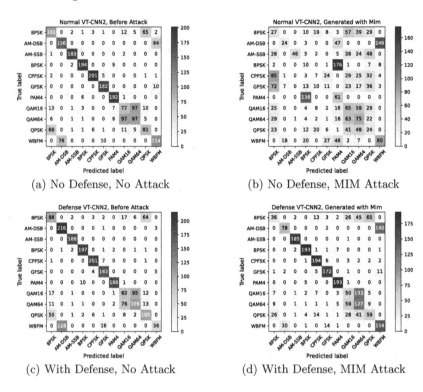

(a) No Defense, No Attack

(b) No Defense, MIM Attack

(c) With Defense, No Attack

(d) With Defense, MIM Attack

Fig. 5. Confusion Matrix of VT-CNN2 in different scenarios. Note the SNR = 10 dB and perturbations magnitude $\varepsilon = 0.0015$.

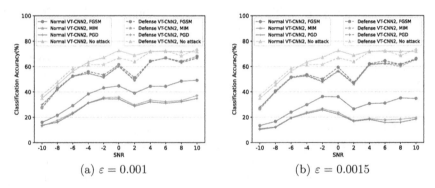

(a) $\varepsilon = 0.001$

(b) $\varepsilon = 0.0015$

Fig. 6. Classification accuracy of VT-CNN2 at different SNRs.

no more than 10% at almost all SNRs compared to the case where there is no attacks.

To further quantify the defense effect of the proposed approach against the adversarial attack algorithms, we calculated the average classification accuracy of the Normal VT-CNN2 and the Defense VT-CNN2 on adversarial examples under

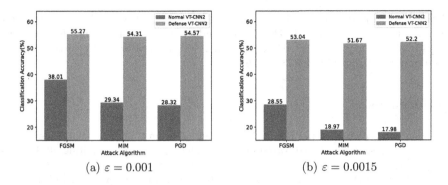

(a) $\varepsilon = 0.001$ (b) $\varepsilon = 0.0015$

Fig. 7. Average accuracy of VT-CNN2 under all SNRs.

all SNRs. The results are shown in Fig. 7. It can be seen clearly that our Defense VT-CNN2 is extremely robust to FGSM, MIM, and PGD attacks. Compare to the Normal VT-CNN2, the classification accuracy of the Defense VT-CNN2 is improved by about 17% for FGSM and by nearly 25% for MIM and PGD when perturbations magnitude $\varepsilon = 0.001$. With the increase of perturbations magnitude ε, this defense effect is more significant. As shown in Fig. 7b, when perturbations magnitude $\varepsilon = 0.0015$, the classification accuracy of the Defense VT-CNN2 is improved by about 34% under the iterative-step attacks (i.e. MIM and PGD).

This results show that the Normal VT-CNN2 is more sensitive to the perturbations magnitude ε of the attack algorithms, since it's average classification accuracy decreased by almost 10% when the perturbations magnitude ε increased from 0.001 to 0.0015 while the classification accuracy of Defense VT-CNN2 nearly remains unchanged. It is worth noting that, although the iterative-step attacks are stronger, our Defense VT-CNN2 achieves almost the same accuracy under one-step attack (FGSM) and iterative-step attacks (MIM and PGD), which is about 52%.

5   Conclusion

In this work, we evaluated the security problems on automatic modulation recognition based on deep learning and demonstrated the efficacy of using an appropriate high temperature within the softmax layer as a defense method against adversarial attacks. We analyzed the reason why this defense method works and determined an "optimal" temperature for the VT-CNN2 model through experiment. Our empirical findings showed that using an appropriate high temperature during training can significantly reduce the successfulness of adversarial attacks against automatic modulation recognition classifiers. Moreover, it nearly maintains the accuracy rates of VT-CNN2 on benign examples. Lastly, this defense technique is extremely easy to implement and introduces no overhead for training after the "optimal" temperature is chosen.

Acknowledgment. This work was supported by National Natural Science Foundation of China (Nos. 62171334, 62001359), Fundamental Research Funds for the Central Universities (No. XJS211502) and Guangxi Key Laboratory of Cryptography and Information Security (No. GCIS201716).

References

1. Yin, S.L., Zhang, X.L., Zuo, L.Y.: Defending against adversarial attacks using spherical sampling-based variational auto-encoder. Neurocomputing **478**, 1–10 (2022)
2. N.P., et al.: Deepsig dataset: RadioML 2016.10a (2016). https://www.deepsig.io/datasets
3. Allen-Zhu, Z., Li, Y.: Feature purification: how adversarial training performs robust deep learning. In: 62nd IEEE Annual Symposium on Foundations of Computer Science, FOCS 2021, Denver, CO, USA, 7–10 February 2022, pp. 977–988. IEEE (2021)
4. Carlini, N., Wagner, D.A.: Towards evaluating the robustness of neural networks. In: 2017 IEEE Symposium on Security and Privacy, SP 2017, San Jose, CA, USA, 22–26 May 2017, pp. 39–57. IEEE Computer Society (2017)
5. Warde-Farley, D., Goodfellow, I., Hazan, T., Papandreou, G., Tarlow., D.: Adversarial perturbations of deep neural networks, pp. 311–342 (2017)
6. Dong, J., Zhou, P.: Detecting adversarial examples utilizing pixel value diversity. In: Asian Hardware Oriented Security and Trust Symposium, AsianHOST 2021, Shanghai, China, 16–18 December 2021. pp. 1–6. IEEE (2021)
7. Dong, Y., et al.: Boosting adversarial attacks with momentum. In: 2018 IEEE Conference on Computer Vision and Pattern Recognition, CVPR 2018, Salt Lake City, UT, USA, 18–22 June 2018, pp. 9185–9193. Computer Vision Foundation/IEEE Computer Society (2018)
8. FCC: Notice of proposed rule making and order. ET, Docket No 03-222 (2003)
9. Goodfellow, I.J., Shlens, J., Szegedy, C.: Explaining and harnessing adversarial examples. In: Bengio, Y., LeCun, Y. (eds.) 3rd International Conference on Learning Representations, ICLR 2015, San Diego, CA, USA, 7–9 May 2015, Conference Track Proceedings (2015)
10. Gui, G., Huang, H., Song, Y., Sari, H.: Deep learning for an effective nonorthogonal multiple access scheme. IEEE Trans. Veh. Technol. **67**(9), 8440–8450 (2018)
11. Guo, C., Rana, M., Cissé, M., van der Maaten, L.: Countering adversarial images using input transformations. In: 6th International Conference on Learning Representations, ICLR 2018, Vancouver, BC, Canada, 30 April–3 May 2018, Conference Track Proceedings. OpenReview.net (2018)
12. Hashemi, A.S., Bär, A., Mozaffari, S., Fingscheidt, T.: Transferable universal adversarial perturbations using generative models. CoRR abs/2010.14919 (2020)
13. Jdid, B., Hassan, K., Dayoub, I., Lim, W.H., Mokayef, M.: Machine learning based automatic modulation recognition for wireless communications: a comprehensive survey. IEEE Access **9**, 57851–57873 (2021)
14. Li, Y., Tang, T., Hsieh, C., Lee, T.C.M.: Detecting adversarial examples with Bayesian neural network. CoRR abs/2105.08620 (2021)
15. Liang, B., Li, H., Su, M., Li, X., Shi, W., Wang, X.: Detecting adversarial image examples in deep neural networks with adaptive noise reduction. IEEE Trans. Dependable Secur. Comput. **18**(1), 72–85 (2021)

16. Lin, Y., Zhao, H., Ma, X., Tu, Y., Wang, M.: Adversarial attacks in modulation recognition with convolutional neural networks. IEEE Trans. Reliab. **70**(1), 389–401 (2021)
17. Madry, A., Makelov, A., Schmidt, L., Tsipras, D., Vladu, A.: Towards deep learning models resistant to adversarial attacks. In: 6th International Conference on Learning Representations, ICLR 2018, Vancouver, BC, Canada, 30 April–3 May 2018, Conference Track Proceedings. OpenReview.net (2018)
18. Moosavi-Dezfooli, S., Fawzi, A., Fawzi, O., Frossard, P.: Universal adversarial perturbations. CoRR abs/1610.08401 (2016)
19. Moosavi-Dezfooli, S., Fawzi, A., Frossard, P.: DeepFool: a simple and accurate method to fool deep neural networks. In: 2016 IEEE Conference on Computer Vision and Pattern Recognition, CVPR 2016, Las Vegas, NV, USA, 27–30 June 2016, pp. 2574–2582. IEEE Computer Society (2016)
20. O'Shea, T.J., West, N.: Radio machine learning dataset generation with gnu radio (2016)
21. O'Shea, T.J., Corgan, J., Clancy, T.C.: Convolutional radio modulation recognition networks. In: Jayne, C., Iliadis, L. (eds.) EANN 2016. CCIS, vol. 629, pp. 213–226. Springer, Cham (2016). https://doi.org/10.1007/978-3-319-44188-7_16
22. Papernot, N., Faghri, F., Carlini, N., et al.: Technical report on the CleverHans v2.1.0 adversarial examples library. arXiv preprint arXiv:1610.00768 (2018)
23. Papernot, N., McDaniel, P.D., Wu, X., Jha, S., Swami, A.: Distillation as a defense to adversarial perturbations against deep neural networks. In: IEEE Symposium on Security and Privacy, SP 2016, San Jose, CA, USA, 22–26 May 2016, pp. 582–597. IEEE Computer Society (2016)
24. Poursaeed, O., Katsman, I., Gao, B., Belongie, S.J.: Generative adversarial perturbations. In: 2018 IEEE Conference on Computer Vision and Pattern Recognition, CVPR 2018, Salt Lake City, UT, USA, 18–22 June 2018, pp. 4422–4431. Computer Vision Foundation/IEEE Computer Society (2018)
25. Samangouei, P., Kabkab, M., Chellappa, R.: Defense-GAN: protecting classifiers against adversarial attacks using generative models. In: 6th International Conference on Learning Representations, ICLR 2018, Vancouver, BC, Canada, 30 April–3 May 2018, Conference Track Proceedings. OpenReview.net (2018)
26. Szegedy, C., et al.: Intriguing properties of neural networks. In: Bengio, Y., LeCun, Y. (eds.) 2nd International Conference on Learning Representations, ICLR 2014, Banff, AB, Canada, 14–16 April 2014, Conference Track Proceedings (2014)
27. Tramèr, F., Kurakin, A., Papernot, N., Boneh, D., McDaniel, P.D.: Ensemble adversarial training: attacks and defenses. CoRR abs/1705.07204 (2017)
28. Wang, X., He, X., Wang, J., He, K.: Admix: enhancing the transferability of adversarial attacks. In: 2021 IEEE/CVF International Conference on Computer Vision, ICCV 2021, Montreal, QC, Canada, 10–17 October 2021, pp. 16138–16147. IEEE (2021)
29. Wu, W., Su, Y., Lyu, M.R., King, I.: Improving the transferability of adversarial samples with adversarial transformations. In: IEEE Conference on Computer Vision and Pattern Recognition, CVPR 2021, virtual, 19–25 June 2021, pp. 9024–9033. Computer Vision Foundation/IEEE (2021)
30. Zhong, Y., Deng, W.: Towards transferable adversarial attack against deep face recognition. IEEE Trans. Inf. Forensics Secur. **16**, 1452–1466 (2021)

PF-Net: Personalized Filter for Speaker Recognition from Raw Waveform

Wencheng Li, Zhenhua Tan$^{(\boxtimes)}$, Zhenche Xia, Danke Wu, and Jingyu Ning

School of Software, Northeastern University, Shenyang 110819, China
{liwencheng,xiazhenche,wudk2019}@stumail.neu.edu.cn,
{tanzh,ningjy}@mail.neu.edu.cn

Abstract. Speaker recognition using i-vector has been replaced by speaker recognition using deep learning. Speaker recognition based on Convolutional Neural Networks (CNNs) has been widely used in recent years, which learn low-level speech representations from raw waveforms. On this basis, a CNN architecture called SincNet proposes a kind of unique convolutional layer, which has achieved band-pass filters. Compared with standard CNNs, SincNet learns the low and high cut-off frequencies of each filter. This paper proposes an improved CNNs architecture called PF-Net, which encourages the first convolutional layer to implement more personalized filters than SincNet. PF-Net parameterizes the frequency domain shape and can realize band-pass filters by learning some deformation points in frequency domain. Compared with standard CNN, PF-Net can learn the characteristics of each filter. Compared with SincNet, PF-Net can learn more characteristic parameters, instead of only low and high cut-off frequencies. This provides a personalized filter bank for different tasks. As a result, our experiments show that the PF-Net converges faster than standard CNN and performs better than SincNet. Our code is available at github.com/TAN-OpenLab/PF-NET.

Keywords: Speaker recognition · Raw waveform · Personalized filters · Deep learning

1 Introduction

In our daily life, we are always receiving and conveying a variety of information from the outside world, and voice information is an important part of it. Audio signal processing plays an important role in the field of artificial intelligence and machine learning. Because each person's voice organs are different, their voices and tones are different. Apart from physical differences, each person has his own unique way of speaking, including using a specific accent, rhythm, intonation style, pronunciation mode, vocabulary selection, and so on. Together, these make up a distinct feature for everyone [1–3].

This work was funded by the National Key Research and Development Program of China under Grant No. 2019YFB1405803.

Y. Chenggang et al. (Eds.): MobiMedia 2022, LNICST 451, pp. 362–374, 2022.
https://doi.org/10.1007/978-3-031-23902-1_28

In the early days, speaker recognition used models such as Dynamic Time Warping (DTW) [4] to calculate the similarity of speakers. Gaussian Mixture Model- Universal Background Models (GMM-UBM) [5,5,6] has improved on this basis. i-vector [7] reduces the computational cost by compressing the speaker vector and can make better use of the channel compensation algorithm. Most speaker recognition requires pre-processing steps. Incorrect pre-processing of recorded speech input can reduce classification performance [8]. Some common methods include noise removal, endpoint detection, pre-emphasis, framing, and normalization [9,10] can be used in pre-processing. After the rise of neural networks, researchers applied DNN [11] directly to speaker classification tasks. This method has the characteristics of large parameters and unclear timing information. The fully connected layer in d-vector was replaced by a feature extraction method similar to one-dimensional convolution in [12–14], which reduces the computational cost. CNNs pays more attention to the speaker information between frames to achieve a better effect. Some networks used artificial features such as MFCC [15,16] and LPCC [17]. However, these features may cause the classifier to miss some speaker-specific information. In order to alleviate this shortcoming, some works used the spectrogram as the input of the network, the others directly used the raw waveform in their network. In order to process the raw waveform, a common choice for researchers is to apply CNNs. Because of the weight sharing feature, the convolution kernel can find a invariant and robust representation. In recent years, there have been many studies on speaker recognition based on the time-domain characteristics of audio using related neural networks [18,19]. Some studies have introduced ResNet [20,21] to deal with more and more complex network structures. However, they are not special in dealing with the first layer of neural network, and are usually the same as other layers in the network. SincNet [22] uses multiple sets of parameterized filters as the first layer of the convolutional network to obtain a personalized solution of the filter. However, SincNet uses the Sinc function as a filter, which only considers limited parameters.

RawNet [23] mixes CNN with LSTM to get better performance. Its input layer is still the same as SincNet, which has the same limitation. This paper alleviates the constraints of the Sinc function on the filter, and enables the filter to directly fit the shape in the frequency domain. This is formed by a set of parameterized linear filtering constraints. This method gives the filter more freedom and enables it to learn more peculiar features.

Our experiments were conducted under challenging but realistic conditions, which are characterized by few data (12–15 s per speaker) and short test sentences (lasting 2 to 6 s). The results show that the filter achieves better final performance.

The remainder of the paper is organized as follows. The PF-Net architecture is described in Sect. 2. Section 3 discusses the relation to prior work. The experimental setup and results are outlined in Sect. 4 and Sect. 5 respectively. Finally, Sect. 6 discusses our conclusions.

2   The SincNet Architecture

For speech time series signals, the standard first-layer CNN structure is regarded as a time-domain convolution operation [24], which is defined as follows:

$$y[n] = x[n] * h[n] = \sum_{l=0}^{L-1} x[l] \cdot h[n-l] \tag{1}$$

where $x[n]$ is the speech signal, $h[n]$ is the filter of length L, and $y[n]$ is the output of the filter. In the standard CNN structure, the L elements of each filter are learned from the data.

In the SincNet structure, the convolution operation uses a predefined function g, where g contains only a few learnable variables, defined as follows:

$$y[n] = x[n] * g[n, \theta] \tag{2}$$

SincNet uses the low and high frequencies to filter the original audio in segments. The g function is defined as a rectangular bandpass filter in the text, and its frequency domain characteristics are as follows:

$$G[f, f_{beg}, f_{end}] = rect\left(\frac{f}{2f_{end}}\right) - rect\left(\frac{f}{2f_{beg}}\right) \tag{3}$$

where f_{beg} and f_{end} are start cut-off frequency and end cut-off frequency respectively, both of which are learnable.

Unlike SincNet, the filter in PF-Net convolution operation reconstructs the function g so that g contains more learnable variables. This is achieved by inserting learnable deformation points in the waveform segments at different low and high frequencies, and divide a frequency domain into multiple one can learn small line segments. The frequency domain characteristics of each segment are expressed as follows:

$$G[f, f_k, f_{k+1}] = \frac{h_{k+1} - h_k}{f_{k+1} - f_k}(f - f_k) + h_k \tag{4}$$

f_k and f_{k+1} represent the low and high frequencies of each segment, h_k and h_{k+1} are their corresponding amplitude intensity in frequency domain. f_k, f_{k+1}, h_k and h_{k+1} are learnable, and the value of f is within $[f_k, f_{k+1}]$.

When f is not in the interval $[f_k, f_{k+1}]$:

$$G[f, f_k, f_{k+1}] = 0, \tag{5}$$

Accumulate each line segment to get the whole frequency band that can be learned. The expression is as follows:

$$G[f, f_{beg}, f_{end}] = \sum_{k=beg}^{end-1} G[n, f_k, f_{k+1}] \tag{6}$$

After inverse Fourier transform [24], the above formula about each line segment is transformed into the time domain expression form as:

$$g[n, f_k, f_{k+1}] = \frac{\Delta(cos(2\pi f_{k+1}n) - cos(2\pi f_k n))}{4\pi^2 n^2}$$
$$- \frac{h_{k+1} sin(2\pi f_{k+1}n) - h_k sin(2\pi f_k n)}{2\pi n} \tag{7}$$

where:

$$\Delta = \frac{h_{k+1} - h_k}{f_{k+1} - f_k} \tag{8}$$

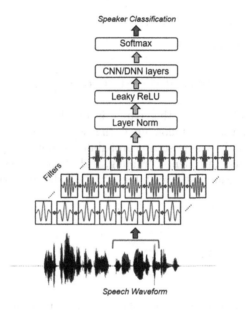

Fig. 1. Network Architecture of SincNet [22], PF-Net differs from it only in the filter part

The time domain expression of the entire filtering frequency band is:

$$g[f, f_{beg}, f_{end}] = \sum_{k=beg}^{end-1} g[n, f_k, f_{k+1}] \tag{9}$$

Among them, the cutoff frequencies is initialized to a value in the range of $[0, f_s/2]$, and f_s is the sampling rate of the signal. In fact, in order to better extract effective information from low frequencies, both the cutoff frequency and the deformation point frequency are initialized with Mel frequency. To constrain the shape of the filter, h_k is expressed as:

$$h_k = 1 + \Delta h \tag{10}$$

By constraining the value of Δh, the value of h can be constrained indirectly. This paper uses Δh instead of h as the learnable parameters, so that h_k always learns with 1 as the center. The value of Δh is initialized randomly between $[-0.1, 0.1]$. In this way, the deep neural network can learn the shape of each filter. As shown in Fig. 2, the initial shape of the filter in the frequency domain is the same as that of SincNet. After learning, the deformation points set in the frequency band begin to move in different directions by changing the abscissa and ordinate of the points (both of which are learnable parameters). Therefore, PF-Net can obtain richer information than the cut-off frequency.

Finally, in order to smooth the truncation characteristics of the g function, multiply the g function by a window function:

$$g_w[n, f_{beg}, f_{end}] = g[n, f_{beg}, f_{end}] \cdot w[n]. \tag{11}$$

Adopt Hamming window [25]:

$$w[n] = 0.54 - -0.46 \cdot cos\left(\frac{2\pi n}{L}\right). \tag{12}$$

The neural network used in this paper is divided into two parts, the first part is the filter layer, the follow-up is the neural network part composed of CNN/DNN, and finally the posterior probability is output by Softmax. Preprocessing includes removing silence, framing, and maximum normalization operations. Among them, the first layer filter is the key design part, and the network structure is as Fig. 1.

Fig. 2. Learning process of a filter in frequency domain.

2.1 Model Properties

- **Flexible parameters:** PF-Net can control the number of parameters in the first convolutional layer. For example, if we consider a convolutional layer with F channels, each channel uses a filter of length L, and the number of deformation points is S, the standard CNN uses F·L parameters, SincNet uses 2F parameters, and PF-Net uses L·F·S parameters, if F = 80, L = 200, S = 5, CNN has 16000 parameters, and SincNet has 160. PF-Net has 800 parameters, somewhere in between. If you change the value of S, you can change the number of parameters without changing the number of channels. Moreover, if we filter twice the length L, twice the parameter count of the standard CNN, while the amount of parameters of PF-Net remains unchanged. This provides a very selective filter without actually adding parameters to the optimization problem. In addition, as the number of parameters increases, the PF-Net network has a more powerful fitting function, and at the same time, it is more difficult to train. The user can freely set the number of deformation points according to the data and actual needs.

- **Interpretability:** Same as SincNet, the features obtained by PF-Net in the first convolutional layer are more interpretable and readable than other methods. The reason for this property of PF-Net is that all deformation points have corresponding positions in frequency domain.

3   Related Work

In the process of speaker recognition, feature extraction has attracted much attention. Researchers always assume that the input signal has a stable property in a short enough time interval. Therefore, segmenting the input signal into multiple short-term frames and extracting their feature sequences can better model the audio signal [26]. In the past, people mainly used manual features such as MFCC [15,16], LPCC [17], and PLP [27]. These methods will inevitably lose part of the speaker information. In the field of CNN, there have been many attempts to process audio using amplitude spectrograms [28–32]. Compared with manual features, the amplitude spectrogram retains more speaker features. However, this method requires careful adjustment of some key hyperparameters such as frame window length, overlap, and type. Therefore, it has become a trend to conduct deep learning directly through raw audio [33–37] has proved its feasibility.

SincNet [22] uses a set of parameterized Sinc filters to directly learn from the original audio. Liu proposed a learnable MFCC [38], but only carried out experiments in speaker verification. In order to obtain the timing characteristics in the original audio, many neural networks [18,19] used to process timing signals are used for speaker recognition. To deal with more complex neural networks, ResNet [20,21] was introduced into speaker recognition. These networks pay more attention to the deep structure, but pay less attention to the first layer structure of the network. RawNet [23] mixes CNN with LSTM to get better performance, which has the same first layer as SincNet. However, for each filter, SincNet only has two parameters that can be learned.

In this paper, a neural network which called PF-Net is proposed to learn the shape of the filter by inserting deformation points into each filter. PF-Net can actively control the number of learnable parameters by controlling the number of deformation points. This kind of filter has a good effect on speaker recognition, especially in the scene with several seconds samples. Each speaker provides a short test statement.

4   Experimental Setup

On some public datasets (TIMIT and Librispeech), PF-Net was compared with different baseline systems. In the following sections, we show the detailed settings of the experiment.

W. Li et al.

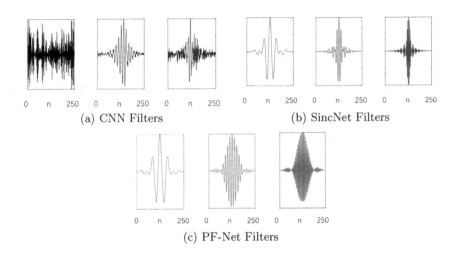

(a) CNN Filters   (b) SincNet Filters

(c) PF-Net Filters

Fig. 3. Time domain representation of different channel filters earned by neural networks.

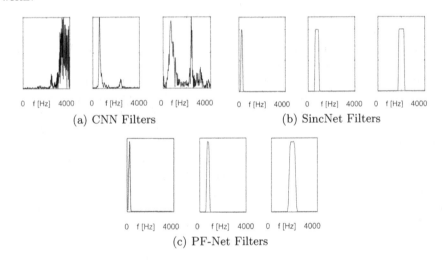

(a) CNN Filters   (b) SincNet Filters

(c) PF-Net Filters

Fig. 4. Time domain representation of different channel filters earned by neural networks.

4.1 Corpora

This paper conducts experiments on the following two datasets.

TIMIT corpora [39], the voice sampling rate of the TIMIT dataset is 16 kHz, which contains a total of 6300 sentences, and 70% of the speakers are male. Most of the speakers are adult whites. Use the TIMIT dataset training set part for the speaker recognition task (same as SincNet), After deleting TIMIT's calibration sentences (same sentences), each speaker had 8 sentences, of which five sentences were used to train the model, and the remaining three were used for testing.

Librispeech corpora [40], which is a corpus of about 1000 h of 16 kHz reading English speech. It contains 2484 speakers, and the sampling rate is 16 kHz. The training and test speech in the dataset are used in the experiment. After removing the silent part, each sentence lasts for 2–6 s.

4.2 PF-Net Setup

Speech signal is divided into frames (frame length 200 ms, overlapping 10 ms) and then input into PF-Net. We insert five deformation points in each filter. As Fig. 2, The filter layer uses 80 filters of length 251, which are calculated by the formula in Sect. 2. Subsequently, the CNN part used two standard convolutional layers, the number of channels was 60, and the size of the convolution kernel was 5. Layer normalization [41] was used for input samples and for all convolutional layers (so is the filter layer). Next, we used 3 fully connected layers containing 2048 neurons, which normalized with batch normalization [42]. The activation function used leaky-ReLU [43]. The transformation point was initialized with mel-scale. We used softmax classifier to output the posterior probability of each frame. On this basis, the results of sentence-level classification were obtained by voting. The RMSprop optimizer was applied, and the learning rate lr = 0.001, $\alpha = 0.95$, $\varepsilon = 10^{-7}$. The batch size is 128. All hyper-parameters are optimized on TIMIT, as is Librispeech. The speaker verification system can directly take the softmax posterior score corresponding to the claimed identity [44].

4.3 Baseline Setups

This paper compares PF-Net with several different systems.

First of all, CNN network with raw waveform as input was applied. Its network structure is the same as PF-Net in this paper, but the first layer convolution was replaced by PF-Net convolution. Secondly, we compared with manual features, this paper uses Kaldi toolkit [45] to calculate 40 FBANK features, which were calculated every 25 ms, with an overlap time of 10 ms, forming a context window of 200 ms. Layer normalization was also used in FBANK network and processed by CNN network. Finally, Sinc function was used to replace the first layer convolution of CNN. Except for the first layer, the network structure and hyperparameters of PF-Net were all the same as SincNet [22]. For speaker verification experiments, the enrollment and test phase is conducted on Librispeech.

5   Results

This section reports the experimental validation of the proposed SincNet. First, we perform a comparison between the filters learned by a SincNet and by a standard CNN. We then compare our architecture with other competitive systems on speaker recognition tasks.

5.1 Filter Analysis

Figure 3 and Fig. 4 are visual representations of the time-frequency domain of the filters learned by CNN, SincNet and PF-Net in the librispeech dataset, respectively. Through the analysis of them, we can find that PF-Net has the advantages of both original CNN and SincNet. Figure 3 represents the time-domain waveforms of the three filters. Through observation, we can conclude that the filters learned by standard CNN are always noisy. In contrast, PF-Net and SincNet can learn more interpretable filters. In the time domain, In the time domain, SincNet found a narrower waveform while PF-Net found a wider one. In the frequency response shown in Fig. 3, the standard CNN is more difficult to interpret, and the noise is almost distributed in all frequency bands. For SincNet structure, although the filter can learn the corresponding response of a specific frequency band, its model remains unchanged in amplitude intensity. Figure 4(c) shows that PF-Net is different from both. It not only realizes band-pass filtering, but also is not invariable in amplitude intensity.

5.2 Speaker Identification

Table 1. Classification Error Rates (CER%) of PF-Net on two datasets

Model	TIMIT	LibriSpeech
CNN-FBANK	0.86	1.55
CNN-Raw	1.65	1.00
SINCNET	0.85	0.96
PF-NET	**0.72**	**0.77**

Table 1 shows the comparison of Classification Error Rates (CER%). This table shows the comparison of PF-Net with other networks on the LibriSpeech dataset and TIMIT dataset. The network using CNN raw has a lower accuracy rate on the TIMIT dataset and a higher accuracy rate on the LibriSpeech dataset, which indicates the advantage of the original filter, that is, it is more suitable for datasets with large data volume, which is also a feature of the neural network. CNN network using fbank performs well on data sets with small data volume due to the use of manually extracted features. However, it is not as good as CNN on larger datasets. Sincnet and PF-net are both manually designed features and retain learnable parameters. Both of them combine the learnability of neural network and the experience of manual design. Therefore, in two datasets of different sizes, the CER can still be kept low. Among them, because PF-net has designed more parameters that can be learned, it can learn more complex filter banks, which makes PF-net outperform sincnet in datasets. This is because larger datasets need more complex filters for characterization. Due to the small amount of data in TIMIT, Sincnet is not very different from PF-net. However, with the increase of the amount of data, simple bandwidth learning cannot adapt to more complex data, which makes a greater gap between the two in LibriSpeech.

The LibriSpeech dataset was fast in the first 500 rounds. Although the speed slowed down thereafter, there was still a performance improvement, and the training ended in the 2900th round. The Frame Error Rate (FER%) of LibriSpeech is 0.3, which is better than the result on the TIMIT dataset.

5.3 Speaker Verification

Table 2 shows the comparison of Equal Error Rate (EER%). This table shows the performance of the PF-Net on the LibriSpeech dataset. It can be seen that PF-Net performs better than both a CNN trained on standard FBANK coefficients and CNN trained or the raw waveform in speaker verification task. Although the performance of PF-Net is close to SincNet in this task, it still has certain advantages. Through the above experiments, it can be seen that PF-net improves the baseline in speaker identification more than in speaker verification, which may be because the speaker verification task is more prone to over fitting than speaker recognition.

Table 2. Equal Error Rates (EER%) of PF-Net on two Librispeech dataset.

Model	LibriSpeech
CNN-FBANK	0.37
CNN-Raw	0.36
SINCNET	0.32
PF-NET	**0.30**

6 Conclusion

In this paper, PF-Net is proposed, which is a neural architecture for directly processing waveform audio. Our model is a change of SincNet, which forms a loose constraint on the shape of the filter through effective parameterization and retains a certain order. Compared with SincNet, PF-Net has more freedom and can adjust the number of parameters freely. PF-Net has carried out extensive evaluation for challenging speaker recognition tasks, showing its performance advantages in speaker recognition. In addition to improving the performance, PF-Net and SincNet have the same advantages, that is, the convergence speed of standard CNN is improved, and the computational efficiency is improved by using the symmetry of the filter. In future work, we plan to evaluate PF-Net performance on datasets in other languages (such as Cn-Celeb) or in more challenging environments (such as VoxCeleb). Although only speaker recognition experiments are carried out in this paper, in theory, PF-Net, a time series processing method, should also work in other fields. Therefore, our future work will be extended to emotion recognition and singer recognition. We have ever uploaded the earlier version of this paper in arXiv, and now we have the opportunity to publish it in MobileMedia. We also open related codes in Github (github.com/TAN-OpenLab/PF-NET).

References

1. Atal, B.: Automatic recognition of speakers from their voices. Proc. IEEE **64**(4), 460–475 (1976). https://doi.org/10.1109/PROC.1976.10155
2. Shriberg, E., Ferrer, L., Kajarekar, S., Venkataraman, A., Stolcke, A.: Modeling prosodic feature sequences for speaker recognition. Speech Commun. **46**(3), 455–472 (2005). https://doi.org/10.1016/j.specom.2005.02.018. Quantitative Prosody Modelling for Natural Speech Description and Generation
3. Furui, S.: An overview of speaker recognition technology. In: Lee, C.H., Soong, F.K., Paliwal, K.K. (eds.) Automatic Speech and Speaker Recognition. The Kluwer International Series in Engineering and Computer Science, vol. 355, pp. 31–56. Springer, Boston (1996). https://doi.org/10.1007/978-1-4613-1367-0_2
4. Rabiner, L., Rosenberg, A., Levinson, S.: Considerations in dynamic time warping algorithms for discrete word recognition. IEEE Trans. Acoust. Speech Signal Process. **26**(6), 575–582 (1978). https://doi.org/10.1109/TASSP.1978.1163164
5. Reynolds, D.A., Quatieri, T.F., Dunn, R.B.: Speaker verification using adapted gaussian mixture models. Digit. Signal Process. **10**(1), 19–41 (2000). https://doi.org/10.1006/dspr.1999.0361
6. Pathak, M.A., Raj, B.: Privacy-preserving speaker verification and identification using Gaussian mixture models. IEEE Trans. Audio Speech Lang. Process. **21**(2), 397–406 (2013). https://doi.org/10.1109/TASL.2012.2215602
7. Liu, G., Hansen, J.H.L.: An investigation into back-end advancements for speaker recognition in multi-session and noisy enrollment scenarios. IEEE/ACM Trans. Audio Speech Lang. Process. **22**(12), 1978–1992 (2014). https://doi.org/10.1109/TASLP.2014.2352154
8. Singh, N.: A critical review on automatic speaker recognition. Sci. J. Circ. Syst. Signal Process. **4**, 14 (2015). https://doi.org/10.11648/j.cssp.20150402.12
9. Yilmaz, E., McLaren, M., van den Heuvel, H., van Leeuwen, D.A.: Language diarization for semi-supervised bilingual acoustic model training. In: 2017 IEEE Automatic Speech Recognition and Understanding Workshop (ASRU), pp. 91–96 (2017). https://doi.org/10.1109/ASRU.2017.8268921
10. Cutajar, M., Gatt, E., Grech, I., Casha, O., Micallef, J.: Comparative study of automatic speech recognition techniques. IET Signal Proc. **7**(1), 25–46 (2013). https://doi.org/10.1049/iet-spr.2012.0151
11. Variani, E., Lei, X., McDermott, E., Moreno, I.L., Gonzalez-Dominguez, J.: Deep neural networks for small footprint text-dependent speaker verification. In: 2014 IEEE International Conference on Acoustics, Speech and Signal Processing (ICASSP), pp. 4052–4056 (2014). https://doi.org/10.1109/ICASSP.2014.6854363
12. Poddar, A., Sahidullah, M., Saha, G.: Speaker verification with short utterances: a review of challenges, trends and opportunities. IET Biometr. **7** (2017). https://doi.org/10.1049/iet-bmt.2017.0065
13. Dehak, N., Kenny, P.J., Dehak, R., Dumouchel, P., Ouellet, P.: Front-end factor analysis for speaker verification. IEEE Trans. Audio Speech Lang. Process. **19**(4), 788–798 (2011). https://doi.org/10.1109/TASL.2010.2064307

14. Debnath, S., Soni, B., Baruah, U., Sah, D.K.: Text-dependent speaker verification system: a review. In: 2015 IEEE 9th International Conference on Intelligent Systems and Control (ISCO), pp. 1–7 (2015). https://doi.org/10.1109/ISCO.2015.7282386

15. Balpande, M., Sansare, R., Padelkar, T., Shinde, V.: Speaker recognition based on mel-frequency cepstral coefficients and vector quantization. In: 2021 IEEE Bombay Section Signature Conference (IBSSC), pp. 1–6 (2021). https://doi.org/10.1109/IBSSC53889.2021.9673167

16. Zhang, N., Yao, Y.: Speaker recognition based on dynamic time warping and gaussian mixture model. In: 2020 39th Chinese Control Conference (CCC), pp. 1174–1177 (2020). https://doi.org/10.23919/CCC50068.2020.9188632

17. Rodriguez-Porcheron, D., Faundez-Zanuy, M.: Speaker recognition with a MLP classifier and LPCC codebook. In: Proceedings of the 1999 IEEE International Conference on Acoustics, Speech, and Signal Processing, ICASSP99 (Cat. No.99CH36258). vol. 2, pp. 1005–1008 (1999). https://doi.org/10.1109/ICASSP.1999.759872

18. Zhao, Y., Zhou, T., Chen, Z., Wu, J.: Improving deep CNN networks with long temporal context for text-independent speaker verification. In: ICASSP 2020–2020 IEEE International Conference on Acoustics, Speech and Signal Processing (ICASSP), pp. 6834–6838 (2020). https://doi.org/10.1109/ICASSP40776.2020.9053767

19. Utomo, Y.F., Djamal, E.C., Nugraha, F., Renaldi, F.: Spoken word and speaker recognition using MFCC and multiple recurrent neural networks. In: 2020 7th International Conference on Electrical Engineering, Computer Sciences and Informatics (EECSI), pp. 192–197 (2020). https://doi.org/10.23919/EECSI50503.2020.9251870

20. Jakubec, M., Lieskovska, E., Jarina, R.: Speaker recognition with ResNet and VGG networks. In: 2021 31st International Conference Radioelektronika (RADIOELEKTRONIKA), pp. 1–5 (2021). https://doi.org/10.1109/RADIOELEKTRONIKA52220.2021.9420202

21. Zhou, T., Zhao, Y., Wu, J.: ResNeXt and Res2Net structures for speaker verification. In: 2021 IEEE Spoken Language Technology Workshop (SLT), pp. 301–307 (2021). https://doi.org/10.1109/SLT48900.2021.9383531

22. Ravanelli, M., Bengio, Y.: Speaker recognition from raw waveform with SincNet. In: 2018 IEEE Spoken Language Technology Workshop (SLT), pp. 1021–1028 (2018). https://doi.org/10.1109/SLT.2018.8639585

23. Weon Jung, J., Heo, H.S., ho Kim, J., Jin Shim, H., Yu, H.J.: RawNet: advanced end-to-end deep neural network using raw waveforms for text-independent speaker verification (2019)

24. Rabiner, L., Schafer, R.: Theory and Applications of Digital Speech Processing, 1st edn. Prentice Hall Press, USA (2010)

25. Mitra, S.K.: Digital Signal Processing. McGraw Hill (2006)

26. Malik, S., Afsar, F.A.: Wavelet transform based automatic speaker recognition. In: 2009 IEEE 13th International Multitopic Conference, pp. 1–4 (2009). https://doi.org/10.1109/INMIC.2009.5383083

27. Li, Q., Huang, Y.: An auditory-based feature extraction algorithm for robust speaker identification under mismatched conditions. IEEE Trans. Audio Speech Lang. Process. **19**(6), 1791–1801 (2011). https://doi.org/10.1109/TASL.2010.2101594

28. Zhang, C., Koishida, K., Hansen, J.H.L.: Text-independent speaker verification based on triplet convolutional neural network embeddings. IEEE/ACM Trans. Audio Speech Lang. Process. **26**(9), 1633–1644 (2018). https://doi.org/10.1109/TASLP.2018.2831456
29. Kadyrov, S., Turan, C., Amirzhanov, A., Ozdemir, C.: Speaker recognition from spectrogram images. In: 2021 IEEE International Conference on Smart Information Systems and Technologies (SIST), pp. 1–4 (2021). https://doi.org/10.1109/SIST50301.2021.9465954
30. Nehra, N., Sangwan, P., Kumar, D.: Speaker identification system using CNN approach. In: 2021 International Conference on Industrial Electronics Research and Applications (ICIERA), pp. 1–6 (2021). https://doi.org/10.1109/ICIERA53202.2021.9726767
31. Dinkel, H., Chen, N., Qian, Y., Yu, K.: End-to-end spoofing detection with raw waveform CLDNNS. In: Proceedings of ICASSP, pp. 4860–4864 (2017)
32. Seki, H., Yamamoto, K., Nakagawa, S.: A deep neural network integrated with FilterBank learning for speech recognition. In: Proceedings of ICASSP, pp. 5480–5484 (2017)
33. Palaz, D., Magimai-Doss, M., Collobert, R.: Analysis of CNN-based speech recognition system using raw speech as input. In: Proceedings of Interspeech (2015)
34. Sainath, T.N., Weiss, R.J., Senior, A.W., Wilson, K.W., Vinyals, O.: Learning the speech front-end with raw waveform CLDNNs. In: Proceedings of Interspeech (2015)
35. Hoshen, Y., Weiss, R., Wilson, K.W.: Speech acoustic modeling from raw multi-channel waveforms. In: Proceedings of ICASSP (2015)
36. Sainath, T.N., Weiss, R.J., Wilson, K.W., Narayanan, A., Bacchiani, M., Senior, A.: Speaker localization and microphone spacing invariant acoustic modeling from raw multichannel waveforms. In: Proceedings of ASRU (2015)
37. Tüske, Z., Golik, P., Schlüter, R., Ney, H.: Acoustic modeling with deep neural networks using raw time signal for LVCSR. In: Proceedings of Interspeech (2014)
38. Liu, X., Sahidullah, M., Kinnunen, T.: Learnable MFCCS for speaker verification. In: 2021 IEEE International Symposium on Circuits and Systems (ISCAS), pp. 1–5 (2021). https://doi.org/10.1109/ISCAS51556.2021.9401593
39. Garofolo, J.S., Lamel, L.F., Fisher, W.M., Fiscus, J.G., Pallett, D.S., Dahlgren, N.L.: DARPA TIMIT acoustic phonetic continuous speech corpus CDROM (1993)
40. Panayotov, V., Chen, G., Povey, D., Khudanpur, S.: Librispeech: an ASR corpus based on public domain audio books. In: Proceedings of ICASSP, pp. 5206–5210 (2015)
41. Ba, J., Kiros, R., Hinton, G.E.: Layer normalization. CoRR abs/1607.06450 (2016)
42. Ioffe, S., Szegedy, C.: Batch normalization: accelerating deep network training by reducing internal covariate shift. In: Proceedings of ICML, pp. 448–456 (2015)
43. Maas, A.L., Hannun, A.Y., Ng, A.Y.: Rectifier nonlinearities improve neural network acoustic models. In: Proceedings of ICML (2013)
44. Muckenhirn, H., Magimai.-Doss, M., Marcell, S.: Towards directly modeling raw speech signal for speaker verification using CNNs. In: 2018 IEEE International Conference on Acoustics, Speech and Signal Processing (ICASSP), pp. 4884–4888 (2018). https://doi.org/10.1109/ICASSP.2018.8462165
45. Povey, D., et al.: The Kaldi speech recognition toolkit. In: Proceedings of ASRU (2011)

Retrospective Evaluation of COVID-19 Therapeutics

Yuhan Gao[1,2] ⓘ, Zunjie Zhu[1], Yaoqi Sun[1], Dongmei Yu[3], Peiwu Qin[4,5], Cai Cheng[6], Ming Xu[7], Yuhan Dong[7], Jiyong Zhang[2], and Mang Xiao[8(✉)]

[1] Lishui Institute of Hangzhou Dianzi University, Hangzhou, Zhejiang, China
[2] Department of Automation, Hangzhou Dianzi University, Hangzhou, Zhejiang, China
[3] Shandong University, Weihai, Shandong, China
[4] Tsinghua Shenzhen International Graduate School, Shenzhen, Guangdong, China
[5] Tsinghua-Berkeley Shenzhen Institute, Shenzhen, Guangdong, China
[6] Tongji Hospital, Tongji Medical College, Huazhong University of Science and Technology, Wuhan, Hubei, China
[7] Tsinghua University, Beijing, China
[8] Sir Run Run Shaw Hospital, Zhejiang, China
joelxm@zju.edu.cn

Abstract. The pandemic outbreak of COVID-19 created panic all over the world. As therapeutics that can effectively wipe out the virus and terminate transmission are not available, supportive therapeutics are the main clinical treatments for COVID-19. Repurposing available therapeutics from other viral infections is the primary surrogate in ameliorating and treating COVID-19. The therapeutics should be tailored individually by analyzing the severity of COVID-19, age, gender, comorbidities, and so on. We aim to investigate the effects of COVID-19 therapeutics and to search for laboratory parameters indicative of severity of illness. Multi-center collaboration and large cohort of patients will be required to evaluate therapeutics combinations in the future.

This study is a single-center retrospective observational study of COVID-19 clinical data in China. Information on patients' treatment modalities, previous medical records, individual disease history, and clinical outcomes were considered to evaluate treatment efficacy. After screening, 2,844 patients are selected for the study. The result shows that treatment with TCM (Hazard Ratio (HR) 0.191 [95% Confidence Interval (CI), 0.14–0.25]; $p < 0.0001$), antiviral therapy (HR 0.331 [95% CI 0.19–0.58]; $p = 0.000128$), or Arbidol (HR 0.454 [95% CI 0.34–0.60]; $p < 0.0001$) is associated with good prognostic of patients. Multivariate Cox regression analysis showed TCM treatment decreased the mortality hazard ratio by 69.4% ($p < 0.0001$).

Keywords: COVID-19 · Therapeutics · Single-center retrospective observational study

© ICST Institute for Computer Sciences, Social Informatics and Telecommunications Engineering 2022
Published by Springer Nature Switzerland AG 2022. All Rights Reserved
Y. Chenggang et al. (Eds.): MobiMedia 2022, LNICST 451, pp. 375–400, 2022.
https://doi.org/10.1007/978-3-031-23902-1_29

376 Y. Gao et al.

1 Introduction

The quick spread and highly contagious nature of COVID-19 created a severe crisis worldwide. The absence of specific treatment for this decrease further raises the public concerns. Therefore, governments the world over utilize all the possible measures to prevent the infection and decrease the disease's devastating outcomes. Although the current therapeutics and vaccines have made promising progress, supportive therapeutics are the main methods for COVID-19 clinically [1]. There is still a long way for therapeutic optimization and understanding of diverse therapeutic approaches under the high risk of the second COVID-19 wave.

As the diseases caused by the SARS-CoV-2 range from asymptomatic, mild pneumonia to acute severe respiratory distress syndromes (ARDS), septic shock, and multiple organ dysfunction syndromes (MODS) [2]. The clinicians widely use antiviral, antibacterial, and TCM therapies to treat patients. Antivirals generally act through two paths: first path directly attacks the virus and interrupts its replication machinery or its ability to attack host cells, and second path blocks the host–viral interactions on the host side. Lopinavir (LPV), a protease inhibitor of 3CLpro, showed an antiviral effect against the SARS-CoV-2 virus with the estimated EC50 (half-maximal effective concentration) at 26.63 μM. LPV is commonly administered in coformulation with the structurally related ritonavir (LPV/r), a mutagenic guanosine analog that inhibits cytochrome P450 metabolism of LPV and boosts lopinavir concentrations [3]. Arbidol blocks virus replication by inhibiting the fusion of the virus's lipid membrane with the host cells, which blocks viral entry and post-stages of entry by targeting viral proteins or virus-associated host factors [4]. Arbidol targets the SARS-CoV-2 spike glycoprotein and impedes its trimerization [5]. Arbidol may induce structural rigidity for binding at the RBD/ACE2 interface, which will inhibit the conformational dynamics required during virus entry [6]. Besides, it can also regulate the immune system by promoting interferon release from cells and continuing to play an antiviral role [7].

Fluoroquinolones are broad-spectrum antibiotics [8]; their mechanism of action is by inhibiting the activities of p prokaryotic DNA gyrase–topoisomerase II and topoisomerase IV, which are involved in replication transcription and DNA synthesis [9]. Ciprofloxacin and moxifloxacin may interact with COVID-19 Main Protease [10]. Fluoroquinolones have limited ability to inhibit the replication of SARS-CoV-2 and MERS-CoV in cultured cells [11]. Azithromycin is an orally active synthetic macrolide antibiotic with a wide range of antibacterial, anti-inflammatory and antiviral properties. Azithromycin increased rhinovirus 1B- and rhinovirus 16-induced interferons and interferon-stimulated gene mRNA expression and protein production, and reduced rhinovirus replication and release [12]. Macrolides's antibacterial action is through inhibition of protein synthesis via binding to the 50S subunit of bacterial ribosomes [13]. Antibacterial therapy will be adopted to prevent bacterial co-infection and secondary bacterial infection are critical risk factors for the severity and mortality rates of COVID-19. It may increase drug resistance and raise the risks of allergic reactions.

TCM is an important weapon to contain the pandemic in Chinese history, which has been widely used to treat a variety of infectious diseases such as SARS, H1N1, and H5N1 [14, 15]. TCM can mitigate clinical symptoms, alleviate fever, shorten average hospitalization time, and slows down mild to severe transition [16]. Some plants have been observed to be effective in laboratory or animal studies; however there is a need to be aware that plant products may interact with other drugs [17]. Heparin and vitamin C are effective natural products and TCM-based therapies for combating the COVID-19 and immune boosters [18]. The compound from Qingfei Paidu Decoction may directly interfere with Toll-like receptor 4 and regulate the downstream signaling pathways, leading to the inhibition of release of proinflammation factors [19]. Lianhuaqingwen exerted its anti-coronavirus activity by inhibiting virus replication, affects virus morphology and reducing the cytokine release from host cells [20]. The mortality rate of patients receiving TCM treatment was lower than those not receiving TCM treatment [21].

This study explores the factors that correlate with disease severity and hospitalization mortality, and reveals the impact of different therapies on patient clinical outcomes. It shows that treatment with TCM and antiviral therapy is associated with good prognostic of patients benefits from main therapeutic methods for moderate patients are antiviral and TCM therapy. Antibacterial therapy had reduced survival rate since antibiotics are ineffective at suppressing bacterial infections and antimicrobial resistance may be associated with harm to patients. The physiological parameters of patients such as MPV, PT-INR, K^+, EOS#, BASO#, BASO%, Ca, ALB/GLO, Lymph#, and EOS% are closely related to the severity of the disease.

2 Methods

2.1 Study Design and Participants

This study was a retrospective, observational study based on clinical data from Tongji Hospital in Wuhan. The severity of patients' illness is determined by WHO interim guidance with positive SARS-CoV-2 RNA detection in throat swab specimens. We categorize patients into three groups and analyze the data by statistical methods. Specifically, we analyzed the relationship of the treatment modalities, past medical history, individual disease history, and clinical outcomes among patients with different disease severity. We studied the correlation between the severity of illness and laboratory parameters as well as the relationship between laboratory parameters and patient survival rate.

Inclusion and exclusion criteria are as follows: we included (1) RCTs or (2) cohort or case-control studies reporting on the adjusted effect estimates of the association between CST using in COVID-19 patients and one of the following a-priori outcomes: (1) in-hospital mortality, (2) mechanical ventilation, (3) ICU admission, (4) viral shedding and (5) composite outcomes if reported.

2.2 Data Collection

We collect the clinical data for 3337 COVID-19 patients. Data were ascertained from hospital's electronic medical record and recorded in a standardized electronic case report form. The data include all the diagnostic, pathological, and therapeutic information. Baseline data (such as demographics, medical history, individual disease history, and physical examination), laboratory, treatment, and outcome data are extracted from electronic medical records. Laboratory tests include routine blood tests, biochemical tests, coagulation tests, blood gas analysis, cytokine tests, ferritin, erythrocyte sedimentation rate, hypersensitive C-reactive protein, procalcitonin, etc. The treatment mainly includes TCM, immunotherapy, antiviral therapy, antibacterial therapy, and supportive therapy.

2.3 Statistical Analysis

Descriptive data contains normal and non-normal distributed types. The first type is expressed in terms of mean and standard deviation. Others are presented by median and interquartile range. Categorical variables were presented as percentages. We applied the Analysis of Variance or Kruskal-Wallis rank-sum for two kinds of data, respectively, comparing groups with varying disease severity. The chi-square test was performed to compare count data. We use Kaplan-Meier to plot to visualize survival curves, Log-rank test to compare the survival curves of two or more groups, and Cox proportional hazards regression for survival analysis to describe the effect of variables on survival.

Kaplan-Meier curves and log-rank tests – are examples of univariate analysis. They describe the survival according to one factor under investigation, but ignore the impact of any others. Additionally, Kaplan-Meier curves and log rank tests are useful only when the predictor variable is categorical. They don't work quickly for quantitative predictors. An alternative method is the Cox proportional hazards regression analysis, which works for both quantitative predictor variables and categorical variables. Furthermore, the Cox regression model extends survival analysis methods to simultaneously assess several risk factors' effect on survival time.

Assess the association between different drugs and in-hospital mortality in patients admitted with COVID-19 using a Kaplan-Meier method. The Cox proportional hazards regression analysis was used to extend survival analysis methods to assess the effect of several risk factors for in-hospital mortality simultaneously. All statistical analyses were conducted using the R language.

3 Results

We collect the clinical data for 3337 COVID-19 patients from Tongji Hospital in Wuhan. The data include all the diagnostic, pathological, and therapeutic information, which is screened to finalize the patients' cohort for further statistical analysis. Patients were excluded because they have asymptomatic or mild clinical symptoms without pneumonia on CT imaging since they do not need therapeutic intervention for recovery. Patients who are not sick enough to be hospitalized or lack of clinical records are excluded in this study. 2,844 (85.23%) patients after screening were grouped into categories in this study: moderate, severe, and critical ill according to the severity of COVID-19 (Fig. 1). The definition of COVID-19 severity follows the WHO standards. The various therapeutics have been used to treat three groups of patients, including 242 moderate, 1995 severe, and 607 critically ill patients.

For our study, the most commonly used combination for critically ill patients is ventilator, oxygen-therapy, TCM, hormone therapy, antiviral therapy and antibacterial therapy. The combination of oxygen therapy, TCM, antiviral therapy and antibacterial

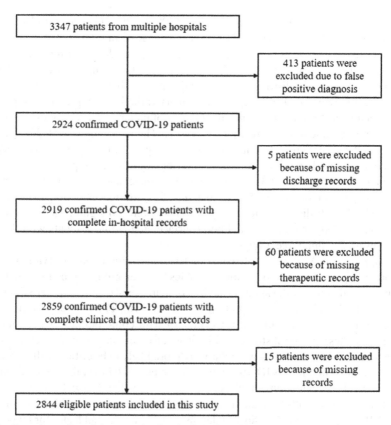

Fig. 1. Overview of participants selection included in this cohort. Some patients are excluded due to following factors such as missing important information and non-treatment cases for self-recovery.

therapy is most common for seriously ill patients. Moderate patients used a combination of TCM and antivirals at most.

The main therapeutic methods for moderate patients are antiviral (88.4%) and TCM (79.8%) therapy. Same patients receive a combination of different treatments, which causes the total percentage is greater than 100%. The therapeutics for severe patients are antiviral therapy (97.1%), oxygen therapy (89.3%), TCM (88.0%), and antibacterial therapy (72.8%). The treatment methods for critically ill patients are: oxygen therapy (98.7%), antiviral therapy (95.4%), antibacterial therapy (92.4%), hormone therapy (80.1%), and TCM (78.4%). Patients in less severity group have fewer therapeutics since some treatments are invasive, only applicable in severe conditions, and side effects. Oxygen therapy was used in a large proportion of patients (2508, 88.2%), while ventilator, intubate, hemodialysis, ECMO, and CRRT were mainly used in critically ill patients. 848 (29.8%) patients were treated with gamma globulin, 2,424 (85.2%) with TCM, 1,295 (45.5%) with hormone, 455 (16.0%) with immunotherapy, 2,119 (74.5%) with antibacterial therapy, and 2,731 (96.0%) with antiviral therapy for all three groups. The five most widely used antiviral drugs are Arbidol (1800, 63.3%), Ganciclovir (191, 6.7%), Oseltamivir (201, 7.1%), Interferon (126, 4.4%), and Kaletra (269, 9.5%).

Descriptive data was presented as mean with standard deviation for normally distributed continuous variables, where the standard deviation is in the bracket following mean. For non-normally-distributed data, we list the variable median with interquartile range in the following bracket. Categorical or binary variables were presented as percentages. For a different group of patients, the number of patients is listed followed with the percentage of treatment or nontreatment (Table 1). The mean age was 58.74 years (SD 15.28), and the severe group has higher mean age. Aging is associated with endothelial dysfunction and weak immune protection, contributing to vascular pathologies and cardiovascular diseases [22]. 1393 cases (49.0%) were male, and the group of critically ill patients comprised more males (57.2%) patients. Sex differences in immune responses underlie COVID-19 disease outcomes [23]. There were no significant differences in height, weight, body mass index, and body surface area among patients with different disease severity within three groups.

We applied the Analysis of Variance or Kruskal-Wallis rank-sum (variables with non-normal distribution) for continuous variables between groups with different disease severity. The chi-square test was performed to compare count data. There were significant differences ($p < 0.01$) in the proportion of patients with previous disease history in different disease severity. Patients in COVID-19 with comorbidities of hypertension, coronary, diabetes, chronic obstructive pulmonary diseases, malignancy, cerebrovascular disease, trauma history, or cardiovascular were more likely to be critically ill, associated with poorer outcomes in COVID-19 patients. Diabetes (13.7% overall) is associated with immunological dysregulation, which is potentially equivalent to accelerated aging, and could therefore potentially explain the poor prognosis in patients with diabetes mellitus and COVID-19. Preexisting cardiovascular diseases is an essential factor for myocardial injury as approximately 30% and 60% of patients with cardiac injury have coronary heart disease and hypertension previously [3, 4]. Patients with underlying cardiovascular disease, including hypertension, coronary heart disease, and cardiomyopathy are more likely to develop more severe adverse outcomes when myocardial injury occurs after COVID-19 infection and face a higher risk of death [24].

It is known that there is no effective therapeutics against COVID-19, and it will be informative to compare the available supportive treatment in the reduction of mortality and hospitalization time. We use Kaplan-Meier plots to visualize and Log-rank test to compare the impact on mortality by Arbidol, Ganciclovir, Oseltamivir, Interferon, Kaletra, antibacterial therapy, and TCM. There were significant differences ($p < 0.0001$) in patients survival rate treated with or without Abidiol, antibacterial, or TCM. Patients who had been treated with either Arbidol or TCM had improved survival likelihood, whereas antibacterial therapy had reduced survival rate. The phenomenon about patients who receive antibacterial therapy shows bacterial infection symptoms reacts SARS-CoV-2 infection weaken the immune system that increases the risk of bacterial infection. However, the current antibacterial are not effective for the inhibition of bacterial infection (Fig. 2).

A separate univariate Cox regression evaluated each factor to show the statistical significance of each variable with overall survival. Univariate Cox regression yielded

Table 1. Statistics on baseline characteristics, treatment, and comorbidities among patients with different severities and overall.

	Level	Moderate	Severe	Critical	Overall	p
n		242	1,995	607	2,844	
Age (mean (SD))		48.88 (14.42)	57.70 (14.64)	66.10 (14.51)	58.74 (15.28)	<0.001
Inhospital length (mean (SD))		10.43 (6.94)	22.10 (12.06)	29.03 (16.64)	22.59 (13.66)	<0.001
Sex (%)	Female	126 (52.1)	1065 (53.4)	260 (42.8)	1451 (51.0)	<0.001
	Male	116 (47.9)	930 (46.6)	347 (57.2)	1393 (49.0)	
Height (median [IQR])		168.00 [160.00, 170.00]	165.00 [160.00, 170.00]	167.00 [160.00, 170.00]	165.00 [160.00, 170.00]	0.067
Weight (median [IQR])		65.00 [59.00, 72.88]	65.00 [57.00, 70.00]	64.00 [55.00, 70.00]	65.00 [57.00, 70.00]	0.322
BMI (median [IQR])		23.66 [21.92, 25.26]	23.44 [21.48, 25.50]	23.03 [20.92, 25.10]	23.44 [21.47, 25.39]	0.163
BSA (mean (SD))		1.81 (0.17)	1.80 (0.34)	1.79 (0.18)	1.80 (0.30)	0.798
Ventilator (%)	No	239 (98.8)	1902 (95.3)	263 (43.3)	2404 (84.5)	<0.001
	Yes	3 (1.2)	93 (4.7)	344 (56.7)	440 (15.5)	
Intubate (%)	No	241 (99.6)	1978 (99.1)	415 (68.4)	2634 (92.6)	<0.001
	Yes	1 (0.4)	17 (0.9)	192 (31.6)	210 (7.4)	
Oxygen therapy (%)	No	115 (47.5)	213 (10.7)	8 (1.3)	336 (11.8)	<0.001
	Yes	127 (52.5)	1782 (89.3)	599 (98.7)	2508 (88.2)	
Hemodialysis (%)	No	242 (100.0)	1992 (99.8)	524 (86.3)	2758 (97.0)	<0.001
	Yes	0 (0.0)	3 (0.2)	83 (13.7)	86 (3.0)	
ECMO (%)	No	242 (100.0)	1994 (99.9)	592 (97.5)	2828 (99.4)	<0.001
	Yes	0 (0.0)	1 (0.1)	15 (2.5)	16 (0.6)	

(continued)

Table 1. (*continued*)

	Level	Moderate	Severe	Critical	Overall	p
CRRT (%)	No	242 (100.0)	1994 (99.9)	530 (87.3)	2766 (97.3)	<0.001
	Yes	0 (0.0)	1 (0.1)	77 (12.7)	78 (2.7)	
Gamma globulin therapy (%)	No	220 (90.9)	1521 (76.2)	255 (42.0)	1996 (70.2)	< 0.001
	Yes	22 (9.1)	474 (23.8)	352 (58.0)	848 (29.8)	
TCM (%)	No	49 (20.2)	240 (12.0)	131 (21.6)	420 (14.8)	<0.001
	Yes	193 (79.8)	1755 (88.0)	476 (78.4)	2424 (85.2)	
Hormone therapy (%)	No	202 (83.5)	1226 (61.5)	121 (19.9)	1549 (54.5)	< 0.001
	Yes	40 (16.5)	769 (38.5)	486 (80.1)	1295 (45.5)	
Immunotherapy (%)	No	209 (86.4)	1740 (87.2)	440 (72.5)	2389 (84.0)	<0.001
	Yes	33 (13.6)	255 (12.8)	167 (27.5)	455 (16.0)	
Antiviral therapy (%)	No	28 (11.6)	57 (2.9)	28 (4.6)	113 (4.0)	<0.001
	Yes	214 (88.4)	1938 (97.1)	579 (95.4)	2731 (96.0)	
Arbidol (%)	No	150 (62.0)	631 (31.6)	263 (43.3)	1044 (36.7)	<0.001
	Yes	92 (38.0)	1364 (68.4)	344 (56.7)	1800 (63.3)	
Ganciclovir (%)	No	237 (97.9)	1874 (93.9)	542 (89.3)	2653 (93.3)	<0.001
	Yes	5 (2.1)	121 (6.1)	65 (10.7)	191 (6.7)	
Oseltamivir (%)	No	227 (93.8)	1848 (92.6)	568 (93.6)	2643 (92.9)	0.627
	Yes	15 (6.2)	147 (7.4)	39 (6.4)	201 (7.1)	
Interferon (%)	No	229 (94.6)	1914 (95.9)	575 (94.7)	2718 (95.6)	0.338
	Yes	13 (5.4)	81 (4.1)	32 (5.3)	126 (4.4)	
Kaletra (%)	No	228 (94.2)	1819 (91.2)	528 (87.0)	2575 (90.5)	0.001

(*continued*)

Table 1. (*continued*)

	Level	Moderate	Severe	Critical	Overall	p
	Yes	14 (5.8)	176 (8.8)	79 (13.0)	269 (9.5)	
Antibacterial therapy (%)	No	137 (56.6)	542 (27.2)	46 (7.6)	725 (25.5)	<0.001
	Yes	105 (43.4)	1453 (72.8)	561 (92.4)	2119 (74.5)	
Smoking (%)	No	242 (100.0)	1976 (99.0)	603 (99.3)	2821 (99.2)	0.265
	Yes	0 (0.0)	19 (1.0)	4 (0.7)	23 (0.8)	
Past disease (%)	No	136 (56.2)	956 (47.9)	181 (29.8)	1273 (44.8)	<0.001
	Yes	106 (43.8)	1039 (52.1)	426 (70.2)	1571 (55.2)	
Infectious disease (%)	No	231 (95.5)	1934 (96.9)	582 (95.9)	2747 (96.6)	0.269
	Yes	11 (4.5)	61 (3.1)	25 (4.1)	97 (3.4)	
Allergic history (%)	No	226 (93.4)	1818 (91.1)	571 (94.1)	2615 (91.9)	0.046
	Yes	16 (6.6)	177 (8.9)	36 (5.9)	229 (8.1)	
Blood transfusion history (%)	No	242 (100.0)	1980 (99.2)	601 (99.0)	2823 (99.3)	0.313
	Yes	0 (0.0)	15 (0.8)	6 (1.0)	21 (0.7)	
Past surgery (%)	No	201 (83.1)	1666 (83.5)	482 (79.4)	2349 (82.6)	0.064
	Yes	41 (16.9)	329 (16.5)	125 (20.6)	495 (17.4)	
Hypertension (%)	No	203 (83.9)	1448 (72.6)	344 (56.7)	1995 (70.1)	<0.001
	Yes	39 (16.1)	547 (27.4)	263 (43.3)	849 (29.9)	
Coronary (%)	No	237 (97.9)	1860 (93.2)	544 (89.6)	2641 (92.9)	<0.001
	Yes	5 (2.1)	135 (6.8)	63 (10.4)	203 (7.1)	
Diabetes (%)	No	222 (91.7)	1733 (86.9)	500 (82.4)	2455 (86.3)	0.001
	Yes	20 (8.3)	262 (13.1)	107 (17.6)	389 (13.7)	

(*continued*)

Table 1. (*continued*)

	Level	Moderate	Severe	Critical	Overall	p
COPD (%)	No	241 (99.6)	1977 (99.1)	593 (97.7)	2811 (98.8)	0.01
	Yes	1 (0.4)	18 (0.9)	14 (2.3)	33 (1.2)	
Malignancy (%)	No	238 (98.3)	1950 (97.7)	579 (95.4)	2767 (97.3)	0.004
	Yes	4 (1.7)	45 (2.3)	28 (4.6)	77 (2.7)	
CKD (%)	No	239 (98.8)	1989 (99.7)	599 (98.7)	2827 (99.4)	0.007
	Yes	3 (1.2)	6 (0.3)	8 (1.3)	17 (0.6)	
Cerebrovascular disease (%)	No	237 (97.9)	1954 (97.9)	555 (91.4)	2746 (96.6)	<0.001
	Yes	5 (2.1)	41 (2.1)	52 (8.6)	98 (3.4)	
Immunodeficiency disease (%)	No	242 (100.0)	1,995 (100.0)	607 (100.0)	2,844 (100.0)	NA
Hepatitis (%)	No	234 (96.7)	1963 (98.4)	592 (97.5)	2789 (98.1)	0.107
	Yes	8 (3.3)	32 (1.6)	15 (2.5)	55 (1.9)	
Tuberculosis (%)	No	238 (98.3)	1961 (98.3)	592 (97.5)	2791 (98.1)	0.458
	Yes	4 (1.7)	34 (1.7)	15 (2.5)	53 (1.9)	
Trauma history (%)	No	241 (99.6)	1953 (97.9)	583 (96.0)	2777 (97.6)	0.004
	Yes	1 (0.4)	42 (2.1)	24 (4.0)	67 (2.4)	
Cardiovascular (%)	No	194 (80.2)	1363 (68.3)	305 (50.2)	1862 (65.5)	<0.001
	Yes	48 (19.8)	632 (31.7)	302 (49.8)	982 (34.5)	

Abbreviations: Body Mass Index, BMI; Body Surface Area, BSA; Extracorporeal Membrane Oxygenation, ECMO; Continuous Renal Replacement Therapy, CRRT; Chronic Obstructive Pulmonary Diseases, COPD; Chronic Kidney Disease, CKD.

similar results as survival analysis. Besides, we found differences in the characteristics of the patients' ventricle, intubate, hemodynamics, ECMO, CRRT, gamma globulin therapy, hormone therapy, infectious disease, coronary, malignant, CKD, or cerebrovascular disease had a significant impact (p < 0.01) on survival. Treatment with TCM (HR 0.191 [95% CI 0.14–0.25]; p < 0.0001), antiviral therapy (HR 0.331 [95% CI 0.19–0.58]; p = 0.000128), or Arbidol (HR 0.454 [95% CI 0.34–0.60]; p < 0.0001) is associated with good prognostic of patients, and others were associated with poor outcome or a higher risk of death (Table 2).

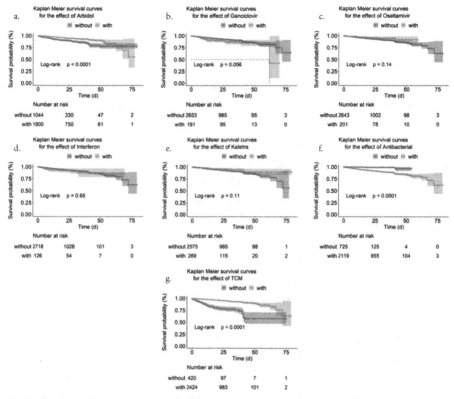

Fig. 2. Kaplan-Meier survival curves. Kaplan Meier survival curves and log rank tests for the effect of Arbidol (a), Ganciclovir (b), Oseltamivir (c), Interferon (d), Kaletra (e), Antibacterial therapy (f), and TCM (g) treatments on mortality.

Table 2. Univariate Cox regression of baseline characteristics, treatment, and comorbidities.

	Beta	HR (95% CI for HR)	wald.test	p. value
Ventilator	3.86	47.6 (29–77)	243	9.82E−55
Intubate	2.99	19.9 (15–27)	399	1.07E−88
Oxygen therapy	17.2	28100000 (0-Inf)	0	0.99
Hemodialysis	2.28	9.75 (7.1–13)	199	4.23E−45
ECMO	1.23	3.43 (1.6–7.4)	9.69	0.00186
CRRT	2.4	11 (8–15)	224	1.17E−50
Gamma globulin therapy	1.15	3.17 (2.4–4.2)	60.3	8.15E−15
TCM	−1.66	0.191 (0.14–0.25)	130	3.40E−30

(continued)

Table 2. (*continued*)

	Beta	HR (95% CI for HR)	wald.test	p. value
Hormone therapy	2.07	7.95 (5–13)	76.7	2.01E−18
Immunotherapy	−0.121	0.886 (0.62–1.3)	0.45	0.5
Antiviral therapy	−1.1	0.331 (0.19–0.58)	14.7	0.000128
Arbidol	−0.79	0.454 (0.34–0.6)	31.2	2.39E−08
Ganciclovir	0.42	1.52 (0.99–2.4)	3.58	0.0584
Oseltamivir	−0.502	0.605 (0.31–1.2)	2.16	0.141
Interferon	0.14	1.15 (0.63–2.1)	0.2	0.653
Kaletra	−0.421	0.656 (0.39–1.1)	2.45	0.117
Antibacterial therapy	2.18	8.81 (3.6–21)	23	1.62E−06
Smoking	−0.856	0.425 (0.059–3.1)	0.72	0.395
Past disease	0.361	1.43 (1.1–1.9)	5.78	0.0162
Infectious disease	0.833	2.3 (1.3–4)	8.41	0.00374
Allergic history	−0.518	0.596 (0.32–1.1)	2.55	0.11
Blood transfusion history	1.2	3.3 (1.2–8.9)	5.6	0.018
Past surgery	0.113	1.12 (0.79–1.6)	0.41	0.522
Hypertension	0.178	1.2 (0.9–1.6)	1.48	0.224
Coronary	0.609	1.84 (1.2–2.8)	8.38	0.00379
Diabetes	0.108	1.11 (0.77–1.6)	0.32	0.569
COPD	0.249	1.28 (0.47–3.5)	0.24	0.624
Malignancy	0.743	2.1 (1.2–3.7)	6.66	0.00988
CKD	1.38	3.97 (1.5–11)	7.42	0.00643
Cerebrovascular disease	0.754	2.13 (1.3–3.5)	8.77	0.00306
Hepatitis	0.551	1.73 (0.77–3.9)	1.76	0.184
Tuberculosis	0.562	1.75 (0.78–4)	1.84	0.175
Trauma history	−0.0835	0.92 (0.38–2.2)	0.03	0.854
Cardiovascular	0.335	1.4 (1.1–1.8)	5.57	0.0183

Besides, we used multivariate Cox regression analysis to describe how these factors work together to influence survival. Multivariate Cox regression analysis showed that treatment with TCM decreased the mortality hazard ratio by 69.4% (p < 0.0001), while supportive treatment ventilator or intubate use was statistically associated with a higher risk of mortality due to COVID-19 (Table 3).

We constructed new data frames with two rows according to TCM treatment or not, and other covariates were fixed as used (not used). The resulting survival curve again indicates a strong relationship between TCM therapy and decreased risk of death (Fig. 3).

Table 3. Multivariate Cox regression analysis of baseline characteristics, treatment, and comorbidities.

	exp (coef) [confint]	coef	se (coef)	z	p.value
Ventilator	20.213 [11.273, 36.244]	3.006	0.298	10.091	6.08E−24
Intubate	3.267 [2.269, 4.705]	1.184	0.186	6.363	1.98E−10
Hemodialysis	1.511 [0.888, 2.569]	0.413	0.271	1.524	0.127617286
ECMO	0.660 [0.296, 1.471]	−0.415	0.409	−1.016	0.309832551
CRRT	0.791 [0.465, 1.346]	−0.234	0.271	−0.864	0.387582057
Gamma globulin therapy	0.725 [0.526, 1.000]	−0.322	0.164	−1.962	0.049745714
TCM	0.306 [0.225, 0.414]	−1.186	0.155	−7.633	2.30E−14
Hormone therapy	1.202 [0.702, 2.060]	0.184	0.275	0.670	0.502639462
Antiviral therapy	0.562 [0.302, 1.045]	−0.576	0.317	−1.821	0.068572796
Arbidol	0.794 [0.590, 1.068]	−0.231	0.151	−1.524	0.127407379
Antibacterial therapy	1.438 [0.557, 3.708]	0.363	0.483	0.751	0.452801778
Infectious disease	2.264 [1.260, 4.069]	0.817	0.299	2.732	0.006303463
Coronary	1.186 [0.773, 1.822]	0.171	0.219	0.782	0.434423283
Malignancy	1.305 [0.722, 2.357]	0.266	0.302	0.882	0.377638162
CKD	0.816 [0.293, 2.268]	−0.204	0.522	−0.390	0.696198216
Cerebrovascular disease	0.929 [0.534, 1.616]	−0.074	0.283	−0.262	0.793590892

Exp (coef): the exponentiated coefficients; coef: the regression coefficients; se (coef): standard error of the regression coefficient; z: coef/se (coef).

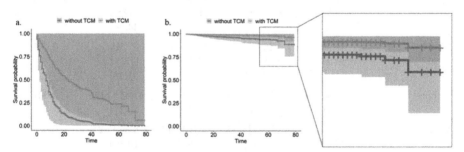

Fig. 3. Visualized survival curves for the new data frames. The latest data framework only kept the values of TCM, modified the other parameters to the same value; the left panel was based on the different treatments all used or had comorbidity, the right panel is the opposite.

A total of 77 indicators derived from laboratory tests including routine blood tests, biochemistry, coagulation, blood gas, cytokines, ferritin, erythrocyte sedimentation rate, hypersensitive C-reactive protein, and procalcitonin were included in this study. Except for Mean Corpuscular Hemoglobin (MCH), Monocyte count (Mono#), Actual bicarbonate (AB), Standard bicarbonate (SB), Base excess (BE), Standard base surplus (SBE), Blood carbon dioxide content, and Interleukin-1β (IL-1β), the other 69 indices were significantly different ($p < 0.001$) between patients with varying severities of disease (Table 4, Fig. 4).

Table 4. Statistics on laboratory indices among patients with different severities and overall.

	Moderate	Severe	Critical	Overall	p
N	242	1,995	607	2,844	
WBC#	5.69 [4.77, 6.72]	5.67 [4.82, 6.86]	8.04 [6.00, 10.97]	5.96 [4.95, 7.49]	< 0.001
RBC#	4.28 [3.98, 4.72]	4.08 [3.75, 4.45]	3.74 [3.33, 4.14]	4.04 [3.68, 4.42]	< 0.001
MCV	89.24 [86.59, 91.71]	90.00 [87.35, 92.66]	90.94 [87.90, 93.92]	90.13 [87.37, 92.84]	< 0.001
MCHC	342.00 [336.00, 348.00]	342.00 [335.33, 349.00]	339.73 [331.47, 346.62]	341.33 [334.84, 348.33]	< 0.001
MCH	30.60 [29.60, 31.50]	30.87 [29.80, 31.82]	30.85 [29.80, 31.92]	30.83 [29.78, 31.80]	0.021
RDW-CV	12.72 [12.13, 13.24]	12.63 [12.10, 13.22]	13.46 [12.70, 14.54]	12.78 [12.20, 13.50]	< 0.001
RDW-SD	41.30 [38.92, 43.51]	41.15 [38.98, 43.55]	44.05 [41.29, 48.02]	41.63 [39.30, 44.30]	< 0.001
Lymph%	31.30 [25.87, 36.21]	26.88 [21.28, 32.50]	15.46 [7.41, 21.17]	25.30 [18.71, 31.35]	< 0.001
Lymph#	1.74 [1.35, 2.11]	1.49 [1.18, 1.81]	0.99 [0.68, 1.33]	1.41 [1.08, 1.78]	< 0.001
Mono%	8.52 [7.44, 9.66]	8.90 [7.63, 10.37]	7.39 [5.14, 9.06]	8.64 [7.25, 10.10]	< 0.001
Mono#	0.48 [0.41, 0.58]	0.50 [0.41, 0.61]	0.52 [0.40, 0.68]	0.50 [0.41, 0.62]	0.004
Neut%	56.32 [51.56, 62.51]	61.21 [54.97, 67.30]	74.98 [67.39, 86.80]	63.03 [56.00, 70.50]	< 0.001

(continued)

Table 4. (*continued*)

	Moderate	Severe	Critical	Overall	p
Neut#	3.27 [2.59, 4.03]	3.46 [2.74, 4.47]	5.99 [4.20, 9.06]	3.73 [2.86, 5.12]	< 0.001
Hct	38.10 [35.88, 41.70]	36.75 [34.05, 39.42]	33.82 [30.33, 37.13]	36.40 [33.43, 39.22]	< 0.001
Eos%	2.30 [1.40, 3.21]	1.77 [1.10, 2.70]	1.06 [0.35, 2.18]	1.70 [0.95, 2.65]	< 0.001
Baso%	0.49 [0.30, 0.60]	0.40 [0.28, 0.58]	0.25 [0.16, 0.40]	0.40 [0.24, 0.55]	< 0.001
Eos#	0.13 [0.08, 0.19]	0.10 [0.06, 0.15]	0.08 [0.03, 0.14]	0.10 [0.05, 0.15]	< 0.001
Baso#	0.03 [0.02, 0.04]	0.02 [0.01, 0.03]	0.02 [0.01, 0.03]	0.02 [0.01, 0.03]	< 0.001
Hb	131.50 [122.00, 143.00]	125.50 [115.67, 135.50]	114.87 [102.16, 126.27]	124.00 [113.33, 134.75]	< 0.001
PLT#	227.00 [199.00, 264.17]	231.38 [192.00, 277.20]	196.47 [135.96, 254.97]	224.83 [183.50, 273.00]	< 0.001
MPV	10.40 [9.90, 11.00]	10.50 [9.97, 11.10]	11.06 [10.35, 11.80]	10.60 [10.00, 11.23]	< 0.001
PDW	12.00 [10.96, 13.30]	11.93 [10.81, 13.34]	13.03 [11.43, 15.00]	12.13 [10.95, 13.58]	< 0.001
Thrombocytocrit	0.24 [0.21, 0.27]	0.24 [0.20, 0.29]	0.22 [0.16, 0.27]	0.24 [0.20, 0.28]	< 0.001
P-LCR%	28.02 [23.89, 33.21]	28.52 [24.17, 33.60]	33.08 [27.27, 38.88]	29.38 [24.55, 34.64]	< 0.001
ALT	21.17 [13.88, 36.00]	23.63 [15.24, 37.00]	27.55 [18.22, 42.69]	24.00 [15.67, 38.00]	< 0.001

(*continued*)

Table 4. (*continued*)

	Moderate	Severe	Critical	Overall	p
AST	20.00 [16.00, 26.50]	22.00 [17.33, 28.85]	29.50 [22.14, 41.90]	23.00 [18.00, 31.20]	< 0.001
GGT	24.58 [16.00, 41.87]	28.33 [18.00, 47.75]	40.75 [25.50, 66.93]	30.00 [19.00, 51.00]	< 0.001
TBil	8.80 [6.93, 11.57]	8.50 [6.68, 11.00]	10.80 [8.02, 15.05]	8.84 [6.90, 11.77]	< 0.001
DBIL	3.30 [2.71, 4.10]	3.46 [2.80, 4.44]	5.07 [3.60, 7.29]	3.63 [2.90, 4.90]	< 0.001
IBIL	5.57 [4.24, 7.40]	4.97 [3.80, 6.60]	5.44 [4.22, 7.56]	5.13 [3.90, 6.82]	< 0.001
ALB	41.80 [40.00, 43.80]	37.64 [34.70, 40.65]	33.62 [30.84, 35.80]	37.10 [33.93, 40.50]	< 0.001
GLO	27.92 [26.15, 30.31]	30.00 [27.27, 32.92]	32.14 [28.40, 35.72]	30.13 [27.27, 33.40]	< 0.001
TP	69.78 [67.46, 72.93]	68.10 [65.15, 70.95]	65.67 [61.62, 69.26]	67.80 [64.63, 70.85]	< 0.001
ALB/GLO	1.49 [1.36, 1.66]	1.26 [1.09, 1.46]	1.07 [0.91, 1.24]	1.25 [1.05, 1.45]	< 0.001
Crea	67.67 [58.00, 77.00]	67.50 [57.00, 79.58]	72.88 [57.67, 93.89]	68.33 [57.00, 82.00]	< 0.001
Urea	4.50 [3.90, 5.60]	4.35 [3.60, 5.19]	6.20 [4.70, 9.83]	4.60 [3.78, 5.70]	< 0.001
UA	321.00 [256.00, 387.15]	271.33 [221.60, 330.42]	233.79 [173.73, 310.33]	268.17 [214.44, 333.35]	< 0.001
TC	4.44 [3.81, 5.07]	4.13 [3.60, 4.71]	3.57 [2.93, 4.31]	4.05 [3.47, 4.68]	< 0.001
K^+	4.22 [4.07, 4.47]	4.25 [4.00, 4.48]	4.33 [4.06, 4.66]	4.26 [4.02, 4.50]	< 0.001
Na^+	140.80 [139.70, 141.80]	140.17 [138.75, 141.50]	139.49 [137.40, 141.57]	140.13 [138.60, 141.53]	< 0.001

(*continued*)

Table 4. (*continued*)

	Moderate	Severe	Critical	Overall	p
Cl⁻	102.20 [100.90, 103.50]	101.72 [100.10, 103.22]	100.38 [98.04, 102.99]	101.60 [99.72, 103.22]	< 0.001
Ca	2.27 [2.20, 2.33]	2.19 [2.13, 2.24]	2.13 [2.06, 2.19]	2.18 [2.12, 2.25]	< 0.001
Glu	5.09 [4.75, 5.50]	5.54 [5.03, 6.54]	6.94 [5.87, 9.08]	5.69 [5.07, 6.99]	< 0.001
LDH	182.00 [162.00, 201.50]	206.00 [178.00, 241.25]	290.20 [234.50, 429.20]	213.85 [181.68, 260.83]	< 0.001
ALP	63.42 [53.50, 76.00]	65.75 [55.40, 78.50]	76.80 [61.36, 99.83]	67.00 [56.40, 81.94]	< 0.001
CKD-EPI formula	98.65 [90.65, 108.77]	93.79 [82.80, 103.90]	86.18 [67.35, 97.70]	93.30 [80.76, 103.50]	< 0.001
TT	16.10 [15.40, 16.60]	16.50 [15.90, 17.18]	16.51 [15.76, 17.80]	16.45 [15.80, 17.20]	< 0.001
PT	13.30 [13.00, 13.70]	13.53 [13.10, 14.00]	14.37 [13.67, 15.62]	13.63 [13.20, 14.20]	< 0.001
APTT	38.10 [35.90, 40.70]	38.20 [35.74, 41.30]	40.10 [36.79, 44.53]	38.50 [35.90, 41.80]	< 0.001
PT-INR	1.01 [0.98, 1.05]	1.03 [1.00, 1.08]	1.12 [1.04, 1.24]	1.04 [1.00, 1.10]	< 0.001
D-Dimer	0.26 [0.22, 0.39]	0.55 [0.30, 1.11]	2.27 [1.05, 4.27]	0.66 [0.32, 1.59]	< 0.001
Fbg	3.10 [2.74, 3.64]	4.06 [3.34, 4.89]	4.32 [3.58, 5.22]	4.03 [3.28, 4.90]	< 0.001
PTA	98.00 [92.75, 103.42]	95.00 [89.00, 101.00]	84.67 [73.00, 93.71]	93.67 [86.33, 100.00]	< 0.001
PaO2	110.00 [92.60, 137.00]	116.00 [96.07, 149.33]	102.33 [77.82, 139.07]	112.00 [90.40, 144.00]	< 0.001

(*continued*)

Table 4. (*continued*)

	Moderate	Severe	Critical	Overall	p
SaO2	98.20 [97.30, 99.00]	98.30 [97.10, 99.10]	96.58 [92.73, 98.60]	97.90 [95.96, 99.00]	< 0.001
PaCO2	42.50 [40.20, 44.80]	41.20 [37.85, 43.90]	38.45 [34.31, 43.61]	40.70 [36.60, 43.80]	< 0.001
AB	24.70 [23.20, 25.90]	24.50 [22.92, 25.81]	24.60 [21.90, 26.86]	24.50 [22.70, 26.02]	0.572
SB	24.30 [23.55, 25.10]	24.40 [23.20, 25.40]	24.82 [22.80, 26.75]	24.50 [23.20, 25.86]	0.107
BE	−0.10 [−1.05, 0.80]	−0.10 [−1.40, 1.10]	0.55 [−1.90, 2.60]	0.10 [−1.50, 1.70]	0.067
SBE	0.10 [−0.90, 1.20]	0.10 [−1.40, 1.38]	0.40 [−2.22, 2.60]	0.20 [−1.50, 1.80]	0.317
Blood carbon dioxide content	21.00 [19.90, 21.60]	21.50 [20.30, 23.00]	21.90 [19.40, 23.90]	21.60 [20.00, 23.35]	0.258
Calcium ion-PH correction	2.33 [2.19, 2.42]	2.30 [2.19, 2.41]	2.35 [2.23, 2.44]	2.32 [2.20, 2.42]	< 0.001
IL-6	2.79 [1.89, 5.26]	5.18 [2.79, 12.50]	24.90 [9.50, 76.53]	6.64 [3.10, 20.44]	< 0.001
IL-10	6.45 [6.12, 7.90]	7.20 [5.90, 9.78]	10.60 [7.66, 18.30]	8.30 [6.30, 12.96]	< 0.001
IL-8	9.00 [7.05, 13.12]	11.00 [7.90, 17.52]	19.60 [12.21, 40.29]	12.28 [8.30, 21.30]	< 0.001
TNF-α	7.30 [6.07, 8.80]	7.80 [6.30, 9.90]	10.59 [8.00, 15.48]	8.25 [6.58, 10.60]	< 0.001

(*continued*)

Table 4. (*continued*)

	Moderate	Severe	Critical	Overall	p
IL-1β	9.75 [7.20, 15.15]	8.70 [6.40, 12.10]	9.11 [6.80, 15.41]	8.80 [6.60, 13.20]	0.074
IL-2R	293.25 [234.25, 405.00]	441.50 [310.00, 623.50]	780.61 [519.26, 1179.76]	473.50 [317.00, 705.47]	< 0.001
Ferr	240.30 [121.80, 394.30]	428.80 [232.40, 682.65]	908.59 [496.69, 1620.17]	484.30 [266.97, 864.76]	< 0.001
ESR	9.00 [5.50, 17.25]	25.00 [12.00, 46.00]	37.00 [21.25, 60.00]	26.50 [13.00, 49.90]	< 0.001
HS-CRP	1.23 [0.60, 3.32]	5.87 [1.48, 20.08]	38.49 [16.14, 83.70]	7.91 [1.67, 28.37]	< 0.001
PCT	0.05 [0.04, 0.06]	0.06 [0.04, 0.08]	0.15 [0.07, 0.61]	0.06 [0.04, 0.10]	< 0.001
NT-ProBNP	37.50 [18.25, 69.00]	78.25 [34.00, 180.00]	552.12 [187.52, 1923.39]	101.50 [41.00, 312.25]	< 0.001
Mb	31.20 [26.45, 40.65]	32.30 [25.08, 44.75]	70.00 [38.17, 165.09]	35.03 [26.20, 56.80]	< 0.001
CK	66.25 [48.56, 90.88]	52.00 [37.00, 74.75]	59.92 [36.38, 126.54]	54.63 [37.60, 83.00]	< 0.001

(*continued*)

Table 4. (*continued*)

	Moderate	Severe	Critical	Overall	p
CK-MB	0.60 [0.40, 0.82]	0.60 [0.40, 0.90]	1.15 [0.63, 2.53]	0.67 [0.40, 1.10]	< 0.001
HS-CTNI	3.15 [2.40, 4.65]	4.60 [2.90, 8.50]	15.56 [5.61, 71.00]	5.65 [3.20, 12.90]	< 0.001

WBC#: White Blood Cell Count; RBC#: Red Blood Cell Count; MCV: Mean Corpuscular Volume; RDW−CV: Red Cell Volume Distribution Width-Coefficient of Variation; RDW-SD: Red Cell Volume Distribution Width-Standard Deviation; Lymph%: Lymphocyte Percentage; Mono%: Monocyte Percentage; Neut%: Neutrophil Percentage; Neut#: Neutrophil Count; Hct: Hematocrit; Hb: Hemoglobin; PLT#: Platelet Count; PDW: Platelet Distribution Width; P-LCR%: Platelet Large Cell Ratio; ALT: Alanine Aminotransferase; AST: Aspartate Aminotransferase; GGT: Gamma-Glutamyltransferase; TBil: Total Bilirubin; DBIL: Direct Bilirubin; IBIL: Indirect Bilirubin; ALB: Albumin; GLO: Globulin; TP: Total Protein; Crea: Creatinine; UA: Uric Acid; TC: Total Cholesterol; K^+: Potassium Ions; Glu: Glucose; LDH: Lactate Dehydrogenase; ALP: Alkaline Phosphatase; CKD-EPI formula: Estimation of Glomerular Filtration Rate; TT: Thrombin Time; PT: Prothrombin Time; APTT: Activated Partial Thromboplastin Time; Fbg: Fibrinogen; PTA: Prothrombin Time Activity; PaO2: Partial Pressure of Oxygen; SaO2: Oxygen Saturation; PaCO2: Partial Pressure of Carbon Dioxide; IL: Interleukin; TNF-α: Tumor Necrosis Factor-α; Ferr: Ferritin; ESR: Erythrocyte Sedimentation Rate; HS-CRP: Hypersensitive C-reactive Protein; PCT: Procalcitonin; NT-ProBNP: N-Terminal Pro-Brain Natriuretic Peptide; Mb: Myoglobin; CK: Creatine Kinase; CK-MB: Creatine Kinase Isoenzyme MB; HS-CTNI: Hypersensitive Cardiac Troponin I.

By univariate Cox regression, several indexes including RBC#, MCH, Mono#, Neut#, UA, Fbg, PaCO2, Calcium ion -PH correction, and ESR showed lower statistical significance ($p > 0.01$). Larger MPV, PT-INR, and K + are associated with lower survival, whereas larger Eos#, Baso#, Baso%, Ca, ALB/GLO, Lymph#, and Eos% are associated with better survival (Table 5).

4 Discussion

Aging is associated with endothelial dysfunction, contributing to vascular disease and cardiovascular disease in the elderly [22]. Sex differences in immune response are the basis of COVID-19 disease outcomes [23]. High physiological concentrations of the steroid hormones 17β-estradiol and progesterone are powerful immunomodulators [25]. The combination of 17β-estradiol and progesterone is a potential therapeutic approach. Diabetes is associated with immune disorders, which may equate to accelerated aging. Patients with underlying cardiovascular disease, including hypertension, coronary heart disease, and cardiomyopathy are more likely to develop more severe adverse outcomes when myocardial injury occurs after COVID-19 infection and face a higher death risk [24]. Consider prioritizing and more aggressive treatment for COVID-19 patients based on the presence of underlying cardiovascular disease.

The P value of antiviral therapy was not less than 0.01 in multivariate COX analysis results, and reached significant level in univariate COX, which may be affected

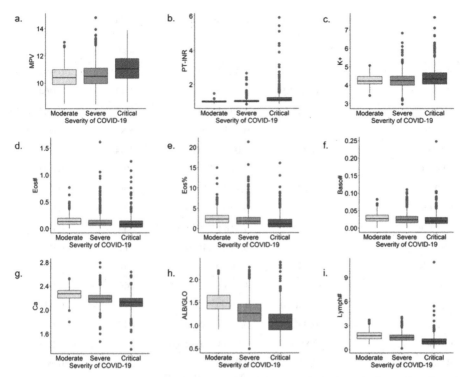

Fig. 4. Boxplots of laboratory indices and severity of COVID-19. A-plot to i-plot are boxplots of indicator MPV (a), PT-INR (b), K^+ (c), Eos# (d), Eos% (e), Baso# (f), Ca (g), ALB/GLO (h), and Lymph# (i) for different covid-19 severities, respectively.

by the difference of multiple antiviral drugs. Kaplan-Meier plots showed a significant improvement in the likelihood of survival of patients treated with Arbidol. Arbidol showed beneficial effects on fever recovery, viral clearance and shorter hospital stay in these patients, especially in males [26]. Arbidol monotherapy is more effective than lopinavir/ritonavir in treating COVID-19 [27]. Arbidol significantly contributed to clinical and laboratory improvement compared to Kaletra in a recent randomized controlled trial (IRCT 20180725040596N2) [28].

We used the Kaplan-Mayer method and Cox regression analysis to show the positive effect of TCM treatment on the patients' prognosis. This indication may increase the testing of the efficacy of TCM in clinical trials. Early combination of Lianhuaqingwen and Arbidol significantly accelerated recovery in patients with moderate COVID-19, but not in patients with severe COVID-19 [29]. SARS-CoV-2 infection weakens the immune system and increases the risk of bacterial infections. Patients treated with antibiotics showed a symbiosis of bacterial infections. However, current antibiotics are ineffective at suppressing bacterial infections, which may be influenced by the very high rate (74.5%) the use of antimicrobial therapy in critically ill patients [30]. For example, prescription drugs are significantly higher than the estimated prevalence of mixed bacterial infections; unnecessary antibiotic use may be high in patients with COVID-19; and antimicrobial

Table 5. Univariate Cox regression of laboratory indices.

	Beta	HR (95% CI for HR)	wald.test	p. value
WBC#	0.29	1.34 (1.3–1.4)	679	<0.001
RBC#	0.000851	1 (1–1)	3.43	0.0641
MCV	0.0679	1.07 (1–1.1)	19.6	<0.001
MCHC	−0.0152	0.985 (0.97–1)	6.85	0.00889
MCH	0.0592	1.06 (1–1.1)	3.34	0.0677
RDW-CV	0.198	1.22 (1.2–1.3)	99.2	<0.001
RDW-SD	0.0917	1.1 (1.1–1.1)	160	<0.001
Lymph%	−0.279	0.756 (0.74–0.78)	391	<0.001
Lymph#	−3.97	0.0188 (0.013–0.028)	384	<0.001
Mono%	−0.671	0.511 (0.48–0.54)	511	<0.001
Mono#	0.00404	1 (1–1)	3.65	0.056
Neut%	0.195	1.22 (1.2–1.2)	466	<0.001
Neut#	0.000191	1 (1–1)	4.5	0.0338
Hct	−0.0989	0.906 (0.88–0.93)	44.3	<0.001
Eos%	−2.89	0.0553 (0.039–0.079)	245	<0.001
Baso%	−9.33	8.91e−05 (2.6e−05–0.00031)	218	<0.001
Eos#	−28.5	4.2e−13 (5.8e−15–3.1e−11)	170	<0.001
Baso#	−26.5	3.01e−12 (1.8e−17–5e−07)	18.7	<0.001
Hb	−0.0284	0.972 (0.96–0.98)	48.6	<0.001
PLT#	−0.0205	0.98 (0.98–0.98)	370	<0.001
MPV	1.09	2.97 (2.6–3.4)	247	<0.001
PDW	0.378	1.46 (1.4–1.5)	283	<0.001
thrombocytocrit	−18.4	1.06e−08 (1.3e−09–8.7e−08)	294	<0.001
P-LCR%	0.137	1.15 (1.1–1.2)	229	<0.001
ALT	0.00245	1 (1–1)	36	<0.001
AST	0.00416	1 (1–1)	149	<0.001
GGT	0.00434	1 (1–1)	20.5	<0.001
TBil	0.0148	1.01 (1–1)	203	<0.001
DBIL	0.021	1.02 (1–1)	218	<0.001

(*continued*)

Table 5. (*continued*)

	Beta	HR (95% CI for HR)	wald.test	p. value
IBIL	0.0286	1.03 (1–1)	98.2	<0.001
ALB	−0.351	0.704 (0.68–0.73)	518	<0.001
GLO	0.0849	1.09 (1.1–1.1)	38.5	<0.001
TP	−0.163	0.849 (0.83–0.87)	171	<0.001
ALB/GLO	−4.75	0.00866 (0.0044–0.017)	186	<0.001
Crea	0.00239	1 (1–1)	110	<0.001
Urea	0.108	1.11 (1.1–1.1)	631	<0.001
UA	0.00146	1 (1–1)	3.65	0.0561
TC	−1.29	0.275 (0.23–0.32)	243	<0.001
K^+	1.44	4.21 (3.2–5.5)	115	<0.001
Na^+	0.15	1.16 (1.1–1.2)	129	<0.001
Cl^-	0.119	1.13 (1.1–1.2)	57.8	<0.001
Ca	−7.05	0.000871 (0.00044–0.0017)	417	<0.001
Glu	0.182	1.2 (1.2–1.2)	319	<0.001
LDH	0.00494	1 (1–1)	856	<0.001
ALP	0.00486	1 (1–1)	99	<0.001
CKD-EPI formula	−0.0361	0.965 (0.96–0.97)	195	<0.001
TT	0.0452	1.05 (1–1.1)	56.6	<0.001
PT	0.17	1.19 (1.2–1.2)	505	<0.001
APTT	0.112	1.12 (1.1–1.1)	191	<0.001
PT-INR	1.31	3.69 (3.3–4.2)	433	<0.001
D-Dimer	0.21	1.23 (1.2–1.3)	422	<0.001
Fbg	0.0398	1.04 (0.92–1.2)	0.38	0.539
PTA	−0.0874	0.916 (0.91–0.92)	717	<0.001
PaO2	−0.0282	0.972 (0.97–0.98)	61.1	<0.001
SaO2	−0.108	0.897 (0.88–0.91)	147	<0.001
PaCO2	−0.0153	0.985 (0.96–1)	0.96	0.327
AB	−0.143	0.867 (0.82–0.92)	25	<0.001
SB	−0.189	0.828 (0.78–0.88)	35.3	<0.001
BE	−0.152	0.859 (0.82–0.9)	42.5	<0.001
SBE	−0.148	0.862 (0.82–0.91)	35.7	<0.001

(*continued*)

Table 5. (*continued*)

	Beta	HR (95% CI for HR)	wald.test	p. value
Blood carbon dioxide content	−0.127	0.88 (0.83–0.94)	15.7	<0.001
Calcium ion−PH correction	0.959	2.61 (0.9–7.6)	3.13	0.0769
IL-6	0.00279	1 (1–1)	302	<0.001
IL-10	0.00571	1.01 (1–1)	48.8	<0.001
IL-8	0.00132	1 (1–1)	88.8	<0.001
TNF-α	0.0454	1.05 (1–1.1)	232	<0.001
IL-1β	0.0179	1.02 (1–1)	14.5	<0.001
IL-2R	0.000974	1 (1–1)	318	<0.001
Ferr	0.000183	1 (1–1)	148	<0.001
ESR	0.00563	1.01 (1–1)	3.27	0.0704
HS-CRP	0.0208	1.02 (1–1)	823	<0.001
PCT	0.147	1.16 (1.1–1.2)	207	<0.001
NT-ProBNP	9.06E−05	1 (1–1)	252	<0.001
Mb	0.00532	1.01 (1–1)	461	<0.001
CK	0.000887	1 (1–1)	116	<0.001
CK-MB	0.0348	1.04 (1–1)	147	<0.001
HS-CTNI	0.000605	1 (1–1)	179	<0.001

resistance may be associated with harm to patients [31]. All these results indicate a more rational use of antibacterial.

We found that larger MPV, PT-INR, and the higher K^+ concentration were associated with lower survival, while larger EOS#, BASO#, BASO%, Ca, ALB/GLO, Lymph#, and EOS% were associated with better survival, indicating greater attention to these physiological parameters during the patient's disease course.

To sum up, from this perspective studies, the doctors need to increase attention to elderly patients and patients with comorbidities, expand the use of TCM and rationalize the use of antibacterial in clinical practice, and pay attention to the changes of physiological parameters such as MPV, PT-INR, K^+, EOS#, BASO#, BASO%, Ca, ALB/GLO, Lymph#, and EOS%.

References

1. Naja, M., Wedderburn, L., Ciurtin, C.: COVID-19 infection in children and adolescents. Br. J. Hosp. Med. (Lond) **81**(8), 1–10 (2020)
2. Chen, N., et al.: Epidemiological and clinical characteristics of 99 cases of 2019 novel coronavirus pneumonia in Wuhan, China: a descriptive study. Lancet **395**(10223), 507–513 (2020)

3. Chu, C.M., et al.: Role of lopinavir/ritonavir in the treatment of SARS: initial virological and clinical findings. Thorax **59**(3), 252–256 (2004)
4. Yang, C., et al.: Effectiveness of arbidol for COVID-19 prevention in health professionals. Front Public Health **8**, 249 (2020)
5. Vankadari, N.: Arbidol: A potential antiviral drug for the treatment of SARS-CoV-2 by blocking trimerization of the spike glycoprotein. Int. J. Antimicrob. Agents **56**(2), 105998 (2020)
6. Padhi, A.K., Seal, A., Masood Khan, J., Ahamed, M., Tripathi, T.: Unraveling the mechanism of arbidol binding and inhibition of SARS-CoV-2: Insights from atomistic simulations. Eur. J. Pharmacol. **894**, 173836 (2021). https://doi.org/10.1016/j.ejphar.2020.173836
7. Blaising, J., Polyak, S.J., Pécheur, E.I.: Arbidol as a broad-spectrum antiviral: an update. Antiviral Res. **107**, 84–94 (2014)
8. Wolfson, J.S., Hooper, D.C.: The fluoroquinolones: structures, mechanisms of action and resistance, and spectra of activity in vitro. Antimicrob. Agents Chemother. **28**(4), 581–586 (1985)
9. Correia, S., et al.: Mechanisms of quinolone action and resistance: where do we stand? J. Med. Microbiol. **66**(5), 551–559 (2017)
10. Marciniec, K., Beberok, A., Pęcak, P., Boryczka, S., Wrześniok, D.: Ciprofloxacin and moxifloxacin could interact with SARS-CoV-2 protease: preliminary in silico analysis. Pharmacol. Rep. **72**(6), 1553–1561 (2020). https://doi.org/10.1007/s43440-020-00169-0
11. Scroggs, S.L.P., et al.: Fluoroquinolone antibiotics exhibit low antiviral activity against SARS-CoV-2 and MERS-CoV. Viruses **13**(1), 8 (2020). https://doi.org/10.3390/v13010008
12. Schögler, A., et al.: Novel antiviral properties of azithromycin in cystic fibrosis airway epithelial cells. Eur. Respir. J. **45**(2), 428–439 (2015)
13. Gielen, V., Johnston, S.L., Edwards, M.R.: Azithromycin induces anti-viral responses in bronchial epithelial cells. Eur. Respir. J. **36**(3), 646–654 (2010)
14. Wang, C., et al.: Oseltamivir compared with the Chinese traditional therapy maxingshiganyinqiaosan in the treatment of H1N1 influenza: a randomized trial. Ann. Intern. Med. **155**(4), 217–225 (2011)
15. Zhou, Z., et al.: Honeysuckle-encoded atypical microRNA2911 directly targets influenza a viruses. Cell Res. **25**(1), 39–49 (2015)
16. Zhang, D., et al.: The clinical benefits of Chinese patent medicines against COVID-19 based on current evidence. Pharmacol. Res. **157**, 104882 (2020)
17. Akalın, E., et al.: Traditional Chinese medicine practices used in COVID-19 (Sars-cov 2/Coronavirus-19) treatment in clinic and their effects on the cardiovascular system. Arch. Turk. Soc. Cardiol. **48**(4), 410–424 (2020)
18. Nile, S.H., Kai, G.: Recent clinical trials on natural products and traditional chinese medicine combating the COVID-19. Indian J. Microbiol. **61**(1), 10–15 (2020). https://doi.org/10.1007/s12088-020-00919-x
19. Yang, R., et al.: Chemical composition and pharmacological mechanism of Qingfei Paidu Decoction and Ma Xing Shi Gan Decoction against Coronavirus Disease 2019 (COVID-19): in silico and experimental study. Pharmacol. Res. **157**, 104820 (2020)
20. Runfeng, L., et al.: Lianhuaqingwen exerts anti-viral and anti-inflammatory activity against novel coronavirus (SARS-CoV-2). Pharmacol. Res. **156**, 104761 (2020)
21. Shu, Z., et al.: Clinical features and the traditional Chinese medicine therapeutic characteristics of 293 COVID-19 inpatient cases. Front. Med. **14**(6), 760–775 (2020). https://doi.org/10.1007/s11684-020-0803-8
22. Ungvari, Z., et al.: Endothelial dysfunction and angiogenesis impairment in the ageing vasculature. Nat. Rev. Cardiol. **15**(9), 555–565 (2018)
23. Klein, S.L., Marriott, I., Fish, E.N.: Sex-based differences in immune function and responses to vaccination. Trans. R Soc. Trop Med. Hyg. **109**(1), 9–15 (2015)

24. Guo, T., et al.: Cardiovascular implications of fatal outcomes of patients with coronavirus disease 2019 (COVID-19). JAMA Cardiol. **5**(7), 811–818 (2020)

25. Mauvais-Jarvis, F., Klein, S.L., Levin, E.R.: Estradiol, progesterone, immunomodulation, and COVID-19 outcomes. Endocrinology **161**(9), bqaa127 (2020). https://doi.org/10.1210/endocr/bqaa127

26. Gao, W., et al.: Clinical features and efficacy of antiviral drug, Arbidol in 220 nonemergency COVID-19 patients from East-West-Lake Shelter Hospital in Wuhan: a retrospective case series. Virol. J. **17**(1), 162 (2020)

27. Zhu, Z., et al.: Arbidol monotherapy is superior to lopinavir/ritonavir in treating COVID-19. J. Infect. **81**(1), e21–e23 (2020)

28. Nojomi, M., et al.: Effect of Arbidol (Umifenovir) on COVID-19: a randomized controlled trial. BMC Infect. Dis. **20**(1), 954 (2020)

29. Fang, J., et al.: Efficacy of early combination therapy with Lianhuaqingwen and Arbidol in moderate and severe COVID-19 patients: a retrospective cohort study. Front. Pharmacol. **11**, 560209 (2020)

30. Langford, B.J., et al.: Antibiotic prescribing in patients with COVID-19: rapid review and meta-analysis. Clin. Microbiol. Infect. **27**(4), 520–531 (2021). https://doi.org/10.1016/j.cmi.2020.12.018

31. Majumder, M.A.A., et al.: Antimicrobial stewardship: fighting antimicrobial resistance and protecting global public health. Infect. Drug Resist. **13**, 4713–4738 (2020)

Author Index

Printed in the United States
by Baker & Taylor Publisher Services